Reformation Writings of Martin Luther

Vol. I: The Basis of the Protestant Reformation

translated by

Bertram Lee-Woolf

James Clarke & Co., Ltd
Cambridge

Published by
James Clarke Co., Ltd
P.O. Box 60
Cambridge
CB1 2NT
England

e-mail: **publishing@jamesclarke.co.uk**
website: **http://www.jamesclarke.co.uk**

ISBN 0 227 17168 3 hardback
ISBN 0 227 17167 5 paperback

British Library Cataloguing in Publication Data:
A catalogue record is available from the British Library.

First published 1952 by The Lutterworth Press
reprinted 2002

PREFACE

THE present English translation of a selection of Luther's works is made exclusively from the definitive Weimar Edition which, begun on the fourth centenary of Luther's birth in 1483, is still in course of publication, though almost completed. Some eighty volumes, magnificently produced in large quarto, each of between 600 and 800 pages, have been published complete with historical and literary introductions and critical apparatus to all the separate writings; an indication, in itself, of the personal greatness, the immense labours, and the religious force of the man who wrote them over 400 years ago.

At first, Luther wrote always in Latin. Not long after he had "found his public", however, he began to write more frequently in German and, incidentally it may be remarked, created the standard by which "good German" has been judged ever since, granted only the changes due to the passage of time. Whether he wrote in German or Latin much was immediately rendered into the various languages (especially Spanish, Italian, and French) and dialects of Europe. As an exception, curiously little was put into English until a generation or more after his death. Henry VIII actually himself took up the foils against Luther,[1] and the devout people of town and country were given few opportunities of reading his works. Some, like Tyndale, went to Wittenberg to do so. Most of the learned looked to the great but unattractive Erasmus for leadership. When, at last, the strong hands of the Tudors were replaced by the thin fingers of the Stuarts, what might have been the direct influence of Luther had been taken over by Calvin.

The most considerable of Luther's works translated into English during the sixteenth century was the longest, but not the best, of his three commentaries on the epistle to the Galatians; indeed this translation appears to be the only one still readily available in Great Britain. Various selections

[1] Cf. *infra*, pp. 205

6 PREFACE

of his works, mostly sermons, commentaries, or polemical writings, appeared in English as time went by, and helped to form the tradition of the great "doctor"; but none seems to have been translated with close attention to precision, or edited on historical and critical principles. Indeed a popular and very unreliable edition of his Table Talk was all that had a considerable sale in the nineteenth century.

The most scholarly selection published in England during the same period was that edited by Wace and Buchheim, which came to be regarded as a standard work and as sufficient for most students. It was confined to a single volume of what the editors called Luther's *Primary Works*.[1] From to-day's standpoint, the selection seems meagre and rather arbitrary, and scarcely to reflect Luther's true contribution to the Protestant Reformation. The works were not arranged in chronological order, nor otherwise well suited for modern methods of historical study. Their text lacked the critical precision since made available in the Weimar Edition.

The United Lutheran Publication House of Philadelphia, U.S.A., began, in 1910, a selection of Luther's works, apart from commentaries and sermons, which was to be published in six volumes. The enterprise was brought to a conclusion in 1932, and, with the special introductions written by the various translators, it has laid all English-speaking students of Luther under a considerable obligation. This selection was more comprehensive than anything of its character that had been published in Great Britain, and it was intended to be the "Standard Edition of Luther in the English Language". Unfortunately, not all the work was on the highest level, some of the texts used could not be regarded as critical, nor was the selection, in other respects, well suited for scientific study.

Since the great Weimar Edition first began to appear in 1883, large quantities of original matter, hitherto for the most part unknown for centuries, have come into the open; even unknown portraits of Luther have been discovered. The

[1] The works chosen were as follows, and printed in this order: *The Short* and the *Great Catechisms*, 1529; *An Address to the German Nobility, The Liberty of a Christian*, and *the Babylonian Captivity of the Church*, all of 1520 but not first published in that order; the *Ninety-five Theses*, 1517

result is that the publishers and the editors of the different documents and volumes have frequently issued, far on in the series at first intended to be strictly chronological, matter of all kinds which belonged to earlier years. It follows that the reader may find himself at any time confronted with a formidable task in finding his particular objective, and everything relevant to it; for there is as yet no index to the whole.

In addition to about 60 volumes of general, edificatory, and devotional writings, sermons, prefaces, commentaries, notes, and what not else, there are to date six volumes of Table Talk (with complete index), eleven volumes of correspondence, and seven volumes of the Bible. The commentaries, when collected together, cover the whole of the Bible in one way or another; the Psalms and the customary lectionaries, in detail. Much of this immense material covers the same ground several times; yet until the end or nearly so, it loses little of its freshness and immediacy, and continues to afford much insight into Luther's mind. It also reflects the mind of the German reformers and the progress of the Reformation in the first half of the sixteenth century, in Germany and beyond. No one can be said to know Luther's works or understand his personality, if, as is too usual, his reading has been largely confined to the earlier polemical works, and uncritical editions of the Table Talk (the least reliable of the Lutheran corpus) which form so exiguous and so unrepresentative a selection of the whole.

Several selections of the works of Luther based on a broad knowledge of the Weimar Edition, sometimes using its text in its medieval form, sometimes in a modernized version, have been published in Germany in recent years; several are of the highest scholarship, and the greatest value to students, not least for their introductions, notes, and vocabularies. But we in Great Britain, always rather remote from Luther, require a selection made to suit our needs, and especially our needs in times of religious decay and cynicism, the modern counterpart of what Luther knew very thoroughly.

The publishers issue the present volume as a selection, taken in chronological order, from 1517 to 1520, the four years after the movement had really begun. It comprises, apart from the first commentaries on the epistle to the Galatians, the most important of the early writings, or those which afford a clear view of Luther at work laying foundations. It shows the gathering momentum before the dramatic climax at the imperial council at Worms in 1521.

Every translator of Luther is faced with the problem of working without a proper lexicon. The publishers of the Weimar edition promised that boon in 1938, but the work, although declared indispensable for understanding what Luther wrote and said, has not yet appeared. In these circumstances, when all else failed, I have thought it best to rely very largely on my acquaintance with Luther's German Bible, that monument to his mastery of his native idiom. It will be no small pleasure to me if I have succeeded in reproducing, though it be still from afar, something of the marvellous freshness and force of language which comes tumbling out like a sunlit cataract, whenever one reads his own words in their original form.

I wish to record my best thanks to the publishers of the Weimar Edition, now Messrs. Hermann Böhlaus Nachfolger in Weimar, for their kind permission to make free use of their *Historisch-kritischen Gesamtausgabe von Luthers Werken*; to Mr. and Mrs. Andre Santo, formerly of Vienna, for help in many difficult passages; to the Rev. Gordon Rupp, of Richmond College, for kind criticisms and advice; to Mr. Harry Cowlishaw for reading both the original MS and the printed proofs, and making many improvements; to Mr. S. D. Charles, M.A., for his matchless sense of the value of words; to the Rev. G. H. Gordon Hewitt, M.A., Editorial Secretary of the Lutterworth Press during the time that the project has been in preparation; and to Miss Hilda M. Wilson, his assistant, for helpfulness far beyond what could have been asked; and to my wife who, as ever, has made it possible for me to carry through the labour when otherwise I could not but have failed.

BEACONSFIELD   B.L.W.
   January, 1952.

CONTENTS

ABBREVIATIONS

in references to the Weimar Edition of
Luther's Works

W.   The main section of the *Werke*, or general works, now
nearly complete in about seventy volumes.

Br.   The *Briefwechsel*, or correspondence, in eleven volumes
so far published.

Bi.   Luther's *German Bible*, in seven volumes.

T.R.   The *Tischreden*, or Table Talk, in six volumes.

GENERAL INTRODUCTION

MORE than half his life had already been lived before Martin Luther, at the age of thirty-four, became known beyond Wittenberg, a town of 2,000 inhabitants, or the monastic circles of the Augustinian order. Within these limits, he was already trusted and admired. Since 1512, he had been in charge of the parish church, and had won the esteem of the congregation. Even so, he was still relatively obscure, a petty friar (*fraterculus*) as the great ones called him even when they could no longer ignore him. His strength of character, his depth of religious experience, his grasp of the meaning of divine grace, his understanding of the common man, were all quite unusual; they were the materials on which his towering influence was later to be built, but they do not amount to an explanation of that influence. Here was a strong and likeable man, contented with his lot, enjoying every moment of life except perhaps for occasional "moods"; and yet it was he, and not one of his eminent contemporaries, that came to act in such a way as opened up the Reformation.

While this much is the plain verdict of history, he himself is commonly regarded as an enigma, an enigma different from that presented by most of the great figures of history, since greatness is always enigmatic to the common man. But it has become the fashion, since early in the twentieth century, to regard him as having been discredited, and as presenting a repellent personality to the unbiassed eye of the historian.[1] We ourselves believe that this is to do immeasurable injustice, not only to Martin Luther himself, but to the intelligence, perspicacity, and religious quality of his contemporaries and those who came under his influence—including such figures, among others, as William Tyndale, John Calvin, John Bunyan, and John Wesley. These are men whose opinions cannot be trifled with, and whose

[1] Eg. Hartmann Grisar, *Luther*, 6 vols. 1914–17 (Roman Catholic); Peter F. Wiener, *Martin Luther, Hitler's Spiritual Ancestor*, 1945

acknowledged debts to Luther create insoluble problems for the detractors.

The different ways in which Luther has been recently understood or misunderstood may be partly explained by certain facts: in former centuries, religious leaders read hundreds of his sermons and all his commentaries, which covered the whole Bible; whereas few read his sermons to-day and no translations of his commentaries—even on Galatians—have been readily available in Great Britain for a hundred years. The next important fact explaining the twentieth century fashion is that, apart from his commentaries, he has never yet been read in full;[1] reliance has been placed on various selections, and even on dubious and uncritical versions of a few works; seldom have his writings been studied in a truly comprehensive way, as in the epochmaking, critical work of Karl Holl,[2] whose massive studies leave no room for doubt as to Luther's place among religious leaders of the Christian church or, indeed, among the great figures of western civilization.

It would seem however that, as gradually revealed by the definitive Weimar Edition during the seventy years in which it has been in process of publication (since 1883), the wide range and great accuracy of his knowledge, and the scientific character of his methods of study, will now cause the enigma to take a different shape: it will probably be seen, not to be due to a host of apparent self-contradictions, often violent and coarse, but to the rushing torrents of evangelical teaching, preaching, and writing, with all that these astounding labours implied for the rebirth of religion and the new moral sensibility which arose in its wake. Many a former scholar has become like a boy caught in mid-stream when the flood waters broke.

No attempt can be made here to do anything more than indicate a few of the aspects of Luther study which have struck our special attention. We maintain that the real Luther must have been much more like the beloved and

[1] If only because he has not yet been published in full, though this argument is not stressed here

[2] Cf. *Gesammelte Aufsätze*, Vol. I, *Luther*

trusted "doctor" of the best tradition, than like some of the portraits and interpretations produced in the first half of the twentieth century.

The outstanding quality in Luther's character was his honesty. He was stubbornly honest, with himself in the first instance, and then with the facts he studied; this honesty is of the essence of scientific method. He combined it with a great intelligence, a highly trained mind, and a power of swift decision. His honesty and intelligence together go far to explain his very special, personal piety. The exhaustive character of his long period of religious doubt was due to this kind of honesty in a deeply religious man; his power of decision, and the firmness of his step as he followed each new gleam of light, showed his attachment to the truth. His combination of insight, honesty, and forthrightness, was precisely the instrument needed to cut through the thickets which obscured the religious landscape, where far too many institutions, activities, traditions, and ideas, were masquerading as genuine heirs of the Christian faith.

This honesty with himself led Luther into depths of religious experience such as have been searched by only the greatest souls. There is a direct similarity between Paul, Augustine, Luther, and again, Bunyan and Wesley. The poignancy of Luther's experience finds its testimony in several characteristics. Firstly, his reading of the Bible; no man could have read the Bible so attentively, so minutely, so diligently, just for the sake of acquaintance with the subject matter. It would have been an impossible task for him to read it through minutely twice a year for the greater part of his life, unless it had been a necessity, and a sustaining experience, for him to do so. He read, learned, and digested, to an extent in which he is without rival; and always as he read, he listened for God's voice. That voice meant not only authoritative command; it also meant life to him.

Another testimony to the deep character of his religion was his choice of subject for his first publications: a commentary on the seven penitential Psalms, in A.D. 1517. The choice, no less than the commentary itself, was significant of his profound sense of sin and of the greatness of God's mercy.

Then there is, even more remarkably, the strength which he gave to his lectures on Romans. He seems never to have been satisfied that he had plumbed the depths of the epistle, although his more popular introduction to it[1] is what converted John Wesley 220 years later. The lectures themselves were not published during his life-time——nor indeed till nearly 400 years after their first delivery.[2] Galatians was his favourite epistle; on it he published three commentaries, which are, at the same time, commentaries on his doctrine of divine grace.

Equally revealing of the depth of his religious experience are the subjects to which he constantly returned throughout life in preaching and teaching: the Ten Commandments, The Apostles' Creed and the Lord's Prayer; and on these he wrote with extraordinary power. It is in works like these, rather than in snippets from this or that work, or quotations from this or that passage, that we best grasp his doctrine of *sola fide*.

His intense religious experience had remarkable qualities of its own. Although he was, of course, absorbed in that experience, he never lost his sense of the reality of this world. He was averse to that mystic rapture and ecstasy which were so earnestly sought as the goal of medieval religious exercises. When he saw the light of divine truth at what may be called the time of his conversion, he was in full possession of his senses. Reason and religion were equally active when the meaning of God's righteousness[3] dawned on him; and the Bible leapt into new life as he swiftly absorbed what was now the plain meaning of page after page. The assurance of God's mercy, His immediate, personal mercy, His mercy on the man there in the monastic cell; His will to forgive and redeem just for love's sake; His love and mercy revealed in Christ; all this in addition to the direct experience of the divine power apart

[1] Published with his translation of the New Testament in 1522, and often revised; cf. *Bi.*, Vol. VII, 2-27. In itself, the document is a masterpiece
[2] By J. Ficker, 1908, reproducing as accurately as possible the Latin notes as they occur between the lines and in the margins of Luther's copy of the Latin printed Bible, and the continuous notes that follow. The whole is so complex and difficult to tease out into its separate strands, that a translation probably remains impossible; cf. also *W.*, Vol. LVII (1938)
[3] Cf. Rom. 1:17 and 3:25

from any "means of grace", except the word of God in Holy Scripture. On it his intelligence seized and his heart fed. His stature increased with his delight, and his faith with his stature. He could cry triumphantly with Paul, "I can do all things through Christ that strengtheneth me;" and "Life means Christ to me". There is a vital contagion and an essential element of religious leadership in such a delight in God. It is what Luther meant by faith.

There was in him also a profound conviction of God's wisdom, a boundless trust in His providence, and an adamant certainty of His protection. With his simple and direct mind, Luther had no mental reservations—the curse of medievalism; and no hypothetical clauses—the affliction imposed by the Humanists. For him, God was God indeed, the God of "my own Psalm",[1] namely, the God who knew all, who was able to do all, and whose concern was over all. To rely entirely on God was not an exercise of "blind faith", but of plainest common sense; and it gave him a settled peace. His "nerves" were never "on edge", although he had many long periods of despondency. The secret of Luther's courage is to be sought, not in his pugnacity, which was far less than is often assumed, but in his faith in a God who was indeed "able to keep all that he committed unto Him". That is also the secret of a humility and a selflessness in which he was in marked contrast to the majority of contemporary leaders of church or state, and which helped countless thousands to look to him as the father of his people.

His battles with himself, and his consequent estrangement from his father, on the question of his entering a monastery[2] tended to increase the firmness with which he trod the path as it opened out step by step. This firmness of mind together with a prodigious memory, which enabled him to reproduce long passages of books he had read years earlier, meant that he knew what he knew; he knew what a writer had said and, more notably, he knew what a writer had never said. This self-confidence and this ability helped him to gain a firm grasp

[1] Ps. 118, read in the light of the New Testament, and of Luther's own experience

[2] Cf. Luther's own Preface to de votis monasticis, W., VIII, 573–669

of the salient issues that had engaged the minds of the great thinkers. He had, moreover, an exquisite sense of the meaning of words, whether in his native German or in the Latin of scholarly intercourse; and a minute knowledge of the Old and New Testaments.[1] An equipment of this character made him a formidable opponent in debate, and a magnetic champion of the common people.

His theology, too, was expressed in such terms, and was of such a character, that it could be intelligently discussed by ordinary people and, indeed, to discuss it came to be their most fascinating pre-occupation: Christ died for your sake. You lay hold of Christ by your faith. By your faith you commit your life to Him; and, for His sake, God's grace flows to you. You can now live the good life acceptable to God, and do so in a masculine way. All else in religion is but the implementation of these basic facts, and the Romanist system an imposition making you depend on doubtful intermediaries.[2]

The *annus mirabilis*, 1520, was one during which Luther poured out more writings than many great writers in a decade. Several of these writings were of classical importance, not only for the Reformation, but also for revitalizing Germany. The influence of his *Appeal to the Ruling Class*[3] is impossible to assess. His *Prelude to the Pagan Servitude of the Christian Church*[4] abashed his friends (e.g. the Elector, Frederick the Wise), alienated the fearful (e.g. Erasmus), provoked a royal rejoinder (Henry VIII), but gave the people a grasp of the central points at issue in the Romanist sacramental system. On the other hand, *The Freedom of a Christian*[5] showed the essential simplicity of the evangelical faith; and it has retained its value as a classical document. His essay *On Good Works*,[6] though hasty and uneven, put ethics in the texture of the Decalogue and the Sermon on the Mount—a refreshing change from Aristotle—and provided at

---

[1] Most of the marginal references familiar in our Bibles come direct from Luther in the first instance

[2] For a further discussion on faith and works, cf. *infra*, pp. 83f. and oft; *The Freedom of a Christian, infra*, pp. 349ff.

[3] Cf. *infra*, pp. 101ff.   [4] Cf. *infra*, pp. 201ff.   [5] Cf. *infra*, pp. 349ff.

[6] Much of the thought is contained in briefer form in the *Short Exposition*, cf. *infra*, pp. 67ff.

least the groundwork of a genuinely Christian system of morals. Violent language was the order of the day in controversy;[1] yet he used vituperation only when attacked in this way.[2] Nay, the mildness, or the silent contempt with which he responded to some of his enemies' worst efforts, is what strikes the reader to-day;[3] while in his polemical writings he answered fools according to their folly, that being then regarded as the essence of vigour and high spirits, yet when Luther won the confidence of the multitudes, it was by other means. As is the case to-day, men were timid, fearful of endangering their precious skins, and unwilling to commit themselves till they saw how others would fare. These, the great majority of his adherents, he won by the plain, factual truth of his assertions, the temperance of his claims, and, especially, by the deeply religious character of the issues that he placed before their consciences. They were led into profounder and more satisfying experiences than any they had hitherto known, experiences of an evangelical, liberating faith, which meant life, power, and peace. His sermons, by the thousand, bear witness to the loftiness of his appeal to men's hearts, not playing on their fears or prejudices or passions; but, rather, evoking their faith and confidence. In fact, the clarity, swiftness, and firmness of his style are outstanding. His principle and practice in this regard was "to ask the mother in the home, the children in the streets, and the ordinary man in the market-place. . . . We must take the words from their very lips. . . . Then the people will understand".[4] His readers and his hearers alike felt that he

[1] One prior said of Luther, "Would that I could fasten my teeth in Luther's throat: I should not fear to go to the Lord's supper with his blood in my mouth", P. Smith, *Luther's Correspondence*, pp. 70f., qd. G. Rupp, *Luther's Progress*, p. 79; the remark shows incidentally the horror with which heretics were regarded

[2] One of the most striking examples is to be found in his exchanges with Emser, cf. *W.*, II, 655/7–79; VII, 259/62–265; 266/70–283; 614/20–688

[3] Cf. his reply to Prierias *W.*, II, 48/49–56; his burning of the bull of excommunication, together with his apology thereafter in Latin, and then in German, cf. *W.*, VI, 595–629; so also his prompt publication of the lampoon which falsely proclaimed his death in 1545, accompanied by all manner of terrestrial, celestial, and subterranean phenomena, cf. O. Clemen's selection of Luther's works, Vol. IV, pp. 388ff., reproduced from the Erlangen edition, Vol. XXXII, pp. 426ff.

[4] *W.*, XXX, ii, p. 737

B

was speaking to them personally. Bunyan said of the commentary on Galatians that it was "as if the book had been
written out of my own heart".[1]

Luther was quite remote from demagogism. A man of
learning, he called learning to his side, and poured it into his
sermons and writings. His main purpose was to instruct his
people. His constant readiness to submit his teachings to the
test of Scripture was a severe and sobering thing to his
challengers, but quietening and satisfying to his followers; it
sent the more serious and inquiring minds to study the Bible
more deeply for themselves. The importance of the Bible had
come to be confined, increasingly among scholars since Origen,
and similarly among the ordinary clergy of the medieval
church, to isolated passages used as keystones to support those
dogmas which were of greatest value, either to theological
discussion, or to ecclesiastical polity. To read the Bible as a
whole was a long-forgotten practice. The Bible as a book the
whole of which contained God's message and showed the
wide sweep of God's will through history, was a concept
which Luther was the first to seize in its immense significance.
It was this, rather than any isolated texts and passages,
which enabled him to grasp the nature of God's redemptive
righteousness, His gracious forgiveness, and His power to
save. Luther was not a man of snap texts, or of one book to
the exclusion of others. To him, the Psalter was a "clear
mirror of Christianity", Romans "quintessential gospel", and
Galatians "my own epistle"; yet he was a man of the whole
Bible and the Bible as a whole. He found that every book of
the Bible directed his thought and faith to God's redemptive
love as brought to historical reality in the cross of Christ.
For him, the Old Testament was not the narrow record of an
ancient history, or of the early phases of a particular religion;
nor was the New Testament merely the literary deposit of the
life of Jesus, the apostles, and the early church. He found the
Old Testament in the New, and the New Testament in the
Old; and he believed that what was so true, so revealing, and
so reassuring in his own case, was exactly that which all men
needed, and to which, under God, they would respond; and

[1] G. Rupp, *op. cit.*, qd. p. 106

he was right. Although his German translation of the New Testament cost the equivalent of about £2 per copy when first published in September, 1522, the whole of the first edition of 5,000 was bought out in a few days, and reprints sold by the ten-thousand. In the last analysis, it was his Biblical work that made his influence monumental, and gave him his place among the great leaders of men.

In public and private, he discussed what all men were discussing, but with a new authority: the issues raised by the celibacy of the clergy; the disequilibrium of society due to the excessive development of monasticism; the needs of popular education; the artificial barriers placed on marriage by vows, consanguinities, and the like; and the church's arbitrary claims to "bind and loose" in matters of pure ethics. He felt that what ultimately ailed his times was a stifling spiritual climate; and he showed himself, not only able to rise above the miasma, but also capable of lifting his contemporaries into the upper air. He found that the Bible contained a commentary on his own times, and he saw how the Bible could teach the people to form sound opinions for themselves.

Then, as if he was aware that he who makes the songs of the people shapes their lives, he discovered, when already forty years of age, his power of hymn-writing. He proceeded to give the people hymns in which, for the first time for a thousand years, they could pour out their hearts in their mother-tongue. Nor was his work a mere versifying of religious tales and sentiments; it was gratitude, faith, prayer, praise, and joy expressed in songs uplifted to God; and Luther often composed the melody. Thomas à Jesu, the Carmelite, dismayed at their effect, said, "It is marvellous to see how Luther's hymns further Luther's cause. They are sung, not only in churches and schools, but also in the homes and the workshops, on the streets and market-places, and on the farms."[1] Three quarters of the first, small, vernacular hymn-book, published in 1524, came from his pen. The best of his hymns still rank among the greatest of the Christian church. His greater and smaller *Catechisms*, of 1529, possessed

[1] Qd. W. J.Kooiman, *Maarten Luther*, 2nd ed., Amsterdam, 1948, p. 104; E.T., Lutterworth Press, 1952, Chap. 16

a value which can never be told in shaping the thought of both high and low, young and old. He also provided a new liturgy centred, not on the Mass as hitherto, but on the sermon; and the sermon was to be an exposition of the message of the Bible.

It is possible to get a glimpse of what the impact must have been like in the sixteenth century, but it is impossible to give the whole answer to the question how Luther was able to remain one of the people and yet to rise to such towering heights, and to accomplish such immense labours. The answer is too closely connected with the secrets of personality, and with the hidden nexus between soul and soul. That is the true enigma of Luther.

The great issue had been joined in 1517, and decided, in principle, before the end of 1520. He had attacked "the crown of the pope, and the bellies of the monks",[1] as Erasmus explained to Frederick the Wise. It was a clever epigram, but it only skimmed the surface of the flood; it did not plumb its depths. For, by this time, Luther was the leader of his people by virtue of the truth of the gospel which he preached and the power with which he pressed it home. Evangelical truth was now planted in the hearts of countless multitudes, and the argument which Luther had voiced was for ever part of the education of mankind.

[1] In an interview between Erasmus and Frederick at Cologne on October 5, 1920, and reported by Spalatin; c.f. *T.R.*, Vol. I, pp. 55, 131, and H. P. Smith, *Erasmus*, p. 235

1

THE NINETY-FIVE THESES

Introduction

THE *Ninety-five Theses* is the name which Luther gave to
the series of propositions which he announced for public
debate in accordance with established custom. The title was
transliterated when the propositions were translated into
the vernacular, and has become traditional. Otherwise, some
such title as "The Ninety-five Propositions" would be more
suitable as the heading of a modern translation such as the
present. Luther's usual title was *"Disputatio de . . ."*; e.g.,
Disputatio de lege et fide (1519); *Disputatio de circumcisione*
(1520); *Disputatio de fide infusa et acquisita* (1520); etc. Why
Luther should not have used his more customary title on
the present occasion is unknown. It is quite clear, however,
that the practice of holding such public debates was common
throughout the later Middle Ages, and public interest in them
was often profound and sustained. As a consequence, the
method was, and still is, employed as a device for instructing the people, especially in matters of importance to religion
and the church.

Strictly speaking, a *disputatio* was a syllogistic act
between a proponent and a respondent to establish a point
or proposition, and that remained the primary meaning.
From the days when he first matriculated at Erfurt in 1503,
Luther had been acquainted with the method of disputations, which were prescribed as regular weekly exercises, and
which he seems greatly to have enjoyed; they not only made
a student familiar with the different questions that could
be raised, but sharpened his wits, and gave him confidence.
Luther introduced the method to Wittenberg when he
became professor in 1508, and used it as a means of training his students in logical thinking and in ready debate. In
fact, he used the method so widely that he earned for himself the nickname of "the philosopher".

But logical thought and alert wits were also required in
the very preparation of the scheme that was to be debated.

For the most effective use of the method, the teacher must see to it that all the main points regarding a subject were brought well out into the open, and that all the pros and cons were thoroughly discussed. He must also see to it that the conclusions reached at each stage would knit together at the end into a satisfactory demonstration. Meanwhile the points must be so presented that interest did not flag; this would be particularly important in public debates, as distinct from those of the class-room. Considerable skill was required. As is obvious, the problem was more than that of seizing on the most important of the debatable elements of a subject, or assembling a number of points in dispute and arranging them in logical order; the real problem was so to arrange the sequence of the propositions that the conclusions arrived at in regard to them would hang together and have a cumulative effect.

This skill was demanded merely in the true interests of objective inquiry and the furtherance of good learning. But, once a certain skill had been acquired in the method, it could be readily employed either to test a person's knowledge, as in an examination for a degree, or to demonstrate the truth and the superiority of any special doctrine. And however sincerely Luther may have asserted that his purpose in proposing the Ninety-five Theses was academic in character,[1] there can be little room for doubt that he intended that his doctrine of salvation by faith should "get across". Granted that he wanted to learn the truth of the points in dispute, yet he also wanted to make his own views known among responsible people, and so to test them in the thorough manner which this method permitted. It is not satisfactory to maintain that the propositions, being drawn up in Latin, were therefore intended only for the educated, i.e., the clergy and higher-school students. There is a popular streak in students, and also in the most learned, which no good preacher ignores; and any point, however academic it may be in the first instance, which makes a vivid appeal to this side of human nature, has a way of making itself rapidly known among the people at large. There can be little real

---

[1] Cf. Dedication to Leo X, *infra*, p. 63

doubt but that this consequence was in the back of Luther's mind, even if he felt it would be necessary to publish the conclusions later in a formal manner. It would be wrong, however, to say that Luther's purpose was polemical: rather, it was primarily an academic inquiry, as shown by its form and high seriousness; and his aim was only ultimately evangelical.

The Ninety-five Theses were directed to the question of indulgences, which had developed into one of the most extraordinary issues in the whole history of the church whether before or since Luther's time. This is not the place to discuss the theological principles that were involved, or the unparalleled abuses that came into practice.[1] It is rather uncertain to what extent Luther was aware, at that moment, of the sordid background,[2] or of the cynical terms of the Bull of Indulgence of 1515, and also of Albert's commendation of it, probably written in 1517.[3] What is certain is that Luther was perturbed by the moral effects on the populace at large, and made more keenly conscious than ever of the difference between his own presentation of the gospel and that which represented religion among the people. Hence, he was stirred by two impulses. Of these, the first was theological and academic in character, and had to do with an inquiry into truth and error in the whole question of indulgence and grace, of sin and its annulment, of redemption and human salvation; and the standards to be found in the Bible, in the early Fathers, and in natural morality. In sallying forth under this impulse, Luther appears as a warrior armed with

[1] This complex and difficult subject is best studied in its historical development; the main relevant documents have been conveniently assembled by W. Köhler, *Dokumente zum Ablassstreit*, Tübingen, 1902. The substance of the Theses is discussed by T. M. Lindsay, *History of the Reformation*, Vol. I, 216–236, J. Mackinnon, *Luther and the Reformation*, Vol. I, 297f. The Roman Catholic standpoint is perhaps best represented by Hartmann Grisar S. J., *Luther*, E.T., 2nd ed. 1914, Vol. I, pp. 327–355

[2] I.e., the arrangement between Albert of Mainz and Leo X on the one hand, and between Albert and the Fuggers on the other, whereby Leo took half the proceeds, while the Fuggers' representative, who travelled with Tetzel, took the other half (after going into the accounts, each evening), in satisfaction of the loan made to Albert to enable him to meet the cost of his pluralities

[3] Cf. Köhler, *op. cit.*, 83ff., 104ff.; and cf. 124ff.

all the equipment which he had forged for himself during twenty years of hard study, and ten years of brilliant academic teaching. He knew every aspect of his subject, and he was an acknowledged master in the art of teaching. The second impulse was that of a man profoundly concerned for the well-being of the people themselves. He had been born and bred among them; he understood them and loved them. His repute as a preacher, which soon became considerable, was largely due to the way in which he could speak directly to them. He had been District-Vicar of his Congregation since 1515, a responsibility which not only threw on him the general administration of eleven monasteries, but, more importantly, which caused him to move to and fro throughout the district. He was therefore very different from a mere scholarly recluse, whose work was confined to his study and his classroom; for he was personally familiar with the needs of the people: he understood how they felt in regard to the problems, the aspirations, the practices, and the abuses of the times in central Germany. He was zealous in correcting excesses and rectifying wrongs; and the winsomeness of his personal bearing, acknowledged at that time by all, lent much weight to his counsel of mildness and clemency, especially towards erring brethren.[1] And his sympathies for his fellow Germans had been increased and indeed fired, by his visit, in 1510, to Italy and Rome.

The first real signs of his reforming interest in questions of morals were shown in a sermon preached over five years earlier at Litzka.[2] His lectures on the Seven Penitential Psalms, delivered during the winter of 1515-16, constitute an urgent plea for personal repentance and faith as sufficient means of grace.[3] He preached directly on Indulgences in July, 1516,[4] and on the church's need of power from God in August of the same year.[5] He discussed the abuse of Indulgences in February, 1517,[6] and then began a series on the Ten Commandments which he expounded with much originality from the same general standpoint. The whole issue was therefore of great moment to him—and

[1] Cf. Letter to Lang, Oct. 26, 1516   [2] W., I, 9   [3] W., I, 154ff.
[4] W., I, 65   [5] W., I, 69   [6] W., I, 138

now Tetzel,[1] licensed by his own archbishop, was stirring all Germany, and drawing near.

Roused in this way, therefore, Luther must be presumed to have set out his Theses with a clear head but a trembling hand. It had become the custom in the University of Wittenberg on Fridays for the professors to take their turn in dealing in public with matters of academic importance or general interest. It would seem that they followed a regular rota, and Luther would be well aware when he was due to lead. On this occasion, it was to be All Saints Day, November 1, at noon; a day specially important also as the "foundation day" or "anniversary" of the church. In view of the fact that Tetzel was already almost in the neighbourhood, and preaching the new Indulgence in the name of the pope and under the authority of Albert of Mainz, Luther's subject was almost chosen for him: Indulgences and Divine Grace.[2]

It is perfectly true to say that the Theses are not a clearly reasoned statement of theological doctrine; still less are they the programme of a scheme of reformation. But it is very wrong to go on and say: "They are simply ninety-five sledgehammer blows directed against the most flagrant ecclesiastical abuse of the age."[3] They are not analogous to the muscular deliveries of a blacksmith; nor were they plied with any idea of merely smashing the hated thing to pieces; nor are they without a proper arrangement. Rather, they are like the leaps and the strokes of a skilled fencer: there are thrust and parry, attack and feint; quick advances, and, apparently, sudden retreats. They twist and turn, sometimes demanding assent, sometimes dissent. Sometimes the responder must argue strenuously for the proposition, only to find himself called, on his own premises, to deny the next with all his resources. The theses change from gentle suggestion to biting

[1] John Tetzel (c. 1465–1519), a German Dominican preacher of papal Indulgences, whose only historical significance is that he roused Luther to protest. The later rightly said that "The child (i.e. the indulgence arranged between the pope and Albert of Mainz) had another father" when T. proclaimed it in 1516 and 1517. T. died in 1519, broken-hearted at the mischance which had followed his efforts. Luther wrote a kindly letter which comforted him on his deathbed   [2] *Vide infra*, pp. 49ff.
[3] T. M. Lindsay, in *Cambridge Modern History*, II, 129

irony, from what is granted by the common consent of all mankind, to the most extreme claims of the pontiff's privilege. Neither is humour lacking; nor its companion, pathos. Here is, in fact, all the material for a new display of Socratic irony.

It follows that the propositions, even when taken as a whole, do not present a case, nor set forth a doctrine; that is not their purpose. Their purpose, rather, is to elicit a clear understanding, or to bring to birth many ideas with which the times themselves were pregnant. The propositions are only partial, whether taken singly or as a whole; they are complete only when they are accompanied by the responder's reply. It is a proof of the skill of the challenger if he can compel those replies to take the form which harmonizes with his own conviction. Luther's superior skill in this respect is immediately apparent when one compares the reply attempted by Prierias[1] in his *Epitoma* the following year, which Erasmus stigmatized as "a bungling answer";[2] or the arrogant and abusive style of the *Obelisks*, which was Eck's[3] opening attack on Luther's teaching.

The detailed arrangement of the propositions, therefore, is determined by the psychology of debate, and by what the challenger feels will best build up his case in the conditions that are likely to obtain on that particular occasion. But the broad outline must be kept steadily in mind, even though this may be only partially visible in the terse and fragmentary notes constituting the propositions themselves. To a certain extent, the challenger must conceal his deeper purpose as he passes from point to point. The fundamental scheme of the Ninety-five Theses may perhaps be stated in the following terms:[4]

[1] Sylvester Prierias, really Mazzolini, from Prierio in Piedmont (1456–1523), Dominican theologian, became Grand Inquisitor and Censor in 1515. He was very active in writing against Luther 1518–20. Not a true scholar, as L. easily showed; *vide infra*, p. 337, n.1
[2] Cf. Letter to Lang, Oct. 17, 1518
[3] John Eck (1486–1543) from Egg (hence Eck or Eccius) in central Germany; really his name was Mair. He was the most eminent Romish theologian in Germany in the sixteenth century. At 24 he became professor in Ingoldstadt. Friendly with Luther in their early days, he became his most able and trenchant opponent
[4] With acknowledgments to the scheme attributed to T. Brieger

1. What is the real nature of the call made by Christ to a sinner? (Theses 1–7.)

2. How has the Church really dealt with the problem of sin and its punishment? (Theses 8–19.)

3. What powers are exercised in fact, and what should be exercised, by the pope in this respect? (Theses 20–29.)

4. What is the truth in the matter of Indulgences for the living? (Theses 30–80.) And, in particular,

5. What is their nature as preached to-day? (Theses 30–55.)

6. What is the truth of the "treasury of the Church"? (Theses 56–66.)

7. What is the duty of the leaders of the Church? (Theses 67–80.)

8. What are the objections widely felt against the traffic in the present Indulgences? (Theses 81–90.)

9. What is the way out of the present evil? (Theses 91–95.)

The Theses were somewhat arbitrarily divided into four groups, in harmony with the medieval custom of dividing a sermon, a lecture, or a discussion under four "heads"; in the present instance the divisions may be assumed to indicate the times when it would be convenient for intervals. No doubt, Luther chose the number 95 because Albert had put out 94 arguments (although not explicitly so numbered) in his *Instructio summaria* to subcommissioners and others in commendation of the Bull of Indulgences.[1] But whatever may be the value of these artificial features, Luther's profoundly religious spirit and his intense sincerity of purpose were plain to all readers, from the first proposition onwards. The first proposition raises the question of the central purpose of the work of Christ on earth. Luther's spirit and purpose were also plain in his reminder, as the Theses develop, that the question of the nature of Christian life is a profoundly serious matter (e.g., Theses 30, 49); in the crux of the problem as expressed in Theses 36 and 37;

[1] Cf. Köhler, *op cit.*, pp. 104ff.; and W. J. Kooiman, *op. cit.*, chaps. 7 and 8

and in his conclusion, which conceives of that life in terms of a difficult, spiritual pilgrimage.

It must have been with many a good-humoured smile that Luther wrote out these propositions, and, in accordance with custom, nailed them to the church door on the day previous to the public debate. The date was Thursday, October 31, 1517, a date which, years later, was recognized by Melanchthon as that on which it could be said that the Reformation began.

Fortunately, or unfortunately, there was no debate; for no one took up the challenge. But it would seem that some of Luther's own students copied out the propositions, after many had noticed their freshness and force. A translation, or translations, were soon made and, without Luther's consent, the press seized on them. They were soon known throughout Germany. Early in January, 1518, Bernhard Adelmann[1] possessed a copy which he thought had been printed in Basel. They were also printed, perhaps earlier, in Latin and German, at Nüremberg, the translation being done by Caspar Nützel. But not a single copy of these early prints is extant.

Meanwhile, as in duty bound, Luther had apprised Albert of the "Disputation" he proposed to hold, and had sent him a copy of his propositions.[2] Also, on the afternoon of the same day when he "posted" the Theses on the church door, he preached in the church itself on the substance of his contention: Indulgences and Grace.[3] And once the subject had in a certain sense became a public issue, Luther plunged with amazing and apparently boundless energy into the business of making his convictions known. Already for something like five years, now, the subject had been gestating in his mind, and coming to clearer and clearer expression in his lectures and sermons. But the time had come to write and publish; and the very multitude and power of his writings for the next few years are enough to overwhelm

---

[1] Bernhard Adelmann (c. 1457–1523) born near Württemberg. A humanist; adherent of Reuchlin and Erasmus. Like these, he welcomed Luther's early protests and actions; he wrote against Eck. In 1520, he submitted to the pope, and was absolved. He remained, however, well-disposed to Luther
[2] Cf. *infra*, pp. 44f.   [3] Cf. *infra*, pp. 49ff.

the student. Luther actually kept three printing presses entirely occupied. In spite of the stir created by the polemical writings into which he was at first more or less decoyed, partly by the insults of Eck, his main work consisted in the constructive presentation of his convictions. This took the form of numberless sermons to the people, lectures on the Bible to students and others; discussions of traditional theological doctrines, and of topical issues; repeated exposition of the Decalogue, the Apostles' Creed, and the Lord's Prayer; the most famous of all his published commentaries, that on Galatians; the epoch-making monographs[1] of A.D. 1520; and, after the dramatic episode at Worms, crowned by his classic translation of the New Testament, which, incredible though it may seem, was begun and ended in ten weeks. All this was the historical consequence, perhaps the logical result, of posting the Ninety-five Thesis.

[1] *Vide supra*, p. 16

Text and Notes

Oᴜᴛ of love and concern for the truth, and with the object of eliciting it, the following heads will be the subject of a public discussion at Wittenberg under the presidency of the reverend father, Martin Luther,[1] Augustinian, Master of Arts and Sacred Theology, and duly appointed Lecturer on these subjects in that place. He requests that whoever cannot be present personally to debate the matter orally will do so in absence in writing.[2]

1. When our Lord and Master, Jesus Christ, said "Repent",[3] He called for the entire life of believers to be one of penitence.

2. The word cannot be properly understood as referring to the sacrament of penance, i.e., confession and satisfaction, as administered by the clergy.

3. Yet its meaning is not restricted to penitence in one's heart; for such penitence is null unless it produces outward signs in various mortifications of the flesh.

4. As long as hatred of self abides (i.e., true inward penitence) the penalty of sin abides, viz., until we enter the kingdom of heaven.

[1] Luther spelled his name in various ways; the form used in the preamble to the *Theses* was Lutther

[2] Unfortunately, no one responded and there was no debate; but Luther preached that day in the Castle Church on the subject of Indulgences and Grace, cf. pp. 49ff., *infra*

[3] This quotation from Matt. 4:17 was known throughout Europe in its Latin form: *poenitentiam agite*. Unfortunately, the phrase was capable of two meanings: repent; and, do penance. Although the two meanings were originally indistinguishable, the second became predominant, and, when taken alone, as only too frequently, opened the door to all the abuses against which Luther protested. The double meaning of the phrase is felt in many of the theses that follow, and sometimes occasions differences of translation

5. The pope has neither the will nor the power to remit any penalties beyond those imposed either at his own discretion or by canon law.

6. The pope himself cannot remit guilt, but only declare and confirm that it has been remitted by God; or, at most, he can remit it in cases reserved to his discretion. Except for these cases, the guilt remains untouched.

7. God never remits guilt to anyone without, at the same time, making him humbly submissive to the priest, His representative.

8. The penitential canons apply only to men who are still alive, and, according to the canons themselves, none applies to the dead.

9. Accordingly, the Holy Spirit, acting in the person of the pope, manifests grace to us, by the fact that the papal regulations always cease to apply at death, or in any hard case.

10. It is a wrongful act, due to ignorance, when priests retain the canonical penalties on the dead in purgatory.

11. When canonical penalties were changed and made to apply to purgatory, surely it would seem that tares were sown[1] while the bishops were asleep.

12. In former days, the canonical penalties were imposed, not after, but before absolution was pronounced; and were intended to be tests of true contrition.

13. Death puts an end to all the claims of the church; even the dying are already dead to the canon laws, and are no longer bound by them.

14. Defective piety or love in a dying person is necessarily accompanied by great fear, which is greatest where the piety or love is least.

[1] Matt. 13:24ff.

C

15. This fear or horror is sufficient in itself, whatever else might be said, to constitute the pain of purgatory, since it approaches very closely to the horror of despair.

16. There seems to be the same difference between hell, purgatory, and heaven as between despair, uncertainty, and assurance.

17. Of a truth, the pains of souls in purgatory ought to be abated, and charity ought to be proportionately increased.

18. Moreover, it does not seem proved, on any grounds of reason or Scripture, that these souls are outside the state of merit, or unable to grow in grace;

19. Nor does it seem proved to be always the case that they are certain and assured of salvation, even if we are very certain of it ourselves.

20. Therefore the pope, in speaking of the plenary remission of all penalties, does not mean "all" in the strict sense, but only those imposed by himself.

21. Hence those who preach indulgences are in error when they say that a man is absolved and saved from every penalty by the pope's indulgences;

22. Indeed, he cannot remit to souls in purgatory any penalty which canon law declares should be suffered in the present life.

23. If plenary remission could be granted to anyone at all, it would be only in the cases of the most perfect, i.e. to very few.

24. It must therefore be the case that the major part of the people are deceived by that indiscriminate and high-sounding promise of relief from penalty.

25. The same power as the pope exercises in general over purgatory is exercised in particular by every single bishop in his bishopric and priest in his parish.

(*The second series*)

1 (26). The pope does excellently when he grants remission to the souls in purgatory on account of intercessions made on their behalf, and not by the power of the keys (which he cannot exercise for them).

2 (27). There is no divine authority for preaching that the soul flies out of purgatory immediately the money clinks in the bottom of the chest.

3 (28). It is certainly possible that when the money clinks in the bottom of the chest avarice and greed increase; but when the church offers intercession, all depends on the will of God.

4 (29). Who knows whether all souls in purgatory wish to be redeemed in view of what is said of St. Severinus[1] and St. Paschal?[2]

5 (30). No one is sure of the reality of his own contrition, much less of receiving plenary forgiveness.

6 (31). One who *bona fide* buys indulgences is as rare as a *bona fide* penitent man, i.e., very rare indeed.

7 (32). All those who believe themselves certain of their own salvation by means of letters of indulgence, will be eternally damned, together with their teachers.

8 (33). We should be most carefully on our guard against those who say that the papal indulgences are an inestimable divine gift, and that a man is reconciled to God by them.

[1] Pope, 638–40, successor to Honorius I
[2] Paschal I, pope 817–24. The legend is that he and Severinus were willing to endure the pains of purgatory for the benefit of the faithful

9 (34). For the grace conveyed by these indulgences relates simply to the penalties of the sacramental "satisfactions" decreed merely by man.

10 (35). It is not in accordance with Christian doctrine to preach and teach that those who buy off souls, or purchase confessional licences, have no need to repent of their own sins.[1]

11 (36). Any Christian whatsoever, who is truly repentant, enjoys plenary remission from penalty and guilt, and this is given him without letters of indulgence.

12 (37). Any true Christian whatsoever, living or dead, participates in all the benefits of Christ and the Church; and this participation is granted to him by God without letters of indulgence.

13 (38). Yet the pope's remission and dispensation are in no way to be despised, for, as already said, they proclaim the divine remission.

14 (39). It is very difficult, even for the most learned theologians, to extol to the people the great bounty contained in the indulgences, while, at the same time, praising contrition as a virtue.

15 (40). A truly contrite sinner seeks out, and loves to pay, the penalties of his sins; whereas the very multitude of indulgences dulls men's consciences, and tends to make them hate the penalties.

16 (41). Papal indulgences should only be preached with caution, lest people gain a wrong understanding, and think that they are preferable to other good works: those of love.

---

[1] This is what Tetzel appears to have preached; it appears also to have had the support of Wimpina at the public debate on Indulgences at Frankfort-on-Oder, Jan. 20, 1518. It was not sound Roman doctrine according to Grisar, *Luther*, I, 344

17 (42). Christians should be taught that the pope does not at all intend that the purchase of indulgences should be understood as at all comparable with works of mercy.

18 (43). Christians should be taught that one who gives to the poor, or lends to the needy, does a better action than if he purchases indulgences;

19 (44). Because, by works of love, love grows and a man becomes a better man; whereas, by indulgences, he does not become a better man, but only escapes certain penalties.

20 (45). Christians should be taught that he who sees a needy person, but passes him by although he gives money for indulgences, gains no benefit from the pope's pardon, but only incurs the wrath of God.

21 (46). Christians should be taught that, unless they have more than they need, they are bound to retain what is necessary for the upkeep of their home, and should in no way squander it on indulgences.

22 (47). Christians should be taught that they purchase indulgences voluntarily, and are not under obligation to do so.

23 (48). Christians should be taught that, in granting indulgences, the pope has more need, and more desire, for devout prayer on his own behalf than for ready money.

24 (49). Christians should be taught that the pope's indulgences are useful only if one does not rely on them, but most harmful if one loses the fear of God through them.

25 (50). Christians should be taught that, if the pope knew the exactions of the indulgence-preachers, he would rather the church of St. Peter were reduced to ashes than be built with the skin, flesh, and bones of his sheep.

(The third series)

1 (51). Christians should be taught that the pope would be willing, as he ought if necessity should arise, to sell the church of St. Peter, and give, too, his own money to many of those from whom the pardon-merchants conjure money.

2 (52). It is vain to rely on salvation by letters of indulgence, even if the commissary, or indeed the pope himself, were to pledge his own soul for their validity.

3 (53). Those are enemies of Christ and the pope who forbid the word of God to be preached at all in some churches, in order that indulgences may be preached in others.

4 (54). The word of God suffers injury if, in the same sermon, an equal or longer time is devoted to indulgences than to that word.

5 (55). The pope cannot help taking the view that if indulgences (very small matters) are celebrated by one bell, one pageant, or one ceremony, the gospel (a very great matter) should be preached to the accompaniment of a hundred bells, a hundred processions, a hundred ceremonies.

6 (56). The treasures of the church, out of which the pope dispenses indulgences, are not sufficiently spoken of or known among the people of Christ.

7 (57). That these treasures are not temporal is clear from the fact that many of the merchants do not grant them freely, but only collect them;

8 (58). Nor are they the merits of Christ and the saints, because, even apart from the pope, these merits are always working grace in the inner man, and working the cross, death, and hell in the outer man.

9 (59). St. Laurence said that the poor were the treasures of the church, but he used the term in accordance with the custom of his own time.

10 (60). We do not speak rashly in saying that the treasures of the church are the keys of the church, and are bestowed by the merits of Christ;

11 (61). For it is clear that the power of the pope suffices, by itself, for the remission of penalties and reserved cases.

12 (62). The true treasure of the church is the Holy Gospel of the glory and the grace of God.

13 (63). It is right to regard this treasure as most odious, for it makes the first to be the last.[1]

14 (64). On the other hand, the treasure of indulgences is most acceptable, for it makes the last to be the first.

15 (65). Therefore the treasures of the gospel are nets which, in former times, they used to fish for men of wealth.

16 (66). The treasures of the indulgences are the nets to-day which they use to fish for men of wealth.

17 (67). The indulgences, which the merchants extol as the greatest of favours, are seen to be, in fact, a favourite means for money-getting;

18 (68). Nevertheless, they are not to be compared with the grace of God and the compassion shown in the Cross.

19 (69). Bishops and curates, in duty bound, must receive the commissaries of the papal indulgences with all reverence;

20 (70). But they are under a much greater obligation to watch closely and attend carefully lest these men preach their own fancies instead of what the pope commissioned.

[1] Matt. 20:16

21 (71). Let him be anathema and accursed who denies the apostolic character of the indulgences;

22 (72). On the other hand, let him be blessed who is on his guard against the wantonness and licence of the pardon-merchants' words.

23 (73). In the same way, the pope rightly excommunicates those who make any plans to the detriment of the trade in indulgences.

24 (74). It is much more in keeping with his views to excommunicate those who use the pretext of indulgences to plot anything to the detriment of holy love and truth.

25 (75). It is foolish to think that papal indulgences have so much power that they can absolve a man even if he has done the impossible and violated the mother of God.

(*The fourth series*)

1 (76). We assert the contrary, and say that the pope's pardons are not able to remove the least venial of sins as far as their guilt is concerned.

2 (77). When it is said that not even St. Peter, if he were now pope, could grant a greater grace, it is blasphemy against St. Peter and the pope.

3 (78). We assert the contrary, and say that he, and any pope whatever, possesses greater graces, viz., the gospel, spiritual powers, gifts of healing, etc., as is declared in I Corinthians 12.[1]

4 (79). It is blasphemy to say that the insignia of the cross with the papal arms are of equal value to the cross on which Christ died.

[1] I Cor. 12:28

5 (80). The bishops, curates, and theologians, who permit assertions of that kind to be made to the people without let or hindrance, will have to answer for it.

6 (81). This unbridled preaching of indulgences makes it difficult for learned men to guard the respect due to the pope against false accusations, or at least from the keen criticisms of the laity;

7 (82). They ask, e.g.: Why does not the pope liberate everyone from purgatory for the sake of love (a most holy thing) and because of the supreme necessity of their souls? This would be morally the best of all reasons. Meanwhile he redeems innumerable souls for money, a most perishable thing, with which to build St. Peter's church, a very minor purpose.[1]

8 (83). Again: why should funeral and anniversary masses for the dead continue to be said? And why does not the pope repay, or permit to be repaid, the benefactions instituted for these purposes, since it is wrong to pray for those souls who are now redeemed?

9 (84). Again: surely this is a new sort of compassion, on the part of God and the pope, when an impious man, an enemy of God, is allowed to pay money to redeem a devout soul, a friend of God; while yet that devout and beloved soul is not allowed to be redeemed without payment, for love's sake, and just because of its need of redemption.[2]

10 (85). Again: Why are the penitential canon laws, which in fact, if not in practice, have long been obsolete and dead in themselves,—why are they, to-day, still used in imposing

---

[1] Abelard made the point, *circa* A.D. 1140, that if the pope was willing to remit, on certain conditions, a third or a quarter of the due penance for money, he should be more willing to remit one half or even the whole, for *pietas*. Luther, therefore, in this thesis, is only making a point which had long become traditional

[2] Innocent III issued a Bull after the Lateran Council of 1215, and promised indulgence for those taking part in the Crusade whether at their own or another's expense; and also for paying for someone to take part

fines in money, through the granting of indulgences, as if all the penitential canons were fully operative?

11 (86). Again: Since the pope's income to-day is larger than that of the wealthiest of wealthy men, why does he not build this one church[1] of St. Peter with his own money, rather than with the money of indigent believers?

12 (87). Again: What does the pope remit or dispense to people who, by their perfect penitence, have a right to plenary remission or dispensation?

13 (88). Again: Surely greater good could be done to the church if the pope were to bestow these remissions and dispensations, not once, as now, but a hundred times a day, for the benefit of any believer whatever.

14 (89). What the pope seeks by indulgences is not money, but rather the salvation of souls; why then does he not suspend the letters and indulgences formerly conceded, and still as efficacious as ever?

15 (90). These questions are serious matters of conscience to the laity. To suppress them by force alone, and not to refute them by giving reasons, is to expose the church and the pope to the ridicule of their enemies, and to make Christian people unhappy.

16 (91). If, therefore, indulgences were preached in accordance with the spirit and mind of the pope, all these difficulties would be easily overcome, and, indeed, cease to exist.

17 (92). Away, then, with those prophets who say to Christ's people, "Peace, peace," where there is no peace.[2]

18 (93). Hail, hail to all those prophets who say to Christ's people, "The cross, the cross," where there is no cross.

[1] As early as 1215, Innocent III had spoken against excess in issuing indulgences at the dedication of churches, and for similar causes, lest the power of the keys fell into disrepute
[2] Jer, 6:14

19 (94). Christians should be exhorted to be zealous to follow Christ, their Head, through penalties, deaths, and hells;

20 (95). And let them thus be more confident of entering heaven through many tribulations[1] rather than through a false assurance of peace.

MDXVII.

[1] Acts 14:22

A LETTER TO ALBERT OF MAINZ

Introduction

Albert was an archbishop of the church and a prince of the state; a man of large and liberal ideas, but, towards the end of his life, rather intolerant of the Protestants. When this letter was written, he was still only 27, and obviously one of the men with a future. He was born in 1490 as the younger son of the reigning Elector of Brandenburg. When 23 he was appointed archbishop of Magdeburg, being already bishop of Halberstadt. When 24 he became both archbishop and elector of Mainz; at 28 he was made a cardinal. To hold the archbishoprics in plurality was an offence against Canon Law, and required a special dispensation from Leo X, then only recently elected pope of Rome. But a dispensation required a special fee of some 20,000 guilders besides the usual fees for the installation. To pay the large sums thus required, Albert had resort to the great medieval financiers, Fuggers of Augsburg; and then, to pay off this debt, Albert applied to the Pope for the benefit of an Indulgence, which was granted in 1515 on condition that His Holiness received half the proceeds to enable him to meet the immense cost of building St. Peter's in Rome (on which both Michelangelo and Raphael were then working). The Indulgence, when preached by Tetzel, as he neared central Germany, was the immediate cause leading to Luther's posting of the *Ninety-five Theses*. As archbishop of Magdeburg, Albert was Luther's superior, and it was a piquant situation when Luther, perhaps in all ignorance of the bargain between Leo X and Albert, sent this letter, with a copy of the Theses, as in duty bound, to the young prince. History does not record whether he was amused or embarrassed; probably neither. Rather he would treat the matter in the routine way by ordering it to be sent to the councils that dealt with such things, being quite unaware that the date of the letter, October 31, 1517, was to be one of the two most notable in the history of modern civilization.

While this letter appears to have been always described as the covering letter which Luther sent with a copy of the *Ninety-five*

Theses to Albert, it seems likely that he also wrote a letter of the same content to Jerome Scultetus, bishop of Brandenburg, although this copy seems to have disappeared at an early date.[1] The original of the present text is in the Swedish royal archives at Stockholm, and is the copy which the council at Magdeburg sent, together with the *Ninety-five Theses*, to Albert who was in residence at that time in Aschaffenburg. The archbishop replied on December 13 that, although he had felt little personal offence at the monk's presumption, he had taken appropriate steps at once lest the ignorant be misled: he had sent the *Theses* to the theologians and jurists of his own university at Mainz for an opinion; he had consulted with the council at Aschaffenburg, who had agreed on ordering Luther to abstain from going further; and he had sent an outline of this council's conclusions to that at Magdeburg for their opinion. Should they agree, they were to order Tetzel to tell Luther of the prohibition.

Albert had written to Mainz on December 1, and again on December 11, but the reply was not ready till December 17; hence it was not available to the council of Magdeburg which met on December 13. In the opinion of Mainz, exception was to be taken only to the attempt to limit the authority of the pope to issue *sacratissimarum indulgentiarum elargitionem*, as the limitation was against tradition. But they refused to pronounce a formal condemnation of Luther, urging, rather, that the pope should withdraw the bull of indulgences.

It would seem also that, before writing to the council of Magdeburg on December 13, Albert had already sent the *Ninety-five Theses* to the pope, anticipating that His Holiness would take appropriate action in good time. Kalkoff holds[2] that the *Theses* were received in Rome early in December, and that Cajetan's *tractatus de indulgentiis* published on December 8 was a reply.

Nothing else happened at that time; Albert did not think of appealing to the curia, and setting in motion the necessary processes for declaring Luther heretical. He was content simply to carry out his duty as archbishop and inform headquarters of the way in which Luther had come forward.[3]

Luther's covering letter requests Albert to reprove the indulgence preachers commissioned by him, and to withdraw his

---

[1] Cf. discussion, *Br.*, Vol. I, pp. 113f.

[2] *Zu Luthers römischem Process*; the precise reference has escaped the editor

[3] *Br.*, Vol. I, pp. 114f.

Instructio summaria pro subcommissariis;[1] it encloses the *Ninety-five Theses.*

The text used in the present translation is that given in the Weimar Edition of *Luther's Correspondence* (cited as *Br.*), Vol. I, No. 48, p. 108. An English version is given by Margaret A. Currie (*Letters of Martin Luther, selected and translated*), based on De Wette's text, which is reprinted in Kidd's *Reformation Documents*, pp. 27ff. The selection published by The United Lutheran Publication House of Philadelphia gives a version (Vol. I, pp. 25-8) which appears to be based on a text very similar to that of the definitive Weimar Edition.

The Letter

To the Most Reverend Father in Christ, the most Illustrious Lord, Baron Albert, Archbishop and Primate of the Churches of Magdeburg and Mainz, Marquis of Brandenburg,[2] etc., my own Superior and Pastor in Christ, held in all due honour and respect, most gracious.

Jesus[3]

May God give you all the grace and mercy that exist, most reverend Father in Christ, and most illustrious Prince. Pardon me, if I, a man of no standing, should yet have the temerity to think of writing to your Sublime Excellency. The Lord Jesus is my witness that I am well aware that I am of mean condition and no consequence; and I have therefore long deferred doing what I am now making bold to do. Above all else, I am urged by my duty of loyalty to you, a duty which I acknowledge I owe you, my most Reverend Father in Christ. Perhaps then, your Excellency will deign to look on me who am but dust, and, of your episcopal clemency, give heed to my request.

Papal indulgences for building St. Peter's are being carried round under the authority of your most distinguished self.

---

[1] Th. Brieger, quoted *ibid.* p. 108, *Das Wesen d. Ablasses*, 1897, p. 1

[2] Cf. *infra*, p. 49, 175n.

[3] It was Luther's almost invariable custom to invoke the name of Jesus before settling down to write. The name was given a full line to itself and was set out distinctly, and apart from the rest

The purpose of the protest I am now making is not concerned with the substance of the message which the preachers proclaim so loudly; for I have not myself actually heard them; but I do deplore the very mistaken impressions which the common people have gained, and which are universally current among the masses. For example, the poor souls believe that if they buy these letters of indulgence, their own salvation is assured.[1] Again, that souls are liberated from purgatory at the very moment that contributions are cast into the chest.[2] Further, that these indulgences are of so effective a grace that there is no sin too great to be wiped out by them, even if, as they say, *per impossible*, it consisted in having violated the mother of God.[3] Again, that these indulgences free a man from all punishment and guilt.[4] God have mercy on us! That is how those committed to your care, good Father, are taught to regard death. It will be very hard for you to render your account for them all, and it will grow still harder.[5] That is why I have not been able to keep silence any longer about these things. For no man is assured of salvation by a gift, be it conferred by a bishop, since such an assurance is not given even by the infused grace of God; rather the Apostle bids us always to work out our salvation in fear and trembling,[6] and, we read, "the righteous shall scarcely be saved".[7] Moreover, so narrow is the way that leads to life[8] that the Lord, speaking through the prophets Amos[9] and Zechariah,[10] calls those who shall be saved "brands plucked from the burning". Indeed the Lord points everywhere to the difficulty of being saved. Why then do the preachers utter those falsehoods, and give promises of pardons, and make the people feel safe and unafraid? At no time do indulgences give anything advantageous to the salvation or sanctity of the soul; at best they only do away with the external punishments, which it has hitherto been the custom to impose according to canon law.[11]

Moreover, works of piety and love are infinitely preferable to indulgences.[12] Yet it is not of these that they preach with

---

[1] Thesis No. 32   [2] No. 27   [3] No. 75   [4] No. 21   [5] No. 70
[6] Phil. 2:12   [7] 1 Pet. 4:18   [8] Matt. 7:14   [9] 4:11   [10] 3:2
[11] Cf. Thesis No. 5   [12] No. 43

great pomp and authority; rather, they pass these works over in silence, in order to proclaim the indulgences. Nevertheless, the prime and sole duty of all bishops is to teach the people the gospel and the love of Christ. Christ nowhere commands the preaching of indulgences, but He insistently commands that the gospel should be preached. Then what a dreadful thing it is, and how great the peril of a bishop, who says nothing about the gospel, but readily allows indulgences to be noised abroad among his people in preference to the gospel! Will not Christ say to him, "You are straining at a gnat and swallowing a camel"?[1]

In addition, there is this fact, Most Reverend Father in the Lord, that an "Instruction"[2] to the sub-commissioners has been issued in your name, Reverend Father, but surely without the knowledge and consent of your Fatherly Reverence. This "Instruction" declares that one of the chief graces of these indulgences is God's incalculable gift, whereby a man is reconciled to God, and all the pains of purgatory are abolished; also, that there is no need for contrite hearts on the part of those who pay for souls to be redeemed from purgatory, or who buy the tickets of indulgence.[3]

What am I to do, best of primates and most illustrious of princes, except pray your Most Fatherly Reverence in the name of Jesus Christ to deign to give your paternal attention to this matter, and totally withdraw those summary instructions altogether, and order the indulgence preachers to adopt another style of preaching. Otherwise, it may happen that someone will arise, publish his own summary instructions, and confute those preachers and the present instructions. This will bring your Most Illustrious Sublimity into the greatest disrepute, an event which I should heartily detest; yet I fear that it will happen unless appropriate steps are taken immediately.

I beg your Most Illustrious Grace to accept my humble and dutiful respects in the manner of a prince and a bishop: with the utmost clemency, since I put them forward in good

[1] Matt. 23:24
[2] *Instructio summaria pro subcommissariis*, etc.; cf. W. Köhler, *Dokumente zum Ablassstreit*, 1902, pp. 104–24
[3] Cf. W. Köhler, *op. cit.*, p. 110

faith, and I am entirely devoted to your Most Fatherly
Reverence; and because I am also a member of your flock.
May the Lord Jesus guard your Most Fatherly Reverence
for ever. Amen.

Wittenberg, 1517. Eve of All Saints. If it please your
Fatherly Reverence, you may glance at the theses of mine
enclosed herewith, and see how dubious is the question of
indulgences, although these people are broadcasting them
as if it were most indubitable.

Your unworthy son,

Martin Luther,

Augustinian, Doctor of Sacred' Theology.

A SERMON ON INDULGENCE AND GRACE

(*preached at Wittenberg, October* 31, 1517)

Introduction

As it has come down to us, this document is not so much a
sermon as a tract, and not so much a tract as a few headings
with brief explanatory remarks added. As it stands, it is too terse
to be readily understood to-day. But to the people who were
discussing the Ninety-five Theses and the growing furore about
them; or, especially, to the people who had heard Luther preach
in the chapel of the monastery on the very day when he had
nailed the Theses to the door of the Castle Church, these notes
would keep the main issue, and Luther's teaching about it, in
the very middle of the arena. For us to understand the sermon
in our day, we must read it in close connection with the Ninety-
five Theses themselves (plus our Introduction) and with the letters
written by Luther regarding them. The "sermon" is then seen
to be Luther's simple presentation of his whole case regarding
indulgences and grace.

Luther did not send these notes to the press at once. Rather
he waited, though in vain, for a reply to the letter[1] which he
had sent to his superior, Albert of Mainz. Receiving no reply

---

1 *Vide supra*, pp. 44f.

within what seemed a reasonable time, he sent the notes to the press in their original form; it is known that a copy was in Albert's hands before December 13, 1517. But during the next few weeks, the last section seems to have been added, and the present form published during Lent, which began on February 17, 1518. The addition was made because, early that year, certain enemies had begun to accuse Luther of blasphemy. These accusations were the first rumbles of the coming storm.

The sermon does not appear to have been previously translated into English, although it ran through numerous editions in Germany and Switzerland even before 1520. It was printed in the Basel edition (probably edited by Beatus Rhenanus) of several of Luther's pamphlets, and was published in October, 1518. Tetzel's "Reply" is given by W. Köhler, *Documente vom Ablass-streit von 1517*, p. 146ff.

The text followed in the present translation is that given in the Weimar Edition of Luther's Works, Vol. I, pp. 239–46.

The Sermon

The first point to note is that certain recent teachers, such as Peter Lombard, St. Thomas, and their school, regard repentance as consisting of three parts. These are contrition, confession, and satisfaction. Neither this analysis nor this point of view can be based readily, if at all, on Holy Scripture, or on the doctrines of the ancient Christian Fathers. However, we shall let that pass, and adopt the above analysis for the sake of argument.

Secondly: those recent teachers say that indulgences do not render either the first or the second element unnecessary, namely, contrition or confession; but only the third, satisfaction.

Thirdly: they further divide satisfaction itself into three sub-sections, namely: prayer, fasting, and almsgiving. Prayer is a term used in this connection to cover all kinds of spiritual activity, e.g., reading, meditation, hearing God's word, preaching, teaching, and the like. Fasting similarly covers all forms of disciplining one's body, e.g., watching, working, a hard bed, simple and shabby clothes, etc. Almsgiving covers all varieties of works of love and mercy towards our neighbours.

Fourthly: if all of them are right in affirming that indulgences abrogate all need for these "satisfactions" which were due or prescribed for sin; and that the indulgences render these works entirely superfluous, then no good works would remain for us to do.

The fifth point is that many hold a view, widespread, but still not agreed upon by all, that indulgences do away with rather more than these prescribed good works; namely, they abrogate the penalties prescribed for sin as required by the divine righteousness.

In the sixth place: for the time being I shall not refute this view of theirs. My point is that it is impossible to prove from Scripture that the divine righteousness requires or demands any penalty or satisfaction from a sinner, excepting only his own heartfelt, genuine contrition and reform. It is assumed that, henceforward, he will carry Christ's cross and exercise the good works mentioned above, and therefore not prescribed by any human being. Speaking through Ezekiel, Christ says: "If the sinner reforms, and does what is right, I will remember his sins no more."[1] Moreover, Christ Himself forgave each and all of the following: Mary Magdalene,[2] the man sick of the palsy,[3] the woman that was a sinner,[4] and others. I should like to know what other meaning can really be attached to these facts in spite of what certain scholars have trumped up as explanations.

Seventhly: granted, we find that God in His righteousness still punishes certain persons, or causes them to repent by the penalties He imposes. Thus in Psalm 88: "If his children sin, I will visit their transgression with the rod, but my mercy will I not utterly take from them."[5] It remains no one's power except God's to remit this punishment. And He will not remit it, but declares in advance that He will impose it.

In the eighth place: no man is able to name the punishment thus referred to, for no one knows just what it will be. Hence, it is not to be identified with the penalty under discussion, nor with the good works mentioned above.

[1] Cf. Ezek. 18:21; 33:14–16   [2] Luke 7:36ff.; Mark 14:3–9; Matt. 26:6–13
[3] Mark 2:1–12; Matt. 9:1–8; Luke 5:17–26
[4] John 7:53–8:11   [5] Cf. Ps. 89:31–4

In the ninth place: even if the Christian church to-day decided and declared outright that indulgences do something besides rendering the works of satisfaction superfluous, nevertheless I assert that it would be a thousand times more preferable if no Christian bought or wanted indulgences. An indulgence only excuses, and can do nothing further than remit, good works and wholesome punishments, and there is nothing else it can do; and these it were better to accept than to avoid. Certain of the recent preachers have discovered two different punishments, reformative and retributive,[1] i.e., some are penalties appropriate to satisfaction, and others are for our good. But we are more at liberty to disdain (praise God) suchlike small talk than they are to use it; for every form of punishment, indeed everything laid on us by God, is for our good, and can be borne by Christians.

In the tenth place: it is pointless to say that the appropriate penalties and works are too many for a man to carry out in this short life, and therefore that indulgences are necessary. My answer is that that assertion is a mere unfounded piece of fiction. Neither God nor Holy Church imposes more on a man than he is able to bear. St. Paul himself says that God will not suffer any man to be tempted above what he can bear.[2] It brings not a little contempt upon the Christian faith when it is accused of laying more on us than we can bear.

In the eleventh place: even if penance were at this stage to be introduced into the canon with the effect of imposing a seven years' penance for every deadly sin, yet Christendom[3] would still have to legislate in such a way as not to impose anything beyond what a particular individual could bear. And before this legislation is passed, all the more care must be taken not to impose a greater burden than each can well bear.

In the twelfth place: there is a saying that a sinner, who has incurred too great a penalty, must either pay in purgatory, or else have recourse to indulgences. Our reply is that there are also many other things said without reason or proof.

[1] Lat. medicinas, satisfactorias
[2] 1 Cor. 10:13   [3] I.e., in this case, a general council

Thirteenth: it is a great mistake for anyone to think he can make amends for his own sins; so God always forgives them freely out of His infinite grace, requiring nothing more than a blameless life afterwards. The Christian church should give help; and so it may and should pronounce forgiveness, and not impose any severe or intolerable penance.

Fourteenth: indulgences make a place for themselves because there are many imperfect and indolent Christians, who refuse to do good works[1] diligently or who are indifferent and careless. Indulgences do not help to make people better, but tolerate their imperfections and let them remain. Hence indulgences ought not to be condemned; but, on the other hand, no one ought to be urged to use them.

Fifteenth: the ground is much safer, and it is far better, when a man, just for God's sake, makes a gift to the building of St. Peter's, or whatever is specified, than if he buys an indulgence with that object. The danger is that he will make the gift for the sake of the indulgence, and not for God's sake.

Sixteenth: it is much better to do a good work to someone in need than to make a gift towards the building of St. Peter's; and much better than buying an indulgence for that purpose. For, as I have said, it is much better to do one good work than to be excused many. An indulgence, however, excuses many a good work, but otherwise effects nothing.

I would like to make this point quite clear to you; so please note: if you are minded to make a gift, your very first obligation is to an indigent neighbour, and not to the building of St. Peter's, or to buying an indulgence. Should it be the case, however, that there is no one in your town in need of help (which never happens, in God's sight), then you should make your choice of something in your own town, and give to the churches, the altars, the church-ornaments, or the poor fund. Where no object of this kind is forthcoming, then, in the last resort, and quite at your choice, you may give to the building of St. Peter's, or the like. But even then let it not be for the sake of obtaining an indulgence. St. Paul says: "If any provideth not for his

[1] In the sense of Paul's "fruits of the spirit" Gal. 5:22, cf. Eph. 5:9

own, he is no Christian, and is worse than an unbeliever."[1] Beware of anyone who tells you otherwise. He is misleading you, or else he is trying to find your soul in your purse. But if he finds a farthing there, he will prefer that to any amount of soul!

Perhaps you will say: in that case, I ought never to buy an indulgence. My answer is: I have already said that my own inclination, desire, request, and advice are that no one should buy indulgences. Leave indulgences to Christians who are indolent and asleep. You go about your own business.

Seventeenth: indulgences are not among the things commanded or advised, but belong to the class of things allowed or permitted. They are not works for which the church requires our obedience, nor are they meritorious; they are an appendix to obedience. Hence, although no one should prevent another from buying them, nevertheless one ought to draw all Christians aside from them, and urge and help them to do those works and labours which are otherwise neglected.

Eighteenth: whether souls are delivered from purgatory by indulgences, I do not know; nor do I believe it, in spite of some recent scholars who affirm it. But it cannot be proved, nor has the church pronounced on it. Wherefore, for the sake of greater certainty, it were much better for you to pray and labour for those souls yourself; this course is more worthy, and is safe.

Nineteenth: I have no doubt as to the above points, and they are adequately based on Scripture. Hence there is no need for you, on your part, to feel any dubiety.[2] Let the learned scholastics be scholastics. The whole body of them have not sufficient material in their opinions to compose a single sermon.

[1] 1 Tim. 5:8

[2] This remark is not intended to be boastful; rather it shows Luther as a true pastor, concerned for the peace of mind of his congregation. It was designed to relieve the anxieties of those who possessed a simple loyalty to the church; who felt, fearfully, that they were being led into strange places; who themselves had no knowledge of Scripture, probably never having had a Bible in their hands; and who would value the assurances of their own pastor, himself a Doctor of Holy Scripture, and, as such, authorized to teach the people

Twentieth: some people to-day seem to be accusing me of heresy, because the truth I speak has a very bad effect on the church's treasure chest. Nevertheless, I set no great store by such idle talk, especially that of a few thick-heads who have never pored over the Bible, never read the Christian Fathers, never understood their own teachers, but have well-nigh gone mouldy in their own moth-eaten and juristical notions. If they had any understanding of the Fathers, they would have known that they ought not to accuse anyone of heresy unheard and unrefuted; but may God grant them and us the right understanding. Amen.

A LETTER TO JOHN STAUPITZ

enclosing a copy of the *Resolutiones* to the *Ninety-five Theses*, Wittenberg, May 30, 1518

Introduction

It is not known when John von Staupitz was born, but he was probably elderly at the time when he first comes into our purview. He certainly seems to have been rather a weary man in 1520, and he died in 1524. He exercised immense influence for many years as the Vicar-General of the Augustinian Order of monks in Germany, and he filled many other positions with distinction. The shrewd and urbane nobleman was a welcome guest at many a princely board, and he is said to have been "reverent in worship, and merry at table". He had played an important part in Electoral Saxony at the time when Frederick the Wise founded his new university at Wittenberg in 1502. This town was chosen as its site partly because of the Augustinian monastery there, which would provide a good supply of teachers of philosophy and theology. Staupitz became the first dean of the faculty of theology in 1503, and one of the professors of the faculty. As dean he was responsible for the appointment of Luther in 1508 to teach Aristotelian logic and ethics; and as Vicar-General he was responsible for sending Luther to Rome in 1510 on delicate business for the Augustinian Order. In 1512, Staupitz resigned his professorship into Luther's hands, and went south.

He cannot have done other than exercise a far-reaching influence on the young Luther, and the present letter shows the warm relation existing between them six years later (although it broke down when the controversy became heated). In the course of conversation at table on one occasion when Luther was present, Staupitz expressed the view that in former times the phrase *poenitentiam agere*, as in Matthew 4:17, had meant "be repentant in your heart", and not merely "do the prescribed penances". This interpretation had come as a great shock to Luther, set his mind working in a new direction, and did much to shape his opinions. These opinions were seriously at variance with the sermons preached on indulgences by the papal envoys and by the priests under their instructions; and this variance caused Luther to seek a public debate in a first attempt to get the issue clear. Luther proposed the Ninety-five Theses, and these became known fairly rapidly throughout Germany; when they had come to be the subject of universal discussion and even of the dread charge of heresy, he wrote a detailed defence, the *Resolutiones disputationum de indulgentiarum virtute*,[1] and reaffirmed his position at all points. It is rather a lengthy document; it shows that Luther knew exactly his own mind, that he believed himself quite in accord with orthodox tradition, and that this was what he would have tried to prove if the Ninety-five Theses had issued in a public debate. The present letter asks Staupitz to transmit these explanations and this defence of his theses to the pope.

The letter is of the greatest interest in itself, because it recalls that vital bit of exegesis which Staupitz passed on quite casually, and gives us Luther's account of its far-reaching effect upon himself in driving him to seek if these things were so. It also reveals the general state of affairs on the eve of the Reformation, whether on the traditional side, or on that of Luther and his friends. Its date was May 30, 1518.

The text from which the present translation is made is that given in the Weimar Edition of Luther's Works, Vol. I, pp. 325–7.

The Letter

To the Reverend and Beloved Father, John Staupitz, Professor of Sacred Theology, Vicar of the Augustinian Order, Friar Martin Luther, his pupil, sends greeting.

Among your pleasant and helpful talks, with which the Lord Jesus often gives me wonderful satisfaction, I remember

[1] *W.*, Vol. I, p. 522–628; cf. also Vol. IX, pp. 171–5

one occasion, Reverend Father, when you happened to mention the term *poenitentia*.[1] What pity we then felt for the consciences of many, and for those aggravating persons who gave innumerable rules, which could not be kept, and pretended to teach a mode of confession.[2] Then it sounded like a voice from heaven when we heard you say that true repentance begins only with the love of righteousness and of God; and that this love, which others hold to be the final end and consummation of penitence, is rather its beginning.

These words of yours stuck fast in me like "a sharp arrow of the mighty";[3] I began to look up the passages of Scripture which teach penitence, and I soon found my heart flooded with happiness. Words came from all parts of the Bible to sport with me; they laughed and leaped round the phrase. Formerly, I had found scarcely a word in the whole of Scripture which had a bitterer taste than "penitence" (although I had been sedulously trying, in God's sight, to pretend I could produce a forced and fictitious love); but now, no word sounded sweeter or more gracious to me than penitence. God's commandments grow sweet indeed when we understand how to read them, not so much in books, as in the wounds of our loved Redeemer.

The next thing was that, by the kindly co-operation of the scholarly men who teach us[4] Greek and Hebrew, I learned that the Greek word μετάνοια is derived from μετά and νοῦς, i.e., "after" and "mind" or "understanding", so that penitence, or μετάνοια, meant "coming to oneself again", or "to understand our own sinfulness after being punished and acknowledging our error". It is impossible for this to take place without a change in our very disposition and, similarly, in the objects of our affection. All this harmonized so well with the Pauline theology that, at least in my

---

[1] An ambiguous term meaning either repentance, penitence, or penance; each meaning having its own independent importance for the individual member of the church

[2] The *modus confitendi* taught what sins were to be confessed to a priest and how to do so. Luther dealt with the subject in his *Kurze Unterweisung wie man beichten soll*, 1518. *W.*, II, 57ff., and in a Latin version *Confitendi ratio* (1520). *W.*, VI, 159–69

[3] Ps. 120:4

[4] In the University of Wittenberg; with special reference to Melanchthon

judgment, scarcely anything else was more fitted to throw light on Paul.

Then I went further, and found by digging deeper that the roots of the word μετάνοια, besides meaning "after" and "mind", also meant "beyond" and "mind", so that the combination, μετάνοια, would mean a changing of the mind and disposition to something beyond; and this seemed to suggest, not only the change of disposition, but also the mode of the change, i.e., the grace of God. The transformation of the mind, i.e., genuine penitence, is of very frequent occurrence in Scripture. Christ made quite plain what that ancient term "Passover"[1] had once signified.[2] Long before, Abraham had been a type of it when he came to be called a pilgrim,[3] i.e., a Hebrew, or one who passed through into Mesopotamia, as Paul of Burgos[4] so learnedly teaches. This is also borne out by that Psalm where the title introduces Jeduthun,[5] i.e., the pilgrim, as the singer.

By holding firmly to these results, I dared to think those men were in the wrong who ascribed so much to penitential works that they left us scarcely a relic of penitence, properly so-called, beyond a few dull "satisfactions" and a "confession" very laboriously made. They may have been misled by the Latin term, because *poenitentiam agere* speaks of the doing of an act rather than a change of the disposition; and it does not express the real meaning of the Greek word.

While my mind was quite in a fever with thinking of these things, suddenly trumpets and bugles sounded a great clangour all about us again, and certain persons began proclaiming indulgences and pardons; but the bugles were not intended to fill us with a keen and martial ardour. In brief, the preachers said never a word about the true meaning of penitence, but had the effrontery to make much, not of penitence, nor even of that least significant part of penitence which is known as "satisfaction"; all they had in mind was

---

[1] Exod. 12:11   [2] 1 Cor. 5:7   [3] Cf. Gen. 12:5-9

[4] Paul of Burgos (1353–1435), the son of rich Jewish parents, became a Christian in 1390, and eventually bishop of Burgos. He was famous as an exegete largely on account of his knowledge of Hebrew, a rare accomplishment for a Christian

[5] Ps. 39:1

to proclaim how we could be excused even this least significant part. They extolled this "pardon" in unheard-of terms,
and proclaimed doctrines that were impious, false, and
heretical. They did it, moreover, with such authority (not
to say temerity) that it was felt that anyone who uttered
a syllable in contradiction would be immediately consigned
to the flames as a heretic, and be accursed for ever.

For my part, being unable to quell their tempestuosity,
I decided to put in a modest demurrer, and call their doctrines into question. I relied on the opinion of all scholars,
and of the whole church, that to render satisfaction was
better than to have satisfaction remitted: by the buying of
indulgences. No one has ever taught the contrary. Consequently, I published[1] my *Theses*; but the only effect was to
bring on my head all the curses, high, middle, and low,
which these men, greedy for money (of course "souls" is the
word I should use), could impose and call down upon me. So
very courteous are these men, so well equipped with the most
specious adroitness that, since they could not controvert
what I had put forward, they pretended that, in my *Theses*,
I had calumniated the authority of the Supreme Pontiff.

These are the reasons, Reverend Father, why I have reluc-
tantly come out into public at the present juncture. I have
always been one who loved a place apart. I have preferred
to watch the splendid interplay of the talented men of the
present day rather than to be seen and get myself laughed
at. But it seems I must be a square peg in a round hole,[2]
and a black among the whites—on account of my comeliness
and charm!

I beg, therefore, that you will accept this poor effort of
mine, and be good enough to take the trouble of sending it
to his Excellency, Pope Leo X. I want it to act as my
advocate, pleading my cause against the designs of my
detractors. Not that I would want you to be endangered
along with me, for I wish this to be done at my risk only.
Christ will see to it whether to acknowledge that what I have

[1] Not in the sense of making them public in print, but by nailing a copy
in public view on the church door
[2] Lat. *colchorum inter hera*

said is true. Without His consent, even the Supreme Pontiff cannot utter a word, nor is the heart of a king at his own disposal. It is Christ's own verdict that I await from the Roman see.

Meantime I have nothing to say in reply to the threats of those friends of mine, except Reuchlin's[1] remark: "A poor man fears nothing and can lose nothing." I have no possessions, nor do I desire them. Repute and fame, even if I had them, are things of the kind that the Destroyer is to-day busily destroying. All that remains to me is but one, small mortal frame, weak and worn with constant hardships. If by God's will they were to do away with it by violence or villainy, they would make me the poorer by perhaps an hour or two of life. Enough for me is Jesus Christ, my sweet Saviour and atoning Lord, to whose praise I shall sing as long as I live. What is it to me if there is someone who refuses to join my song? If he prefers a solo, let him screech alone. May the Lord Jesus Himself have you ever in His keeping, Gracious Father.

Wittenberg, Holy Trinity.[2]   MDXVIII.

A LETTER TO POPE LEO X

Introduction

GIOVANNI de' Medici (1475–1521), younger son of Lorenzo the Magnificent, was elected pope (Leo X) at the early age of thirty-eight, after having been a cardinal for twenty-five years. Yet he was only ordained after his election to the Holy See, and in order that he might celebrate (his first) mass. He was held in high esteem: "Leo, noble by birth and education, brought many aptitudes to the papacy, especially a remarkable knowledge of classical literature, humanity, kindness, the greatest liberality, an avowed intention of supporting artists and learned men."

[1] Johann Reuchlin (1455-1522), a scholar regarded by the humanists as their leader, rivalled only by Erasmus, his younger contemporary. He was a fine Greek scholar, and the pioneer of the study of Hebrew in Germany. A man of high character, his life was embittered by a quarrel, long drawn out, with a charlatan called Pfefferkorn

[2] In 1518, Holy Trinity fell on May 30. Hence we have the precise date of the present letter and the approximate date of the Dedication to the pope (cf. *infra*, p. 61)

This favourable opinion, expressed by Sarpi, was entertained by Leo's contemporaries and long held the field in history. Recent critical studies have served greatly to modify that judgment; but, at the time when the present letter of dedication was written, Luther doubtless shared to the full the popular contemporary view. In sending Leo the *Resolutiones*, he was really appealing from Peter ill-informed to Peter well-informed and, therefore, ready to decide in Luther's favour. Luther can have had but little idea that, at that stage, if he bothered about the unrest in Germany at all, Leo regarded it still as a "squabble among the friars", and was rather amused by the violence of the contending parties.

But the *resolutiones disputationum de indulgentiarum virtute* show that Luther was in full earnest. Together with the *protestatio* which introduces the actual document, it presents the case which Luther would have endeavoured to set forth if it had come to the public debate on his Ninety-five Theses. And it was this case, rather than the Theses, with their thrust and parry, their direct charge and their witty innuendo, which was the real matter in dispute. The *resolutiones* "aimed as definitely as possible to prove the doctrinal errors and the practical mistakes of the preachers of the Indulgences"[1] then licensed in Germany.

It will be noted that the letter is dated shortly before May 30, 1518.[2] It shows that much heat and no little fire had been generated since the *Ninety-five Theses* had been made public seven months earlier, but the letter also shows the great naturalness and simplicity with which Luther approached the Holy See, and that his heart was entirely undivided in its allegiance to Holy Church. He believed the church was being wronged and travestied, not that it was itself wrong and the source of evil; and he certainly believed that the present pope, whatever may have been the case with his predecessors, was one to put right at once any malpractice performed in his name. This is the letter in which Luther puts himself personally at the disposal of the pope; he says, in the closing paragraph: "I shall acknowledge the voice of God speaking through you. If I merit death, I shall not refuse to die."

The text from which the present translation is made is that given in the Weimar Edition of Luther's Works, Vol. I, pp. 527–9, where it is immediately followed by the *Protestatio* which introduces the *Resolutiones*.

[1] Kalkoff, *Zu Luthers römischem Process*, p. 117; for an excellent discussion, cf. pp. 118ff.
[2] Cf. discussion of the date of letter to John Staupitz, *supra*, p. 56

The Letter

To the most blessed father Leo X, *pontifex maximus*, Friar Martin Luther, Augustinian, wishes eternal welfare.

Holy Father, the worst of reports are in circulation about my own self. I understand that even certain friends of mine have seriously defamed my reputation, and put me in bad odour with you and those around you. I am made out to be one who is undermining the authority and power of the keys and the supreme bishop. Consequently I have been called heretic, apostate, infidel, and 600 other ignominious names. I am horrified and astounded by what I hear and see. Nevertheless, my confidence remains unshaken on account of the fact that I have kept an innocent and peaceful conscience. Moreover, my foes are saying nothing new, even when those whose own consciences are very uneasy, have thrown at me, even in this district, the kind of epithets that would suit themselves. They have tried to impose their own monstrosities on me, and to make their own baseness shine and look splendid in contrast with what they call my shame. But you will deign to hear the truth of the matter from me, though I am but a child and ignorant of courtly language.

The Indulgences of the Apostolic Jubilee have been preached among us quite recently. Matters have already gone to such a length that the preachers have come to think they possessed every licence, owing to the authority attaching to your name; they have even openly dared to teach very impious heresies. This has caused the most serious scandal, and brought derision on the church's authority. They act as if the decretal, *de abusionibus quaestorum,*[1] in no way applied to them. Nor have the preachers been satisfied with spreading this poison of theirs orally, for they have published pamphlets and distributed them among the masses. I will pass over the insatiable and unheard-of avarice with which almost every word they utter positively reeks; but, in these pamphlets, they put forward the same impious heresies as they preach. They put them forward and enjoin them in such a way that priests in confessional are bound

[1] Dealing with the method of collecting funds for the church

by oath to teach them to the people, word for word[1] and most insistently. I am speaking the truth, and none can deny it. The pamphlets are there and cannot be disowned. They sold so well, and the people were carried away so completely by false hopes, that, as the prophet says, "they tore the flesh from the people's bones".[2] Meanwhile the preachers themselves enjoyed the richest and most comfortable fare.

They allayed scandal by one means only, viz.: the honour in which your name is held, the threat of the stake, and the shame of being called heretic.[3] It is unbelievable how prone the preachers are to utter threats, even when they are aware that it is only their own nonsensical notions that are really in question; as if this kind of preaching were the way to allay scandal, and not rather to cause schisms and seditions by their very arrogance!

In spite of all, however, tales began to spread in the taverns about the greed of the priests, and other things derogatory to the keys and the Supreme Pontiff, as witness common talk everywhere hereabouts. I confess that I myself was on fire out of zeal for Christ, as it seemed to me, or out of the hotheadedness of youth, as you may think. Yet I did not think that it was my place to make a public protest. Therefore I gave a private warning to certain prelates of the church. I was heeded by some, laughed at by more, and regarded askance by others. The honour in which your name was held, and the threat of ecclesiastical censure, prevailed upon them to do nothing. Then, when no other course was open, I thought it right to show at least a modicum of opposition to the preachers; I therefore called their doctrines into question, and proposed a public debate. I therefore published a list of theses, and invited only the more scholarly to a discussion with me, if they so wished. This should be obvious, even to my adversaries, from the preface to those very theses.[4]

That is the fire which, they complain, has set the whole world alight. Perhaps, they are indignant with me because,

[1] Lat. *fidelissime* [2] Cf. Micah 3:2
[3] In the Middle Ages heretics were regarded almost like lepers and with a superstitious horror
[4] Cf. *supra*, p. 32

as a teacher of theology by your own Apostolic authority, I have the right to conduct public debates. This is customary in all universities and the whole church. I have the right, not only to debate indulgences, but also God's power, His forgiveness, and His mercy, which are incomparably greater matters. Yet I am not greatly disturbed that they should envy my having been granted this privilege by the authority of your Holiness. Unfortunately, I cannot avoid accusing them of far more serious matters, viz.: that they mix up irrelevant notions of Aristotle's with matters theological, and put forward purely nonsensical arguments contrary to, and beyond, the terms of reference which they have received.

I am at a loss, indeed, to know why it is fated that these particular theses of mine and no others, whether of mine or of any other teachers, should have spread throughout almost the entire country. They were made public at the university of Wittenberg, and intended only for this university. They were made public in such a manner that it seems incredible that all and sundry could understand them. They are theses; they are neither teachings nor doctrines;[1] as is customary, they are cast in obscure and ambiguous language.[2] If I could have foreseen what would happen, I should certainly have done my part to see that they were more fully intelligible.

As things are, what am I to do? I cannot recall them; and yet I see that I have inflamed against myself an astonishing amount of ill-will once they were published and sold among the masses. I am unwilling to stand or fall by the mere voice of popular opinion with its dangers and differences, especially as I am not a learned man, but a person of dull wits and poor scholarship. In these flourishing times, with the skill in letters and learning that now prevails,[3] it would be easy to corner even Cicero, although in his own time he was held in no mean public esteem. But I am constrained to speak by necessity, though I must croak like a crow among blackbirds.

[1] *Vide supra,* pp. 27f.
[2] *Vide supra,* p. 28
[3] A remark reflecting the exhilaration felt by the spread of the Renaissance

Thus, in order to mollify adversaries and meet the wishes of many friends, I am sending herewith these all too inadequate explanations of my theses. I am sending them, too, Holy Father, in order that I may be the safer by having your approval as my defence, and your shadow as a protection. By these means, all who so desire will understand that I am simply seeking to maintain the authority of the church and only wanting to add to the respect for the Keys. At the same time also, all mankind will understand how sinful and false it has been when my adversaries have spoken about me in disgraceful terms. If I had been of the sort they try to make me out; and if, on the contrary, I had not done everything strictly in accordance with the regulations for public disputations, that Most Illustrious Prince, Frederick Duke of Saxony, Imperial Elector, etc., would not possibly have suffered me to be a nuisance in his university. He himself holds Catholic and Apostolic truth too dear. Nor would the keen and learned men of this university have borne with me. But I have been able to do what has been done because these men, very loyal to your court as they are, do not fear the outcome even although the prince and the university risk being involved openly in the same opprobrium as I myself. Wherefore, Holy Father, I fling myself prostrate at the feet of your Holiness with all that I am and all that I have.[1] Revive, kill, call, recall, approve, reprove, as it pleases you. I shall acknowledge your voice as the voice of the Christ who is enthroned in you, and who speaks through you. If I merit death, I shall not refuse to die. For the earth is the Lord's and the fullness thereof.[2] He is blessed for ever. Amen, and may He have you for ever in His keeping.

ANNO MDXVIII

[1] Not exaggerated phraseology, but a mere description of the usual method of approach. It was precisely thus that Luther prostrated himself, first prone, then on invitation rising to his knees, and then standing, when he had audience of Cajetan at Augsburg on Oct. 8 (7), 1518

[2] Ps. 24:1

E

2

A SHORT EXPOSITION

OF

THE DECALOGUE
THE APOSTLES' CREED
THE LORD'S PRAYER

Introduction

Iᴛ was typical of the character of Luther that he should issue
a challenge to debate the Ninety-five Theses, for he had a passion
for knowledge of the truth; similarly, it was typical that he should
eventually face the emperor and the court at Worms with firmness, courage, and yet humility, for faith in God and obedience
to His will as he grasped it were matters of a conscience which
had always been scrupulous; similarly, it was typical of his quality
that his lecture-rooms at Wittenberg should be crowded, for his
learning was massive and his manner vivid and direct; but it
was equally characteristic of Luther that, however he might be
engrossed otherwise, he was profoundly concerned for the religious
life of the people. In the effort to teach them the truth of which
the gospel really consisted, he delivered a series of sermons on
the Ten Commandments. This occupied him from Midsummer,
1516, to Shrovetide, 1517. In Lent, he went on to deal similarly
with the Lord's Prayer. The substance of these sermons was
afterwards published, and a good deal of the original presentation can still be seen in the printed form. In the following years,
he went over the same ground again in a somewhat different
way and, in 1520, he also treated of the Apostles' Creed. Thus
it was that the present document came into being. Not primarily
academic but evangelical, it nevertheless reveals the scholar as
plainly as the evangelist and pastor of souls.

Luther's monograph on *Good Works* (also of A.D. 1520), has
received more attention, and it is indeed of great historical
importance. It attacks and refutes the medieval conception that
the most holy "works", or "fruits" of the Christian religion, are
things like the monastic life, the diligent observance of the
canonical hours, the ornamentation of churches and altars, presenting jewels or vestments to the clergy, praying the rosary, invoking
the saints, and going on pilgrimage. These were indeed among
the most outstanding characteristics of the "age of religion";
whereas the duties of one's calling, and the claims of normal life,
were regarded as of a lower order. Luther did an indispensable
work in refuting this religious theory, and he devoted the first
seventeen paragraphs of the *Good Works* to that purpose. But
the more constructive part of the treatise, that devoted to showing

what good works really are in the Pauline sense, consists of a long and elaborate exposition of the Decalogue. He makes it a genuine *praeparatio evangelica*; nay, indeed, when rightly followed, it is the foundation of sound Christian conduct, and is of the essence of an active Christian life.

The *Short Exposition of the Decalogue, the Creed, and the Lord's Prayer* gives all the essential, positive instruction of the *Good Works*, and has the advantage that it is even more revealing of Luther's personal religion, and more searching of the reader's conscience. With all his emphasis on salvation by faith, Luther never for a moment forgot that God is the lord and master of our life, to command what He would. In later years, when he felt that the doctrine of *sola fide* could no longer be successfully assailed, although still liable to abuse, he gave more frequent and emphatic expression than hitherto to his sense of God's majesty. In the *Short Exposition*, both features are plain. We see the infinite tenderness of Luther's conscience and his humble obeisance to God's holy will; his profound insight into human sin and failure, and into their causes and consequences; his immediate awareness of the marvel and miracle of the love and the grace of God. It includes, in stirring words, a powerful, personal confession of the assurance which his own faith gave him.[1]

There is nothing more intense in all Luther's writings than his *Short Exposition*, and nothing that has better preserved its original freshness. Of the documents belonging to the strenuous year, 1520, this is one that gives a clear reflection of his inner life, and of his abiding concern for the religion of the people. It is well worthy of a place side by side with those works which have long been known as his three principal Reformation writings.

The *Short Exposition* summed up much of Luther's preaching and writing in the years 1517–19. It is used again, in altered form, and otherwise carried further, in the *Betbüchlein* of 1522,[2] and in the varying editions of the *Deutsch Catechism*[3] and the *Enchiridion (Kleiner Catechismus)*[4] first published in 1529, and the *Simple Forms of Prayer*[5] of 1535.

The text here translated is that of the definitive Weimar Edition of Luther's Works, Vol. VII (1897), pp. 194/204–29.

[1] His letter to Melanchthon from Coburg Castle, June 30, 1530, is also in place here
[2] Cf. *W.*, Vol. X, Part iv, pp. 375–482
[3] Cf. *W.*, Vol. XXX, Part i, pp. 123–238
[4] Cf. *W.*, Vol. XXX, Part i, pp. 239–425
[5] Cf. *W.*, Vol. XXXVIII, pp. 351–75

A SHORT EXPOSITION OF

THE DECALOGUE, THE APOSTLES' CREED AND THE LORD'S PRAYER[1]

Text and Notes

PREAMBLE

SURELY it has been specially ordained by God that the people in general, who cannot read the Scriptures for themselves, should learn, and know by heart, the Ten Commandments, the Apostles' Creed, and the Lord's Prayer. They contain the whole substance of the Scriptures, and should be expounded time and again. They also contain everything that a Christian needs to know; they put the essentials in summary form; and also they are quickly and easily grasped. Thus there is no room for complaint; nor can anyone make the excuse that what he was required to know for his own salvation was either too much to remember, or else too difficult to comprehend.

There are three essentials that a man should know in order to be saved: (1) He should know what his duties are, and what they are not. (2) When at last he comes to understand that, by virtue of his own strength alone, he can neither keep this particular commandment, nor avoid yielding to that particular temptation, he should know where he can seek, and find, and obtain what he needs, so as to achieve the one, and withstand the other. (3) He should know how to set about seeking to obtain what he needs. The case is similar to that of a sick man: his first requirement is a

---

[1] The Short Exposition should be compared with that in the *Betbüchlein*, *W.*, X.ii, 1. Notes on p. 338 draw special attention to certain passages in *W.*, VII, pp. 206.64, 211.24, 212.27, 218.2–18, 223.18, 228.4. Compare these with the parallel passages in *W.*, X.ii, pp. 375–482. N.B.—Was it this version of remarks on the Ten Commandments which the humanists published 1518–19 through Froben, with a number of Luther's pamphlets, etc.? Cf. H. P. Smith, *Erasmus*, 217

diagnosis of his illness, and to know what he should do and
what he should avoid. Next, he requires to know where the
medicine is that will help him to do or to avoid things in
the way that would be natural if he were in good health.
In the third place, he must desire that medicine, seek and
fetch it, or have it brought. In a similar way, (i) the Decalogue teaches a man to know what is wrong with himself,
until he sees and feels what he should or should not do,
what he can or cannot dispense with; and to know himself
to be a sinful and unrighteous man. Then (ii) the Creed
shows and teaches him where to find the medicine, i.e., divine
grace, which will help him to become devout and to keep
the Commandments; this grace will help him to know God,
and also the mercy revealed and offered in Christ. And (iii)
the Lord's Prayer teaches him to yearn for this grace, to
seek it, and take it to heart. This he will do by regular,
humble, strengthening prayer. Then he will receive grace,
and, in this way, by fulfilling God's Commandment, he will
be saved.

These are the three great things taught by the Scriptures
as a whole. We begin, therefore, firstly, by learning the
Commandments; thereby we are taught to recognize our sins
and our unrighteousness, i.e., the spiritual maladies which
cause us to fall into sins of commission as well as sins of
omission.[1]

The First Table of Moses: That on the Right Hand[2]

This includes the first three commandments, in which we
learn how we should live in God's sight, what we owe God,
and what we ought to do or avoid doing.

1. The first commandment teaches us how we should feel
in our hearts towards God, i.e., what our thought about Him
should always be like, what should be our conduct and what
our reverence. In particular, we should look to Him for all

[1] Luther discussed the Decalogue and its practical implication very fully
in *Von den guten Werken* (On Good Works), which he published a few
weeks later, i.e., at the beginning of June, A.D. 1520. Cf. *W.*, VI, 202–76
[2] As customarily inscribed on the walls of churches near the altar in a
form abbreviated from Exod. 20:1-17 conflated with Deut. 5:6-21

that is good, as if to a father or a kindly friend, in all loyalty, and faith, and love. We must be always watchful not to displease Him, but to act like a child towards its father. Nature teaches that there is but one God[1] who gives us every good thing, and helps us in every difficulty. This is shown even by the heathen in their very worship of idols. The Commandment therefore says: THOU SHALT HAVE NO OTHER GODS, ETC.

2. The second commandment teaches how we should bear ourselves towards God outwardly, in words spoken in the hearing of others; but also inwardly, in our own hearts, viz.: we must remember His name and keep it holy. No one can make God's nature plain either to himself or to other people. We can only repeat His names.[2] The commandment therefore says: THOU SHALT NOT TAKE THE NAME OF THY GOD IN VAIN.

3. The third commandment teaches what our outward relation should be to God as seen in our works, i.e., in God's service. It says: REMEMBER THE SABBATH TO KEEP IT HOLY.

Thus the three commandments already spoken of teach us how to live in God's sight, in thought, word, and deed; i.e., in the whole of our life.

The Second Table of Moses: That on the Left Hand

This contains the following seven commandments, in which we are taught our obligations both to mankind and also to our neighbour, whether in positive action, or in self-restraint.

4. The first teaches our bearing to all those in authority, being, as such, God's representatives.[3] That is why this commandment precedes the rest, and follows immediately after

[1] The idea of the natural knowledge of God was one of the theological axioms of the Middle Ages. Modern scepticism was as yet unborn, though certain Humanists were already freethinkers, e.g., Filelfo, Poggio, Valla, and others; cf. Mackinnon, *Luther and the Reformation*, Vol. I, pp. 240ff. *Camb. Mod. Hist.*, I, chap. xvi; II, chap. xix

[2] All names had meanings originally, or described some function, e.g., Yahweh Sabaoth, El Shaddai, etc. Thus the "names" of God refer to the attributes of God; and this is what Luther implies, besides the sense of awe

[3] Cf. Rom. 13. This teaching is characteristic of Luther's theory of legal authority; and accounts for much of his attitude in the Peasants' Rising of 1525, and for the attitude of the Reformers in general; cf. also G. Rupp, *The English Protestant Tradition* (1947), p. 83

the first three commandments, which relate to God Himself. The "authorities" are our father and mother; our masters, whether spiritual or temporal; etc. The commandment, therefore, says: *HONOUR THY FATHER AND THY MOTHER.*

5. The second teaches us how to bear ourselves towards our equals and our neighbours, having regard to the person of each, so that we do him no injury, but, where needful, give support and help. It therefore says: *THOU SHALT NOT KILL.*

6. The third teaches us how to conduct ourselves towards the most cherished possessions which our neighbour has after his own person, i.e., his lawful wife, his children, and his friends. We must do them no harm, but hold them in all possible honour. It therefore says: *THOU SHALT NOT COMMIT ADULTERY.*

7. The fourth teaches us how to conduct ourselves towards our neighbour's temporal property—not to take possession of his goods, nor interfere with him, but help him forward. It says: *THOU SHALT NOT STEAL.*

8. The fifth teaches us how to conduct ourselves in regard to our neighbour's good standing and repute. These we must not undermine, but increase, protect, and preserve. It therefore says: *THOU SHALT NOT BEAR FALSE WITNESS AGAINST THY NEIGHBOUR.*

Thus we are forbidden to do damage to any of our neighbour's possessions; rather, we are commanded to forward his welfare. If at this point we consider the natural law,[1] we shall find that all these commandments are proper and equitable. For not all that is commanded here in our attitude to God or man differs from what any would wish for himself,[2] if he were in God's place, or in that of his fellow man.

9 and 10. The last two commandments teach in what way human nature is evil; and that we must be quite free from lascivious passions, and a greedy, acquisitive spirit. This, however, means struggle and effort as long as we live. These commandments therefore say: *THOU SHALT NOT COVET THY*

[1] Cf. Rom. 2:12. Luther means not the law of cause and effect as in modern usage, but the order of the universe recognized apart from divine revelation
[2] Cf. Matt. 7:12

*NEIGHBOUR'S HOUSE, THOU SHALT NOT COVET HIS WIFE, HIS
MANSERVANT, HIS MAIDSERVANT, HIS CATTLE, OR ANYTHING
THAT IS HIS.*

Short Conclusion to the Ten Commandments

Christ Himself said:
"What ye would that men should do to you, do ye also the
same unto them. This is the whole law and the prophets."[1] No
one readily bears ingratitude for a kindness, or allows another
to injure his repute. No one readily endures arrogance. No
one readily bears disobedience, anger, the unfaithfulness of
his wife, the theft of his property; or lying, deception, and
slander; rather, everybody seeks love and friendship, gratitude and assistance, truth and loyalty, from his neighbour.
And all these are what the Ten Commandments require of us.

How the Ten Commandments are Broken

The First: *Thou shalt have no other Gods.*

By taking to witchcraft, magic, or the black arts, when
in difficulty.

By making use of mystic letters, signs, herbs, magic words,
charms, and the like.

By using divining rods, incantations, crystal-gazing, cloak-
riding, or milk-stealing.[2]

By ordering one's life and work in accordance with lucky
days, astrological signs, and the views of fortune-tellers.

By using prayers and adjurations to the evil spirits to
protect oneself, one's cattle, house, children, and all else,
from wolves, war, fire, flood, and other kinds of harm.

By attributing misfortune and difficulties to the devil, or
to the wickedness of men; and by not accepting hardships
with love and gratitude, whether pleasant or unpleasant, as
from God alone; and by not acknowledging them to Him
with thanks and ready submissiveness.

By tempting God, and putting oneself into needless danger
to body and soul.

[1] Matt. 7:12
[2] Witches were supposed to use cloaks to make them invisible, etc., and
to steal the milk from cows' udders

By spiritual pride, or conceit about other spiritual gifts.

By forgetfulness of the needs of the soul, or only honouring God and the saints for the sake of temporal benefits.

By not trusting God always, and by not expecting to receive God's blessing in everything we try to do.

By a wavering faith, or by doubting God's grace.

By not shielding others from unbelief and doubt; by not helping them, as far as possible, to have faith and to trust in God's grace.

ALL forms of unbelief, doubt, and heresy break this commandment.

The Second: *Thou shalt not take the name of thy God in vain.*

To swear oaths without necessity, or by habit.

To swear falsely, or to break one's oath.

To vow or swear to do something evil.

To curse in God's name.

To tell foolish anecdotes about God, and lightly pervert the words of Scripture.

Not to call on the name of God in difficulty; and not to bless Him, whether in joy or sorrow, in success or failure.

To seek fame and honour and repute on account of one's religious devotion, one's knowledge, etc.

To call on God's name in pretence, like the heretics and all who suffer from religious pride.

Not to praise God's name in every event of life.

Not to disapprove of those who dishonour God's name, use it treacherously, or do evil in His name.

Vaingloriousness, boastfulness, and spiritual pride, break this commandment.

The Third: *Remember the Sabbath day to keep it Holy.*

To be given to gluttony, drinking, gambling, dancing, idleness, and debauchery.

To be lazy; to sleep during divine service; not to attend church; to go for a walk instead, or to gossip.

To work or transact business unnecessarily on Sunday.

Not to pray, nor to meditate on Christ's passion; not to repent of one's sins, nor to seek forgiveness; in short, to observe the day only outwardly by one's clothes, food, or conduct.

In all we do, and in all that befalls us, not to be content that God's own will should be done.

Not to help others to do the same, and not to hinder their doing the opposite.

Indifference to public worship also breaks this commandment.

The Fourth: *Honour thy father and thy mother.*

To be ashamed of one's parents because of their poverty, their uncultured manners, or their humble station.

Not to provide them with food and clothing when they are in need; even worse: to curse them, speak evil of them, slander them, or hate and disobey them.

Not to hold them in high esteem in all earnestness, for God's sake.

Not to respect them, even when they are unjust and harsh.

Not to observe the rules of the Christian church in regard to fast days, and feast days, etc.

To be disrespectful to the priesthood, to slander and insult it.

Not to be respectful towards one's superiors or governors; to be disloyal and disobedient to them, no matter whether they are kind or unkind.

This commandment also refers to all the heretics, schismatics, the excommunicated, and to hardened sinners, etc.

Not to help others to keep this commandment, and not to resist those who transgress it.

All forms of pride and disobedience should be included here.

The Fifth: *Thou shalt not kill.*

To be angry with one's neighbour.

To call him *Raca*, a word meaning all kinds of anger and dislike.[1] To call him *"fatue"*, "you fool", which includes all kinds of bad language, cursing, slander, libel, judging, criticizing, contemptuous references, and the like.

To censure one's neighbour's sins or transgressions, and not to overlook or minimize them.

[1] Matt. 5:22

Not to forgive one's enemies; not to pray for them; not to be friendly toward them, nor seek their welfare.

Under this commandment come all sins of anger and hatred, e.g., murder, war, robbery, arson, quarrelsomeness, irritability, regretting one's neighbour's success, and taking pleasure in his misfortune.

Not to practise works of mercy, even towards one's enemies.

To provoke or set men against each other.

To sow discord or suspicion among others.

Not to try to reconcile those unfriendly to each other.

Not to restrain, or ward off, anger and unfriendliness wherever possible.

The Sixth: *Thou shalt not commit adultery.*

To seduce virgin girls, to commit adultery, incest, and similar immoral practices.

To use unnatural means or persons to satisfy one's passions (these are known as the "unspeakable sins").

To use obscene words, catches, tales, or pictures, to rouse or exhibit sensual passion.

To rouse one's own sensual feelings, and defile oneself by prying, by touching, or by perverted thoughts.

Not to avoid whatever causes immorality, such as gluttony, toping, indolence, laziness, sleeping too long, and intimate contact with the persons of women or men.

To use extravagant dress or gestures and the like to rouse others to sensuality.

To provide house-room, space, opportunity, or assistance for doing such things.

Not to help in guarding another's purity by word or act.

The Seventh: *Thou shalt not steal.*

To practise theft, and robbery, and usury.

To use false weights and measures, or to sell poor quality as good.

To accept bequests or incomes dishonestly.[1]

To withhold earnings and deny debts.

[1] Such legacies as were often made to the church, and were therefore a special subject of temptation to the clergy

Not to lend to a needy neighbour, or not to do so without demanding interest.

Every form of greediness, or haste to be rich; and all other ways of keeping the property of others, or seizing it.

Not to resist what causes loss to another man.

Not to warn another against loss.

To hinder another's advantage.

To begrudge his gain.

The Eighth: *Thou shalt not bear false witness against thy neighbour.*

To conceal or suppress the truth before the bench.

To lie or deceive, and do harm thereby.

Similarly all seductive flattery, innuendos, and double dealings.

To explain away and lampoon the goodly life, words, or works of one's neighbour.

To give occasion and encouragement to evil speaking of that kind, instead of resisting it.

Not to speak in defence of the repute of one's neighbour.

Not to censure a slander.

To be silent about the good of anyone, and to speak about any evil.

To conceal the truth, or not to defend it.

The Last Two: *Thou shalt not covet thy neighbour's wife,* etc.

The last two commandments have no place in the confessional, but are set before us as the aim and goal of our pilgrimage. Every day we should strive to overcome evil, with God's help and by His Grace; for the tendency to evil never dies out of us until our body returns to the dust, and becomes a new creature.

The "five senses" come under the fifth and sixth commandments; the "six works of mercy" under the fifth and seventh. As to the "seven deadly sins", pride comes under the first and second; uncleanness under the sixth; wrath and hatred under the fifth; gluttony under the sixth; indolence under the third, and, really, under all of them. The "sins through others" are dealt with in all the commandments, for all the commandments may be sinned against by inciting, urging, and helping others to break them. The "crying sins" and the "unspeakable sins" come under the fifth, sixth, and seventh commandments;[1] and so on.

All such trespasses reveal nought but self-love; they deprive both God and man of their due; nor does such love render to God or man anything that it has, or is, or can do. Well did Augustine say: "All sin begins in self-love."

The inference from the whole of the foregoing is that the commandments only command love and forbid self-love; and that they are only fulfilled by love, and transgressed by self-love. That is why St. Paul says that "love is the fulfilment of the law",[2] just as perverted love is the transgression of every commandment.

How to fulfil the Ten Commandments

The First: *Thou shalt have no other Gods.*

You must fear and love God with unalloyed faith, and trust Him firmly at all times and in all your doings; and be entirely, perfectly, and wholly undisturbed, no matter what happens, good or bad.[3]

Everything said in the whole Bible about faith, and hope and the love of God, applies to keeping this commandment; it summarizes all its teaching.

The Second: *Thou shalt not take the Name . . .*

Praise, glorify, bless, and call upon God's name; count your own name and glory as nothing at all if only God be praised; for He alone comprises all things, and brings all things to pass.

Everything taught in the Scriptures about praising God, glorifying Him, and giving Him thanks; and about His name and the joy He gives, applies to keeping this commandment.

The Third: *Remember the Sabbath Day.*

Prepare for worshipping God, and for seeking His grace by prayer, attending mass, hearing the gospel, and meditating

---

[1] A medieval classification of sins used in the late Middle Ages for instructing the ignorant; it was, of course, familiar to Luther's readers and obviously in his mind in writing the above passage

[2] Rom. 13:10 (R.V.)

[3] Cf. the ending of Luther's letter to the pope, *supra*, p. 65

on the cross of Christ. These make you spiritually ready to attend the sacrament; for this commandment requires the soul to be "poor in spirit".[1] The soul must offer its nothingness to God, and find within itself His own works, and His own name, as taught in the first two commandments.

The above includes every ordinance in regard to divine worship, listening to the preaching of God's word, doing good works, and keeping the body in subjection to the spirit; so that all we do may belong to God, and not to ourselves.

The Fourth: *Honour Thy Father and Thy Mother . . .*
Willing obedience, humility, submission to all due authority, in order that we may be well-pleasing to God, as the Apostle Peter says.[2] And this we must do without any protest, complaint, or grumbling.

Everything in Scripture about obedience, humility, subjection, and doing reverence, applies to keeping this commandment.

The Fifth: *Thou shalt not kill.*
Patience, gentleness, kindliness, peaceableness, mercifulness, at all times, a sweet and friendly disposition without any hatred, wrath, or bitterness towards anyone whatsoever, including enemies.

All teachings of patience, gentleness, peace, and harmony, apply to keeping this commandment.

The Sixth: *Thou shalt not commit adultery.*
Modesty, self-control, chastity, whether in actions, words, bearing, or thought; also moderation in eating, drinking, sleeping; and all that promotes modesty.

All teachings are in place here about modesty, fasting, moderation, temperateness, prayer, watching, working, and whatever harmonizes with modesty.

The Seventh: *Thou shalt not steal.*
Lowliness of spirit, self-restraint, willingness to lend or give one's property, and to live without any greed or acquisitiveness.

[1] Matt. 5:2   [2] Cf. 1 Pet. 2:18; also Titus 2:9

F

All teachings are in place here which deal with greed, unlawful possessions, usury, sharp practice, deceit, injury to, and prevention of, the temporal well-being of our neighbour.

The Eighth: *Thou shalt not bear false witness.*

A peaceable and commendable mode of speech, hurtful to none, helpful to all, reconciling foes, excusing and defending the insulted; in short, truth and simplicity in speech.

This includes everything that teaches when to speak and when to be silent in regard to our neighbour's honour, rights, business, and felicity.

The Last Two.

Perfect purity of spirit, and superiority to all temporal pleasures and possessions, are of the kind which, properly speaking, are only brought to completion in the life to come.

There is only one motive operating in all these actions, whether to friend or foe, namely, love for both God and man. Love seeketh not its own, but what is due to God and one's neighbour. It gives itself liberally for each to use as his own, for his service, and at his disposal.

It is therefore clear that the Ten Commandments comprise, in an orderly and succinct manner, all the teachings which are needful in the course of human life. If a man means to keep them, he will be busy in good works day by day. He will have no need to choose some other occupation, to go from place to place,[1] or do anything not mentioned in the commandments.

All this is brought to our notice by the fact that the Ten Commandments never teach what a man should do, refuse to do, or desire of others for himself; but rather what he should do, or refuse to do, for others, for God, and for mankind. Thus it is borne in upon us inevitably that their fulfilment consists in love for others and not for ourselves. For a man does or refuses to do things, or seeks them in excess, when it is all for himself; and so what our nation needs is not teaching, but restraining in this regard. Therefore, the

[1] In the sense of "go on pilgrimages"

best life is one lived quite without regard for oneself, and
the worst life is one lived for oneself; and that is why the
Ten Commandments give their teaching as they do. They
show how few men live good lives; indeed, as man, no one's
life is good. Once we see this, we must go on to learn where
we can obtain that which will enable us to live a good life,
and fulfil the Commandments.

Jesus

The Creed is divided into three sections[1] corresponding to
the three persons of the holy and divine Trinity of whom it
tells. The first section bears witness to the Father, the second
to the Son, and the third to the Holy Spirit; for belief in
the Trinity is the principal article of faith, and all the other
articles depend on it.

We should not fail to notice at this point, however, that
there are two ways of believing. Firstly, our belief may be
about God, as is the case when I accept what is said about
Him, in the same way as I accept what is said about the
Turks, or the devil, or hell. This kind of believing is not
faith, so much as a sort of knowledge, or the taking note of
something. On the other hand, we may believe *in* God. This
is the case where I do not merely accept what is said about
God, but I put my faith in Him, I surrender myself to Him;
I venture to enter into association with Him, believing without any hesitation that He will be to me, and act towards
me, just as we are taught He will. This is not the form of
my belief in regard to the Turks, or mankind in general, no
matter how high their repute. It is easy for me to believe
that a certain person is good; but I do not, on this account,
build on him as my foundation. The kind of faith which
dares to accept what is said of God, even if doing so means
risking life or death, is the faith which alone makes a man

[1] In so dividing the creed, according to its subject matter, Luther was
making what the people must have felt to be a momentous innovation; it
was customary in the Middle Ages to divide the creed into twelve articles,
according to the number of the apostles

a Christian; through it, all his desires are satisfied by God. This kind of faith is unknown to those who are evil and sinful at heart, for it is a living faith. It is enjoined in the first commandment, which says: "I am thy God; thou shalt have no other gods." That is why the little word "in" is placed there, and is to be taken in all earnest, so that we do not say: "I believe God the Father" or "about the Father", but "in God the Father", "in Jesus Christ", "in the Holy Spirit". We cannot place this kind of faith in another man, but in God alone. That is how we know that Jesus Christ and the Holy Spirit are divine; it is because we believe *in* them, just as we believe *in* the Father. And since we have the same faith *in* each of the three persons, it follows that the three persons are in God.

The First Section

I believe in God the Father Almighty, Creator of heaven and earth.

This means:

I repudiate the devil, all idolatry, all sorcery, and all heresy;

I put my trust in no man on earth; not in myself, nor in my strength, talent, property, piety, or whatever else is mine;

I put my trust in no created being, whether in heaven or on earth;

I make bold to put all my trust only in the one wholly invisible and incomprehensible God, who created heaven and earth, and who alone is above every created thing;

Nor am I afraid of any wickedness on the part of the devil and his angels, for my God is above them all;

Even though I am forsaken by all men and persecuted, I shall nevertheless believe in God;

Even though I am poor, without wisdom, untaught and despised, or lacking in all other respects, nevertheless I shall believe in God;

Even though I am sinful, nevertheless my faith in God shall not falter. My faith must and shall soar above everything, whether near or far; above sin and virtue, and all else; in order that it may remain, purely and simply, faith in God, as required by the first commandment.

Nor do I seek a sign from Him, for that would be to tempt God. I trust in Him abidingly, no matter how I must wait; and I do not prescribe for Him the goal, the time, the degree or the manner; but I place all at the disposal of His divine will, with a faith genuine and unconstrained.

Since He is almighty, there is nothing I need that He cannot give me, or do for me.

Since He is the creator of heaven and earth, and Lord of all, who is there that can deprive me of anything, or do me harm? Yea, there can be no event whatsoever, but that it will all turn out to my benefit, and serve me, since He, whom everything obeys and serves, Himself seeks my good.[1]

Just because He is God, He can do what is best for me, and knows how best it should be done.

Just because He is Father, He wills to do it, and He does it graciously.

Just because I do not doubt these things, but put my trust in Him, I am assuredly His son, His servant, and His heir, through all eternity; and, according as I believe, so will it be done unto me.[2]

The Second Section

And in Jesus Christ, His only Son our Lord, who was conceived by the Holy Ghost, Born of the Virgin Mary, Suffered under Pontius Pilate, Was crucified, dead and buried, He descended into hell; and the third day He rose again from the dead. He ascended into heaven and sitteth on the right hand of God the Father Almighty; From thence He shall come to judge the quick and the dead.

This means:

I believe that Jesus Christ is the son of the one true God, begotten from eternity in an eternal divine nature and substance; and also that the Father has put all things in subjection to Him. According to His manhood, Christ is made my Lord, and the Lord of all things; according to His godhead, He, with the Father, created them all.

[1] Rom. 8:28   [2] Matt. 8:13

I believe that it is beyond anyone to believe in the Father, or to come to the Father, by virtue of his own ability, acts, or intelligence; nor by anything else which may be mentioned in heaven or on earth, except in and through Jesus Christ, His only Son; which means, through faith in His name and in His lordship.

I believe firmly that, for my sake, He was conceived by the Holy Spirit without any act of man's or of the flesh, without human father or any coition, in order that He might cleanse my own conception, and that of all believers in Him, from sin, concupiscence,[1] impurity, and damnation; and make them spiritual by the gracious will of Himself and the Almighty Father.

I believe He was born for my sake from Mary, the immaculate virgin, without prejudice to her virginity in either body or soul; and this, in order that my birth, and that of all believers in Him, might receive a blessing, be made innocent and pure by Him, in accordance with the merciful decree of the Father.

I believe that He bore His sufferings and endured the cross for my sake and that of all believers; and, in so doing, blessed all suffering and every cross, and rendered them, not merely innocent, but also salutary and highly meritorious.

I believe that He died and was buried in order completely to annul and bury my sins, and those of all believers in Him; and, in addition, I believe that He slew bodily death, and not only made it entirely harmless, but even advantageous and salutary.

I believe that He descended into hell to subdue and imprison the devil and all his angels, and the devil's cunning and his wickedness, for my sake and that of all believers in Him; in order that henceforth the devil would be unable to do me any harm, and that He might redeem me from the pains of hell, and even make them harmless and meritorious.

I believe that, on the third day, He rose again from the dead to give new life to me and to all that believe in Him; and that He has reawakened us with Himself by grace and

---

[1] Luther uses this term predominantly in the sense of desire, greed and avarice, rather than lust as such

in the Spirit, that henceforth we should have no need to sin, but only to serve Him in all grace and goodness.

I believe that He ascended into heaven and received authority and honour from the Father to rule all angels and created things. Therefore He sits at the right hand of God, i.e., He is king and lord over all that belongs to God in heaven, in hell, and on earth. Thereby He can help me, and all believers, in all our necessities, and against all our adversaries and enemies.

I believe He will come from thence, from heaven, on the last day, to judge those who will be found still alive, and the dead who have died meanwhile.

I believe that all men, all the angels and devils, must appear before His judgment seat and see Him bodily; and that He will redeem me, and all that believe in Him, from bodily death and from all our transgressions; and punish eternally our enemies and adversaries, and free us eternally from their power.

The Third Section

I believe in the Holy Ghost, one holy Christian Church, one Fellowship of the Saints, one Forgiveness of sins, Resurrection of the Body, and a Life Everlasting. Amen.

This means:

I believe, not only that the Holy Spirit is the only true God together with the Father and the Son; but also that, apart from the operation of the Holy Spirit, no one can come to God, nor receive any of the blessings effected through Christ, His life, cross, and death, and whatever else is ascribed to Him. Through Him, the Father and the Son move me and all others that are His. Through the Holy Spirit, the Father and the Son rouse, call, and draw us; and, through and in Christ, give us life and holiness, and make us spiritually-minded. Thus the Holy Spirit brings us to the Father, for He it is by whom the Father, through Christ and in Christ, does all things, and gives life to all.

I believe that, here below and throughout the world, there is only one Christian church, the church universal, and that this church is identical with the universal fellowship of the

saints, i.e., the devout believers everywhere on earth. This
church is gathered, sustained, and ruled by the Holy Spirit
as aforesaid, and strengthened day by day through the
sacraments and the Word of God.

I believe that no one can be saved who does not belong
to this universal fellowship, and keep in unison with it in
faith, word, and sacrament; in hope and love; and that no
Jew, heretic, heathen, or sinner, will enjoy its salvation,
unless he abandons his hostility, joins its fellowship, and
conforms to it in every respect.

I believe that, in this universal fellowship of Christendom,
all things are in common, and the property of any belongs
to all, and no one has anything of his own. Therefore all
the prayers and good works of the entire fellowship must
be of benefit to me and every believer, and must assist and
strengthen us, and this at all times in life or death. Thus
all bear one another's burdens, as St. Paul says.[1]

I believe that forgiveness of sins is to be found within
this universal fellowship, and nowhere else. Outside this
fellowship, no matter how many and important are the good
works, these do not avail for forgiveness of sin; but within
this fellowship, no matter how much, or how greatly, or how
often, a man may sin, forgiveness is not prejudiced, for it
abides wherever the one universal fellowship abides, and as
long as it lasts. Christ gave it "the keys" and said, in Matthew
18: "What you bind on earth shall be bound in heaven."[2]
Similarly He said to the one individual, Peter, in the room
of and standing for the one and only church (Matthew 16):
"Whatsoever thou shalt loose . . .", etc.[3]

I believe there will be a resurrection of the dead, in which
all mankind will be raised from the dead by the Holy Spirit;
that all men in the body or the flesh, whether they were
good or wicked, shall be raised and quickened in the body
or the flesh, meaning thereby the very flesh which died,
was buried, rotted away, and however else it came to
nought.

I believe that, after the resurrection of the dead, there
awaits eternal life for the holy, and eternal death for the

[1] Gal. 6:2   [2] Matt. 18:18   [3] Matt. 16:19

sinful. Throughout all, I am certain that the Father, through Jesus Christ, His Son and our Lord, with and in the Holy Spirit, will bring all these things to pass. That is what *Amen* means, namely, it is verily and certainly true.

Now follows:

THE LORD'S PRAYER[1]

The Preface and Preparation for offering the seven petitions to God

Our Father which art in heaven

Its meaning:

O Almighty God, because of Thine unbought mercy, Thou hast not left us to ourselves, but hast given us commandments and hast taught us through Thine only beloved Son, Jesus Christ our Lord. Through His merits, and with Him as our mediator, we may worship Thee and call Thee Father. Thou mightest justly be a stern judge of our sins. We have oftentimes grievously offended against Thy divine and perfect will, and incurred Thy wrath; yet, of that same mercy, do Thou comfort our hearts, and assure us of Thy Fatherly love. Let us taste that most precious flavour, and grant us that sweetness of childlike assurance in which we rejoice to call Thee Father; and let us know Thee, love Thee, and cry unto Thee, in all our necessities. Keep us ever as Thy children so that we fall into no sin, and lest we make Thee, our Father most to be loved, into a Judge much to be feared; and lest we transform ourselves from children to enemies.

It is also Thy will that we should not only call Thee "Father", but also "our Father", the common Father of us all; and that we should pray to Thee together and in unity. Therefore grant us a harmonious, brotherly love that we may recognize and respect each other as true brothers and sisters, and know Thee as the beloved Father of all alike. We pray for one another, each and all, as one child prays for another to its father. Let none among us be selfish in our desires, or forget our fellows before Thee; but, putting aside all hatred,

---

[1] Matt. 6:9-13, Lk. 11:2-4

envy, and quarrelsomeness, let us love one another as true and dutiful children of God. So may we say with one heart, not merely "My Father", but "Our Father".

Yet Thou art not a human father whose home is on earth, but a spiritual Father in heaven, who never dies and who is never uncertain. Thou art not one who cannot help himself like an earthly and human father, and Thou dost make plain to us that Thou art an exceeding better father, and teachest us to regard parenthood, native land, friends, goods, our own flesh and blood, as small things beside Thee. Therefore grant us, O Father, that we, on our part, may be Thy heavenly children; teach us to attend only to our souls and our heavenly heritage, in order that our temporal motherland and material heritage may not deceive us, nor lay hold on us and hinder us, and so make us wholly into children of this world. Grant us the right and true grounds for saying: "O Thou, our Father who art in Heaven"; that we may be truly Thy heavenly children.

The First Petition

Hallowed be Thy Name

Its meaning:

O Almighty God, our dear Father in heaven, in this unhappy vale of tears, Thy Holy Name is in so many ways profaned, dishonoured, and despised; attached to so many things which are not to Thy honour; and is also sinfully misused on so many occasions, till even those who bear Thy holy name lead infamous lives, which violate and dishonour it. Therefore, so grant us Thy divine grace that we may be kept from everything that does not redound to the honour and praise of Thy holy name. Help us to set aside all witchcraft and incantations. Help us to cease adjuring the devil or his creatures through Thy name. Help us to root out all wrong belief and superstition. Let it be that all heresy and false doctrine, which only bear Thy name as a disguise, may come to nought by Thy help. Grant that no false appearance of truth, piety, or holiness may deceive any one. Grant that no one shall use Thy name to swear or tell lies or deceive others. Defend us from all false confidence, all pretence of sheltering under Thy name. Keep us from all spiritual pride, all vain honouring of temporal fame and repute. Grant that, in all our necessities and infirmities, we may call upon Thy holy name. Grant that, in distress of conscience, and in the hour of death, we may not forget Thy name. Grant that, in all we have, or say, or do, we may praise and honour Thee alone, and not endeavour to promote our own repute or seek our own fame; but only Thine, to whom all things belong. Keep us from the shameful wrong of ingratitude. Grant that, through our good works and life, all others may be roused to praise, not our own selves, but Thyself in us, and to glorify Thy name. Grant that our evil deeds and infirmities may provoke no one to dishonour Thy name, or to neglect Thy praise. Prevent us from desiring anything, whether in time or eternity, which is not to Thy honour and glory; and if we pray for such things, answer us not according to our folly. Grant that our lives be such that we are found to be true children of God, and that Thy name of Father be not named over us falsely or in vain. Amen.

All the Psalms are in place in this petition, and all prayers in which God is praised, glorified, lauded, or thanked, together with the whole of the *Te Deum*.

The Second Petition

Thy Kingdom Come

Its meaning:

The present life with its afflictions is ruled by every kind of sin and wickedness, a realm where the evil one holds sway, and which is chiefly responsible for all wickedness and wrong. But Thy Kingdom is a kingdom entirely of grace and goodness where Christ Jesus, Thy beloved Son, is Lord, and is the Head and source of every grace and virtue. Therefore, help us and have mercy on us, beloved Father. Before all else, give us a true and steadfast faith in Christ, undismayed hope in Thy compassion on all the blindness of our sinful conscience, a pure and fervent love toward Thee and all men.

Keep us from unbelief, and doubt, and envy of worldly things. Preserve us from the base desire for anything unchaste, and give us a love for all continence and all modesty. Preserve us from all quarrelsomeness, war, and unrest; and let the blessings of Thy kingdom come, with peace, unity, and tranquillity. Grant that neither anger, nor any bitterness of spirit, overcome Thy Kingdom within us; but, of Thy grace, let a simple sweet-reasonableness and a brotherly faithfulness, together with all forms of friendliness, gentleness, and tenderness, abide and rule in us. Grant that we be not given to a resentful spirit, nor to moodiness; but fill us with joy and gladness in Thy grace and loving-kindness.

Finally, and in order to turn aside every sin from us, and that we, by Thy grace, may be full of every virtue and all good works, let Thy Kingdom come. So may we, with all our heart and mind and understanding, serve Thee obediently; and do so with all our strength, without and within, according to Thy will and Thy commandments. Then may we give ourselves to be ruled by Thee alone, and not follow our own inclinations, nor the world, the flesh, and the devil.

Grant that this Kingdom of Thine may begin in us and grow, and daily increase and improve; that we be not overcome by wicked and cunning excuses for ourselves, nor by a slothful spirit in serving God, lest we fall away again; but give us earnestness of purpose, and the power, not only to begin a spiritual life, but also to go forward courageously, and complete the work; as the prophet says: "Enlighten mine eyes that I fall not asleep, nor become slothful in the good life which I have begun, lest the Enemy once more gain power over me."[1]

Grant that we may remain steadfast in this way, so that, when Thy Kingdom comes, it may finish and complete the kingdom within our hearts which Thou hast already begun. Deliver us from the dangers of this sinful world; help us to yearn for the life to come, and to hate the present one. Help us not to fear death, but to long for it. Turn us from loving and clinging to this life, that thus Thy Kingdom may come, above all within our hearts.

[1] Psalm 13:3f.

This petition includes all the psalms, verses, and prayers, in which we beseech God to give us grace and virtue.

The Third Petition

Thy will be done on earth as it is in heaven

Its meaning:

Our will, when compared with Thy will, is never good, but always evil. But Thy will is always entirely good; it is to be loved and sought in the highest degree, and beyond all else. Therefore have mercy on us, O our Father, and do not allow anything to happen merely according to our own will. Give us patience, and teach us to persevere therein if our own desires are denied or delayed. When anyone speaks or remains silent, does or neglects to do anything contrary to our will, help us not to become angry or ill-tempered, not to swear or complain, not to cry out or criticize, not to condemn or contradict, etc. Help us humbly to accommodate our will to our opponents and to those who hinder us; and subduing our own will, may we praise, bless, and benefit them as persons who bring about, not our will, but Thy divine will, which is always the best.

Give us grace willingly to bear every sort of illness, poverty, contempt, suffering, and adversity, and to recognize that these are Thy divine will, and sent to crucify our will. Help us also to bear injustice cheerfully, and keep us from taking our revenge. Permit us not to repay evil with evil, or to meet force with force. Help us rather to take delight in this Thy will which brings these things upon us, and to praise and thank Thee. Help us not to ascribe to the devil or to human wickedness anything that happens to us contrary to our own will; but to ascribe it only to Thy divine will, which ordains all these things so as to hinder our own will, and to promote holiness in Thy kingdom.

Help us to be willing and happy to die, and to accept death cheerfully in accordance with Thy will, lest we become disobedient to Thee by impatience or reluctance. Grant that none of our members—our eyes, tongue, heart, hands, or feet —be allowed their own desires and will; but let them be seized by Thy will, held fast, and conquered. Keep us from everything in our own will which, just because it is our own, is evil, refractory, harsh, stubborn, and self-assertive.

Grant us true obedience, a complete and simple and abiding serenity, whether of our hearts and minds, or of outer circumstances, whether of time or of eternity. Keep us from the terrible vice of backbiting, from slander, evil speaking, cursing, or breaking our promises to others. O fend far off from us the great misfortune, and the great plague, of these ways of speaking. But when we see or hear anything blameworthy or displeasing to us in others, teach us to say nothing about it, to keep it to ourselves, to cry to Thee alone, and to give place to Thy will. Thus may we forgive from our hearts all who trespass against us, and may we feel sympathy for them.

Teach us to understand that no one can hurt us, without first doing himself a thousand times more harm in Thy sight. May we be moved thereby more to pity for him than to anger; rather to sorrow for him than to seek revenge. Grant that we may not rejoice when things go wrong with those who have not done what we wished, or when evil falls on those who have not done our will, or have done us evil; or when they fall otherwise into difficulties in their lives. Grant also that we be not disappointed when they prosper.

This petition includes also all the psalms, verses, and prayers which we offer in our hearts against sins and other enemies.

The Fourth Petition

Give us this day our daily bread

Its meaning:

The bread is our Lord Jesus Christ who nourishes and comforts the soul. Therefore, O heavenly Father, grant by Thy grace that the life of Christ, His words, His works, and His cross may be preached to us and to all mankind, and so be made known and revered. Help us to keep His words and work before us throughout life as an inspiring example, and a mirror of every virtue. Help us when we suffer, or are in adversity, to find strength and comfort through and in His sufferings and His cross. Help us, in firmness of faith, to rise through His death or be superior to our own, and thus fearlessly to follow our beloved pioneer into the life beyond.[1] Grant Thy grace to all preachers so that they may preach Christ and Thy Word effectively to all mankind, and with power to save. Help all hearers of Thy preached Word to learn of Christ, and truly to amend their lives. It is also by Thy grace that Thou dost will to drive from the holy Church all preaching foreign to itself, and all doctrines which do not teach Christ. Be merciful unto all bishops, priests, and ministers of the gospel, and unto all in authority over us, that, illumined by Thy grace, they may give us proper instruction and guidance by their words and their sound example. Guard all whose faith is feeble, lest they be led astray by any false example of those in authority. Guard us from heretical and schismatical teachers, that we may be united, partaking of the same daily bread, namely, the same doctrine and the same Word of Christ. Teach us by Thy grace rightly to understand the cross of Christ, to hold to it with all our hearts, to form our lives upon it to our salvation. On the day of our death, suffer us not to be robbed of the holy and true body of Christ. Help all priests to administer and apply the most precious sacraments worthily, so as to bring salvation and edification to the whole Christian community. Help us and all Christians to receive the holy sacraments at their due season, and to be blessed by their grace. And, all in all, give us our daily bread, that Christ may abide eternally in us and we in Him, and that we may worthily bear the name of Christian, which we have received from Him.

This petition includes all the prayers and psalms on behalf of those who rule over us, and particularly those for protection against false teachers, and those on behalf of Jews, heretics, and all the wayward; also those on behalf of all who are afflicted, and all who suffer, knowing no consolation.

[1] John 14:6

The Fifth Petition

And forgive us our debts, as we forgive our debtors

Its meaning:

A certain condition is appended to this petition: that we should previously forgive our debtors. When we have done that, we may then pray: "Forgive us our debts." This prayer is also included in the *third* petition already discussed: that God's will be done. The purpose of that will is that we should bear everything patiently, and not return evil for evil, nor seek our revenge; but return good for evil, as is done by our Father in heaven. For He makes His sun to rise on the good and on the evil, and sends His rain upon those who thank Him and those who do not.[1] Therefore we pray Thee, O Father, comfort our hearts both now and on the day of our death; for on account of our sins and Thy judgment, we are in great fear now, and will be so when we die. Give our hearts Thy peace, that we may await Thy judgment with joy. Deal not with us in the strictness of Thy judgment, for then no man shall be found righteous. Teach us, dear Father, not to trust in our good works, or depend on our merits; but simply and firmly to rely on and humbly accept Thine unfathomable mercy. Likewise, let us not lose courage because of our sinfulness and guilt, but esteem Thy mercy as higher, wider, and stronger than all else in our lives.

Help all men who are in dire need, and those attacked by sore temptation; and especially (So and so) and (So and so). Have mercy on all poor souls in Purgatory, especially (So and so) and (So and so); forgive them and us all our debts; comfort them and receive them in Thy mercy. Give us Thy good things in spite of our evil, as Thou hast commanded us also to do. Silence that terrible calumniator and accuser, the Evil One who magnifies our sins. Silence him both now and in our hour of death, and whenever our conscience troubles us; for we on our part will refrain from speaking evil of others, and enlarging on their sins. Judge us not according to the charges of the devil, or of our unhappy consciences. Listen not to the voice of our enemies who

[1] Matt. 5:45

accuse us day and night unto Thee, for we also will not listen to those who speak evil of others, or bring charges against others.

Take from us the heavy burden of all our sins and of our uneasy consciences, so that we may rejoice with light hearts, suffering or doing all we can, in entire confidence in Thy mercy. So may we live and die.

This petition includes all the psalms and prayers which call on God for His mercy on our sins.

The Sixth Petition

And lead us not into temptation

Its meaning:

We are subject to three kinds of temptations or spiritual attacks: the world, the flesh, and the devil. So we pray: Heavenly Father, give us grace to overcome the wiles of the flesh. Help us to resist when we are tempted to eat, drink, and sleep to excess, or to give way to idleness and laziness. Help us to control our desires by fasting, by moderation in eating, clothing, and sleeping, and during our waking and working hours; and thus to keep our body under, ready for doing anything good.

Help us to smite its evil inclination to uncleanness, and all its passions and lusts, and slay them by the crucified Christ, so that we do not consent to any of its temptations, nor follow them. When we see an alluring person or picture or other excitement, let not temptation rise within us; help us to learn to love purity and to praise Thee in Thy creatures whenever we hear something enticing and we feel its attraction. Help us lest our passions be roused thereby; rather, may we seek Thy praise and glory. Keep us from the grievous vices of greed and of yearning for the riches of this world. Keep us from seeking place and power in this world, or succumbing to such inclinations. Defend us, lest the faithlessness of men, or the false shows and enticements of the world, move us to follow them. Defend us in the evils and disappointments of life from falling into impatience, or

G

revenge, or anger, or other wrongdoing. Help us to put aside (as we said when we were baptized) the falsehoods of the world, its deceits, pretences, unfaithfulness, and all worldly things, whether good or evil in themselves; and so to grow in strength daily that we may resist these things.

Protect us from the suggestions of the devil, lest we give way to pride, to seeking our own good pleasure, or to despising others, all for the sake of wealth, rank, power, skill, fashion, or any other good things which Thou hast given. Keep us from falling into hatred or envy for any cause. Sustain us when we are tempted to unbelief; defend us from doubt both now and when death overshadows us.

We commend unto Thee, Heavenly Father, all those who strive and struggle against great and manifold temptations. Strengthen those who stand, and grant new help to those who have fallen and are prostrate. Give to all of us Thy grace, that, afflicted and insecure as we are, and continually surrounded by many foes, we may steadily wield our sword with a firm and knightly faith, and win the eternal crown.

The Seventh Petition

But deliver us from evil

Its meaning:

This petition is offered because of all the evils of torment and punishment, just as is done by the holy Church herself in the litanies. Deliver us, O Father, from Thy eternal wrath and the pains of hell. Deliver us from Thy stern judgment at our death, and at the last day. Shield us from quick and sudden death. Guard us from water and fire, from lightning and hail. Deliver us from famine, and times of high prices. Spare us from Thy great plagues; from pestilence, from syphilis,[1] and other serious maladies. Guard us from all afflictions and torments of the body. And in all these things, may Thy name be glorified, Thy Kingdom come, and Thy divine will be done.

Amen.

[1] Syphilis was extremely prevalent in the fifteenth and early sixteenth centuries

Amen

Grant, O God, a most certain answer to all these petitions, and let us not doubt that Thou hast heard, and wilt hear, us when we offer them; and that, in answer, Thou wilt grant them and not refuse them, or leave us in doubt. So with joy we say: "Amen; it is true and assured."

Amen.

POSTSCRIPT[1]

Finally, you must remember always to say the "Amen" definitely; and you must not doubt that God will most certainly hear you with all His Grace, and answer your prayer. Consider further that you are not alone in kneeling and standing there, but the whole of Christendom, and all good Christians, are with you; and you are among them in unanimous and single-minded prayer which God cannot despise. And, when you pray, always think to yourself: I am assured and certain of that. That is the meaning of "Amen".

Of course, you will understand that I do not wish that all these words which I have written should be uttered in your prayers, for that would end in your merely uttering the formal language found in a book. Rather I hope I have stirred up your hearts and taught you what kind of thoughts are comprised in the Lord's Prayer. But the heart can express these thoughts in many other words, and indeed in either fewer or more numerous words. For I do not bind even myself to use just these words, but to-day I speak in one way and to-morrow use other words, according to what my heart moves me.

[1] From *Anweisung wie man beten solle*, Leipzig ed., Vol. XXII, but often included in popular reprints as providing a less abrupt conclusion

3

AN APPEAL TO THE RULING CLASS OF GERMAN NATIONALITY

AS TO THE AMELIORATION OF THE STATE OF CHRISTENDOM

Introduction

HITHERTO, Luther had confined himself entirely to teaching religion, and had sought to show what was the essence of the Christian faith. Only when stung by the attacks of his enemies did he enter into polemics, and at first with reluctance and restraint. But in his replies to Prierias[1] and to John Eck,[2] among others, he seems to have discovered his powers of invective, which he gradually came to use in their full vigour. He had already become widely known among the people as a teacher and writer, and many were beginning, but only beginning, to look at the Christian faith through his eyes.[3] His advent was given a warmer welcome in other quarters, to which he had already made a certain appeal. In the course of the *Sermon on Good Works* he had addressed a paragraph or two to the kings, princes, and noblemen, and had called on them to attack the real Turks, i.e. the pope's entourage; and, without seeking any personal advantage, to attempt to improve the state of Christendom. He had said very similar things in another tract in which he discussed the state of the papacy in Rome. Many young men, of the upper classes in particular, were strongly possessed by the new spirit of nationality then just beginning to be felt; they seem quickly to have realized that Luther was a man they must support. Among others, von Sickingen[4] wrote and offered Luther protection in case of need. Whatever assurance Luther may have gained from these interchanges, there can be little doubt but that they must have influenced the direction of his thoughts during the present, almost incredibly strenuous year, 1520. After the religious teaching, framed primarily for the people at large, teaching which he had given in the *Good Works* and the *Short Exposition,* he now turned to the upper class. He did so because he thought they were in a position to implement a reformation of the crying scandals which were being perpetrated in the name of religion, and under the aegis of the church.

Luther was not stirred by nationalism, but by sympathy for the multitudes of poor people suffering needlessly in body and

[1] *Supra,* p. 28   [2] *Supra,* p. 28   [3] *Supra,* pp. 16ff.
[4] Franz von Sickingen (1481–1523) a man of debonair character, many enthusiasms, and a stormy career. Drawn by Ulrich von Hutten to support the humanist movement and the effort to reform the church. Died of wounds after a siege

soul owing to the enormities of the times. His sympathy had gained content from the psalms and the prophets of the Old Testament, and had been illumined by the gospels and epistles of the New Testament. His compassion was aroused by the poor and the blind and the halt and the helpless just because of their condition, and only in a secondary fashion because they were fellow-Germans. Indeed, one rather gains the impression that it is because the poorer Germans were despised that he felt called to speak a special word on their behalf. For centuries, responsibility for the poor and the ignorant had been in the hands of the church; and, in many respects, this responsibility was far from having been evaded. The majority of the prelates and pastors felt a genuine concern for the well-being of their flock. But, by the nature of the case, these priests and prelates were more or less remote in mind from the place-holders and the place-seekers and the policy-makers. They may have protested in the privacy of their parsonages; or, like Wessel Gansfort,[1] they may have timidly expressed their dissent in academic terms; yet, on the whole, they kept themselves to themselves with many a pious hope, no doubt, that someone would do something about it.

Meanwhile, it should be noted that several of the princes and other members of the ruling class in the state and in the church, and many of the scholars belonging to the Humanist movement, now in full bloom, were markedly in sympathy with Luther's teachings, and admired the courage with which he had taken his stand. But the authority of the church was universally accepted, and its responsibility for the welfare of Christendom prevented dissatisfaction from gathering to effective force. Any open protest, indeed, would border on insurrection and on sacrilege. Never, in all the history of the church, had there been a moral appeal addressed at the same time both to the secular authorities on behalf of the people, and also against the head of the church which was their guardian. The very idea was novel. Apart from the church, there was scarcely any such thing as a public opinion of an ethical character, not even among those actually discharging the duties of administration or attending to the well-being of the people at large. Yet, as a practical alternative to the princes of the church, there were the members of the ruling class, the

---

[1] (1420–89) a "reformer before the Reformation". One of the great scholars of the humanist movement; after study and teaching at Heidelberg, Paris, he returned to Zwolle, where he was one of the Brethren of the Common Lot. His cautious character enabled him to escape the inquisition. Luther greatly admired his writings; cf. Miller & Scudder, *Wessel Gansfort: His Life and Writings*, 2 vols, 1917

class to whose power the authorities of the church themselves appealed to carry out their decrees. This class, of course, was "Christian"; the age was still the "age of faith". All men belonged to the church, and heretics were regarded with a certain horror, as if they were moral lepers. Within the ruling class itself, naturally, there were degrees and differences: some persons were dominated by loyalty to the established order and to Holy Church, but others were leavened by the religious ideas of the reforming preachers and teachers, of whom Luther was now chief. If a common platform and a common programme could be found, there was at least a hope of an amelioration of the abuses under which both the state and its members were suffering. It was to the more forward-looking that Luther determined to appeal; and, in making his appeal, he wrote what was both the first tractate on social reform, as well as the first outline of a Christian policy in the conduct of public affairs. But his interest was purely religious, and not at all "social" in the modern sense of that term. He was concerned about men's souls; for the rest, he was content if the poor had enough to keep them from starvation. Poverty as such was neither a hardship nor an evil in his eyes; and inequality, far from being of the essence of injustice, was something belonging to the nature of things. Order and peace in the state were of far greater consequence than a mere egalitarianism.

Nevertheless, of all Luther's writings, this document is that which is most egalitarian, for it elaborates more fully than in any other writing his doctrine of the priesthood of all believers:[1] all Christians are Christian by virtue of their baptism and their baptismal vows; each therefore possesses, in principle, all the grace which God gives through Christ. It follows that all Christians are essentially equal, and possess equally all the treasures which God has committed to men. The differences that exist between them are those of accident or function, and are based, ultimately, on the common consent or choice of the Christian community. Even the religious offices bear the same stamp, including that of hearing confession and administering the sacraments. Apart from the exercise of the function or office which had been delegated to him, a priest or a prelate was on the same standing as his fellow-Christians.

In the earlier part of the discussion, Luther brings out this doctrine with great power; it may indeed be said that his

[1] Cf. *infra*, pp. 113ff., *and Pagan Servitude*, pp. 318ff.; *Freedom*, pp. 366ff.

arguments have often been denied, but not that they have been refuted: they have only been ignored and passed over. Here, in fact, is fundamental Christian teaching. In the last part of the treatise, however, where Luther attempts to apply his main principles to the habits of the wealthy, he is on less exalted ground, and his reasons are less purely religious; we cannot avoid a certain disappointment that he attempted to discuss issues that we ourselves recognize to be economic in their character, complex in their ramifications, and, at that date, completely obscure in principle. But in pleading for the education of girls as well as boys, and that encouragement should be given to the brighter minds, he shows himself the genuine pastor of souls. His proposals in the present treatise reveal Luther as an independent thinker and a practical pioneer. It is impossible to over-estimate the influence of the *Appeal* on succeeding generations.

The main part of the *Appeal*, however, and the one that makes it a document of the greatest importance in the actual reformation of religion, is Luther's indictment of the Roman hierarchy for the abuses under which all western Christendom was grievously suffering. Although the abuses were not universal, they were sufficiently widespread and gross to be called scandalous without qualification; and that they, or any one of them, should be made legitimate by a single prelate, apart from the question of their being practised by the Roman curia itself, constitutes one of the most astounding enigmas in the history of the Christian church. No matter what the historical "explanation", the situation was one for which there was neither excuse nor pardon. If we consider the enormity of the case, on the one hand, and, on the other, the disquiet felt by multitudes of responsible men, we can only marvel at the moderation of Luther's tone, and at the close, factual character of his statements. For his indictments are not based merely on a few, casual observations made by a recluse who had once gone on a delegation to Rome; the tone of his statements reveals precise documentation, and trustworthy personal information, although most of the charges that Luther marshals were simply matters of common knowledge among educated men. Valla's refutation of the *Donation of Constantine* reveals far more than the historical fraud which it discloses. The writings of Erasmus, whether the *Colloquies*, the *Praise of Folly*, or the *Julius Exclusus*, cannot be understood on any other basis than that of gross public scandal. Similarly the *Letters of Obscure Men*, or Jakob Wimpheling's *Responsa et replicae*, his *Gravamina*

Germanicae Nationis, as well as many anonymous and unidentified writings, show the depravity which had become commonplace.

As to the more personal information which Luther received: much was conveyed in letters that friends were writing him from Rome, one of whom was probably John Hess.[1] After a long residence in Rome, Hess arrived early in 1520 in Wittenberg, where he had personal intercourse with both Luther and Melanchthon. Another important source of personal information was John von der Wick, who had been in Rome as Reuchlin's lawyer in his affair with the Dominicans. Luther actually mentioned him when writing to Spalatin on June 10, 1520. Then, of course, Luther's own duties gave him many opportunities of observation in different parts of Germany. But, whether drawn from actual documents, or from the accounts of others, or from his own personal observation in the course of visitations as district-vicar, or from his journeys for the purpose of attending meetings, and keeping other engagements in numerous towns during the last ten years, it is abundantly plain that Luther was thoroughly acquainted with the facts, and satisfied as to their veracity. The facts were indeed terrible enough in themselves without any further emphasis.

Of course, many of his acquaintances were fearful of the consequences if he published the present tract. In particular, his old friend, John Lang, urged him not to do so, but wrote just too late. By August 18, at the moment when the princes were beginning to assemble for the coronation of Charles V, Melchior Lotther had already printed a first edition and sold 4,000 copies; and less than a week later, on August 23, Luther seems to have followed a hint from Spalatin and introduced other passages into the second edition on which the publisher was already at work (*vide* pp. 59ff., 112f., 125).

In this way, an epoch-making document was given forth to the world. It was both the prophecy and the pioneer of the Protestant Reformation.

The original text of the present translation is to be found in the Weimar Edition of Luther's Works, Vol. VI, pp. 381–403, 404–69.

(NOTE: The original title reads: *An den christlichen Adel deutscher Nation von des christlichen Standes Besserung, 1520.* The term *Adel* means persons of good birth whatever their particular rank;

[1] (1490–1547) born in Nüremberg. Became the Reformer of Breslau as an ardent disciple of Luther, although he retained the humanist leanings which he had acquired as a student in Leipzig

but in the present document Luther has in mind, not their blood, but the fact that they constituted the rulers and administrators; hence the translation "ruling class" seems to be a nearer equivalent than the term "nobility" which does not in itself connote "rulers". It will be noticed that the familiar term "Address" does not occur; and in fact this tract is not an address but an appeal, and well deserves to be so entitled. This must also be one of the earliest instances of the word "nation" used approximately in its modern sense; it reflects the birth of national consciousness so characteristic of the modern, as distinct from the medieval, world.)

Text and Notes

Jesus

Dedicated by Dr. Martin Luther to his dear friend, the honourable and worthy gentleman, NICHOLAS von AMSDORFT,[1] Licentiate in Holy Scripture, and Canon in Wittenberg.

The Salutation

MAY the grace and peace of God be yours, my honourable, worthy, and dear friend.

The time for silence is over, and the time for speech has come, as Ecclesiastes[2] says. In accordance with our project, I have put together a few paragraphs on the amelioration of the condition of Christendom. I intend the writing for the consideration of Christians belonging to the ruling classes in Germany. I hope that God will grant help to His church through the laity, since the clergy, who should be the more appropriate persons, have grown quite indifferent. I am sending to your worthy self all I have written. Please examine, and, where desirable, modify it. I know that I shall not escape the criticism that I presume too much, in that I, an unimportant and inferior person,[3] dare to address such a high and responsible class of society on very special and important subjects. I am acting, I confess, as if there were no other in the world than Doctor Luther to play the part of a Christian, and give advice to people of culture and education. But I shall not apologize, no matter who demands it. Perhaps I owe God and the world another

[1] Born in 1483, he was the same age as Luther. They were together as students at Erfurt, and were life-long friends. Amsdorff was a man of strong character and one of the most prominent of the early group of reformers. From 1524 he was superintendent minister of Magdeburg, and in 1542 was consecrated by Luther to be bishop of Naumburg. He died in 1561

[2] Eccles. 3:7

[3] It was very much the case in the sixteenth century, in Germany as elsewhere, that a man of lower rank should "know his place", and should not speak to a superior unless specifically invited; cf. *supra*, p. 65, and n.1

act of folly.[1] For what it is worth, this pamphlet is an attempt
to pay that debt as well as I can, even if I become for once
a Court-fool. No one needs to buy me a fool's cap nor shave
me my poll.[2] The question is, Which of us is to put the bells
on the other? I must act according to the proverb, "A Monk
must be in it whatever the world is doing, even if he has
to be painted in."[3] A fool often says wise things and frequently sages speak very foolishly. St. Paul said: "If any
wishes to be wise, he must become a fool."[4] Moreover, since
I am not only a fool, but also sworn in as a Doctor of Holy
Scripture, I am glad that I have the opportunity to fulfil my
oath even in the guise of a fool. I beg you to make my
apologies to those of average understanding, for I make no
pretence of attempting to win the favour and goodwill of
the super-intelligent. I have often tried hard to do it, but
never again will I attempt it, nor worry about it. God help
us not to seek our own glory but His alone. Amen.

Wittenberg, The Augustinian Monastery, on the eve[5] of
John the Baptist's day, A.D. 1520.

The Appeal

Doctor Martin Luther to His Most Illustrious, Most Mighty
and Imperial Majesty, and to the Christians of the German
Ruling Class.

Grace and power from God to his Illustrious Majesty, and
to you, most gracious and honourable Gentlemen.

It is not due to sheer impertinence or wantonness that
I, a lone and simple man, have taken it upon myself to
address your worships. All classes in Christendom, particularly in Germany, are now oppressed by distress and
affliction, and this has stirred not only me but everyman to
cry out anxiously for help. It has compelled me to beg and
pray that God will endow someone with His Spirit to bring
aid to this unhappy nation. Proposals have often been made
at councils, but have been cunningly deferred by the guile

---

[1] A reference to his "presumption" in publishing the *Pagan Servitude*,
infra, pp. 203ff.
[2] I.e., a monk's tonsure was the equivalent of a jester's cap and bells
[3] As a figure or the back-cloth at a play.   [4] Cf. 1 Cor. 3:18   [5] I.e., June 24

of certain men, and matters have gone from bad to worse. Their artifices and wickedness I intend with God's help to lay bare in order that, once shown up, they may never again present such hindrances or be so harmful. God has given us a young man of noble ancestry to be our head[1] and so has raised high hopes in many hearts. In these circumstances, it is fitting for us to do all we can to make good use of the present time and of God's gracious gift to us.

The first and most urgent thing just now is that we should each prepare our own selves in all seriousness. We must not begin by assuming we possess much strength or wisdom, even if we had all the authority in the world. For God cannot and will not suffer a goodly enterprise to be begun if we trust in our own strength and wisdom. God will surely abase such pride, as is said in Psalm 33,[2] "No king stands by the multitude of his host, and no lord by the greatness of his strength." For this reason, I fear, it came to pass in former times that the good princes, emperors Frederick I and II, and many other German emperors, were shamelessly trodden under foot and oppressed by the popes whom all the world feared. Perhaps they relied more on their own strength than on God, and therefore had to fall. And what else, in our day, has raised the bloodthirsty Julius II[3] so high, if it were not, as I fear, that France, Germany, and Venice depended on themselves? The children of Benjamin slew 42,000 Israelites because they relied on their own strength (Judges 19).[4]

Lest we have the same experience under our noble emperor, Charles, we must be clear that we are not dealing permanently with men in this matter, but with the princes of hell who would fill the world with war and bloodshed, and yet avoid letting themselves be caught by the flood. We must go to work now, not depending on physical power, but in humble

[1] The emperor, Charles V, succeeded in A.D. 1518, at the age of eighteen
[2] Ps. 33:16
[3] Julius II, pope, A.D. 1503-13. The reference is to the war for which the League of Cambrai, A.D. 1508, was the preparation, and the main outcome of which was to establish the temporal power of the papacy. Julius II led his armies in person, and was the "scourge of Italy". *Camb. Mod. Hist.*, Vol. I, pp. 128-43
[4] Judges 20:21 says 22,000

trust in God, seeking help from Him in earnest prayer, with nothing else in mind than the misery and distress of all Christendom suffering over and above what sinful men have deserved. Otherwise our efforts may well begin with good prospects, but, when we get deeply involved, the evil spirit will cause such confusion as to make the whole world swim in blood, and then nothing will be accomplished. Therefore, in this matter let us act wisely, and as those who fear God. The greater the power we employ, the greater the disaster we suffer, unless we act humbly and in the fear of God. If hitherto the popes and Romanists have been able, with the devil's help, to bring kings into conflict with each other, they will be able to do it again now, if we set forth without God's help, and armed only with our own strength and shrewdness.

I. THE THREE WALLS

The Romanists have very cleverly surrounded themselves with three walls, which have protected them till now in such a way that no one could reform them. As a result, the whole of Christendom has suffered woeful corruption. In the first place, when under the threat of secular force, they have stood firm and declared that secular force had no jurisdiction over them; rather the opposite was the case, and the spiritual was superior to the secular. In the second place, when the Holy Scriptures have been used to reprove them, they have responded that no one except the pope was competent to expound Scripture. In the third place, when threatened with a council, they have pretended that no one but the pope could summon a council. In this way, they have adroitly nullified these three means of correction, and avoided punishment. Thus they still remain in secure possession of these three walls, and practise all the villainy and wickedness we see to-day. When they have been compelled to hold a council, they have made it nugatory by compelling the princes to swear in advance that the present position shall remain undisturbed. In addition they have given the pope full authority over all the decisions of a council, till it is a matter of indifference whether there be many councils or none, for they only deceive us with make-believes and sham-fights. So terribly fearful are they for their skins, if a truly free council were held. Further, the Romanists have over-awed kings and princes till the latter believe it would be impious not to obey them in spite of all the deceitful and cunning dodges of theirs.

May God now help us, and give us one of those trumpets with which the walls of Jericho were overthrown;[1] that we may blow away these walls of paper and straw, and set free the Christian, corrective measures to punish sin, and to bring the devil's deceits and wiles to the light of day. In this way, may we be reformed through suffering and again receive God's blessing.

i. Let us begin by attacking the first wall.

To call popes, bishops, priests, monks, and nuns, the religious class, but princes, lords, artizans, and farm-workers the secular class, is a specious device invented by certain time-servers; but no one ought to be frightened by it, and for good reason. For all Christians whatsoever really and truly belong to the religious class, and there is no difference among them except in so far as they do different work. That is St. Paul's meaning, in 1 Corinthians 12, when he says: "We are all one body, yet each member hath his own work for serving others."[2] This applies to us all, because we have one baptism, one gospel, one faith, and are all equally Christian. For baptism, gospel, and faith alone make men religious, and create a Christian people. When a pope or bishop anoints, grants tonsures, ordains, consecrates, dresses differently from laymen, he may make a hypocrite of a man, or an anointed image,[3] but never a Christian or a spiritually-minded man. The fact is that our baptism consecrates us all without exception, and makes us all priests. As St. Peter says,[4] "You are a royal priesthood and a realm of priests",

[1] Joshua 6:20   [2] Cf. esp. 1 Cor. 12:12ff.

[3] *Oelgötzen* really means idols smeared with oil or paint; metaphorically used of false doctrines; and by Luther of "false priests", with a reference to the oil used when they were ordained. The same word is used to mean a dummy, figure-head, a half-wit

[4] 1 Pet. 2:9; cf. *infra*, pp. 318f., 366f.

H

and Revelation, "Thou hast made us priests and kings by Thy blood".[1] If we ourselves as Christians did not receive a higher consecration than that given by pope or bishop, then no one would be made priest even by consecration at the hands of pope or bishop; nor would anyone be authorized to celebrate Eucharist, or preach, or pronounce absolution.

When a bishop consecrates, he simply acts on behalf of the entire congregation, all of whom have the same authority. They may select one of their number and command him to exercise this authority on behalf of the others. It would be similar if ten brothers, king's sons and equal heirs, were to choose one of themselves to rule the kingdom for them. All would be kings and of equal authority, although one was appointed to rule. To put it more plainly, suppose a small group of earnest Christian laymen were taken prisoner and settled in the middle of a desert without any episcopally ordained priest among them; and they then agreed to choose one of themselves, whether married or not, and endow him with the office of baptizing, administering the sacrament, pronouncing absolution, and preaching; that man would be as truly a priest as if he had been ordained by all the bishops and the popes. It follows that, if needs be, anyone may baptize or pronounce absolution, an impossible situation if we were not all priests. The fact that baptism, and the Christian status which it confers, possess such great grace and authority, is what the Romanists have overridden by their canon law, and kept us in ignorance thereof. But, in former days, Christians used to choose their bishops and priests from their own members, and these were afterwards confirmed by other bishops without any of the pomp of present custom. St. Augustine, Ambrose, and Cyprian each became bishops in this way.

Those who exercise secular authority have been baptized like the rest of us, and have the same faith and the same gospel; therefore we must admit that they are priests and bishops. They discharge their office as an office of the Christian community, and for the benefit of that community. Every one who has been baptized may claim that he has

[1] Rev. 5:9f.

already been consecrated priest, bishop, or pope, even though
it is not seemly for any particular person arbitrarily to exercise the office. Just because we are all priests of equal standing, no one must push himself forward and, without the
consent and choice of the rest, presume to do that for which
we all have equal authority. Only by the consent and command of the community should any individual person claim
for himself what belongs equally to all. If it should happen
that anyone abuses an office for which he has been chosen,
and is dismissed for that reason, he would resume his former
status. It follows that the status of a priest among Christians
is merely that of an office-bearer; while he holds the office
he exercises it; if he be deposed he resumes his status in the
community and becomes like the rest. Certainly a priest is
no longer a priest after being unfrocked. Yet the Romanists
have devised the claim to *characteres indelebiles*,[1] and assert
that a priest, even if deposed, is different from a mere layman. They even hold the illusion that a priest can never be
anything else than a priest, and therefore never a layman
again. All these are human inventions and regulations.

Hence we deduce that there is, at bottom, really no other
difference between laymen, priests, princes, bishops, or, in
Romanist terminology, between religious and secular, than
that of office or occupation, and not that of Christian status.
All have spiritual status, and all are truly priests, bishops,
and popes. But Christians do not all follow the same occupation. Similarly, priests and monks do not all work at the
same task. This is supported by Romans 12[2] and 1 Corinthians 12,[3] and by 1 Peter 2,[4] as I showed above. In these
passages, St. Paul and St. Peter say that we are all one body,
and belong to Jesus Christ who is the head, and we are all
members of one another. Christ has not two bodies, nor two
kinds of body, one secular and the other religious. He has
one head and one body.

Therefore those now called "the religious", i.e., priests,
bishops, and popes, possess no further or greater dignity than

[1] Inexpungeable mark or quality. In the bull, *Exultate Deo*, of 1439,
Pope Eugenius IV claimed that "orders" made a priest for ever different
from a layman

[2] Rom. 12:4ff.   [3] 1 Cor. 12:12ff.   [4] 1 Pet. 2:9

other Christians, except that their duty is to expound the word of God and administer the sacraments—that being their office. In the same way, the secular authorities "hold the sword and the rod", their function being to punish evil-doers and protect the law-abiding. A shoemaker, a smith, a farmer, each has his manual occupation and work; and yet, at the same time, all are eligible to act as priests and bishops. Every one of them in his occupation or handicraft ought to be useful to his fellows, and serve them in such a way that the various trades are all directed to the best advantage of the community, and promote the well-being of body and soul, just as all the organs of the body serve each other.

Now let us consider whether it is Christian to affirm and declare that secular authorities do not exercise jurisdiction over religious office-bearers, and should not inflict penalties on them. That is as much as to say that the hand ought to do nothing to help when the eye suffers severely. Would it not be unnatural, or indeed unchristian, for one organ not to help another and not ward off what is destroying it? Rather, the more precious an organ is, the more ought the other to help. Therefore, I maintain, that since the secular authorities are ordained by God to punish evil-doers and to protect the law-abiding, so we ought to leave them free to do their work without let or hindrance everywhere in Christian countries, and without partiality, whether for pope, bishops, pastors, monks, nuns, or anyone else. If, to prevent the exercise of secular authority, it were enough to say that the civil administration was, from the Christian standpoint, a lower function than that of preacher or confessor or the religious status, then surely tailors, shoemakers, stonemasons, carpenters, cooks, manservants, farmers, and all secular craftsmen, being lower still, should be forbidden to make shoes, clothes, houses, things to eat and drink, or pay rents and tributes to the pope, bishops, priests, and monks. But if these laymen are to be allowed to do their work undisturbed, what is the purpose of Romanist writers who make laws by which they exempt themselves from the secular Christian authorities? It is simply that they may do evil unpunished, and fulfil what St. Peter said, "There shall arise false teachers among you, moving among you with false and imaginary sayings, selling you a bad bargain."[1]

Hence secular Christian authorities should exercise their office freely and unhindered and without fear, whether it be pope, bishop, or priest with whom they are dealing; if a man is guilty let him pay the penalty. What canon law says to the contrary is Romish presumptuousness and pure invention. For this is what St. Paul says to all Christians, "Let every soul (I hold that includes the pope's) be subject to the higher powers, for they bear not the sword in vain. They serve God alone, punishing the evil and praising the good."[2] And St. Peter, "Be subject unto every ordinance of man for God's sake, whose will is that it should be so."[3] He has also proclaimed that such men would come, and would contemn secular authority;[4] and this has, in fact, come about through canon law.

That in my view overturns the first wall—of paper. The reason is that the social corpus of Christendom includes secular government as one of its component functions. This government is spiritual in status, although it discharges a secular duty. It should operate, freely and unhindered, upon all members of the entire corpus, should punish and compel where guilt deserves or necessity requires, in spite of pope, bishops, and priests; and whether they denounce or excommunicate to their hearts' desire. That is why guilty priests, before being handed over to the secular arm, are previously deprived of the dignities of their office. This would not be right unless the secular "sword" already possessed authority over them by divine ordinance. Moreover, it is intolerable that in canon law, the freedom, person, and goods of the clergy should be given this exemption, as if laymen were not exactly as spiritual, and as good Christians, as they, or did not equally belong to the church. Why should your person, life, possessions, and honour be exempt, whereas mine are not, although we are equally Christian, with the same baptism, guilt, and spirit and all else? If a priest is killed, a country is placed under interdict; why not also if a farmer is killed? Whence comes such a great difference between two men equally Christian? Simply from human law and fabrications.

[1] 2 Pet. 2:1ff.   [2] Rom. 13:1-4   [3] 1 Pet. 2:13, 15   [4] 2 Pet. 2:10

It cannot have been a man of goodwill who devised such distinctions, and made some sins exempt and immune. For it is our duty to strive as much as we can against the Evil One and his works and to drive him away, for so Christ and His apostles bade us. How comes it then that we are told to hold our peace and be silent when the pope or his supporters design impious words or deeds? Are we, on account of certain men, to neglect divine commands and God's truth which we swore at our baptism to defend with life and limb? Of a truth we shall be held responsible for the souls of all who are abandoned and led astray thereby. Surely, it must be the archdevil himself who propounded that canon law which declares, "Even if the pope were so wicked that he led men in multitudes to the devil, nevertheless he could not be deposed." This is the accursed and impious foundation on which they build at Rome, maintaining that we should sooner let all the world go to the devil than oppose their villainy. If a certain person were not to be penalised on the ground that he was superior to the rest, then no Christian may penalise his fellows, since Christ bade us one and all to serve the meanest and humblest.[1]

There is no longer any defence against punishment where sin exists. St. Gregory himself wrote[2] that, while we are all equal, guilt makes one man subject to others. All this shows plainly how the Romanists deal with Christian people, robbing them of their freedom without any warrant from Scripture, but by sheer wantonness. But God and the apostles made them subject to the secular "sword". Well may we fear that Antichrist has been at work, or is completing his preparations.[3]

---

[1] Matt. 18:4; 20:27; 23:11; Luke 9:48

[2] Pope Gregory the Great (590–604) in the *Regula pastoralis*, II, 6 (Migne, *Patrol. Ser. Lat.*, 77, 34)

[3] Luther shared the common belief in the approach of the Last Judgment as an article of Christian faith; but he held that the precise date was a secret which God reserved to Himself. One pastor, Michael Stifel, calculated that it would come on Sunday, Oct. 19, 1533, at 8.0 a.m.; much unrest and excitement were caused. Luther reproved him sharply, and even deprived him of office for a time
Luther regarded the doctrine of the Antichrist largely as a means of destroying the doctrine of salvation by works, and of making faith in God central to the Christian life. Further, cf. K. Holl, *Ges. Aufs*, I, 326, n. 3

ii

The second wall is more loosely built and less indefensible. The Romanists profess to be the only interpreters of Scripture, even though they never learn anything contained in it their lives long. They claim authority for themselves alone, juggle with words shamelessly before our eyes, saying that the pope cannot err as to the faith, whether he be bad or good; although they cannot quote a single letter of Scripture to support their claim. Thus it comes about that so many heretical, unchristian, and even unnatural laws are contained in the canon law—matters of which there is no need for discussion at the present juncture. Just because the Romanists profess to believe that the Holy Spirit has not abandoned them, no matter if they are as ignorant and bad as they could be, they presume to assert whatever they please. In such a case, what is the need or the value of Holy Scripture? Let it be burned, and let us be content with the ignorant gentlemen at Rome who "possess the Holy Spirit within", who, however, in fact, dwells in pious souls only. Had I not read it, I should have thought it incredible that the devil should have produced such ineptitudes at Rome, and have gained adherents to them. But lest we fight them with mere words, let us adduce Scripture. St. Paul says, I Corinthians 14, "If something superior be revealed to any one sitting there and listening to another speaking God's word, the first speaker must be silent and give place."[1] What would be the virtue of this commandment if only the speaker, or the person in the highest position, were to be believed? Christ Himself says,[2] John 6, "that all Christians shall be taught by God". Then if the pope and his adherents were bad men, and not true Christians, i.e., not taught by God to have a true understanding; and if, on the other hand, a humble person should have the true understanding, why ever should we not follow him? Has not the pope made many errors? Who could enlighten Christian people if the pope erred, unless someone else, who had the support of Scripture, were more to be believed than he?

[1] I Cor. 14:30   [2] John 6:45

Therefore it is a wicked, base invention, for which they cannot adduce a tittle of evidence in support, to aver that it is the function of the pope alone to interpret Scripture, or to confirm any particular interpretation. And if they claim that St. Peter received authority when he was given the keys —well, it is plain enough that the keys were not given to St. Peter only, but to the whole Christian community.[1] Moreover the keys have no reference to doctrine or policy, but only to refusing or being willing to forgive sin. Whatever else the Romanists claim in virtue of the keys is an idle invention. But Christ's word to Peter, "I have prayed for thee that thy faith fail not",[2] cannot be stretched to apply to the pope, seeing that the majority of the popes have had no faith, as they themselves are obliged to confess. Therefore, Christ did not pray for Peter only, but for all apostles and Christians. As He said in John 17, "Father, I pray for those whom Thou hast given me, and not only for them, but for all those who believe on me through their word."[3] Surely these words are plain enough.

Think it over for yourself. You must acknowledge that there are good Christians among us who have the true faith, spirit, understanding, word, and mind of Christ. Why ever should one reject their opinion and judgment, and accept those of the pope, who has neither that faith nor that spirit? That would be to repudiate the whole faith and the Christian church itself. Moreover, it can never be the pope alone who is in the right, if the creed is correct in the article, "I believe in one, holy, Christian church"; or should the confession take the form: "I believe in the pope of Rome"? But this would be to concentrate the Christian church entirely in one man, and that would be in every way an impious, pernicious, error.

In addition, as I have already said, each and all of us are priests because we all have the one faith, the one gospel, one and the same sacrament; why then should we not be entitled to taste or test, and to judge what is right or wrong in the faith? How otherwise does St. Paul's dictum stand,

---

[1] Luther is here only repeating the point made by Erasmus in his note on Matt. 16:19 in his Greek New Testament of A.D. 1516
[2] Luke 22:32   [3] John 17:9, 20

1 Corinthians 2, "He that is spiritual judges all things and is judged by none",[1] and 2 Corinthians 4, "We all have the one spirit of faith"?[2] Why then should we not distinguish what accords or does not accord with the faith quite as well as an unbelieving pope? These and many other passages should give us courage and set us free. We ought not to allow the spirit of liberty—to use St. Paul's term[3]—to be frightened away by pronouncements confabricated by the popes. We ought to march boldly forward, and test everything the Romanists do or leave undone. We ought to apply that understanding of the Scriptures which we possess as believers, and constrain the Romanists to follow, not their own interpretation, but that which is in fact the better. In former days, Abraham had to listen to Sarah,[4] who was more completely subject to him than we are to anyone in the world. Similarly, Balaam's ass was more perspicacious than the prophet himself.[5] Since God once spoke through an ass, why should He not come in our day and speak through a man of faith and even contradict the pope? Moreover, St. Paul upbraided St. Peter as a wrongdoer.[6] Hence it is the duty of every Christian to accept the implications of the faith, understand and defend it, and denounce everything false.

iii

The third wall falls without more ado when the first two are demolished; for, even if the pope acts contrary to Scripture, we ourselves are bound to abide by Scripture. We must punish him and constrain him, according to the passage, "If thy brother sin against thee, go and tell it him between thee and him alone; but if he hear thee not, take with thee one or two more; and if he hear them not, tell it to the church; and if he hear not the church, let him be unto thee as a Gentile."[7] This passage commands each member to exercise concern for his fellow; much more is it our duty when the wrongdoer is one who rules over us all alike, and who causes much harm and offence to the rest by his conduct. And if

[1] 1 Cor. 2:15   [2] 2 Cor. 4:13   [3] 2 Cor. 3:17   [4] Gen. 21:12
[5] Num. 22:28   [6] Gal. 2:11   [7] Matt. 18:15-17

I am to lay a charge against him before the church, then I must call it together.

Romanists have no Scriptural basis for their contention that the pope alone has the right to summon or sanction a council. This is their own ruling, and only valid as long as it is not harmful to Christian well-being or contrary to God's laws. If, however, the pope is in the wrong, this ruling becomes invalid, because it is harmful to Christian well-being not to punish him through a council.

Accordingly, we read in Acts 15 that it was not St. Peter, but all the apostles and elders, who called the Apostolic Council.[1] If that had been the sole right of St. Peter, it would not have been a Christian council, but an heretical *conciliabulum*. Further, the bishop of Rome neither called nor sanctioned the council of Nicea, the most celebrated of all, but the emperor, Constantine. After him, many other emperors did the same, and these councils were the most Christian of all. But if the pope had really had the sole authority, then they would necessarily all have been heretical. Moreover, when I examine decisions of those councils which the pope himself called, I find they did nothing of special importance.

Therefore, when need requires it, and the pope is acting harmfully to Christian well-being, let anyone who is a true member of the Christian community as a whole take steps as early as possible to bring about a genuinely free council. No one is so able to do this as the secular authorities, especially since they are also fellow Christians, fellow priests, similarly religious, and of similar authority in all respects. They should exercise their office and do their work without let or hindrance where it is necessary or advantageous to do so, for God has given them authority over every one. Surely it would be an unnatural proceeding, if fire were to break out in a town, if everyone should stand still and let it burn on and on, simply because no one had the mayor's authority, or perhaps because it began at the mayor's residence. In such a case, is it not the duty of each citizen to stir up the rest, and call upon them for help? Much more ought it to be the

[1] Acts 15:6

case in the spiritual city of Christ, were a fire of offence to break out, whether in the pope's régime or anywhere else. The same argument would hold, if an enemy were to attack a town; that man who called his fellow citizens together at the earliest moment would deserve honour and gratitude. Why then should not honour be accorded to one who makes our infernal enemies known, rouses Christian people, and calls them together?

It is empty talk when the Romanists boast of possessing an authority such as cannot properly be contested. No one in Christendom has authority to do evil, or to forbid evil from being resisted. The church has no authority except to promote the greater good. Hence, if the pope should exercise his authority to prevent a free council, and so hinder the reform of the church, we ought to pay no regard to him and his authority. If he should excommunicate and fulminate, that ought to be despised as the proceedings of a foolish man. Trusting in God's protection, we ought to excommunicate him in return, and manage as best we can; for this authority of his would be presumptuous and empty. He does not possess it, and he would fall an easy victim to a passage of Scripture; for Paul says to the Corinthians, "For God gave us authority, not to cast down Christendom, but to build it up".[1] Who would pretend to ignore this text? Only the power of the devil and the Antichrist attempting to arrest whatever serves the reform of Christendom. Wherefore, we must resist that power with life and limb, and might and main.

Even if some supernatural sign should be given, and appear to support the pope against the secular authority; e.g., if a plague were to strike someone down, as they boast has happened sometimes, we ought only to regard it as caused by the devil on account of our lack of faith in God. It is what Christ proclaimed, "False Christs and false prophets will come in my name, and will do signs and wonders, so as to lead astray, if possible, even the elect."[2] St. Paul says to the Thessalonians[3] that the Antichrist shall, through Satan, be mighty in false, miraculous signs.

[1] 2 Cor. 10:8   [2] Matt. 24:24   [3] cf. 2 Thess. 2:9

Therefore, let us firmly maintain that no Christian authority is valid when exercised contrary to Christ. St. Paul says, "We can do nothing against Christ, but only for Christ."[1] But if an authority does anything against Christ, it is due to the power of the Antichrist and of the devil, even if that authority makes it rain and hail miracles and plagues. Miracles and plagues prove nothing, especially in these latter days of evil, for specious miracles of this kind are foretold everywhere in Scripture. Therefore, we must hold to God's Word with firm faith. The devil will soon abandon his miracles.

And now, I hope that I have laid these false and deceptive terrors, though the Romanists have long used them to make us diffident and of a fearful conscience. It is obvious to all that they, like us, are subject to the authority of the state, that they have no warrant to expound Scripture arbitrarily and without special knowledge. They are not empowered to prohibit a council or, according to their pleasure, to determine its decisions in advance, to bind it and to rob it of freedom. But if they do so, I hope I have shown that of a truth they belong to the community of Antichrist and the devil, and have nothing in common with Christ except the name.

[N.B. The foregoing paragraphs assume a new theory of government, and also of the relation between church and state. Owing to the abuse which the ruling classes made of Luther's theory in the next few decades, it is important to notice the precise terms of Luther's theory. He regarded the existing rulers and their class, *eo ipso*, as essentially Christian in heart, and in their feeling of responsibility to God for their rulership; all this in the evangelical sense. He had grounds for this view in the character and convictions of many of the ruling class that he knew personally; but he showed his naïveté in generalizing these assumptions. The more astute and self-seeking of the class were not slow to take advantage of the support afforded by the simple religious fervour of the new movement, to further their own interests. There is a direct connection between this abuse and the rise of the modern, secular state.

[1] 2 Cor. 13:8

The new relation envisaged between church and state reversed the position, originally due to Ambrose,[1] and regarded them as equal partners with different functions in respect to the welfare of the people. This view was only practicable if both were truly Christian, and indeed in the evangelical sense. Luther's eagerness, doubtless, prevented his seeing that this condition did not obtain, and made him blind to the "unreality" of many details of his position. —Editor.]

II. SUBJECTS TO BE DISCUSSED BY THE COUNCILS

Now let us consider the subjects which might properly be discussed in the councils, or with which popes, cardinals, bishops, and all scholars might well busy themselves day and night if they held Christ or His church dear. Otherwise, Christians at large, and those who exercise authority in the state, ought to do so despite the Romanists' excommunications or fulminations. For one undeserved excommunication is better than ten justifiable absolutions; and one undeserved absolution is worse than ten justifiable excommunications. Therefore let us wake up, my dear fellow countrymen, and fear God rather than men, lest we suffer like all those poor folk who have gone astray so pitiably through the shameless and impious régime of Rome. Under this régime, the devil prospers more and more every day; and, if such a thing were possible, this impious régime must become worse as a consequence, although I still cannot conceive nor believe how.

1. In the first place,[2] it is painful and shocking to see that the head of Christendom, proclaiming himself the Vicar of Christ and the successor of St. Peter, lives in such a worldly

[1] Cf. Lietzmann, *The Era of the Church Fathers*, E.T. 1951, pp. 77ff.
[2] In making this point, Luther goes over well-trodden ground, and is only repeating what had been said often enough. Long before the Reformation, polemical writers had made much of the contrast between Christ and the Antichrist. It was put very forcibly by Wycliffe's *De Christo et suo adversario Antichristo*, and was common among Hussite and Franciscan writers. Luther's use of the idea helped to spread it everywhere among the masses

and ostentatious style that no king or emperor can reach
and rival him.¹ He claims the titles of "Most Holy" and
"Most Spiritual", but there is more worldliness in him than
in the world itself. He wears a triple crown, whereas the
mightiest kings wear only one. If that is like the lowly Christ
or St. Peter, it is to me a new sort of likeness. The Romanists
bleat that it would be heretical to speak against it; they
refuse to consider how unchristian and ungodly such conduct is. In my view, however, if the pope were to pray before
God with fear, he would have to lay aside his triple crown,
for our God tolerates no haughtiness.² Of course, his duty
ought to be nothing less than to weep and pray day by day
for all Christian people, and to show an example of deep
humility.

No matter how his inclinations may lead him, such pomp
is evil; and for the sake of his soul's salvation, the pope ought
to lay it aside, if only because St. Paul says, "Abstain from
all demeanour which is evil",³ and again, "We ought to bring
forth what is good, not only in God's sight, but also before
all men".⁴ An ordinary bishop's crown ought to suffice the
pope. He should be above others in wisdom and holiness,
and leave the crown of pride to the Antichrist, as his predecessors did centuries ago. The Romanists declare he is the
Lord of the earth. That is false; for Christ, whose vicegerent
and steward he boasts of being, said before Pilate, "My kingdom is not of this world."⁵ No vicegerent can have a rulership greater than his lord. Nor is the pope vicegerent on
behalf of the Risen Christ, but of the Crucified Christ, for
Paul says, "For I determined not to know anything among
you save Christ and him crucified";⁶ and, "You ought so
to think of yourselves as you see in Christ, who emptied himself, and took on the mien of a servant",⁷ and again, "We
preach Christ, the crucified".⁸ But now they create the pope
the vicegerent of the Risen Christ in heaven; and some popes

¹ The reigning pope was the Medici, Leo X, under whom the papacy
reached its greatest splendour, far beyond that of any contemporary king,
even Henry VIII. Similar criticisms were not uncommon at the time, cf.
note in *W.*, VI, 415
² Cf. Ps. 101:5; 138:6   ³ 1 Thess. 5:22   ⁴ Rom. 12:17
⁵ John 18:36   ⁶ 1 Cor. 2:2   ⁷ Phil. 2:5-7   ⁸ 1 Cor. 1:23

have let the devil rule in them so fully that they have claimed that the pope is above the angels in heaven and has them at his command; which surely is the work of Antichrist himself.

2. What Christian purpose is served by the ecclesiastics called cardinals?[1] I will tell you. In Italy and Germany there are many wealthy monasteries, institutions, benefices, and parishes. No better way has been devised of bringing them into Rome's possession than by creating cardinals and giving them bishoprics, monasteries, and prelacies as their property, thus destroying the service of God. The consequence is that Italy is now almost devastated; monasteries are in disorder, bishoprics despoiled, the revenues of prelacies and all the churches drawn to Rome, cities devastated, land and people ruined, because no longer are services held or sermons preached. Why so? Because the cardinals must have their revenues. The Turk himself could not have ruined Italy in like manner nor put an end to divine worship to such an extent.

Now that Italy is drained dry, they are coming into the German countries, and beginning with calculated restraint. But let us watch, for the German countries will soon become like Italy. Already we have a few cardinals. They think the drunken Germans will not understand what the game is, till there is not a single bishopric, monastery, parish or benefice, not a cent or farthing, left for them. The Antichrist must take the treasures of the world, as it is written.[2] This is what happens: they take a heavy toll of the bishoprics, monasteries, and benefices. While they do not yet dare entirely to despoil the country, as they have done in Italy, meantime they use such unction and adroitness that they clump ten or twenty prelacies together. They then wrest annual tribute from each, amounting in total to a considerable sum. The priory at Wurzburg pays 1,000 guilders, that at Bamberg also makes a contribution, besides Mayence, Trèves, and others. In this

[1] This question had also been raised by Aeneas Silvius in A.D. 1515, in his *Germania*. Compare also the trenchant criticism in Erasmus, *Praise of Folly* (Gibbings & Co., 1900), pp. 165ff.
[2] Cf. 1 John 2:15–18

way 1,000 or 10,000 guilders may be collected in order that a cardinal shall live in Rome in princely style.

Having reached this stage, they proceed to create thirty or forty cardinals in a single day,[1] give to one the convent on the Mönchberg, near Bamberg, plus the bishopric of Wurzburg, with a few wealthy parishes tacked on, until churches and cities are laid waste; and then they proceed to justify it all by saying, "We are Christ's agents and the shepherds of Christ's sheep. The silly drunken Germans must put up with it."

My way would be to create fewer cardinals, or else let the pope support them at his own expense. Twelve of them would be more than enough, each with 1,000 guilders income. How has it come about that we Germans have to tolerate such robbery, such confiscations of our property? If the kingdom of France has resisted it,[2] why do we Germans let the Romanists make fools and apes of us in this way? It would be more tolerable if they only stole our possessions in this fashion; but they devastate the church by it, rob Christ's sheep of their devout pastors, and debase the service of God and the Word of God. Even if there were not a single cardinal, the church would still not decline. As things are, they do nothing to serve Christendom; they only bargain and quarrel about bishoprics and prelacies just as any thief might do.

3. If ninety-nine per cent. of the papal court were abolished and only one per cent. were left, it would still be large enough to deal with questions of Christian faith. At present there is a crawling mass of reptiles, all claiming to pay allegiance to the pope, but Babylon never saw the like of these miscreants. The pope has more than 3,000 secretaries alone, and no one can count the others he employs, as the posts are so numerous. It is hardly possible to number all those that lie in wait for the institutions and benefices of Germany, like wolves for the

---

[1] Leo X created 31 cardinals on July 31, 1517, for his own personal safety immediately after the discovery of the infamous plot to poison him. Luther's account is overstrained, though the fact remained; *infra*, pp. 165, 339

[2] A reference to the Pragmatic Sanction of A.D. 1438, confirmed by the Concordat of 1516; cf. *Camb. Mod. Hist.*, I, pp. 385–8

sheep. I fear that Germany to-day is giving far more to the pope in Rome than she used to give formerly to the emperors. Some have estimated that more than 300,000 guilders go annually from Germany to Rome, quite uselessly and to no purpose, while we get nothing in return except contempt and scorn. It is not at all astonishing if princes, aristocracy, towns, institutions, country, and people grow poor. We ought to marvel that we still have anything left to eat.

Now that we have come to close quarters, let us pause a while and consider whether the Germans are quite such simpletons as not to grasp or understand the Romish game. For the moment, I shall say nothing by way of deploring the fact that God's commandments and Christian justice are despised in Rome. The state of Christendom, especially in Rome, is not so happy that we should risk calling such exalted matters into question at the present time. Nor am I objecting that natural or secular right and reason are of no avail. The root of the trouble goes altogether deeper. My complaint is that the Romanists do not observe the very canon law which they themselves have devised, though this in itself is simply a piece of tyranny, avarice, and worldly pomp rather than law—as I shall proceed to show.

Many years ago, German emperors and princes granted the pope permission to take the "annates" of all the benefices in Germany, i.e., the half of the first year's income of every single benefice. The permission was granted in order that the pope might gather together sufficient treasure to enable him to make war against Turks and infidels, and to defend Christendom,[1] so that the burden of fighting the war should not press too heavily upon the ruling class, but that the priesthood should also contribute something. The popes have made such use of the praiseworthy and straightforward intentions of the German people that they have taken these revenues now for more than a hundred years, until, to-day, they have converted them into an obligatory tax and impost

---

[1] The German estates meeting in Augsburg in 1518 made the same point. They complained that the annates were only to a small extent applied to resisting the Turks, but that they had nevertheless been paid for many years and were still being paid. The charge was repeated at Worms in 1521. In England, the annates were abolished by parliament in 1532

I

—due as of right. Not only have they accumulated nothing, but they have used the money to found many posts and offices in Rome, and to pay their yearly salaries as out of a fixed rent. If it is now proposed to make war against the Turks, they despatch emissaries to collect money—indulgences being often sent out also with the same pretext of fighting the Turks. Their opinion is that Germans will always be gullible fools, and go on paying the money to satisfy their indescribable greed, and this in spite of the facts now evident to us all, namely, that not a farthing of the annates or the indulgence money or the like contribution will be used against the Turks, but all will go into the bottomless bag. They lie and deceive; they make agreements with us, of which they do not intend to keep a single letter. Yet all is done ostensibly for the sake of the holy name of Christ and St. Peter.

The German nation, including their bishops and princes, should remember that they too are Christian. They should protect the populace whom it is their duty to rule; they should defend them by means of their temporal and spiritual possessions against these ravening wolves who come dressed in sheep's clothing as shepherds and rulers. Further, since the annates are so shamefully misused, and agreements are not kept, the German bishops and princes ought not to allow their country and people to be so pitiably harassed and impoverished without any regard for justice. Rather, by an imperial decree, or a national law, they ought to suspend payment of the annates,[1] or abolish them entirely. Since the pope and his adherents do not keep agreements, they have no right to the annates; rather, the bishops and princes are under an obligation to punish or prevent this theft and robbery, as the law demands.

They ought to stand by the pope if he is willing to receive help to deal with abuses of this character, for perhaps he is not strong enough to deal with them alone; or, should he prefer to defend and maintain these abuses, they should resist and repel him as a wolf and a tyrant, seeing that he has no authority to do or to defend anything evil. Moreover, if it is desirable to accumulate a war chest against the Turks, we

[1] The estates had made this demand at the Diet of Augsburg, 1518

ought then to have wit enough to see that the German people are more able to guard it than the pope, since the German people are numerous enough to wage the war themselves if the funds are there. The case of the annates is similar to that of many another Romish pretence.

Further, the year has been so divided between the pope and the ruling bishops and chapters, that the pope appoints incumbents to those benefices which fall vacant in six months in the year, i.e., during the alternate months; the ruling bishops and chapters being left to make appointment to those which fall vacant in the other six months. The result of this device is that almost all the benefices fall into the hands of Rome, especially the wealthiest livings and dignities. Those which fall to Rome in this way are never relinquished by her, even though afterwards they do not become vacant in the papal months. Hence the chapters receive far too few. This is pure robbery, and the intention clearly is that nothing should escape. This spoliation must now be brought to an end. It is high time to abolish the pope's months, and to reclaim everything which has accrued to Rome in this way. On that account, therefore, princes and peers ought to take steps for the restitution of the stolen property, for punishing the thieves, and cancelling the privileges of those who have abused them. If it is legally valid that the pope, immediately on election, should make rules and regulations in his chancellery to do what he has no moral right to do, i.e., steal our canonries and livings, it should be much more valid for the emperor Charles, immediately on his coronation, to issue rules and regulations forbidding throughout Germany that any further benefices and livings should accrue to Rome by the papal months; and that those which have fallen to Rome should be set free again and liberated from the Roman thief; he has an official right to do so by virtue of his authority as a ruler.

But the Romish pontiff, Avarice and Robbery, has not had patience to await the time when all benefices would fall to him by the device of the papal months. Rather, urged by his insatiable appetite, and in order to snatch them all for himself at the earliest moment, he has devised a plan whereby, in addition to the annates and months, the benefices and livings should fall to Rome in three ways:

(i) If anyone possessing a "free" living should die in Rome or on the way there, that living becomes the property in perpetuity of the Romish—I might say thievish—papacy, and yet he is not to be called a thief, although no one has ever heard or read of more barefaced robbery.

(ii) Similarly, if anyone on the staff of the pope or the cardinals possesses or takes over a benefice, or if anyone has previously possessed a benefice and later enters the service of the pope and the cardinals, that benefice falls to the pope. But who can count the staff of the pope and the cardinals, even when the pope only goes out riding for pleasure? He is accompanied by three or four thousand on mules, as much as any emperor or king. Did Christ and St. Peter go on foot, in order that their Vicar might have the more pomp and pride to display? But His Avarice has developed further cunning devices, and brought it about that many outside Rome are said to belong to the papal staff, just as if they lived in Rome. Thus in every place whatsoever, the roguish little term, "papal staff", may bring all benefices to the Roman pontiff, and pin them there for ever. Are those not vexatious and impious little devices? If we inquire into it, we shall find that Mayence, Magdeburg, and Halberstadt will go comfortably to Rome, and then the cardinals will cost a pretty penny.[1] Soon, all German bishops will be made cardinals so as to make a clean job of it.

(iii) The third device is to initiate a dispute at Rome about some benefice; this seems the commonest way of getting livings into Rome's hands. If no dispute has already arisen, there are innumerable sycophants who will raise a dispute about nothing of moment, and make a grab at livings anywhere. The consequence is that many a faithful priest has

[1] Only two years before, in 1518, Albrecht of Brandenburg had been made cardinal. In 1513 he had been made archbishop of Magdeburg and administrator of Halberstadt; in 1514 he became archbishop of Mayence as well. The recent elevation of this pluralist was still a subject of gossip when Luther wrote

either to lose his living or buy appeasement for a time. When a dispute has been fastened on a benefice in this way rightly or wrongly, it will eventually belong to Rome in perpetuity. Who could be astonished if God were to rain down sulphur and hell-fire from the sky, or plunge Rome into the abyss, as He once did with Sodom and Gomorrah? What value is the pope to Christendom, if he only uses his power for defending and practising such arch-wickedness? O my noble princes and lords, how long will you let these ravening wolves range at will over your land and people?

But even these devices are insufficient to satisfy their greed, for time drags too slowly for them to engulf all the bishoprics. So our good friend Avarice has invented the theory that while it is true that the bishoprics bear provincial names, yet in origin they are indigenous to Rome. No bishop, therefore, can be confirmed in his episcopate unless he pays up heavily for his pallium,[1] and swears a solemn oath binding himself to the personal service of the pope. That is why no bishop dare take any action against the pope. And that was their objective when the Romanists imposed the oath, and explains why the very richest bishoprics fall into debt and ruin. I am told that Mayence pays 20,000 guilders. That is typically Romish, as it seems to me. Some time ago, the canon law decreed that the pallium should be a free gift, that the papal tax should be reduced, disputes made less frequent, chapter and bishop given freedom of action; but this law brought in no money, so they turned the ruling topsy-turvy. All power was taken from bishops and chapters. They sit there like figure-heads and as if without office, authority, or function. The chief transgressors in Rome control everything, almost down to the sextons and bellringers in each church. Every dispute is called to Rome, and everyone who gets the pope's licence does as he likes.

---

[1] The short woollen cape which is the emblem of the rank, and which must be bought in Rome. Canon Law prescribes three months as the period within which the pallium must be secured, and a high fee was demanded. Albert had apparently paid 20,000 guilders before being admitted to the archiepiscopate of Mainz. On the pallium, see further Eusebius, *Eccles. Hist.*, E.T., ed. C. F. Crusé, pp. 225, n.2, 226, n.1

What has happened this very year? The bishop[1] of Strassburg was planning to put his chapter into seemly order, and introduce certain improvements into the divine services. With this in view, he put forward various propositions which were in themselves both religious and Christian. But the dear pope and the saintly see of Rome took this ordinance, reverent and religious though it was, smashed it to bits, and damned it, all at the request of the local priests. What an example of shepherding Christ's sheep! Priests ought to be supported against their own bishops and to be defended in disobeying ungodly regulations! I do not expect even the Antichrist to exhibit contempt of God like that. But that is the pope for you! Is it after your heart? Why does he act like this? Alas, because, if one church were to be reformed, the movement might spread and, perhaps reach Rome! Rather than that, no two priests should be left in agreement, and the custom must be kept up of sowing discord among princes and kings, flooding the world with Christian blood, lest unity among Christian people should enable them to compel the Holy Roman See to reform.

The foregoing gives an idea as to how they deal with livings that fall vacant, and come free. However, too few vacancies occur for their shameful greed. Hence they take measures in advance in regard to benefices still having incumbents. Steps must be taken as if they had already become vacant, although they are not vacant; to this end, several artifices are resorted to:

(a) My Lord Greed lies in wait where fat prebends or bishoprics are held by an aged, ailing incumbent, or by one accused of some trumped-up disqualification. The Holy See presents such a man with a *coadjutor*, i.e., an "assistant", whether wanted or not. It is done for the sake of the coadjutor, because he is on the pope's staff, or has paid for it, or has otherwise earned a reward for some service which

---

[1] William of Honstein was bishop from 1506 to 1541. He was not able to carry out his entirely praiseworthy purpose. Luther wrote him on June 25, 1520, and said, *Argentinensis tragœdiae memor ero satis loco suo.* The above paragraph shows that he kept his word, as well as that he had solid data

the Romanists have forced on him. That ends the free choice of the local chapter or the patron of the living; all goes to Rome.

(b) Then comes the little word *"Commend"*.[1] This means that the pope gives a cardinal, or another of his supporters, a rich abbey or church in charge, just as if I were to put you in charge of a hundred guilders. This does not mean giving or bestowing the abbey, or destroying it, or abolishing divine service, but only to give it in charge. Nor is the nominee obliged to preserve it or build it up; rather, he is to drive out the incumbent, take possession of the properties and income, or install some apostate monk, a truant from his monastery. This man gets paid five or six guilders per annum, but sits in the church during the day, selling sketches and little images to the pilgrims; there is no more chanting or scripture-reading in that church. But if that were described as destroying the abbey or abolishing divine services, the pope would have to be called one who destroys abbeys and does away with divine services, and he certainly does much of this sort of thing. But in Rome this would be thought an impolite way of talking, and so taking an abbey in charge is called a *commend*, i.e., an *order*.

(c) There are certain benefices called *incompatibilia*, which according to the regulations of Canon Law cannot both be in one man's charge, e.g., two parishes, two bishoprics, and so on. At this point, however, the Holy Roman See and Avarice wriggles itself out of the reach of canon law by making glosses[2] called *unio* or *incorporatio*. This means that the pope makes one body of many *incompatibilia*, till they belong to each other as members of one organism, and so

---

[1] To receive an office *in commendam* did not imply any duties, but only a right to the entire income of a living or abbey, when a vacancy occurred. It was most commonly used *re* abbacies. Even Luther's opponents were indignant about this abuse, including Duke George at the Diet of Worms, 1521

[2] At first an explanatory note, usually brief, bringing out the meaning or application of a difficult or doubtful passage; it was the earliest form of commentary. Afterwards the glosses were much expanded, and often became part of the text and of equal authority

are now treated as a single parish. They are no longer incompatibles now, and yet it is all done according to canon law. In fact, canon law is never binding except on those who refuse to buy these glosses[1] from the pope and his *datarius*.[2]

The *unio*, i.e., combination, is of the same character, in that it means coupling up many of these livings like a bundle of sticks, and, because there is now one bundle, they call it one living. Accordingly, there is at present a court follower in Rome who is in sole possession of 22 parishes and 7 priories together with 44 canonries. A clever "gloss" leads to all these results, and at the same time shows the practice is not against canon law. Let each one work it out for himself what the cardinals and other prelates possess. The Germans are now to have their purses emptied and their pride deflated in this same way!

One of the "glosses" is also called *administratio*. The term is applied to a case where a man possesses, in addition to his bishopric, also an abbacy or a dignity[3] together with all the property pertaining to it, simply because he bears the title of *administrator*. For it suffices Rome if the precious titles are recognized, regardless of whether the duties are done; it is just as if I were to announce that a procuress should be called mayoress, but continue to behave as she does now. Peter prophesied this kind of Romish régime when he said,[4] "False teachers will come, and in covetousness shall they, with feigned words, make merchandise of you to get their profits."

The worthy pontiff, Avarice of Rome, has also thought out a certain device whereby a living or a benefice is sold or disposed of on condition that the seller or disposer retains the reversion and promise of it, in such a way that, if the new owner dies, the living reverts gratis to him who had sold it, disposed of it, or surrendered it. Thus they have converted livings into heritable property. Nobody can come

---

[1] I.e., buy the permission of the pope as based on the gloss

[2] The head, usually a cardinal, of a papal office (*Dataria*) registering and issuing, for a fee, of course, certain documents with an appended phrase, *Datum ad Petrum*

[3] Carrying certain rights of precedence and jurisdiction

[4] 2 Pet. 2:3

to possess them except the man to whom the seller is willing
to dispose of them, or to whom they are bequeathed under
his will. There are many who confer the bare title of a benefice,
but on the understanding that, as incumbent, he draws not
a single farthing. It is also an established custom to bestow
a benefice on another, while reserving a certain amount of
the yearly income—a practice formerly called simony. There
is much more of this sort of thing—beyond the telling. The
Romanists traffic in livings more disgracefully than the
Gentiles under the cross trafficked with Christ's garments.[1]

But the whole of the above is almost ancient history at
Rome, and has become a custom. Yet Avarice has devised
one thing more, perhaps the last, for I hope it will choke
him. The pope possesses a refined device called *pectoralis
reservatio*, i.e., his mental reservation, *et properius motus*, i.e.,
and his own free will and power. This is how it works. A certain candidate comes to Rome seeking a specified benefice.
It is duly assigned under seal to him in the customary manner.
Then comes another applicant who either offers to purchase
the same benefice, or makes his claim in consideration of
services rendered to the pope in a way which we shall not
recount. The pope thereupon annuls the appointment already
made, and gives it to the second applicant. If anyone were
to protest that this transaction was an injustice, the Most
Holy Father has to offer some explanation, lest he be accused
of having flagrantly violated the law. He therefore declares
that he had made reservations in his heart and conscience
about that particular benefice, and had retained his control
of it undiminished—and this, though in fact he had never
given it another thought, or heard another word about it.
Such an instance shows that the pope has discovered a worthy
little "gloss", by using which he can tell lies and play tricks
without incurring censure, and can deceive and fool everybody publicly without a blush. Yet all the time he claims to
be the head of the Christian Church, although he is a barefaced liar letting the Evil One dominate him.

This arbitrary and deceptive "mental reservation" on the
part of the pope creates a state of affairs in Rome that beggars

[1] Matt. 27:35

description. You can find there a buying and selling, a bartering and a bargaining, a lying and trickery, robbery and stealing, pomp, procuration, knavery, and all sorts of stratagems bringing God into contempt, till it would be impossible for the Antichrist to govern more wickedly. There is nothing in Venice, Antwerp, or Cairo[1] to compare with the fair which traffics in Rome. In those cities, right and reason enjoy some respect; but here things go on in a way that pleases the devil himself. This kind of morality flows like a tide into all the world. Such people rightly fear a reformation, or an unfettered council. They would rather set kings and princes at odds than that these should unite and bring a council together. No one could bear to have villainies of this kind come to the light of day.

Finally, the pope has built a market-house for the convenience of all this refined traffic, viz.: the house of the *datarius* in Rome. This is where all those resort who deal in this way in benefices and livings. From him they must buy these "glosses" and transactions, and get power to practise their arch-villainy. In former days, Rome was still gracious enough to·sell or suppress justice for a moderate price. But to-day, she has put her prices so high that she lets no one act the villain before he has paid a huge sum. If that is not more like a den of iniquity than any other den one can imagine, then I do not know what a den of iniquity is.

But, if you bring money to this ecclesiastical market, you can buy any of the goods I have described. Here any one can pay and then legally charge interest[2] on loans of any sort. You can get a legal right to goods you have stolen or seized. Here vows are annulled; here monks receive liberty to leave their orders; here marriage is for sale to the clergy; here bastards can become legitimate, and any form of dishonour and shame can achieve dignity; all kinds of iniquity and evil are knighted and ennobled. Here a marriage is permitted which is within the forbidden degrees, or which is otherwise objectionable. O what a jugglery and extortion

---

[1] The greatest trading cities and ports in Luther's time, with very malodorous reputations

[2] Interest on loans of money was regarded as sinful in Luther's time

go on here! until it would seem that all the laws of the canon
were only given to produce gilded nooses, from which a man
must free himself if he would become a Christian. Indeed,
here the devil becomes a saint and a god: what cannot be
done anywhere else in heaven or earth, can be done in this
house. They call the process *compositiones*. Yes, compositions,
really confusions.[1] O how light a tax is the Rhine-toll[2] compared with the exactions of this sacred house!

Let no one imagine I am overdrawing the picture. Everything is public, and people in Rome have to acknowledge
that it is terrible beyond the power to describe. I have not
yet touched, nor do I intend to touch, upon the hellish dregs
of the personal vices; I am dealing only with commonplace
things, and yet I have not space to name them all. The
bishops and priests, and especially the university doctors,
whose salaries are given for the purpose, ought to have done
their duty and, with one accord, written and declaimed
against these things; but they have done the very opposite.[3]

I must come to an end and have done with this section. Because the whole immeasurable greed which I have
recounted is not satisfied with all this wealth, enough probably for three mighty kings, the business is now to be
transferred, and sold to Fugger of Augsburg.[4] Henceforward
bishoprics and livings for sale or exchange or in demand,
and dealings in the spiritualities, have arrived at their true
destination, now that the bargaining for spiritual or secular
properties has become united into a single business. But I
would like to hear of a man who is clever enough to discover
what Avarice of Rome might do which has not already been
done. Then perhaps Fugger would transfer and sell to someone else these two lines of business which are now to be
combined into one. In my view, we have reached the limit.

For to describe what they have stolen in all countries,

[1] A word-play based more or less on the Latin sound
[2] Charged by the various barons living in the castles overlooking the Rhine
[3] Perhaps the most likely translation of the obsolete saying, "Wend das Blatt um, so findest du es"
[4] The Fuggers were bankers to the Roman curia, and by their ability and trustworthiness had now reached great wealth and splendour. They were zealous Romanists, and supported Eck against Luther. The family still exists, has princely connections, with great estates, chiefly in Bavaria

and are still stealing, and extorting, by indulgences, bulls, letters of confession,[1] butter letters,[2] and other *confessionalia*[3]—to describe all this is work for the odd-job man, and is like playing pitch and toss with a devil in hell. Not that it brings in little profit: it is enough to supply ample revenues for a mighty king; but it is not to be compared with the swelling flood of treasure described above. For the time being, I shall hold my tongue, and not say where the Indulgence-money has gone. Later I shall inquire about it. The Campofiore[4] and Belvedere[5] and a few more places probably know something about it.

This wicked régime is not only barefaced robbery, trickery, and tyranny appropriate to the nether regions, but also a destruction of the body and soul of Christendom. Therefore we ought to make every effort to protect Christendom from this hurt and damage. If we are willing to make war on the Turks, let us begin here where they are most iniquitous. If we are right in hanging thieves and beheading robbers, why should we leave Avarice of Rome unpunished? Here is the greatest thief and robber that has ever come or is likely to come on earth, and the scandal is perpetrated in the holy names of Christ and St. Peter. Who can go on tolerating it or keeping silence? Almost all he possesses has been got by theft and robbery. Everything recorded in the histories tells the same story. The pope has never bought properties so great that his income from his ecclesiastical offices should amount to ten hundred thousand ducats, apart from the mines of treasure as already described, and his landed estates. Neither is it that which Christ and St. Peter bequeathed to him, nor that which any one has given or loaned to him; nor has it been acquired by prescription or ancient right. Tell me where he got it? On this point watch what they are seeking for and aiming at when they send out legates to gather funds against the Turks.

[1] Allowing choice of confessor, and of items to confess

[2] Allowing certain foods on fast days

[3] Letters given, for a fee, to excuse a person from various burdensome duties, etc.

[4] Costly restorations done here by Eugenius IV (1431–47)

[5] Part of the Vatican housing many works of art, ancient and modern

III. TWENTY-SEVEN PROPOSALS FOR IMPROVING THE STATE OF CHRISTENDOM

Although I am really of too little consequence to make proposals for the improvement of such a terrible state of affairs, I will go on, although foolishly, to the end, and declare, as far as I understand the case, what might well be done and should be done, either by the secular arm or an ecumenical council.

1. Firstly, I suggest that every prince, peer, and city should strictly forbid their subjects to pay the annates to Rome, and should do away with them entirely. For the pope has broken the agreement about the annates, and so stolen them, to the hurt and shame of the whole German people. He bestows them on his friends, sells them for large sums, and endows certain offices with them. Hence he has lost the right to them, and deserves to be punished. The secular arm is now under obligation to protect the innocent and prevent injustice, as St. Paul teaches,[1] and St. Peter,[2] and, also, the canon law in Case 16, Question 7, *de filiis*.[3] Hence one says to the pope and his adherents, *"Tu ora"*, Thou shalt pray; but to the emperor and his minister, *"Tu protege"*, Thou shalt protect; and to the ordinary man, *"Tu labora"*, Thou shalt work. Not as if praying and protecting and working were not each man's duty, for he who fulfils his own task, prays, protects, and labours; but to each should be assigned a special function.

2. With his Romish practices, viz., commends, coadjutors, reservations, *gratiae expectativae*,[4] "papal months", incorporations, unions, pensions, palliums, rules in chancery, and similar villainies, the pope is engulfing all foundations of German origin, without authority or justice, and bestowing and selling them in Rome to strangers who do nothing for Germany

---

[1] Rom. 13:4   [2] 1 Pet. 2:14
[3] *Re* the misuse of endowment-incomes. Luther wants the same principle to be applied to the annates
[4] A kind of *post obit*: the promise of a living not yet vacant, often made without regard to rights of third parties

141

in return. It follows that the proper incumbents are robbed
of their rights, and the bishops become figureheads[1] and
targets for ridicule. This means acting contrary to Canon
Law, common sense, and reason. The final issue will be that
the livings and benefices will be sold only to coarse ignor-
amuses and scoundrels in Rome, for greed alone. Merit and
wisdom will avail nothing even to devout and learned men,
with the result that the poorer classes of Germany will have
to do without kindly and scholarly prelates, and will perish
eternally. This is sufficient reason for the Christian ruling
classes to set their faces against the pope as a common foe,
who is wreaking destruction in Christendom; and to do so
for the sake of saving the poor, who cannot avoid perishing
under this tyranny. They should decree, command, and ordain
that not another benefice shall in future be transferred to
Rome, and that by no device whatever shall a single further
appointment be obtained there. Rather, the benefices shall
be rescued and kept from this tyrannical power; the proper
incumbents should have their rights and offices restored, so
that those benefices, which belong to Germany, may be
brought into the best possible order. If a legate should arrive
from Rome, he should be given stern orders to keep off, or
jump into the Rhine or the nearest stretch of water, and
give the Romish ban, complete with seals and epistles, a
cold douche. They would then take note in Rome that
Germans are not silly and besotted all the time, but that
they are really converted Christians, and such that they will
no longer tolerate the holy name of Christ to be scoffed at
and scorned, thus permitting rogues to live and souls to
perish. Rather they reverence God's honour more than
man's power.

3. An imperial law should be decreed, whereby no bishop
should go to Rome for his pallium, or for the confirmation
of any other dignity, from now onwards. Instead of this,
the ordinance of Nicea, the holiest and most celebrated of
all the councils, should be re-established. This regulation
declares that a bishop shall be confirmed by the two nearest

[1] *Supra*, p. 135, n. 1

bishops, or by the archbishop. If the pope intends to abolish the statute of this and all other councils, what is the value of having councils? Moreover, who has given him authority to despise and nullify councils? All the more reason for us to depose all bishops, archbishops, and primates, and make plain pastors of them, with the pope as their sole superior, as in fact he is. For he leaves no regular authority or office to the bishops, archbishops, and primates. He appropriates everything for himself, and allows them to retain only the name and the empty title. By using his "exemption",[1] the abbot of a cloister, and the prelates, are made no longer subject to the regular authority of the bishop. This results in lack of system and order in Christendom, with the inevitable consequence, already to be seen, that penalties are lax, and one is free to do all manner of evil. Of a truth, I fear it is possible to call the pope "the man of sin".[2] Who is to blame if, throughout Christendom, there is neither discipline, nor punishment, nor rule, nor order? None other than the pope who, by the arbitrary power he has assumed, extends to them his patronage while depriving them of power; and, by gift or purchase, freeing from their authority those whom they should control.

Lest the pope complain of loss of authority, it should be decreed that if primates and archbishops are not equal to dealing with a problem, or if a dispute should arise between them, the issue must be referred to the pope, if and when it is of sufficient importance. That is what used to be done in earlier times, and was substantiated by the very famous council at Nicea. His Holiness ought not to be burdened with small matters that can be dealt with by others. He should be able to give himself to prayer, to study, and to concern for Christendom; indeed, he claims to do so, just as did the Apostles (Acts 6), who said: "It is not fit that we should forsake the Word of God and serve tables. But we will continue in preaching and prayer, and set others over such work."[3] At Rome preaching and prayer are simply

[1] By which monasteries owed obedience directly to the pope, and not to the local bishop, from whose authority they were "exempted"
[2] 2 Thess. 2:3   [3] Acts 6:2, 4

despised. All is a matter of serving of tables, i.e., subordination to secular profit. The régimes of the Apostles and the pope harmonize together about as well as Christ and Lucifer, heaven and hell, or night and day; and yet he is called the Vicar of Christ and Successor of the Apostles.

4. It should be decreed that no secular matter is to be referred to Rome. All such issues should be left to the secular arm,[1] as the Romanists themselves affirm in their canon laws, which, however, they do not observe. It should be the pope's part, as the man most learned of all in the Scriptures, and as actually and not merely nominally the holiest of all, to regulate whatever concerns the faith and holy life of Christians. He should hold the primates and archbishops to this duty, join them in handling these matters, and bearing these cares. So St. Paul teaches (1 Corinthians 6), and severely reproves them for their concern about secular affairs.[2] For it does intolerable hurt in every country that these cases should be tried in Rome. It makes them more expensive; the judges themselves are ignorant of the customs, laws, and manners of other lands, and so, frequently, force cases to fit with their own.

Besides the above, the gross malpractices of the judges in the ecclesiastical courts ought to be forbidden.[3] They ought to be concerned only with matters of faith and good morals; whereas money, property, life, and honour should be left for the secular judges to deal with. Therefore the secular arm ought not to allow sentences of excommunication or exile, except where matters of faith or good conduct are concerned.

Nevertheless it should be permissible for cases concerning livings and benefices to be tried before bishops, archbishops, and primates. Therefore to settle disputes and quarrels, the

[1] Wimpheling had already made this point in 1515, in his *Responsa et replicae ad Aeneam Silvium*; cf. *W.*, VI, 430, n. 1

[2] 1 Cor. 6:7

[3] Luther had made this protest in 1518 *cf. W.*, I, 634ff. The point was that the ecclesiastical courts claimed jurisdiction in many matters that properly belonged to the secular courts, and usually imposed fines under ecclesiastical censure. Cf. also *Die Beschwerungen des Haylegen Romischen Reyches*, 1521. *W.*, VI, 430, n. 2

primate of Germany should, where possible, hold a general consistory, with auditors and chancellors who, as in Rome, should be the heads of the *signaturae gratiae* and *justitiae;*[1] and these consistories should be the Courts of Appeal to which cases in Germany should be regularly brought and referred. These courts ought not to be maintained, as in Rome, by unspecified presents and gifts, a custom leading to the selling of justice and injustice, as necessarily takes place now in Rome. Since the pope pays them no salary, they have to contrive their own income out of the presents they receive. The result is that nothing in Rome depends on the rights and wrongs of a case, but only whether there is money in it or not. Instead of this financial bribery, the courts might be maintained from the annates, or some other method devised by more eminent and experienced persons than I. My own purpose is to stir up, and give food for thought to, those who can and will help the German people to regain their Christian faith, and to liberate themselves from the wretched, pagan, and unchristian régime of the pope.

5. Not another reservation should hold good, and not another living should be taken possession of by Rome, even if the incumbent die, or a dispute arise about it, or the incumbent is a cardinal, or one of the pope's staff. A court follower must be strictly forbidden, and prevented from beginning, litigation against the holder of any benefice, or citing and disturbing any dutiful priests, or driving them to some compromise. If, as a consequence, Rome pronounces excommunication or exercises spiritual pressure, it should be ignored just as it would be if a thief excommunicated someone who would not let him steal. Indeed, the Romanists ought to be severely punished for blasphemous misuse of excommunication and of God's name in support of their robberies. They devise threats, which are lies, in order to compel us to tolerate and even praise this blasphemy of the divine name and misuse of Christian power, and to make

[1] The two departments through which the pope administered the matters that he claimed as his prerogatives

K

us take part in their wickedness in God's sight. Far from giving them support, our duty before God is to repudiate them. In Romans 1, St. Paul condemns their like as worthy of death.[1] But they not only do such things, but also encourage and legalize them. In particular, the mendacious "mental reservation" is intolerable, because it brings the Christian religion blasphemously and publicly into shame and contempt, when its head acts with unconcealed mendacity, and unashamedly deceives and fools everyone with his favours for the sake of accursed money.

6. The reserved cases (*casus reservati*),[2] which the pope alone can absolve, should be abolished. Not only are the people cheated of much money by them, but the ravenous tyrants ensnare and confuse tender consciences with intolerable harm to their faith in God. Particularly is this true of the ridiculous and childish cases which the bull,[3] *coena domini*,[4] blows up like bladders. They do not deserve to be called "common sins", still less are they sins so great that even the pope cannot absolve them. Examples from the list are: preventing a pilgrim from going to Rome; or providing the Turks with arms; or counterfeiting papal briefs.[5] They fool us with these insulting, silly, and clumsy devices; yet Sodom and Gomorrah, and all the sins that are or may be done against God's commandments—these are not "reserved cases". What God never ordained, but Romanists themselves invented—these forsooth are "reserved cases". The reason is that no one must be prevented from bringing money to

[1] Rom. 1:32

[2] Cases in which only the pope or his special nominees could give absolution. They were listed every Low Thursday at the proclamation of the bull, *in coena domini*. When Luther was himself mentioned as a condemned heretic in this way in 1521, he published a German translation for the benefit of the laity, with introduction, appendix, and marginal notes (*W.*, VIII, 688ff.)

[3] A "bull" is really a capsule, bubble, blister; it is applied to the papal decree on account of the ball of sealing wax with seals, etc., which was appended. Luther puns on this meaning in the present clause, and often elsewhere.

[4] A bull issued at Rome each Maundy Thursday against heretics and those offences which only the pope can absolve

[5] Much the same as papal bulls, but dealing with matters of less importance

Rome, where, safe from the Turks, the Romanists live in luxury, and keep the rest of the world in chains with wanton and useless bulls and briefs.

Really every priest ought to know, and a public decree should declare, that no private and undenounced trespass constitutes a reserved case; and that every priest is empowered to pronounce absolution, no matter what the sin, or whatever it may be called. If it is private, neither abbot, bishop, nor pope has power to "reserve" it to himself; if they presume to do so, their action is null and void. Rather they ought to be punished for it, as interfering without authority in the judgment which God pronounces, and, without cause, binding and burdening the tender consciences of the uninformed. But where the sins are of a public character and widespread, especially those committed against God's commandments, there are perhaps grounds for making "reserved cases"; but they should not be numerous, and not be "reserved" arbitrarily and without cause; for Christ did not provide tyrants but pastors in His church, as St. Peter says.[1]

7. The Holy See of Rome should abolish the *officia*[2] and lessen the creeping and crawling swarms of hirelings in the city. The object of this abolition is that the papal staff should be supported out of the pope's own income, and his court not outvie in magnificence and extravagance that of any king. Regard should be paid to the fact that such a state of affairs has never been of any service to the Christian faith, but has been a very great hindrance to study and prayer, until the court officials now know scarcely anything about Christian faith. This was proved plainly at the last council which was held recently at Rome.[3]

Among many childish and frivolous clauses, they introduced one which declared the human soul immortal, and that a priest was to say prayers once every month or lose his benefice. How can the affairs of Christendom and questions of faith be settled by men who, having been made

[1] 1 Pet. 5:3   [2] Posts and positions on sale
[3] The fifth Lateran Council, A.D. 1512–17

stupid and blind by much avarice, wealth, and worldly splendour, only now for the first time pronounce the soul immortal? It is no small shame, but one that affects all Christendom, when they treat the faith so disgracefully in Rome. If their wealth and splendour were less, they might be more diligent in study and prayer, and become worthy and capable of dealing with questions of faith. This they were in former days, but then they were content to be bishops, and did not pretend to outvie kings in their wealth and splendour.

8. The far-reaching and fearful oaths, which bishops are wrongfully compelled to swear to the pope, should be abolished. They keep the bishops bound like domestic servants. The decree stands with its arbitrary authority and its great stupidity in the worthless and unscholarly chapter entitled *Significasti*.[1] Is it not enough that their numerous foolish laws should burden us in body, soul, and property, to the weakening of faith and the ruin of the Christian estate? But now they make a prisoner of the bishop with his office and duties, including his very investiture. Formerly, this last was performed by the German emperor, and still is carried out by the king in France and other countries. On this point, the Romanists struggled and disputed hotly with the emperors, until at last they had the barefaced effrontery to seize the right and retain it to the present day. They must think the German Christians are, to a greater extent than any others, the household fools of the pope and the papacy, for doing and suffering what no one elsewhere will suffer or do. Since, therefore, this example of oppression and robbery hinders the bishop from exercising his proper authority and is harmful to needy souls, then an obligation falls on the emperor and the ruling classes supporting him, to repel and punish it as a piece of tyranny.

9. The pope should exercise no authority over the emperor, except the right to anoint and crown him at the altar as

---

[1] *Decret. Greg.*, lib I, tit. 6, cap. 4. It deals with the oath of obedience sworn by bishops

a bishop crowns a king. Never again should his iniquitous Arrogance be permitted to make the emperor kiss the pope's feet, or sit at them, or, as it is said, hold the stirrup and bridle of his mule when he mounts to go riding. Still less should he do homage to the pope, and swear faithfulness to him as his liege lord, as the popes shamelessly presume to demand as if by right. The chapter entitled *Solite*,[1] which raises the power of the pope above that of the emperor, is not worth a farthing; nor are any that are based on it or recognize its authority. For what it actually does is to wrest the meaning of the holy Word of God from its proper interpretation to fit their own ambitions, as I have shown in a Latin treatise.[2]

This ultra-excessive, arrogant, and frivolous presumption of the pope's is a device of the devil's to be used betimes as a cover for introducing the Antichrist, and raising the pope above God, as many have already done and are doing. It is not fitting for the pope to arrogate to himself superiority over the secular authorities, except in his spiritual functions such as preaching and pronouncing absolution. In other respects, he is inferior, as Paul teaches (Romans 13),[3] and Peter (1 Peter 2),[4] too, as I have already said.[5] He is not the Vicar of the Christ in heaven, but only of the Christ who lived on earth. Christ in heaven, in His work as king, needs no vicar. For, seated on His Throne, He can see, know, and perform all things. He is omnipotent. But He needs a vicar as a servant, the form in which He Himself walked on earth where He laboured, preached, suffered, and died. But the Romanists turn things inside out, take from Christ the status of heavenly regent, and confer it on the pope, while allowing the idea of servant to fall into oblivion. The pope seems almost the Counter-Christ, called in Scripture the Antichrist, for the whole of his system, his efforts, and his pretensions are contrary to Christ, and directed solely to blotting out and destroying whatever Christ has informed with His spirit, and whatever work He has done.

[1] *Decret. Greg.*, lib. I, tit. 33, cap. 6
[2] *Resolutio Lutheriana super propositione XIII de potestate papae* (1520). *W.*, II, 217ff., following closely the debate with Eck at Leipzig in 1519
[3] Rom. 13:1   [4] 1 Pet. 2:13   [5] See *W.*, VI, p. 409

Further, it is ridiculous and childish for the pope to use stupid and perverse statements in the Decretal *Pastoralis*[1] and claim that he is the legal heir of the empire if the throne becomes vacant. Who gave it to him? Did Christ when He said, "The princes of the Gentiles are lords, but ye shall not be so"?[2] Or did the pope inherit it from St. Peter? It annoys me that we have to read and learn these shameless, gross, and silly untruths in the canon law, and, besides, receive them as Christian doctrine although they are infernal lies. Further, the "Donation of Constantine" is an unheard-of falsification of the same class.[3] It must have been by virtue of a special plague sent by God that so many knowledgeable people let themselves be talked into believing these falsehoods. They are so gross and clumsy that, methinks, a tipsy boor could have told lies more plausibly and with greater slickness. How is it possible to combine and harmonize the ruling of an empire with preaching, praying, studying, and attending on the poor? Of all the offices, these are most characteristic of a pope. They were imposed by Christ so urgently, that he forbade his disciples to carry cloak or money,[4] since any one who was responsible for a single family could scarcely attend to such responsibilities. Yet the pope wants to administer an empire while yet remaining pope. That is what those rogues have conceived who would like to use the pope's name to dominate the world, and would gladly restore the ruins of the Roman empire, through the pope and the name of Christ, to its former condition.

10. The pope should withdraw from temporal affairs, take his finger out of the pie, and lay no claim to the throne of

---

[1] Decreed in A.D. 1313 and afterwards incorporated in the Canon Law, *Clement*, lib. II, tit. 11, cap. 2

[2] Luke 22:25f.

[3] In 1440, Lorenzo (Laurentius) Valla had proved this document to be a forgery in a work which Ulrich von Hutten republished in Germany in 1517, and which probably came into Luther's hands, to his immense indignation, in the spring of 1520. The "Donation" is a document of the eighth century, and pretends to be written by the Emperor Constantine, conveying to the pope the title to Rome, parts of Italy, and the "Islands of the Sea". On it the medieval popes based their claim to temporal power. Luther published an annotated edition of it in 1537

[4] Matt. 10:9f.

the kingdom of Naples and Sicily.[1] He has no more right
to it than I have, and yet wants to be its overlord. It is
robbery by violence, like almost every other of his possessions. Therefore, the emperor ought not to confirm him in
such tenures, and, in cases where he has already done so,
withdraw his support. Instead, let him point the pope to
the Bible and the prayer books. The pope should let temporal
lords rule land and people, while he himself preaches and
prays.

The same principle should also apply to Bologna, Imola,
Vicenza, Ravenna, and everywhere else in the provinces of
Ancona, Romagna, and other parts of Italy, which the pope
has seized by force[2] and keeps without justification, meddling
in these matters contrary to all the commandments of Christ
and St. Paul. For this is what St. Paul says, "No one entang-
leth himself in the affairs of this life who should attend on
the divine order of chivalry."[3] Now the pope should be the
head and the leader of this order of chivalry, yet he intervenes more in worldly affairs than any emperor or king; and
so we must help him to renounce all this, and attend to his
own order of chivalry. Christ Himself, whose Vicar he claims
to be, never was desirous of dealing with the temporal régime.
When a certain man asked Him to decide a question regarding his brother, He said, "Who made me a judge over you?"[4]
But the pope intrudes uninvited, seizes everything as if by
divine right, until he himself no longer really knows what
Christ was, though pretending to be His Vicar.

11. No one should ever again kiss the pope's feet. It is
unchristian, indeed antichristian, that a pitiable and sinful
man should let his feet be kissed by another who may be
a hundred times better than himself. If it is intended to

---

[1] This remark and others in this section shows that Luther was well
versed in contemporary events and their historical background. The claim
to this kingdom had been contested by popes and emperors for several
centuries. As Luther wrote, Francis I of France and Charles V as King
of Spain were both claiming the kingdom; *Camb. Mod. Hist.*, I, esp.
Chaps. IV, VII, XI, and XIX

[2] A reference to the military aggressions of Julius II (1503–13). Cf.
Camb. Mod. Hist., loc. cit.

[3] 2 Tim. 2:4   [4] Luke 12:14

pay tribute to his authority, why does the pope not do it to others as a tribute to their sanctity? Compare them with one another, Christ and the pope; Christ washed and dried His disciples' feet,[1] but the disciples never washed His. The pope, presuming to be higher than Christ, reverses the relation, and with much condescension allows his feet to be kissed. But it would be proper for him, if any one were to ask permission, to refuse at all costs to allow it. Paul and Barnabas at Lystra would not let themselves be worshipped as gods, but declared, "We also are men like you."[2] But the lickspittles have brought matters to such a pass that they have made an idol for us. The result is that now no one fears God so much as he does the pope; no one does God equal reverence. This fact does not trouble the Romanists, and they will not permit the papal splendour to be diminished by the breadth of a hair. If they were Christian, and held God in greater honour than themselves, the pope would never be content to see God's honour despised and his own exalted. Nor would he allow any one to do him honour until he saw that God's honour was again exalted, and raised above his own.[3]

[Another example[4] of the same overweening and scandalous arrogance is the hateful way in which the pope takes exercise in the open air, and is not content with horseback or a carriage although he is strong and well enough. But he prefers to be carried by bearers like an idol and with unheard-of magnificence. Dear readers, how does such satanic pride harmonize with Christ, who went on foot as did all His apostles? Has there ever been a king who travelled with the worldliness and pomp of him who claims to be chief of all those who ought to despise and flee from worldly glory: the Christians? Not that that disturbs us very much as far as he himself is concerned, but surely we are in danger of God's wrath, if we belaud this kind of arrogance and do not

---

[1] John 13:4ff.   [2] Acts 14:11–16

[3] The three following paragraphs were lacking in Luther's earliest edition

[4] This and the next two examples seem to be based on Luther's personal reactions when he visited Rome in 1510. Luther's strictures on the pope, for all their directness, are less extreme than those of Erasmus, e.g., *Praise of Folly*, p. 168, *ed. cit.*

show our indignation. It is enough for the pope himself to indulge in foolish pomp and show of this kind, but it would be inexcusable for us to agree with it and approve it.

Further, what Christian will be happy at heart on watching the pope when he takes communion? He remains seated and looks like a milord; the sacrament is passed to him on a golden staff by a cardinal who bows to him on bended knee. It is as if the holy sacrament were not really worthy of the pope, for, although he is a poor and unclean sinner, he does not stand and do honour in the presence of God. That is how all other Christians, who are much holier than the Most Holy Father the pope, receive it—with every mark of reverence. Would it be astonishing if God sent an epidemic, because we tolerated such dishonour being done to Him, and because we praised it in our prelates, and ourselves participated in this accursed arrogance by our silence and adulation?

Similar things are seen when the pope carries the sacrament round in procession. He must be carried, but the sacrament is put in front of him like a jug of wine at table. In short, Christ counts for nothing in Rome, but the pope counts for everything. Yet the Romanists would urge upon us and threaten us to approve of their antichristian offences, and join in praise and respect them, contrary to God and all Christian teaching. May God grant His aid to a free council to instruct the pope that he, too, is human, and not greater than God, as he now regards himself.]

12. Pilgrimages to Rome[1] should be disallowed. No person actuated merely by curiosity or his own religious feelings should be permitted to make a pilgrimage. Rather, he must be previously recognized by his minister, city council, or liege lord as having sufficient good reasons for making the pilgrimage. I do not say this because pilgrimages are wrong, but because they are ill-advised just now; for what one sees in Rome is not exemplary, but scandalous. The Romanists

[1] The question of pilgrimages, whether to Rome, Compostella, Jerusalem, Canterbury, and other holy places had become an urgent social issue. Erasmus discussed it trenchantly in *Colloquies*, *"On Rash Vows"*, p. 56, also *"Praise of Folly"*, p. 114, *ed. cit.*

themselves have coined the saying, "The nearer Rome, the worse the Christians", and they bring about contempt of God and God's commandments. Another saying runs, "The first time one goes to Rome, one has to look for a rogue; the second time, one finds him; the third time, one brings him back." But they have become so slick by now that the three journeys are made at the same time, and indeed, in Rome they have coined us the catch-phrase, "It would be better not to have seen or known Rome."

Even if this were not true, there is a more cogent reason, namely, these pilgrimages seduce untrained minds into a false idea and a misapprehension of the divine commandments; simple folk hold that pilgrimages are works of rare merit, which is untrue. They are works of little merit, and, if frequently repeated, they are evil and seductive; God never gave such a commandment. But He has commanded that a man should cherish his wife and children, and perform the duties proper to the married state, besides serving and helping his neighbours. This is what happens when a man undertakes a pilgrimage to Rome, which no one has laid on him: it costs him 50 or 100 guilders more or less, while his wife and child, or his neighbour, suffer from distress at home.[1] And yet the silly fellow thinks that his disobedience to, and contempt for, God's commandments will all be atoned for by the pilgrimage, which he undertook on his own responsibility, although it was pure, self-willed, or Satanic seduction. The popes have given this movement a fillip by their deceitful, trumped up, foolish "Golden Years",[2] which stir up the people, blind them to God's commandments, and seduce them into delusive enterprises. In this way, the popes have caused exactly what they should have forbidden. But it brings money in, and fortifies a fictitious authority; therefore it must go on no matter whether it be contrary to the will of God or the salvation of souls.

In order to eradicate this false and seductive faith from

---

[1] Erasmus, *Praise of Folly* (1512), p. 114, *ed. cit.*

[2] The "golden" or "jubilee" years had been instituted by Boniface VIII in 1300 to mark the centuries. But the intervals were soon reduced to fifty, thirty-three, and finally in 1475 to twenty-five years. In these years it was held specially meritorious to worship at the shrines in Rome

untrained Christian minds, and to re-establish a right conception of meritorious works, all pilgrimages ought to be stopped. They are without value; no commandment enjoins them, and canonical obedience does not require them; nay, they give very frequent occasions for sin and for despising God's commandments. They give rise to a large mendicant class, who perpetrate innumerable villainies on these pilgrimages, and learn the habit of begging even when they are not in distress.

This gives rise to vagabondage and further abuses which I will not stay to recount. If any man to-day wants to go on pilgrimages or esteems them highly, let him first go to his pastor or his liege lord and tell him. If it turns out that his purpose is to do a good work, then let the pastor or the liege boldly trample the vow and the work underfoot as a satanic delusion, and tell the man to apply the money and effort required for the pilgrimage to fulfilling God's commandments, and to doing works a thousand times better than a pilgrimage, namely, meet the needs of his family and his poor neighbours. But if his object is only to satisfy his curiosity and go sight-seeing in country and city, let him have his way. If, however, he vowed the pilgrimage during an illness, the vow must be annulled, and set aside. In contradistinction, the divine commandments must be stressed, with the idea that henceforward he will deem it sufficient to keep his baptismal vow to obey God's commandments. Nevertheless, for this once, and in order to satisfy his conscience, he may be allowed to fulfil his foolish vow. Men do not desire to walk in the straight path of God's commandments common to all; each finds new ways, and vows new vows for himself, as if he had already completed his obedience to all God's other commandments.

13. We now come to the great multitudes who swear many vows, but keep few. Do not be angry, my dear readers; I mean nothing wrong. For it is the truth, at once sweet and bitter, that no more mendicant houses[1] should be built. God knows,

---

[1] The monasteries of the mendicant orders which took an oath to live only on what they could beg

there are already far too many of them. Would to God they were all dissolved, or all combined into two or three Orders. There is no merit, and there will never be any merit, in simply walking about over the face of the earth. I would therefore counsel that ten, or as many as may be necessary, should be joined together into one house and made into a single institution. Let this be endowed sufficiently so as to require no mendicancy. There is far more need for concern in what the multitudes of ordinary folk need for their salvation, than in the rules laid down for the mendicant orders by St. Francis, St. Dominic, St. Augustine, or any one else, especially as their purpose has not been fulfilled.

These Orders must also abandon preaching and hearing confessions, unless they are called upon and desired to do so by the bishops, pastors, churches, or the civil authorities. Their preaching and hearing confession has only led to mutual hatred and envy between priests and monks, and this has become a great offence and obstacle to the common people. Hence it is proper, and very desirable, that it should cease because it can be dispensed with. It appears unlikely that the Holy Roman papacy has increased this army inadvertently, but rather that the priests and bishops who are weary of his tyranny should not by any chance become too strong for him, and begin a reformation, a thing which His Holiness could not bear.

At the same time, the numerous sects and differences within the one Order should be abolished. These have often arisen for minor reasons, and been maintained for less; they are struggling with each other with indescribable hate and envy. The outcome is that the Christian faith, which intrinsically contains no such differences, is swept away by both parties. The effect of all this is the view that the essence and meaning of a true Christian life can be found among outer laws, works, and customs; but this can only cause hypocrisy, and lead to decay of the spirit, as everyone can see for himself.

The pope must be forbidden to institute, or set his seal on, any more of these Orders. Indeed, he must be ordered to dissolve some, or force them to reduce their numbers.

For faith in Christ, which is alone the supreme good, and which exists apart from any of the Orders, suffers no small danger. The many different works and customs may easily lead men rather to rely on these works and customs than to care for faith. Without wise prelates in the cloisters caring more for preaching and practising the Christian faith than for the rules of their order, it cannot but be that the Order will do harm to simple folk, and lead them astray, since they only pay attention to works.

But to-day, almost everywhere, the prelates who possessed the faith and who founded the Orders, have passed away. In olden days among the children of Israel, when the Patriarchs had gone who had known God's works and marvellous deeds, their descendants, lacking knowledge of the divine works and faith, immediately began to establish idolatry and their own human works. In the same way, at the present time unhappily, the Orders, now lacking knowledge of the divine works and faith, only torment themselves pitiably, worrying and labouring about their own rules, laws, and customs, without ever reaching a true understanding of what constitutes a religious and virtuous life. This the Apostle foretold when he said (2 Timothy 3): "They have a form of godliness, but there is nothing to support it; ever learning, but never able to come to the knowledge of true godliness."[1] It is better to do without a cloister unless, at its head, is a spiritually-minded prelate versed in the Christian faith. For one who is not so minded cannot rule without doing hurt and harm, and the more so in proportion as he appears saintly and concerned with a godly life as far as his outer conduct goes.

In my view, it is necessary to decree, especially in these dangerous times of ours, that monasteries and priories should return to the way in which they were regulated by the apostles[2] and for a long time afterwards. In those days, each votary was free to stay just as long as he pleased. For monasteries and priories were only Christian schools to teach Scripture and morals according to the Christian way. They

[1] 2 Tim. 3:5–7
[2] This is of course a gross historical error; cf. Lietzmann, *History of the Early Church*, Vol. IV (*The Era of the Church Fathers*), Chap. VI

trained students how to lead the churches, and how to preach. Thus we read that St. Agnes[1] went to school, and we still see it done in certain nunneries, like those at Quedlimburg and elsewhere. In truth, all monasteries and priories ought to be so free, that the brethren might serve God fully, and not under constraint.

Later on, however, they were restricted by vows, and turned into permanent prisoners, until, to-day, greater respect is paid to these vows than to those made at baptism. But day by day, more and more, do we see, hear, read, and learn what sort of fruit they bear. I fear that my opinion will be regarded as altogether foolish, but I shall not worry about that. My view accords with my conscience, no matter who rejects it. I am well acquainted with the ways in which those vows are kept, especially that of continence. This vow is very widespread throughout these cloisters, yet Christ never commanded it. Indeed, both He Himself and St. Paul said that to keep it was given only to few.[2] Would that help were brought to everyone, and would that Christian souls were not taken prisoner by arbitrary customs and rules of human devising!

14. We know also how the priesthood has declined. Many a poor priest is responsible for wife and child, and has a troubled conscience; yet no one lends a hand, although it would be a very kindly act to help them. The pope and the bishop may let these abuses go on untouched, even though ruin ensue, if ruin it must be.[3] So I will obey my conscience, and speak my mind freely, in spite of hurting the pope, the bishops, or anyone else. What I say is that, according to what Christ and the Apostles instituted, each single town should have a pastor or bishop. Paul says this clearly[4] in Titus 1, and also that that pastor shall not be compelled to live without a lawful wife. He may have one, as St. Paul writes in 1 Timothy 3 and Titus 1 and say: "A bishop shall be a man without reproach and the husband of only one

---

[1] Martyred early in the fourth century. She rivalled St. Sebastian in popularity in the Middle Ages
[2] Matt. 19:11; 1 Cor. 7:7; Col. 2:20
[3] Cf. *infra*, *Pagan Servitude*, p. 302   [4] Titus 1:6

wife, having his children in subjection with all gravity, etc."[1] According to St. Paul, a bishop and a pastor are identical, and this is also St. Jerome's testimony. The Scriptures know nothing of the present-day kind of bishops who, by ordinances of the Christian church, have authority over several pastors.

Thus the Apostle teaches us plainly that the method to be followed among Christians is that each separate town should choose from its church a scholarly and devout citizen, and lay upon him the duties of a pastor; his maintenance being cared for by the church. He should be quite free to marry, or not. At his side, he should have several priests or deacons, either married or not, as he prefers, to help him in ministering to the church and the people at large with sermons and the sacraments. This is the custom retained to our own day in the Greek church. There, after apostolic times, when there was much persecution and many disputes with heretics, many of the holy Fathers voluntarily refrained from marriage, in order to devote themselves more fully to study, and to be prepared instantly, either to defend the faith, or to die.

At that point the papacy interfered entirely on its own initiative, and turned this practice into a universal rule; they forbade ordained persons to marry. The devil must have ordered it, for St. Paul declared in 1 Timothy 4, "Teachers will come with doctrines of devils, forbidding to marry."[2] Unfortunately a more lamentable state of affairs has ensued than can be recounted; moreover, it has caused the Greek church to separate off, and multiplied boundless quarrels, sins, shame, and scandal, as always happens with what the devil initiates and incites.

What ought we to do about it? My advice is, Break the bonds, let each follow his own preference whether to marry or not to marry. But then there will have to be quite a different arrangement and order of things in regard to salaries; also the whole of the canon law must be razed to the ground; nor must many benefices become Rome's. I fear that avarice is one reason for the rule of celibacy, lamentable

[1] 1 Tim. 3:2, 4; Titus 1:6   [2] 1 Tim. 4:1–4

and incontinent though that condition is; with the result
that every man wants to be a priest, or wishes his son to
study with that in view. But continence is not the life he
thinks of, for that can be practised without joining the priesthood. Rather the purpose is to receive temporal support
without work or worry, contrary to God's commandment,
Genesis 3, "In the sweat of thy face shalt thou eat bread",[1]
a commandment which the Romanists have coloured to mean
that reciting the liturgy and the administration of the sacraments are their work.

I am not referring just now to the pope, bishops, canons,
and monks: offices which God did not institute. They have
put burdens on themselves, and must carry them. My purpose is to speak of the ministry,[2] which God did institute,
and which was intended to train a church by sermons and
sacraments, with pastors living among the people and keeping house as other people do. Such men should be granted
permission by a Christian council to marry, in order to avoid
temptation and sin. For, if God has not forbidden them, no
man should or may do so, not even an angel of heaven, not
to mention the pope. Anything to the contrary in the canon
law is pure fabrication and idle chatter.

Furthermore, my advice to anyone taking Holy Orders
or adopting any other vocation, is on no account to swear to
the bishop to remain continent. Rather, point out to him
that he has no authority to demand such a vow, and that
it is an act of impious tyranny to demand it. If any prefers
or is compelled to say, as some do, *"Quantum fragilitas
humana permittet"*,[3] let him frankly give it the negative sense
of *"non promitto castitatem"*;[4] for *"fragilitas humana non per-
mittit caste vivere"*;[5] but only *"angelica fortitudo et celestis
virtus"*,[6] in order that his conscience may not be burdened
by any vows.

I do not wish either to encourage or discourage those, who
have as yet no wife, on the question whether they should
marry or remain single. I leave that to be pronounced by

[1] Gen. 3:19   [2] Cf. *infra, Pagan Servitude*, p. 308
[3] "As far as human nature allows"   [4] "I do not promise continence"
[5] "Human frailty does not allow continent living"
[6] "The strength of angels and the heroism of heaven"

an ecumenical, Christian council, and also by the conscience of the man's better self. But I will not conceal my own real view from the many who are distressed, nor will I withhold from them words of comfort. I mean those who have fallen into disgrace with a woman, and have a child, and who suffer grievously in conscience because she is called a priest's prostitute and the children scorned as "priest-brats". My claim to be a court-fool gives me that right.[1]

There is many a duteous priest, otherwise blameless, who, because of his frailty, has fallen into dishonour with a woman. Both are so minded in the depth of their hearts that, if they could only do it with good conscience, they would gladly live faithfully and permanently together in a regular, conjugal union. But, even though they both have to suffer public disrepute, they are certainly espoused in God's sight. I will even add that if the two people are so minded and if, on that basis, they enter into a common life, they should keep their consciences undaunted. Let him take and keep her as if she were his lawful wife, and in other respects live in a regular way with her as a married man. Let him disregard the pope's pleasure or displeasure, and the transgression of canon or man-made law. The salvation of your soul is of greater importance than tyrannical, oppressive, and wanton laws, unnecessary for salvation, and not commanded by God. You must do as did the Children of Israel, who stole the wages they had earned from the Egyptians; or do like a servant who steals his earnings from his wicked master. So, too, you should steal from the pope your conjugal wife and child.

Let him who has faith enough to make the venture, boldly follow my word; I shall not lead him astray. I have not the power of a pope, but I have the power of a Christian to help and advise my neighbour to escape from his sins and temptations; and that not without rhyme or reason. Not every pastor can live without a woman, not just on account of the weakness of the flesh, but much more on account of keeping his house. If, then, he employs a woman, and the pope will

[1] The right to the most complete freedom of speech, without any respect of persons

L

permit him to do this, but will not allow him to have her in marriage, that means nothing else than leaving a man and a woman alone together, and yet forbidding them to yield to temptation. It is like bringing fire and straw together, and trying to forbid blaze or smoke.

The pope in making such a rule has no more power than if he were to forbid eating, or drinking, or the performance of other natural functions, or growing fat. Hence it is no one's duty to obey this rule. On the other hand, the pope is responsible for all the sins which have thereby been committed, for all the souls which have consequently been lost, and for all the consciences which have been confused and tortured. The fact is that he ought to have been chased out of the world long ago, as a man who has throttled so many miserable people with this Satanic halter of his. But I hope that God will be more merciful to multitudes when they die than the pope was to them in their lifetime. Nothing good has ever issued, or will ever issue, from the papacy and its rules.

In spite of being contrary to the pope's ruling, and even if the married state be entered into in spite of the pope's specific ruling, that ruling is null and void, and retains no validity. For God's commandment, which ordains that no one shall separate man and wife, far overrides the pope's ruling. Nor may God's commandment be broken or deferred for the sake of the papal ordinances. Nevertheless, many hare-brained jurists have sided with the pope, devised impediments to marriage, and so have prevented, or destroyed, or confused the conjugal state. God's commandment has consequently been entirely defeated. Is there any need for me to enlarge on this? In the entire canon law, there are not two lines which can teach anything to a devout Christian; and, unfortunately, there are so many erroneous and dangerous regulations, that nothing better could be done than to make a bonfire of them.

If you should object that the marriage of the clergy would be scandalous unless the pope had previously given a dispensation, I would reply that the scandal in it is the fault of the Roman papacy for setting up such a ruling without any right, and against God. In God's sight, and according to Holy Scripture, there is no offence. Moreover, in a case where the pope, with his greed and his oppressive regulations, can grant a dispensation on payment of a fee, in that very instance any Christian whatever may grant a dispensation just for the sake of God and the salvation of souls. For Christ has set us free from all man-made laws, especially when they operate contrary to God and the soul's good, as St. Paul teaches in Galatians 5 and 1 Corinthians 9.[1]

15. Nor would I forget the sad condition of the monasteries. The evil spirit, who to-day confuses all classes by man-made laws and makes life intolerable, has taken possession of certain abbots, abbesses, and prelates. The result is that they so govern the brothers and sisters that they consign them the more speedily to hell; meanwhile, the poor things lead a lamentable existence here on earth, as do all martyrs to the devil. To go into detail, the papists reserve to their own dispensation all, or at least some, of the deadly sins which are committed in private, and from which no friar is allowed to absolve his fellow under his vow of obedience and on penalty of excommunication. Nowhere are people angels all the time, but only men of flesh and blood; and they would rather risk threats and excommunication than confess their secret sins to the prelates and appointed confessors. Over and above this, they take the sacraments, and do so with such consciences that they become *irregulares*,[2] and fall into many other miseries. O blind shepherds, O fatuous prelates, O ravening wolves!

What I say on this point is: It is right for the prelate to punish open and notorious sins; these alone and no others may he reserve to himself, and make exceptional cases of them. But he should have no authority to deal with secret sins, not even the most scandalous. If a prelate claims jurisdiction over these, then he is acting as a tyrant, acting without justification, and invading the judgment of God. Hence I give this counsel to those same poor creatures, whether friars or nuns. If your Superior will not allow you to confess

[1] Gal. 5:1; 1 Cor. 9:4ff., 10:23
[2] A term applied to monks and nuns guilty of offences of three classes: especially those of the body, of neglecting the sacrament, and of 23 specified cases

your secret sins to someone of your own choice, nevertheless take them and bewail them to the brother or sister whom you prefer. Receive your absolution and comfort; go away, follow your bent, and do your duty. Only remain firm in the faith that you have been absolved, and that nothing further is necessary. Do not let yourself be troubled or led astray by threats of excommunication, or of being *"irregulares"*, or anything of this kind. These apply only to public or known sins such as no one wants to confess; they do not apply to you. What are you thinking of, you blind prelates, trying to exclude secret sins by a fence of threats? Leave untouched what you cannot openly deal with; let the judgment and mercy of God work among those who belong to your care. God has not delivered them so completely into your hands that He has let them go from His own. Indeed you have but the smaller share in those under your rule. Let your statutes be statutes, but do not exalt them into heavenly decrees, nor give them the force of divine justice.

16. Further, masses[1] on anniversaries, or at celebrations, and for the dead, ought to be either entirely abolished, or at least reduced in number. It is plain to see that they become merely subjects for contempt, things with which God will be greatly angered, seeing that they will be celebrated only for money, and as an excuse for eating and drinking to excess. How can it be to God's good pleasure when, alas, the vigils and masses are dreadfully gabbled, in a way which is neither reading nor praying? Even when they are treated as prayers, it is not from a loving devotion, or for God's sake, but for the sake of pay, or to carry out a bounden duty. Yet it is impossible for any work to please God, or to serve any purpose with Him, unless offered out of unconstrained love. Therefore, it is always a Christian act to abolish or reduce everything which we see abused, and which provokes God rather than reconciles Him. It would seem to be far preferable, and surely more pleasing to God, as well as much better in itself, that a Chapter, a church, or a cloister, should combine all their annual masses and

[1] Cf. *infra*, p. 174

vigils into a single celebration. On an appointed day, let them hold a real vigil and mass, in earnestness of heart, in devotion and faith, on behalf of all their benefactors; this, rather than observing thousands upon thousands of them every year, with a special mass for each benefactor, but celebrated without any devotion or faith. O beloved Christians, God is not concerned with how often, but with how truly we pray. He even condemns long and frequent prayers, Matthew 6, and says they will only earn the more punishment.[1] But the greediness of priests who cannot trust God gives rise to the familiar state of affairs, as it leads to fear of death from starvation otherwise.

17. Certain of the penances[2] or penalties of canon law ought to be abolished, especially the *interdict* which is undoubtedly a device of the Evil One. Is it not a trick of Satan to wipe away one sin by causing many sins of a worse character? For it is a greater sin to silence God's Word and to abolish serving Him, than to strangle twenty popes at once,[3] not to mention merely killing one priest or keeping back church property. That is another example of the gentle virtues taught in the canon law. The reason that this law is called "spiritual" is that it derives from the spirit—not, however, the Holy Spirit, but the Evil Spirit.

Excommunication must never be employed as a penalty except where the Scriptures prescribe its use, i.e., against those who believe amiss, or who live in open sin; but it should not be used for the sake of temporal advantages. But, to-day, the opposite is the case; everyone lives and believes as he will, most of all those who harass and plunder other people with interdicts; and every one of the bans is pronounced purely for the sake of temporal property, all of it owing to the holy Canon Law of Unrighteousness, with which I have already dealt at greater length in a sermon.[4]

The remaining punishments and penances, suspensions,[5] irregularities, aggravations, re-aggravations, depositions,

---

[1] Matt. 6:7, cf. 23:24   [2] Cf. *infra*, *Pagan Servitude*, pp. 279ff.
[3] A reference to what happened in 1517, cf. *supra*, p. 128, n.1; *infra*, p. 339
[4] *Sermon von dem Bann. W.*, Vol. VI, p. 63ff.
[5] Temporary withdrawals of certain ecclesiastical privileges

lightnings, thunders, cursings and damnings, and whatever else there is of that kind, ought to be buried thirty feet deep underground, till neither their name nor their memory continued on earth. The Evil One, freed from fetters by the canon law, has brought these dreadful plagues and sufferings into the heavenly kingdom of holy Christendom, and has effected nothing thereby except to destroy men's souls or hinder their faith. Christ's word could well be applied to it when He said, Matthew 23: "Woe unto you scribes, you have seized authority to teach, and you close the Kingdom of Heaven to men. You do not enter yourselves and you prevent those who are entering."[1]

18. All festival days should be abolished, and Sunday alone retained. But, if it is preferred to keep the festivals of Our Lady and of the greater saints, they should all be transferred to Sundays, or observed only at morning Mass, after which the whole day should be a working day. The reason for the proposed change is the present misuse of festival days in drinking, gaming, idleness, and all sorts of sins. In this way, we incur the wrath of God more on holy days than on the rest. Thus all is turned upside down till "holy days" are not holy, whereas "working days" are "holy". Not only is no service done to God and His saints, but great irreverence is shown on the numerous "holy" days. Yet certain senseless prelates believe that if, in accordance with their blind feelings of devotion, they observe a festival of St. Ottilia or St. Barbara, they have done a good work; although they would be doing a much better work if, in honour of a certain saint, they turned a holy day into a working day.

In addition, the ordinary man suffers two material injuries over and above this spiritual injury, namely, he neglects his work, and he spends more money than otherwise. He also weakens his body, and makes himself less skilful. We see this happen daily, but no one thinks of reforming it. In a case like this, no one ought to ask whether the pope ordained these festivals, or whether a dispensation or permission is

[1] Matt. 23:13

required in advance. Each community, council, and administration has authority to abolish and prevent, apart from the knowledge or consent of pope or bishop, anything contrary to God, and hurtful to man in body and soul. Persons of the ruling class are also under an obligation to prevent it, on danger to their soul's salvation, even against the will of pope or bishop, who themselves indeed ought to be the first to prevent it.

Especially ought we to root out the anniversaries which celebrate the consecrating of a church. They have become nothing less than occasions for frequenting taverns, fairs, and gaming places, to the increase of irreverence towards God and the dereliction of the soul. It is useless to repeat the argument that it had a good beginning, and it is a good thing to do. God suspended His own law, which He had sent down from heaven, when it was turned into an abuse; and every day He changes what He has ordained, and destroys what He has made, on account of the same sort of abuses. In Psalm 18 it is written of Him, "Thou showest Thyself perverse with the perverse."[1]

19. The grades or degrees within which marriage is forbidden should be altered, such as those affecting godparents,[2] or third and fourth degrees of kinship. Here the pope, in his scandalous traffic, grants a dispensation for a fee, where every individual pastor should be able to grant dispensations without fee, and for the eternal good of the people concerned. Would God that every pastor might do or permit gratis everything that Rome must be paid for. This would untie the monetary strangle-hold of the canon law; e.g., indulgences, letters of indulgence, butter letters,[3] mass letters,[4] and whatever dispensations and deceptions are otherwise to be had in Rome, by which the people, poor things, are tricked and eased of their money. For, if the pope has the right to sell gilded nooses and spiritual snares (I should have said

---

[1] Ps. 18:26
[2] Since this was a spiritual kinship, it was held to serve as a bar to marriage
[3] Granting permission to eat butter, eggs, etc., on fast days
[4] Granting benefits from certain special masses

canonical wares) for money, then, of a truth, a pastor has much more right to tear them apart and tread them underfoot for God's sake. In fact, he has no right, nor has the pope, to sell them like goods at a fair.

In this connection, it should be said that the question of fasting ought to be a matter of free choice, and the foods which may be eaten left unrestricted, as the gospel has ordained.[1] For the people at Rome themselves scoff at fasts, and leave us in the provinces to use as food oil with which they would not grease their shoes. But they sell us permission to eat butter and other things, in spite of the holy apostle who says that the gospel gives us complete freedom to do everything.[2] But with their canon law, the Romanists have bound and robbed us in order that we should have to buy ourselves off again. Meanwhile they have made our consciences so pallid and timid, that it is not felt commendable to preach about this liberty any longer, because the ordinary people soon become greatly alarmed. They think that eating butter is a greater sin than lying, swearing, or committing fornication. All the same, what men have decreed is man-made, no matter where it is said to originate; and no good ever comes out of it.

20. The extra-parochial chapels and churches, away from inhabited parts,[3] should be pulled down. I mean those which have recently become the goal of pilgrimages, e.g., Wilsnack, Sternberg, Trèves, the Grimmenthal, and now Regensburg and many others.[4] Oh, what a heavy and pitiful reckoning inevitably awaits the bishops who agree to these tricks of the devil's own, and get profit out of them! They ought to be the first to stop them. But they regard it as something divine and holy, and do not see that the devil is behind it to increase avarice, to establish a hollow and fictitious faith, to weaken parish churches, to multiply taverns and spread immorality,

---

[1] Matt. 15:11   [2] 1 Cor. 10:25ff.

[3] And therefore having no congregations of their own; built only for pilgrimages

[4] They treasured things such as a holy wafer which occasionally exuded a drop of Christ's blood; some of Christ's own blood; Christ's seamless garment; etc.; cf. T. M. Lindsay, *Hist. of Ref.*, Vol. II, pp. 343f. for England

to waste money and labour to no purpose, and lead humble folk about by the nose. If they had read Scripture as well as they have read the damnable canon law, they would know how to provide a remedy.

It is useless to argue that miracles are seen in these places, for the Evil Spirit can also work miracles, as Christ declared (Matthew 24).[1] If they got to work in all seriousness and forbade things of this kind, the miracles would soon cease. On the other hand, if they were of God, no prohibition would prevent their taking place.[2] If there were no other indication that this custom were not of God, it would be enough in itself that the people go there rowdily and without common sense, in crowds like cattle, which unseemliness would be impossible if it were of God. And as God never commanded anything of the sort, there is neither "obedience" nor merit in doing it. Therefore, the thing to do is to step in boldly and stop the people. For what has not been commanded, but is more concerned for itself than for what God has commanded, is of a truth inspired by the very devil. It also results in harm to the parish churches, in that they are held in less respect. To put it in a nutshell: these things are indications of great unbelief among the people; for, if their faith were as it should be, they would find everything needful in their own churches which it is ordained they should attend.

But what is it my duty to say? Each bishop is only thinking how he can start one of these pilgrimages in his own province, not caring whether the people believe and live as they should; the rulers are like the people, one blind man leads another. Nay, in places where the pilgrimages are poorly attended, a movement is set on foot to canonize saints, but not for the sake of honouring the saints who would be reverenced without canonization; rather it is to draw crowds and cause money to flow. At this point, the pope and bishops lend their aid, indulgences pour in for which there is always enough money. But as to God's commandments, no one is concerned about them, nor follows them, nor has money for them. The pity is that we are so blind that we do not leave the devil alone to play his tricks in his own way; rather, we

[1] Matt. 24:24   [2] Acts 5:39

support him and multiply them. I wish people would leave the saints in peace, and not mislead humble folk. What spirit was it that gave the pope authority to canonize saints? Who tells him whether they are holy or not? Are there not sins enough already on earth without tempting God, interfering when He judges, and setting up the blessed saints as decoys for bringing in money?

In my view, therefore, the saints should be allowed to canonize themselves. Nay, only God should canonize them. Let every one of us stay each in his own parish, where he will discover more useful work than in all the making of pilgrimages, even if they were all combined into one. Here, at home, you will find baptism, sacrament, preaching, and your neighbour; these are more important to you than all the saints in heaven, for all of them have been sanctified by God's Word and by the sacraments. While we continue to despise these great matters, God is just in judging us with His wrath and in allowing the devil to lead us hither and thither, to institute pilgrimages, build chapels and churches, to set about canonizing saints, and other foolish things. Thus we, although having the right faith, fall into new misbeliefs. This is what the devil brought about in olden times when he misled the children of Israel from the temple at Jerusalem to innumerable other places. It was all done in God's name, and with every appearance of sanctity; all the prophets preached against it, and were martyred for doing so. But, nowadays, no one preaches against it, perhaps for fear that bishop, pope, priest, and monk will suffer martyrdom! In pursuance of this practice of canonization, Antonius of Florence, and certain others, are shortly to be sainted and canonized.[1] Hitherto they have only served the glory of God and passed as good examples; but now their sanctity is to be vaunted, and so made to bring in money.

Even if the canonization of a saint were proper in the

[1] So Ulrich von Hutten in *Vadiscus*, "Recently certain preaching friars wanted to have a certain Antonius of theirs canonized. (He had been an eminent archbishop, and had died May 31, 1459.) They asked letters from Maximilian to Leo X to commend their request, and said that money would begin to come in shortly after." Cf. *Opera*, ed. Böcking, IV, p. 232. *W.*, VI, p. 449, n. 1. He was actually canonized by Hadrian VI on May 31, 1523; cf. A. E. Berger, *Grundzüge*, p. 323

early days, it is never so to-day; just as many another thing
was proper in early days, but now hurtful and scandalous;
e.g., feast days, relics treasured in churches, and "ornaments". For it is plain that the objective in canonizing saints
is not the glory of God, nor the reform of Christians, but
money and notoriety. A church wants something special,
more than the rest are or have, and it would be sorry if
another possessed a similar thing, or if what made it outstanding became common property. Spiritual treasures have
been so completely misused, and made to serve the increase
of temporal goods in these wicked, modern days, that everything which can be called by the name of God is made to
serve Avarice. Further, any such special possession only leads
to schisms, sects, and to pride, if one church is different from
the others; and this, again, is accompanied by mutual contempt and self-exaltation. Yet all the things that are good
in God's sight are common to all and equally at their disposal, for they are only meant to serve the whole. But the
pope likes things as they are, and he would be sorry to see
all Christians equal and united.

It is relevant here to say that we should abolish, ignore,
or else make common to all churches, the licences, the bulls, and
whatever else the pope may have for sale in Rome at the
place where he fleeces people. For if he sells or gives rights
to livings, if he grants privileges, indulgences, graces, advantages, faculties, to Wittenberg, Halle, Venice, and especially
to his own city of Rome, why does he not give them to the
churches in general? Is it not his duty to do, without fee
and for God's sake, everything in his power for all Christian
people, even to the extent of shedding his blood for them?
Why is it that he gives or sells to one church, but not to
another? Or must it be the case, in the eyes of His Holiness,
that accursed gold makes a very great difference between
Christians, who, nevertheless, have the same baptism, gospel,
Christ, God, and all else? Are the Romanists trying to blind
us while yet we have eyes to see, and fool us while yet our
reason is unspoiled, till we do obeisance to this greed, and
villainy, and jugglery? A pastor only acts as a pastor if you
have money, but not otherwise; and yet the popes are not

ashamed to forward these villainies with their bulls here, there, and elsewhere.

So my view is, if this tomfoolery is not abolished, that all duteous Christian men and women should open their eyes, and not allow themselves to be led astray by the Romish bulls, seals, and make-believes. Let each stay at home in his own church. Let each be content with the baptism, gospel, faith, Christ, and God he knows. These are everywhere the same. Let the pope remain a blind leader of the blind. Neither angel nor pope can give you as much as God gives you in your own church. Nay, the pope seduces you away from the gifts of God which you receive unpaid for, to his own "gifts" which you must buy; he gives you lead instead of gold, hides instead of meat, the string instead of the purse, wax instead of honey,[1] words instead of goods, the letter instead of the spirit, as you may see with your own eyes but refuse to notice. If you were to think of going to heaven riding on his parchment and wax, your chariot would break only too soon, and you would tumble into hell; but in God's name, No! Be content with the one sure norm; what you have to buy from the pope is neither good nor godly. What comes from God is not only freely given, but all the world suffers and lies under condemnation for not wishing to receive it, although it is free: I mean the gospel and the works of God. We have deserved it from God that we should have been thus led astray, because we have neglected His holy Word and the grace given at our baptism. It is all as St. Paul says, "God will send a great error unto all those who have believed not the truth given for their salvation, that they should believe and follow a lie and villainy",[2] as they deserve.

21. Probably one of our greatest needs is to abolish all mendicancy everywhere in Christendom.[3] No one living among Christians ought to go begging. It would be an easy

---

[1] The lead was in the seal attached to a bull; the hide was the parchment itself; the string attached the seal; the wax attached the string to the parchment

[2] 2 Thess. 2:11f.

[3] It is one of the great merits of the Reformation that it took the sanctity away from mendicancy, and that it laid on the civil authorities the duty of caring for the indigent

law to make, if only we dared, and were in earnest that every town should support its own poor. No outside beggars should be allowed in, whatever they called themselves, whether pilgrims, friars, or mendicant orders. Every town could provide for its own poor, or, if it were too small, the surrounding villages could be urged to contribute. In any case, they are compelled to-day to provide for the same number of vagabonds and wicked rogues under the name of the mendicant Orders. By this means it would be possible to learn who were really poor and who not.

An overseer or guardian would be required. He would know all the poor, and would inform the town council or the pastor what they needed, or what the best arrangements would be. In my view, nowhere else is there so much wickedness and deception as in mendicancy, and yet all of it could be easily done away with. In addition, much woe falls on the common people on account of this open and general mendicancy. I have calculated that each of the five or six mendicant Orders[1] makes a visitation of one and the same place more than six or seven times every year. Besides this there are the common beggars, and those who beg alms in the name of a patron saint,[2] and then the professional pilgrims.[3] This reckons up to sixty times a year that the town is laid under tribute, besides what goes to the secular authorities in rates, taxes, and assessments; all this the Roman papacy steals in offering its bargains, and then consumes to no purpose. To me it is one of the greatest of God's miracles that, in spite of all, we can still live and keep ourselves.

But certain people think that, if my proposals were adopted, the poor would not fare properly, and that fewer great stone houses and cloisters would be built, and fewer so well adorned. All this I can well believe. Nor is any of it

---

[1] Franciscans, Dominicans, Augustinians, Carmelites, and Servites; cf. *Works of Martin Luther* (Holman, U.S.A.), Vol. II, 135

[2] The *"Botschaften"* or *stationarii*, who would enrol contributors as beneficiaries of their patron saint, and promise protection against disease, etc. Protests against them were raised at Worms in 1521, and Nüremberg, 1523. See Holman's Ed. II, 135

[3] They wandered continually from place to place, subsisting entirely on alms; *ibid.*, v. 3

necessary. He who has chosen poverty, ought not to be rich; but if a man chooses wealth, let him put his hand to the plough and get his wealth for himself out of the earth. It is sufficient if the poor are decently provided for, in such a way that they do not die of hunger or cold. It is not seemly that one man should live in idleness on the labours of his fellows, or possess wealth and luxury through the hardships which others suffer, as is the prevailing, perverse custom. St. Paul says, "If a man will not work, neither shall he eat."[1] God has commanded no one to live at another man's expense, except preachers and administrating priests for the sake of their spiritual labours. As St. Paul says in I Corinthians 9, and as Christ said to the Apostles, "Every labourer is worthy of his hire."[2]

22. I am also concerned to think that the numerous masses,[3] which have been endowed in benefices and cloisters, are both of very little use, and greatly incur the wrath of God. For that reason, it would be wise to endow no more of them, but to abolish many of those that are already endowed. For it is obvious that they are only held to be sacrifices and good works in spite of the fact that, like baptism and penance, they are sacraments which are of value, not to others, but only to him who receives them. Yet, nowadays, it has become prevalent to say masses for the living and the dead. Every hope is based on these masses; that is why so many masses have been endowed, and why the state of affairs which we are familiar with, has arisen. My proposal is perhaps too bold and unprecedented, especially for those who fear to lose their trade and livelihood, if masses of this kind were to come to an end. Unfortunately, it is now many years since it became a trade at which one worked for the sake of a temporal livelihood. Therefore, my advice to a man in future would be to become a shepherd, or else learn a handicraft, rather than become a priest or a monk, unless he were well aware in advance what it means to celebrate mass.

What I have said here does not apply to the ancient monasteries and cathedral chapters, which were undoubtedly founded for the sake of noblemen's children. According to

---

[1] 2 Thess. 3:10   [2] I Cor. 9:14; Luke 10:7   [3] Cf. *supra*, pp. 164f. § 16

German custom, only some of a nobleman's issue can
become landowners or rulers, and it was intended that the
rest should enter these monasteries, and there be free to
serve God, to study, to become scholarly people, and to help
others to do so.[1] But my present subject is the recent monasteries, founded only for repeating the liturgy and saying
mass. Their example is pressing itself on the older institutions and imposing similar repetitions of liturgy and mass,
until even these institutions serve little or no useful purpose. But by God's grace, they finally, and deservedly, come
to the drudgery of being mere choral singers and pipe-organ
players, and to the saying of cold and unattractive masses,
—all of them means by which the temporal endowment-
incomes are earned and spent. Surely the pope, the bishops,
and the doctors ought to go into these things and report on
them. But it is precisely they who are responsible for most
of it. They always let it proceed if it brings in money. Always
one blind man leads another. That is what is done by Avarice
and canon law.

Further, it ought no longer to be permitted that one person
should hold more than one canonry or one living. Each should
be content with a moderate position, and leave something
for his neighbour. This would put an end to the excuses of
those who say that, in order to support their station properly,
they require more than one office. But it would be possible
to interpret the term "properly" so broadly, that a whole
country would not suffice to support it. Covetousness and
hidden unbelief, in a case like this, go, of a truth, hand in

[1] Here Luther touches on a point which has been of much importance
in the history of social structure: the appointment of the younger sons of
the upper class to positions in the church. It was not one of the smallest
reasons why some of the younger sons joined the party of the Reformation,
that they were embittered because so many of the suitable foundations
were given to favourites of the pope. Albert of Mainz pointed out to the
pope in 1521 how easy it would be to reconcile many of the upper class if
appropriate protection were given in cases like this. Luther hoped that the
upper class would take such advantage of their prerogatives that, by deep
study of the Bible, by honourable lives, and by direct teaching, they would
impregnate the rulers of the church, no less than the parish priests, with
the evangelical spirit. A portion of the upper class fulfilled his high expecta-
tions, but others strengthened their connection with the Roman church,
and in the end large parts of Germany were closed to the Reformation.
Cf. Berger, *op. cit.*, p. 323

hand, so that what pretends to be the requirements for "proper support" is simply the pretences of greed and unbelief.

23. The "fraternities",[1] indulgences, letters of indulgence, butter-briefs,[2] mass briefs,[3] dispensations and the like,[4] ought all to be drowned and destroyed as containing nothing good. If the pope can grant you a dispensation to eat butter, or from hearing mass, he should allow a pastor the power to grant it; indeed he had no right to deprive him of the power. I am also including (with the pope) the "fraternities" which grant indulgences, say masses, and prescribe good works. My dear friend, when you were baptized, you entered into fellowship with Christ, with all the angels and saints, and with all Christians on earth. Hold fast to it and do what it demands, and you have all the necessary fraternities. Let the other things be as attractive as they may, they are still only counters as compared with coins. But if a "fraternity" were such that it subscribed funds to feed the poor, or otherwise gave help to someone, that "fraternity" would be sound, and would find its indulgences and merits in heaven. At present, however, their privileges only lead to gluttony and drunkenness.

The first thing is to chase out of Germany the papal legates with the "faculties"[5] which they sell to us at a high figure, although the traffic is nought but trickery. As things are, they take the money, and make unrighteousness righteous, dissolve vows, oaths, and agreements, thereby destroying and teaching us to destroy faithfulness and faith, which men have promised one another; and they plead that the pope has authority to do all these things. This means that the Evil One speaks through them; also, that they are selling impious

[1] Associations of laymen for purposes of prayer, and organizing good works; Berger, *op. cit.*, p. 131

[2] See note on p. 167, *supra*

[3] See p. 167, *supra*

[4] Cf. Luther's *Sermon—des Leichnams Christi u. v. d. Brüderschaften, W.*, II, p. 738ff.

[5] Cf. *W.*, VI, p. 453, n. 1, for a truly astonishing extract from *Summarium facultatum Reverendissimi D. Cardinalis de Campegio legati de Latere per dominum nostrum Clementem Papam Septimum concessarum*

doctrine, and taking our money to teach us to sin and to lead us to hell.

If there were no other insidious device making it clear that the pope was the true Antichrist, this particular example would prove it. Do you hear that, O pope, you who are not most holy, but most sinful? Would that God in heaven immediately destroyed your throne, and sent it into the abyss of hell! Who is it that gave you power to exalt yourself above your God? to relax and break His commandments, and to teach Christians, especially those of Germany, whom all the books of history esteem for their noble, steadfast, and faithful character, to be inconstant, perjured traitors, and faithless profligates? God's commandment is that we should keep our vows and our honour even with our enemies. Yet you interfere and pretend to relax this commandment; and you claim, in your heretical and antichristian decretals,[1] that you have power to do so. Satan, the Evil One, uses you as his mouthpiece and scribe to lie as he never lied before. You even force the meaning of Scripture and twist it to suit yourself. Oh Christ, my Lord! look down; let Thy final day come and destroy this nest of devils at Rome. There sits the man of whom St. Paul said (2 Thessalonians 2), "The Man of Sin and the son of perdition shall exalt himself over thee, and sit in thy church setting himself up as God."[2] To exercise papal power as the pope does, what else is it than to teach and multiply sin and wickedness, to lead souls into perdition under God's name and prerogative?

In the days of old, the children of Israel had unknowingly been deceived into swearing an oath with the Gibeonites their enemies, but they had to keep it.[3] King Zedekiah broke his oath with the king of Babylon, and so he and the whole of his people were miserably defeated.[4] Among our own selves, a hundred years ago, Wladislaus, that splendid king of Poland and Hungary, was slain with a large number of his people, because he allowed himself to be misled by the papal legate and cardinal, to break the propitious and

---

[1] Decretals were papal pronouncements on disputed questions of church discipline, and, once given, had the force of canon law

[2] 2 Thess. 2:3ff.   [3] Joshua 9:6ff.   [4] 2 Kings 24:20 and 25:4ff.

M

advantageous treaty which he had sworn with the Turks.[1] Sigismund, the religious-minded emperor, had no success after the council at Constance, when he allowed those rogues to break the safe-conduct which had been given to John Huss and Jerome of Prague.[2] Out of this arose all sorts of trouble between Bohemia and ourselves. And in living memory, God spare us, how much Christian blood has been poured out for the sake of the treaty[3] sworn between Emperor Maximilian and King Louis of France, which Pope Julius instigated, and then broke? How could I possibly recount all the woe which the popes have caused, with presumption like the devil, in breaking oaths and vows made between powerful princes, to suit their own fancy and to the advantage of their own pocket? I hope that the Last Day is at hand; things surely cannot possibly grow worse than what the conduct of the papacy has brought to pass. It has suppressed God's commandments, replacing them with its own. If that is not the Antichrist, let some one else say what it is. But more of this another time and more incisively.

24. It is high time that we took up the Hussite question and dealt with it seriously. We ought to make an earnest effort to get the Hussites to join us, and for us to unite ourselves with them.[4] It would put an end to defamation, hatred, and envy on both sides. In accord with my present

[1] The Turkish treaty was made in 1443, and broken at the instance of Cardinal Julian Cesarine the following year. The king perished at Varna November 10, 1444

[2] Not to Jerome, though he too was burned at Constance, in 1416. John Huss had a safe conduct from Sigismund, but this was overridden, and Huss was burned at Constance in 1415

[3] The League of Cambrai, 1508

[4] The Hussites represented a popular religious movement in Bohemia which became quite vigorous owing to widespread indignation at the burning of John Huss in Constance, July 6, 1415. The more moderate, the Calistines or Utraquists, demanded preaching in the vernacular, communion in both kinds, reform of the clergy, and prohibition of property and secular jurisdiction to the clergy. The extreme party, Taborites, would prohibit the use of images and the worship of saints, condemn purgatory, etc. Luther's contacts with the Hussites were set afoot by the Disputation at Leipzig in the summer of 1519. Two clergymen of the Utraquist persuasion in Prague sent him their good wishes and various presents, including the works of Huss on the church. These were received by Luther on Oct.3, 1519, and had a great effect on his opinions, but he was far from ever becoming a Hussite

boldness, I will be the first to propound an opinion, but I will defer to any one with a better grasp of the situation.

(a) In the first place we must confess the truth faithfully, and stop our self-justification. We must grant the point to the Hussites, that John Huss and Jerome of Prague were burnt at Constance, despite the Christian safe-conduct vouched to them by the pope and the emperor. This was done contrary to God's commandment, and gave the Hussites every cause for embitterment. Of course they ought to have been perfect Christians, and to that extent their duty was to have endured this deep wrong of ours, and this disobedience to God; nevertheless, it was no part of their duty to approve it, or acknowledge it as right. Indeed to-day they ought rather to sacrifice life and limb than agree that it was right to break a Christian safe-conduct vouchsafed by the pope and the emperor, and to act faithlessly against it. While, then, the impatience of the Hussites was a fault, the pope and those who side with him are far more responsible for all the misery, all the wrong-doing, and all loss of life which have ensued since the Council of Constance.

I have no desire to justify at this stage John Huss's propositions or defend his error, although to my way of thinking he wrote nothing erroneous. I do not find it difficult to believe that they who dealt in that faithless way with a Christian safe-conduct, and broke God's commandment, did not pronounce a fair verdict or a righteous condemnation. They were certainly possessed rather by the Evil One than by the Holy Spirit. Nobody can doubt that the Holy Spirit does not work contrary to God's decrees; and nobody is so ignorant as not to know that to break a safe-conduct and a pledge is contrary to God's commandments, even though the promises were given to the devil himself, not to mention a heretic. It is also public knowledge that such a safe-conduct was given to John Huss and the Bohemians, and was not respected. He was burned in spite of it. I am not to be understood as meaning that John Huss was a saint or a martyr, as certain of his fellow-countrymen maintain. But I do declare my belief that he suffered a wrong, and that his books and his teaching were wrongly condemned.

The terrible judgments of God are given in secret, and are such that no other than Himself has a right to reveal and publish abroad. My point is: John Huss may have been a heretic as bad as could be found; nevertheless he was unjustly banned, and was burned contrary to God's will. No one should bring pressure and compel the Bohemians to assent to the act, or we shall reach no agreement. What must unite us is, not an obstinate opinion, but the plain truth. It does not help matters to say, as was done at the time, that a safe-conduct need not be respected if given to a heretic. That would be the equivalent of the self-contradiction of saying that one ought *not* to keep a commandment of God's if one *is* to keep a commandment of God's. The devil has made the Romanists insane and foolish, or they would have understood what it is they were saying and doing. God has commanded that oaths should be respected even though the world fall. How much more when it is only a question of letting a heretic go free. Heretics ought to be persuaded by argument, and not by fire; and this was the way of the early Fathers. If it were wise policy to suppress heretics by burning them, then the executioners would be the most learned teachers on earth. We should have no need to study books any longer, for he who could overthrow his fellow by violence would have the right to burn him at the stake.

(*b*) In the second place, the emperor and princes ought to send the Bohemians an embassy of religious-minded and perspicacious bishops and scholars, but never a cardinal, or papal legate, or inquisitor. These officials are much too unschooled in Christian affairs. Nor do they seek the soul's good, but, like all papal play-actors, only their own power, or advantage, or glory. These persons were also the principal figures in the calamitous business at Constance. But those who constitute the embassy which we ought to send, should inquire among the Bohemians as to the nature of their faith, and whether it would be possible to unite all their sects into a whole. This is where the pope, for the good of his soul, ought long ago to have asserted his authority. Following the statutes of the most Christian Council at Nicea, he ought to have allowed them to choose for themselves an archbishop of Prague, and should have let him be confirmed by the bishop of Olmutz in Moravia, or the bishop of Grau in Hungary, or the bishop of Magdeburg in Germany. It would suffice if he had been confirmed by one or two of these, as was the custom in St. Cyprian's time. The pope has nothing he can say against that; should he oppose it, he would be acting like a wolf and a tyrant. No one should follow him, and excommunication by him should be met by counter-excommunication.

If it is preferred to follow this course only after informing the pope, out of respect for the papacy, let it be done that way. But we must see to it that the Hussites are not required to pay a farthing, and the pope must demand no pledges of them even as little as a hair, and must not tyrannize over them, nor bind them with oaths and vows. This is what he does with all other bishops, contrary to God and the right. If he refuses to be satisfied with the honour of being asked for his consent, then let him simply keep his vows, rights, regulations, and tyrannies to himself. Let the election stand on its own feet, and may the blood of all those who remain in danger cry out against him. No one ought to consent to what is wrong. It is a sufficient mark of respect for a tyrant if we offer him an honour. If no other course is open, remember that the choice and consent of the common people is as good as any confirmation a tyrant can give. Nevertheless, I hope that a popular vote will not be necessary. Surely it will happen ere long that some of the Romanists and the religious-minded bishops and scholars will become aware of the papal tyranny, and repudiate it.

Nor is it my view that the Hussites be compelled to abandon taking the sacraments in both kinds,[1] for that practice is neither unchristian nor heretical. Let them be free to follow that custom if they prefer it. But let the new bishop see to it that no dissension arises in regard to the custom.

---

[1] Claiming the authority of Holy Writ, the Bohemian reformers had insisted on administering communion in both the bread and the wine to the laity, a practice which was one of the greatest difficulties in the contest with the papacy; in the Roman communion, the wine has been withheld from the laity since the sixth century, but not earlier. Luther discusses the issue in full in the first section of the *Pagan Servitude; vide infra*, pp. 215ff.

He should teach them in a kindly spirit, and show that neither practice is wrong. Similarly, there ought to be no quarrel if the priests dress, or live, differently from laymen. The same principle holds good if they are unwilling to observe the canon law of Rome. Pressure should not be brought to bear on them. It should be their prime concern that they live sincerely by faith, and in accord with Holy Scripture. For there can well be both the Christian faith and the Christian status apart from the intolerable papal laws; indeed that faith and status cannot very well exist unless the Romish rules are diminished or abolished. When we were baptized, we were set free, subject only to God's Word. Why should any man use human words and make us prisoner? As St. Paul says: "Ye are bought with a price; become not bondservants of men",[1] namely, of those who rule according to man-made laws.

If I knew that the Beghards[2] held nothing more erroneous about the sacrament of the altar than the belief that the elements remained truly natural bread and wine, while yet the true body and blood of Christ were present under them, then I myself would not condemn them; I would consent to their being recognized by the bishop of Prague. There is no article of faith which declares that bread and wine are not present in the sacrament in their own essence and nature,[3] which delusion St. Thomas Aquinas and the pope maintain. But it is an article of faith that the natural body and blood of Christ are truly present in the natural bread and wine. Hence the preference held by either side ought to be patiently tolerated till the two reach agreement, because there is nothing dangerous in believing either that the bread is there, or is not there. It is our duty to tolerate all varieties of those manners and customs which do not endanger the faith. But if the Hussites held a different creed from us I should prefer to leave them outside the Church, although they ought then to receive instruction in the truth.

Any further errors and dissensions which might be brought

---

[1] I Cor. 6:20; Gal. 5:1
[2] A name here given by Luther to the "Bohemian Brethren", a sect of the Hussites
[3] Cf. *infra*, *Pagan Servitude*, pp. 224ff. for a classic discussion of the matter

to light in Bohemia should be borne with until the arch-bishop had been reinstalled, and had had time to bring the people together again, with one self-consistent doctrine. They will certainly not unite again if we use violence or threats, or act impatiently. Patience and gentleness are needed here. Christ had to associate with His disciples, and bear their unbelief for a long time before they reached the faith that He would rise again from the dead. If only a good bishop and a proper régime were restored to Bohemia, without any Romish despotism, I am confident that there would soon be an improvement.

The temporal possessions, once belonging to the church, should not be demanded back again very strictly. Since we are Christian, and each of us under obligation to help our neighbour, we are empowered, for the sake of harmony, to give or surrender the properties to them as in God's sight and man's. For Christ says: "If two of you agree on earth, there am I in your midst."[1] Would to God that we, on both sides, helped in that direction; that each gave the other his hand in brotherly lowliness; and that we did not stubbornly insist on our authority or our rights! Love is greater and more needful than the papacy at Rome, which is without love; whereas love can do without the papacy. Having said this, I have done all I could to the purpose. If the pope or those around him interfere, they will have to give an account for having preferred their own advantage rather than their neighbour's, contrary to the love of God. The pope ought to be willing to surrender his papacy, all his property and glory, if in so doing he could effect the salvation of one soul. But to-day, he would rather see the world perish than abandon a jot or tittle of his authority; nevertheless he retains the title of "His Holiness". There I leave this subject.

25. The universities need a sound and thorough reforma-tion. I must say so no matter who takes offence. Everything that the papacy has instituted or ordered is directed solely towards the multiplication of sin and error. Unless they are completely altered from what they have been hitherto, the

[1] Matt. 18:19

universities will fit exactly what is said in the Book of
Maccabees: "Places for the exercise for youth, and for the
Greekish fashion."[1] Loose living is practised there; little is
taught of the Holy Scripture or the Christian faith; the blind
pagan teacher, Aristotle, is of more consequence than Christ.
In my view, Aristotle's writings on *Physics, Metaphysics, On
the Soul,* and *Ethics,* hitherto regarded as the most important,
should be set aside along with all others that boast they
treat of natural objects, for in fact they have nothing to
teach about things natural or spiritual.[2] Remember too that
no one, up to now, has understood his teaching, but much
precious time and mental energy have been uselessly devoted
to wasteful work, study, and effort. I venture to say that
a potter has more understanding of the things of nature than
is written down in those books. It pains me to the heart that
this damnable, arrogant, pagan rascal has seduced and fooled
so many of the best Christians with his misleading writings.
God has made him a plague to us on account of our sins.

In his book, *On the Soul,* which is one of his best, the
wretched fellow teaches that the soul dies with the body;
and many have tried, in vain, to defend him. It is as if we
did not possess the Holy Scriptures where we find a superabundance of teaching on the whole subject, of which
Aristotle has not the faintest inkling. Yet this defunct pagan
has attained supremacy; impeded, and almost suppressed,
the Scriptures of the living God. When I think of this

---

[1] 2 Macc. 4:9, 12

[2] This seemingly extraordinary judgment of Aristotle was not due to
Luther's impatience or ignorance. Immediately after graduating M.A. at
Erfurt, he began to teach Aristotle. This was part of his duties which he
undertook on oath. He continued teaching Aristotle when he transferred
to Wittenberg in 1508 and until 1512, when he was appointed Professor
of Holy Scripture. Moreover, the view was shared to a large extent by
Erasmus; cf. *Colloquies, passim.* Nor was it a novelty. "Roger Bacon . .
believed that Aristotle's philosophy was entirely wrong. . . . In Paris, a considerable body of opinion, in the middle of the nineteenth century, regarded
Aristotelianism as mere pedantry," Sir E. Whittaker, *Space and Spirit,*
1946, p. 49, "I believe that nothing could be more absurdly said in
Natural Philosophy than in . . . Aristotle's." T. Hobbes *Leviathan,* p. 522,
"The popularity of Aristotelian logic retarded the advance of physical
science throughout the Middle Ages," A. N. Whitehead, *Science and the
Modern World,* 1926, p. 37. Luther seems to have been in goodly company
when he formed this opinion of Aristotle, though A. remains "the master
of them that know", Dante, *Inferno,* IV, 131

lamentable state of affairs, I cannot avoid believing that the
Evil One introduced the study of Aristotle.

On the same principles, his book on *Ethics* is worse than
any other book, being the direct opposite of God's grace,
and the Christian virtues;[1] yet it is accounted among the
best of his works. Oh! away with such books from any
Christian hands. Let no one accuse me of overstating the
case, or object that I do not understand. My dear sir, I know
well enough what I am saying. Aristotle is as familiar to me
as to you and your like. I have read him and studied him
with more understanding than did St. Thomas Aquinas or
Duns Scotus.[2] Without pride, I can make that claim, and
if needs be, prove it. It makes no difference that for centuries so many of the best minds have devoted their labours
to him. Such objections do not affect me as at one time they
used to do. For it is plain as the day that the longer the
lapse of time, the greater the errors which abound in the
world and the universities.

I would gladly grant the retention of Aristotle's books on
Logic, *Rhetoric*, and *Poetics*; or that they should be abridged
and read in a useful form to train young men to speak and
preach well. But the comments and notes should be set aside,
and, just as Cicero's *Rhetoric* is read without notes and comments, so also Aristotle's *Logic* should be read in its simple
form, and without the lengthy comments. But to-day no
man learns from it how to speak or preach; the whole thing
has become a mere subject of argumentation and a weariness
to the flesh.

Then there are the languages: Latin, Greek, and Hebrew,
the mathematical disciplines, and history. But this is a subject which I commend to men of greater knowledge than
I possess; it will right itself if a reformation is undertaken
seriously; much depends on that. For Christian youth, and
those of our upper classes, with whom abides the future of
Christianity, will be taught and trained in the universities.
In my view, no work more worthy of the pope and the

[1] A criticism of Aristotle's doctrine of virtue as the mean between two
extremes; cf. *Nichomachean Ethics*, ed. D. P. Chase, 1877, p. 74
[2] Both Aquinas and Scotus knew Aristotle only in a Latin translation,
probably made from the Arabic

emperor could be carried out than a true reformation of the universities. On the other hand, nothing could be more wicked, or serve the devil better, than unreformed universities.

I leave the medical men to reform their own faculties, but I claim to speak for the jurists and theologians. In regard to the former, I aver that it would be well if the canon law, in particular the Decretals, were completely blotted out, from the first letter to the last. There is a superabundance of material at our disposal in the Biblical writings, telling what our conduct should be in all circumstances. The pursuit of the other studies only prevents that of the Holy Scriptures; and, moreover, for the most part, the former are tainted with greed and pride. Even if there were much of value in the canon law, it would still be wise to let it perish, because the pope claims to have all the canon laws ensconced in the chambers of his heart. Henceforth, therefore, to study it is a mere waste of time and a self-deception. To-day, the canon law does not consist of what is written in books, but in the arbitrary choices preferred by the pope and his lickspittles. Even if your case is most firmly established according to the written canon law, the pope still retains his *"scrinium pectoris"* superior to it, and by which he will settle what is legal, and rule the world. Often a villain, or even the devil himself, controls that chamber, although the popes proudly claim that the Holy Spirit rules it. That is their way with the humble folk who belong to Christ; they impose many rules, but keep none; they compel other people to observe them, or to buy themselves off for gold.

Since, then, the pope and those about him have rescinded the entire canon law, refusing to respect it themselves, and observing only their own wanton will in despite of the whole world, we ought to follow them, and ourselves reject these books. We shall never be able to know the papal, arbitrary will through and through, which is the present-day substitute for the canon law, alas! But let that law perish, in the name of God, for it has been exalted in the devil's name. Let there be no more *doctores decretorum*,[1] but only *doctores*

---

[1] Doctors of Canon Law

scrinii,[1] i.e., papal play-actors. It is said that no finer secular administration exists anywhere than among the Turks, and they possess neither the canonical nor the temporal law, but only the Qoran. But we must confess that no more scandalous administration exists than our own with its spiritual and temporal laws, till no class of the people now lives in obedience to natural reason, to say nothing of Holy Scripture.

The temporal law! God help us, what a rank growth that has become. Although it is much better, wiser, and more proper than the "spiritual law", in which nothing is good except the name, nevertheless there is far too much temporal law. Surely there would be quite enough law if there were but wise rulers side by side with the Holy Scriptures. As St. Paul says in 1 Corinthians 6, "Is there no one among you who is able to judge his neighbour's cause that you must go to law before the unrighteous?"[2] In my opinion, appeal should be made to common law and established custom rather than to the general law decreed by the emperor; and only in case of necessity should the imperial law be invoked. And just as every land has its own manners and customs, so, would to God, that each had its own laws, and these few and brief. That is what obtained before the imperial laws were introduced, many lands being still without the latter. Rambling and far-fetched laws only burden the people, and are a hindrance rather than a help in settling their cases. But I hope that this subject will be considered and examined by others better fitted than I to discuss it.

Our worthy theologians have ceased from worrying and working; and so they leave the Bible alone and read the *Sententiae*.[3] I should have thought that theological students would have begun with the study of the *Sententiae*, and left the Bible to the doctors, but it is done the other way round. The Bible comes first and is studied till they reach the Bachelor's degree; the *Sententiae* comes last and remains even after reaching the doctorate. A very sacred obligation is attached here. A man who is not a priest may read the

---

[1] Doctors of the Papal Heart   [2] 1 Cor. 6:1ff.
[3] Books on theology, especially those of Peter Lombard

Bible, but a priest must read the *Sententiae*. It looks to me
as if a married man might be a doctor in the Bible, but not
by any means in the *Sententiae*. How can we expect to enjoy
well-being when we act so perversely, and degrade God's
holy Word like this? Moreover, the pope uses very stern
language, and commands that his laws are to be read and
used in the schools and law courts; but he says little of the
gospel. His command is obeyed; with the result that the
gospel lies in the dust in the schools and courts, while the
pope's scandalous laws are alone in force.

If we bear the name and title of Doctors of Holy Scripture, the very name should make it compulsory for us to
teach Holy Scripture alone; this high-sounding and proud
title, however, is too exalted, and no man should boast it,
or be accorded the degree of Doctor of Holy Scripture. It
would only be tolerable if his duties bore out his title. As
it is, however, the *Sententiae* hold the field; and more of
pagan and man-made opinions are to be found among theologians than of the sacred certainties of scriptural doctrine.
What then are we to do about it? I have no other suggestion
to make on this point than to offer humble prayer to God
that He give us real Doctors of Theology. The pope, the
emperor, the universities create Doctors of the Arts, of
Medicine, and of Law; but be assured that no one can make
a Doctor of Holy Scripture, except the Holy Spirit from
heaven; as Christ said in John 6, "They shall all be taught
of God Himself."[1] Now the Holy Spirit asks no questions
about red or brown birettas[2] and other adornments, nor
whether a candidate is young or old, layman or priest, monk
or secular, celibate or married; nay, in olden times, the spirit
spoke through a she-ass against the prophet who rode on it.
Would to God that we were worthy of being given these
doctors, no matter whether they were priests or laymen,
married or celibate. But to-day they try to force the Holy
Spirit to enter the popes, the bishops, and the doctors,
although there is no gleam or glimpse to show that He has
actually entered them.

The number of books on theology must also be reduced,

[1] John 6:45   [2] Doctors' caps

only the best being retained. For neither many books nor much reading make a man learned; but a good book, often read, no matter how short, will give Scriptural scholarship plus religious-mindedness. Even the writings of any one of the holy Fathers or, indeed, all of them, should only be read for a while, and in order that they might lead us to the Bible. To-day, however, we read them alone, and get no further; we never enter on the Bible. Thus we are like those who look at the sign-posts, but never set out on the journey. The intention of the early Fathers in their writing was to introduce us to the Bible; but we use them only to find a way of avoiding it. Nevertheless, the Bible is our vineyard, and there we should all labour and toil.[1]

Above all, the most important and most usual teaching, in both the universities and the lower schools, ought to be concerned with the Holy Scriptures; beginning with the gospels for the young boys. Would to God also that each town had a girls' school where, day by day, the girls might have a lesson on the gospel, whether in German or Latin. Of course, as we read in the accounts of St. Agnes and other saints in olden times, it was with that praiseworthy and Christian purpose that the schools, monasteries, and nunneries were founded. Those were the days of holy virgins and martyrs, and all was well in the Christian community. But now they only use prayers and hymns in those places. Would it not be reasonable for every Christian person on reaching his ninth or tenth year to know the holy gospel in its entirety, since his name and standing as a Christian are based on it? A woman who spins or sews, teaches her craft to her daughter in her early years. To-day, however, great and learned prelates and bishops themselves do not know the gospel.

Oh! how unwisely we deal with our poor young folk, whom we are commanded to train and instruct![2] But we shall have to give a serious account of our stewardship, and explain why we have not set the Word of God before them. Their lot is that of which Jeremiah speaks in Lamentations 2, "Mine eyes do fail with tears, my bowels are troubled, my

---

[1] Cf. e.g. Ps. 80:15, Isa. 5:7, Matt. 20:1ff   [2] Prov. 22:6

liver is poured upon the earth, for the destruction of the daughter of my people, because the young children and the sucklings swoon in the streets of the city. They say to their mothers, Where is corn and wine? When they swooned as the wounded in the streets of the city, when their soul is poured out into their mothers' bosom."[1] We fail to notice the present pitiful distress of the young people. Though they live in the midst of a Christian world, they faint and perish in misery because they lack the gospel in which we should be training and exercising them all the time.

Moreover, even if the universities diligently studied the Holy Scriptures, we should not, as now, send everyone there for the mere sake of having many students, or because everyone wants a doctor in the family. Only the cleverest should be sent, and after having received a good education in the lower schools. The prince and the local town council ought to see to this, and send only those who are well qualified. But I would not advise anyone to send his son to a place where the Holy Scriptures do not come first. Every institution, where the Word of God is not taught regularly, must fail. That is why we observe the kind of people who are now and will continue to be in the universities. It is nobody's fault except that of the pope, the bishops, and the prelates, who have been charged with the care of the young people. For the universities ought to give students a thorough training in the Bible. Some of them might become bishops and pastors, and stand in the forefront against heretics, and the devil, and the whole world. But that is nowhere to be found. I greatly fear that the universities are but wide-open gates leading to hell, as they are not diligent in training and impressing the Holy Scripture on the young students.

[26.[2] I am well aware that the crew in Rome will object and cry aloud that the pope took the Holy Roman empire from the Greek emperor, and transferred it to the German

---

[1] Lam. 2:11, 12 A.V.
[2] This section does not occur in Luther's first edition

people.[1] In exchange for this honour and favour, he deserves, and should have received, our willing submission, and thanks, and every other expression of gratitude. For this reason, they will perhaps attempt to scatter to the winds every effort to reform them, and let nothing happen except things like making a present of the Roman empire. From this starting-point, they have till now persecuted and oppressed many an excellent emperor so arbitrarily and arrogantly that it is distressing to talk of. And they have used the same adroit-ness in making themselves the overlords of every secular authority and government, contrary to the holy gospel. I must therefore say a word on that subject.

It is unquestionable that the real Roman empire perished and ended long ago. This empire and its destruction were predicted in the writings of Moses in Numbers 24, and of Daniel. Thus Balaam clearly prophesied in Numbers 24 when he said, "The Romans shall come and destroy the Jews, and afterwards they themselves shall perish."[2] That took place at the hands of the Goths, but was confirmed when the Turkish empire arose a thousand years ago. In the course of time, Asia and Africa, and afterwards France and Spain, and finally Venice, fell away, and nothing remained to Rome of its former power.

When the pope could no longer force the Greeks and the emperor to suit his arbitrary preferences, he invented the device of robbing him of his empire and title, and transfer-ring them to the Germans who, at that time, were warlike and of good repute. In so doing, the Romanists wished to make the power of the Roman empire subject to themselves, and then give it away in the form of feudal states. All hap-pened according to plan. It was taken from the emperor at Constantinople, and its name and title ascribed to us.Ger-mans. Thereby we became the pope's feudatories, and there is now a second Roman empire, one built by the popes, but

[1] The whole of the following argument depends on the crowning of Charlemagne in Rome by Pope Leo III on Christmas Day, A.D. 800, thereby founding the Holy Roman Empire of the German People, and making a basis for the claim to papal supremacy; cf. Bryce, *Holy Roman Empire*, Chaps. IV and V

[2] Num. 24:24, an interpretation, rather than a quotation

on German foundations. For the other, the first, as I have said, had perished long before.

Thus the Roman pontiff has his way. Rome has been seized, the German emperor driven out and bound under oath not to reside in Rome. He is to be Roman emperor, and yet not live in Rome. Meanwhile he is to be dependent on, and live by, the good pleasure of the pope and his entourage. The result is that we possess the title, and they the land and the towns. All the time, they have misused us in our simplicity to the advantage of their arrogant and despotic ways. They call us "senseless Germans" for letting ourselves be deceived and fooled just as it suited them.

So be it. For God, the Lord, it is a small thing to toss empires and principalities to and fro. He makes so free with them that sometimes He gives a kingdom to an arrant knave, and takes it from one of a religious mind. Sometimes He does this through the treachery of wicked and faithless men, sometimes by the laws of inheritance. This is what we read of the kingdom of Persia, and of Greece, and almost all empires. It says in Daniel 2 and 4, "He who dwelleth in heaven ruleth over all things, and it is He alone who overthroweth kingdoms, tosseth them to and fro, and setteth them up."[1] Since no one can regard it as a great matter that a kingdom has been given to him, especially if he be a Christian, we Germans have no cause for pride if a new Roman empire is apportioned to us. For in God's eyes it is but a poor gift, such as He has often given to the most unworthy, as it says in Daniel 4, "All who dwell on earth are as nothing in His eyes, and in all the empires of men, He has power to give them to whom He will."[2]

In spite of the fact, however, that the pope has used violence and injustice in robbing the true emperor of the Roman empire, or of the title of Roman Emperor, and transferred it to us Germans, it is certain, all the same, that God made use of the pope's wickedness in this matter, in giving such an empire to the German people. After the fall of the first Roman empire, He set up another, that which now exists. While we gave no occasion for the wickedness of the

[1] Dan. 2:21 and 4:19ff.   [2] Dan. 4:35

popes in this transaction, neither did we understand their deceitful purposes and intentions. Nevertheless, we have unhappily paid far too dearly for this empire, through pontifical cunning and unscrupulousness, at the cost of immeasurable bloodshed, with the suppression of our freedom, the loss and theft of our property, especially of our churches and canonries, and the suffering of unspeakable fraud and contempt. We have the title of empire, but the pope has our goods, our honour, our bodies, lives, souls, and all we possess. That is the way to cheat the Germans, and, because they are Germans, to go on cheating them.[1] The popes had this in mind when they wanted to become emperors; when they could not accomplish this, they set themselves above the emperors.

Since, therefore, by the providence of God and the efforts of evil men, the empire has been given us through no fault of ours, I do not believe that we ought to abandon it; but, rather, to administer it properly in the fear of God, as long as it may please Him. For, as I have said, He does not look to see whence an empire arose; His will is that it should be rightly administered. Though the popes took it improperly from others, we did not receive it improperly. It has been given us by God's will through the hands of wicked men. We rely on Him more than on the false intentions which the popes had at the time when their object was to become emperors, and more than emperors themselves, while merely tricking us with the name, and scorning us.

The king of Babylon seized his kingdom by robbery and violence. Nevertheless, God wished it to be ruled by saintly princes, viz., Daniel, Hananiah, Azariah, and Meshach.[2] Much more is it His will that the present empire should be ruled by Christian German princes, no matter whether the pope stole it, or got it by robbery, or established it afresh. It was all done by God's will, and it came to pass before we understood it.

For these reasons, the pope and his entourage have no room to boast that they have conferred great benefit on the

---

[1] An untranslatable pun: *Szo sol die Deutschen teuschen und mit teuschen teuschenn*   [2] Dan. 3:20 and 5:29

N

German people by giving this Roman empire to them. Firstly, because they did not grant it to us for our benefit. Rather, they took advantage of our simplicity when they did so, in order to give support for their arrogance towards the true Roman emperor in Constantinople. The pope took it from him contrary to God and the right, and without authority. Secondly, because the pope's objective was not to give the empire to us, but to keep it for himself, to claim all our power, freedom, property, our bodies and souls; and with us, if God had not prevented it, all the world besides. He has said so himself plainly in the Decretals and tried to carry it out, with many a trick on several German emperors. How beautifully have we Germans been taught our German! While we supposed we were to become masters, we have become serfs of the most cunning tyrant. We have come into possession of the name, the titles, and the coat of arms of empire; but the treasures, the powers, the rights, and liberties of it remain the pope's. So the pope eats the nut while we play with the empty shell.

May God help us, after having received the empire from Him, as I have said, to rule it as we have been commissioned. We must give substance to the name, the title, and the coat of arms, and retrieve our freedom. We must let the Romanists see for once what it is that we have received from God through them. So be it, and be it so! Let the pope give us the Roman empire and all it means, but let our country be free from his intolerable taxes and frauds. Give us back our freedom, our power, our honour, our bodies and souls; and let us be an empire as an empire ought to be, and let there be an end of his word and claims!

If he will not do so, then why does he make moonshine with false pretences and conjuring tricks? Has there not been enough after so many centuries, of insulting a noble people, and leading it about by the nose all the time? It does not follow that the pope should be superior to the emperor by virtue of crowning or instituting him. For, at God's command, the prophet, St. Samuel, anointed and crowned Saul and David king, but still remained their subject.[1] The

---

[1] I Sam. 10:1 and 16:13

prophet, Nathan, anointed king Solomon, and was not made superior to him thereby. Again, Elisha let one of his servants anoint Jehu king of Israel, but yet remained in subjection to him.[1] Nowhere else in all the world, except in the case of the pope, does he who crowns and consecrates a king become his superior.

Even in his own case, the crowning is done by three cardinals, lower in rank than he; nevertheless he remains above them. Why then, in spite of his own example, in spite of the customs of all the world and the teaching of Scripture, does he set himself above the secular authority and the empire, simply on the basis that he crowns and consecrates the emperor? It is enough for the pope to be his superior in divine affairs, i.e., in preaching, teaching, and dispensing the sacraments. In these respects, a bishop or pastor is superior to the rest, as St. Ambrose was superior to the emperor Theodosius in the confessional, and as the prophet Nathan was over David, and Samuel over Saul. Therefore, let the German emperor be a genuine and a free emperor, and let not his authority and government suffer destruction by the purblind claim of the papal dissembler, pretending to be superior to temporal power and to be ruler in all things.]

27. And now I have spoken at sufficient length about the transgressions of the clergy, though you may and will find more of them if you look in the right place. We shall now devote a section to the consideration of temporal failings.

In the first place, there is urgent need of a general order and decree on behalf of the German people against the overflowing abundance and the great expensiveness of the clothing worn by so many nobles and rich folk. To us, as to other people, God has given enough wool, fur, flax, and everything that would provide proper, suitable, and worthy garments for each class. We do not need to waste such huge sums for silk, and velvet, and articles of gold, and other imports from abroad. I believe that, even if the pope did not rob us Germans with his intolerable, fraudulent practices, we should still have had too many of these native

[1] 2 Kings 9:1ff.

robbers, the silk and velvet merchants. As things stand, we
see that each wants to keep up with the others, to the
awakening and increase of pride and envy among us, as we
have deserved. All this and much else that brings misery
would cease if the desire for display would let us be thankful
and content with the good things which God has supplied to us.

In the same way, the spice traffic ought to be reduced,
for it is another of the great channels by which money is
conveyed out of Germany. By the grace of God, more things
to eat and drink are indigenous to our own country than
to any other, and are just as precious and wholesome. Perhaps I am now bringing forward foolish and impossible
suggestions which would endanger the principal trade of the
merchants. But I am expressing my own views. Unless
things improve in the community, let him bring about
improvements who can do so. I do not see many goodly
habits which have ever been introduced into the country
by commerce. In olden days, God caused the children of
Israel to dwell far from the sea, and did not allow them to
engage in much commerce.

But the greatest misfortune suffered by the German people
is certainly the traffic in annuities.[1] If nothing of this kind
existed, much of the silk and velvet, many of the articles
of gold, spices and all sorts of ornaments, would remain
unbought. The trade has not yet been in existence for many
centuries, but it has already brought misery and ruin on
almost all the princes, monasteries, towns, nobles, and their
heirs. If it should continue for another century, it would
be impossible for Germany to keep a single penny, and we
should be compelled to adopt cannibalism! It is a device of
the devil; and the pope, in approving it, has brought woe
upon the whole world. Therefore, I hereby beg and pray
that everyone will open his eyes and look at the ruin of
himself, his children, and his heirs. It does not stand outside at the door, but already haunts the house. Let the
emperor, the princes, the lords, and the towns do their part
to see that this trade be condemned as soon as possible and
henceforth forbidden, no matter whether the pope and all

[1] A method of surmounting the objection to usury

his law or illegality are against the action; nor if benefices and monasteries are founded thereon. It is better to have one benefice in a town founded on proper freeholds or taxes, than a hundred on the annuity system; indeed, one benefice founded on the annuity system is worse and more oppressive than twenty on freeholds. Nay, the annuities are nothing else than a sign and a symbol that, for its many sins, the world has been sold to the devil; therefore, both temporal and spiritual resources must alike fail us. And we take no notice.

At this point, I would say that we must surely bridle the Fuggers and similar trading companies. How can it happen in a godly and righteous manner, and in a single lifetime, that great wealth, worthy of a king, should be accumulated into a single pile? I am no man for figures. But I do not understand how a hundred guilders can make twenty profit in a single year, or even one guilder make another. Nothing like this takes place by cultivating the soil, or by raising cattle, where the increase does not depend on human wits, but on God's blessing. I commend that observation to men of affairs. As a theologian, I have no further reproof to utter on this subject than as regards its wicked and scandalous appearance, about which St. Paul says, "Abstain from every form and appearance of evil."[1] But I do know that it would be much more godly to increase farming and decrease commerce; and that more of those are on the right side, who till the earth as the Bible says, and seek their livelihood in this way. All this was said to us and all others in the case of Adam, "Cursed be the ground wherein thou labourest; thorns also and thistles shall it bring forth to thee, and in the sweat of thy face shalt thou eat bread."[2] There is still much land untilled, and not farmed.

The next thing is the abuse of eating and drinking, a matter which gains us no good repute abroad, but is thought a special failing of ours. Preaching never makes any impression on it, so firmly is it rooted and so well has it gained the upper hand. The waste of money would be its least evil; but it often entails the vices of murder, adultery, robbery, blasphemy, and every form of immorality. Here is something

---

[1] I Thess. 5:22   [2] Gen. 3:17ff.

for the secular government to prevent; otherwise what Christ said will happen, "The last day will come like a secret snare, when they will drink and eat, marry and court, build and plant, buy and sell."[1] To-day it has come to such a pass, that I verily hope the Last Day is at hand, although it is expected by very few at present.

Finally, is it not a lamentable thing that we Christians should openly tolerate in our midst common houses of ill-fame, though we all took the oath of chastity at our baptism? I am well aware of the frequent reply, that it is a custom not confined to any one people, that it would be difficult to stop, and that it is better to have such houses than that married women, or maidens, or others held in greater respect, should be dishonoured. Nevertheless, ought not the secular but Christian government to consider that that is not the way to get rid of a heathen custom? If the children of Israel could exist without such an abomination, surely Christians ought to be much better able to do so! Nay, how do many cities, market towns, villages, and hamlets manage without such houses? Why should it not be the same in the great cities?

In this, and in other matters which I have discussed earlier, I have tried to show how many good works the secular government can perform, and what ought to be the duty of every administration. Everyone might learn from this what a fearful responsibility it is to sit on high and to act as a ruler. What use would it be if some ruler-in-chief were, in himself, as holy as St. Peter, but not also diligent in planning to help those under him in these respects? His very authority would cry out against him. For it is the part of those in authority to see to the good of their subjects. But, if the administrators would concern themselves with bringing young people together in marriage, the hope of marriage would give great help to each to endure, and to resist temptation. But what happens now when a young man is attracted into the ministry? I fear that not one in a hundred has any other reason than the need of a livelihood, plus doubt about being able to support himself as a married man.[2] Hence they

[1] Luke 21:34   [2] Cf. *infra*, p. 317

first lead very disorderly lives, and sow their wild oats, and are sated; but experience shows they tend to sow them within. I think it is a true proverb which says, "Most of the monks and priests are doubters." So things go on, as we see.

But, on account of avoiding the many sins which gnaw their way within us so disgustingly, I will give the faithful advice that neither youths nor maidens should take the vows of continence[1] or the "spiritual" life before they are thirty. It requires a special gift, as St. Paul says.[2] Therefore, unless specially drawn to it by God, delay your becoming a cleric, or taking the vows.[3] Further: I say that if you trust God so little that you doubt whether you could support yourself and a wife, and if that doubt is your only reason for entering the clerical status, then I beg you for the good of your soul not to become a cleric, but rather a farmer; or else make some other choice. Where a simple faith in God is needed in regard to earning your temporal support, there must be ten times as much faith required to sustain the life of a cleric. If you have no confidence that God will provide for you in the world, how are you to trust Him to sustain you as a cleric? Alas, unbelief and distrust destroy everything, and lead into all sorts of misery, as we see among all classes. Much could be said of this misery. Young people have no one to take care of them. Each follows the custom, and the government is of as much value to them as if it were not there, although the care of the young ought to be the prime concern of the pope, the bishops, the ruling classes, and the councils. They want to exercise authority far and wide, and yet they are of no use. Oh, what rarities will lords and rulers be in heaven on this account, even though they build a hundred churches to God and raise to life again all the saints and the dead!

I have said enough for the present. In my little book, *On Good Works*, I have sufficiently discussed what the secular authorities and the nobles ought to do. There is room for better conduct in the way they live and rule, yet there is no comparison between the temporal and the spiritual abuses,

[1] Cf. *supra*, p. 160   [2] 1 Cor. 7:7   [3] Cf. *infra*, *Pagan Servitude*, p. 317

as I have shown there.[1] I am aware that I have spoken strongly, and suggested much that will be felt impossible, and attacked many subjects too severely. But what am I to do? I cannot but speak. If I were able, I would also act. I would rather that the world were wroth with me than that God were. No man can do more than take away my life.[2] Many times heretofore I have proposed peace with my enemies. But as it seems to me, God has used them to compel me to raise my voice even more insistently; and because they are not satisfied, I must speak, shout, shriek, and write till they have had enough. Oh well! I have still a little song[3] about Rome and about them. Their ears are itching for me to sing it to them, and pitch the notes in the treble clef. Do you grasp my meaning, oh worthy Rome?

I have offered to stand and be cross-examined for what I have written, but without avail. Nevertheless, I know that if my cause is just, though of necessity condemned on earth, it must be justified in heaven. For the whole Bible shows that the cause of Christians and Christianity shall be judged by God alone; it has never yet been judged on earth by men, but has always been too great and strong for my enemies. My great concern and primary fear are that my case may remain uncondemned; that would show me it was not yet pleasing to God. Therefore, let them but come boldly forward, whether pope, bishop, priest, monk, or scholar; they are the right people to pursue the truth. They should have done so all the time. God grant to us a Christian mind, and, in particular, God grant a truly religious courage to the ruling class of the German people, to do the best they can for the church that is so much to be pitied.

[1] This passage is not in Luther's first edition
[2] Cf. *supra*, *Letter to the Pope*, p. 65
[3] A reference to the *Pagan Servitude*, which he began to write almost immediately and which he called a "prelude," a musical term; see opposite page, and *infra*, p. 328

Amen.

Wittenberg. A.D. 1520.

4

THE PAGAN SERVITUDE OF THE CHURCH

A FIRST INQUIRY

(De Captivitate Babylonica Ecclesiae Praeludium)

Introduction

It seems to be impossible to determine the exact state of Luther's mind when, late in July, 1520, the present treatise was taking shape. His *Appeal to the Ruling Class* had been out of his hands for a month or more, but was not yet published. Meantime the bull of excommunication[1] had been promulgated (June 15), and the news had reached Luther. Events were moving rapidly, but were at least matched by the speed of Luther's pen across paper. Not that he had yet become a national figure, although that was soon to be the case. To the people at large, he was still mainly known as a forthright preacher, and as a religious teacher with a fresh style and a clear personal message. Some knowledge of the wider implications of the *Ninety-five Theses* had, of course, spread among the populace, but this knowledge was not sufficient to make Luther of great importance. The few polemical writings which he had published, and the two or three "disputations" in which he had figured, had created a stir among some of the leaders, and certain echoes must have penetrated the lower strata of society; but, in the public mind, this was probably a slight matter compared with the numerous, edificatory writings which he had already published: doctrinal and expository sermons, lectures, and commentaries. He was known predominantly for the religious intensity of his writings, whether in exposition of the *Seven Penitential Psalms*, which was his first essay in print,[2] of the Lord's Prayer,[3] of the Ten Commandments,[4] and the Epistle to the Galatians;[5] or in his teaching about the nature and implications of the sacraments,[6] and about more general questions. Over fifty writings of this character had come from his pen in the last three years. It is obvious, therefore, that he was a "positive" preacher, with a genuinely constructive message, that instruction was his main intention and evangelism his chief interest.

The publication of the *Appeal to the Ruling Class* was soon to reveal to the people another direction in the flow of his energy, or rather, a broadening of its current. Luther was now ahead of

[1] *Exsurge domine*, June 15, 1520, cf. Mirbt *Quellen*, pp. 183ff.
[2] Cf. *W.*, Vol. I, pp. 154–220
[3] Cf. *W.*, Vol. II, pp. 74–139; IX, pp. 122–59
[4] Cf. *W.*, Vol. I, pp. 229–38
[5] Cf. *W.*, Vol. II, 436–618
[6] E.g. *W.*, Vol. II, 713–23; 738–58; Vol. VI; 353–78; etc.

the people and, indeed, of his colleagues and friends. Yet after he knew of the publication of the bull, it is doubtful whether he felt himself in any wise cut off from the fellowship of the real church, any more than from its authentic tradition. In mind and heart, he simply refused to be excommunicated. Rather, the bull made clearer the true nature of the church and of the communion of saints. He did not feel, at least yet, that the church as such was mistaken and needed reform; but rather that she was suffering from gross abuses and indefensible accretions which should be abolished; and that some of her essential doctrines were gravely distorted and seriously misapplied, and this by the very people who should have been her strength. Luther's problem was to know how he could best attempt to deal with a situation which was rapidly becoming intolerable, whether from the standpoint of public well-being or that of personal religion.

In the *Appeal to the Ruling Class*, he had dealt with the abuses and scandals rampant in the practice of the church, and widely felt in the body politic. But he had long been profoundly concerned with the deeper issues, among which the medieval doctrine of the sacraments stood in the forefront. It was indeed the crux of medieval life. Luther had often dealt with different sides of sacramental teaching, but felt the time had come for a thorough-going examination of the entire theory and practice. In 1519, he had published sermons dealing with the sacraments of Confession, Baptism, and the Eucharist, but, in a letter to Spalatin on December 18, 1519, he refused his friend's suggestion that he should deal with the other sacraments in the same way; his reason being that the other four sacraments had no foundation in Scripture. He expressed his intention, however, of dealing with them later. He was specially concerned about the misuse of the mass and the correct understanding of that rite. This subject was to prove of insuperable difficulty in Marburg in 1529, and perhaps still remains the most delicate of doctrinal questions.

The immediate urge causing Luther to sit down and write the *Pagan Servitude* was the fact that, about the middle of July, 1520, he had received two documents of similar quality: one by Alveld, an Augustinian friar of Leipzig, dealing with the question of communion in both kinds on the part of the laity; and the other an anonymous tract issuing from Cremona in Italy "revoking" Luther to the Holy See. Luther's opinion about these pamphlets and his immediate reaction are seen in the first few pages of the present writing. He appears to have sat down at once and to have set to work with the utmost vigour and pugnacity. Perhaps it was of this occasion that he was thinking when, in later years, he declared he wrote best when he felt angry or indignant. But this mood served only to launch him upon his tremendous and, withal, dangerous task. As he settled down to write, his gifts of dispassionate analysis prevailed, and it is for its merits in this respect that the *Pagan Servitude* still holds its place as the most important discussion of sacramental doctrine in the history of Protestantism.

Luther wrote this document in Latin. He did so of set purpose, out of regard for the laity, since it contained many passages that were too strong meat for them; he aimed at the attention of the educated (and was successful), and in particular he wrote for the benefit of parish priests and others who acted as Father Confessors. Writing as he did, page after page with scarcely a blot or an erasure, he had finished by the end of August or the first day or two in September.

On Saturday, October 6, 1520, the second of the three great reformation writings was published. To Luther's displeasure, a German translation appeared anonymously in the following year. But he did not accuse the translator of material misrepresentation, although his work was not without errors. Nevertheless he saw that it had been done by one of his bitterest enemies, Thomas Murner, who very soon acknowledged that he had indeed made the translation. Thus Luther's prime objective in using Latin was defeated, and Murner intended that this should be the case. But Luther and his cause suffered none of the damage that had been expected. The laity were learning rapidly and becoming relatively well-instructed. The *Appeal to the Ruling Class* was also, in its way, an appeal to the people in general, who were responding with a growing consciousness of their own rights as opposed to the ecclesiastical hierarchy; and also with a growing power of independent judgment of the issues under discussion amongst the new leaders. It was not long, therefore, before Murner must have seen that, after all, he had played into the hands of Luther and his sympathizers.

The most outstanding person to enter the arena against Luther was, of course, King Henry VIII, who published a *Defense of the Seven Sacraments* in July, 1521. This effort immediately gained for him the title of *Defensor Fidei* in a bull promulgated by Leo X on October 5, 1521; and also aroused Luther, who wrote a vigorous polemic in reply. Henry, however, like Leo, merely laughed at Luther's billingsgate, and said he was only fit to be the fool at the Lord Mayor's banquet; but Henry could not forgive him for questioning his authorship of the book that had gained him his title of Defender of the Faith.[1]

The importance of the writing for the religious ferment of the time is seen in the official notice it attracted and the measures it occasioned. In the middle of December, at the imperial diet of Worms, Hieronymous Aleander, the papal *nuncio*, described as blasphemous Luther's declaration that, in cases where the pope could grant dispensations, the laity could do so to one another. On February 13 of the following year Aleander returned to the charge with great vigour. Erasmus saw that all his efforts for peace were in vain, once the *Pagan Servitude* had been published. The University of Paris came out openly against it in April, 1521, and strongly condemned it. Kaspar Contarini, however, whom Paul III had made cardinal, told the pope that Luther had certain grounds for writing on the *Pagan Servitude*, because it was impossible to conceive anything more contrary to the law of Christ than a system in which Christians were subject to a pope who, at will, made laws, repealed them, or granted dispensations from them. No severer servitude than this could be imposed upon Christian people.

In fact, the *Pagan Servitude* was wholly concerned with the reformation of religion itself, and it deals with the very core of medieval conceptions of Christianity. Here we have the profound convictions of a profoundly religious man. Luther had great insight, both experimental and intellectual, into the essential nature of religion in its highest manifestation. Apart altogether from the question as to what constitutes Christianity, a subject on which instructed opinions may differ, here is great and true insight into the distinction between sacrament and superstition. Moreover, this is real teaching given by a born teacher, and a real lead given by a born leader. The *Pagan Servitude* lacks nothing in simplicity in stating the essential issues; it exhibits clarity and cogency in argument, unconstrained freedom of judg-

---

[1] So Maynard Smith, *Henry VIII*, p. 295. For Henry's *Assertio Septem Sacramentorum*, cf. Donovan's edition, 1908, which also gives the papal bull. The complete English translation provided by Donovan seems to assume that Henry's *Defense* is of a theological interest or value not immediately apparent from the conventional limits within which the thought is confined. But perhaps Henry's real purpose is summed up in a single sentence of his preface: If Luther does not repent and "if Christian princes do their duty, these errors and himself, if he perseveres therein, may be burned in the fire"

ment, and great courage. After the first shock produced by its publication, the world at large gradually realized that something had been said that could never again be unsaid. The way was now open to a far-reaching emancipation, and this in two important respects: (*a*) from a priest-ridden system, and the power of a corrupt church; and (*b*) from moral timidity and self-deception on the part of the common man. Rather, the common man received his own dignity, not so much because of the doctrine of the priesthood of all believers, inestimably important though that was, but because he was led to respect his own powers of moral judgment; and he was led to use them, and so to grow in moral strength and stature. His faith and his practice became masculine. Over and above all this is the sense of God's immediate presence, of His grace and His love, of the utter reasonableness and rightness of God's ways and requirements, and of the wide-open doors of the Kingdom of God ready for the entry of every one that believeth. On the sixth of October, 1520, it could well have been said that the Reformation had begun.

The text on which the following translation is based, is that of Luther's original Latin autograph, as reproduced in the definitive Weimar Edition, Vol. VI, pp. 484–96, 497–573. Thomas Murner's contemporary German translation (*vide supra*, p. 205) has been published by Borcherdt and Merz, *Martin Luther: Ausgewählte Werke*, 1948, Vol. II, 151-254.

Text and Notes

Jesus

Martin Luther, Augustinian, to his friend, Hermann Tulich,[1] greetings.

As long as there are so very many outstanding masters urging me on and making me work, I cannot help becoming more of a scholar every day. It is two years since I wrote on indulgences, but I now greatly regret having published that little book.[2] At that time I was still entangled in the gross superstitions of a masterful Rome, but I still thought that indulgences ought not to be wholly rejected, as they had received the approval of a very large number of people. My attitude was not strange, for otherwise I should have been alone in trying to move the mountain. Afterwards, thanks to Sylvester, and helped by those friars[3] who strenuously defended indulgences, I saw that these were simply impositions on the part of the hypocrites of Rome to rob men of their money and their faith in God. I now wish I could prevail upon the booksellers, and persuade all my readers, to burn the whole of my booklets on indulgences, and, instead of all I have written on this subject, to adopt the following proposition:

Indulgences are Evils devised by the Toadies at Rome

Meantime Eck,[4] Emser,[5] and their compeers began to read me a lesson on the primacy of the pope. Lest I should appear to be ungrateful to such learned men, I hereby confess that

[1] Went to Wittenberg as a student at the same time as Luther arrived as professor. Graduated B.A. in 1511, and D.D. in 1520. He refused episcopal ordination. Rector of Wittenberg 1525-6. After varied career died at Lüneburg, 1540

[2] *Resolutiones disputationum*, 1518, W., Vol. I, pp. 522ff.

[3] Sylvester Prierias was Prior of the Dominicans. He and several others of the order (e.g., Tetzel and Hochstraten) wrote against Luther

[4] Cf. *supra*, p. 28

[5] Jerome Emser (?1477-1527) once a Humanist professor in Erfurt, when Luther was a student; later, secretary to duke George of Saxony

their works have benefited me greatly. Although I denied divine jurisdiction to the papacy, I admitted a human jurisdiction. But when I had heard and read the most ingenious argument put forward by these five gentlemen to establish their idol in a workmanlike manner, and as I am not entirely lacking in intelligence in such matters, I saw clearly that the papacy was to be understood as the kingdom of Babylon and the régime of Nimrod, the mighty hunter. Hence once again, and in order that my friends may be well on the right side, I beg both the booksellers and my readers to burn whatever I have published on this subject. Instead, let them adopt this proposition:

The Papacy provides Grand Hunting for the Bishop of Rome

This is proved by the arguments put forward by Eck, Emser, and the Leipzig lecturer on the Bible.[1]

They pretend to school me in regard to communion in both kinds,[2] and a few other subjects of the highest importance. Here again I had to be watchful that I overlooked nothing while listening to these eminent masters. A certain Italian friar of Cremona[3] has written a *Revocation of Martin Luther to the Holy See*. In this work he makes it sound as if I have revoked something, whereas he means that he recalls me; but that is the way Italians of to-day are writing Latin. Another friar, a German of Leipzig, who is a "Lecturer on the Whole Bible" and one known to you, has written again about the sacraments in both kinds,[4] and, as I hear, is about to produce some bigger books which will be marvels. The Italian has taken the precaution of writing anonymously, perhaps warned by the examples I made of Cajetan[5] and

---

[1] Augustine Alveld: this reference is his chief claim to fame

[2] Consisting of both bread and wine, and not the wafer alone as still offered to the laity in the Church of Rome

[3] Isidoro Isolani, *Revocatio Martini Lutherii Augustini ad sanctam Sedem*

[4] Augustine Alveld, *Tractatus de communione sub utraque specie*

[5] Head of his Order and leader of the school of Thomists, he was regarded as the foremost theologian in Rome. On account of his eminence, he was deputed to deal with the case remitted by Henry VIII. But, in 1518, he had met Luther at Augsburg, and found himself unequal to Luther's arguments based on the Bible

O

Sylvester. But the Leipzig Lecturer, as befits a vigorous and
hefty German, uses a great many lines on his title-page to
proclaim his name, his life, his sanctity, his knowledge, his
fame, his honours, and almost his wooden shoes.[1] Without
doubt, there is much for me to learn from this book, for he
has dedicated it to the Son of God Himself; so intimate are
these saintly men with the Christ who reigns on high. It
seems to me that three magpies are now speaking, the first
in good Latin, the second in better Greek, and the third in
excellent Hebrew. Surely, my dear Hermann, I can do no
other than prick up my ears. The discussion is being con-
ducted in Leipzig by the Observants of the Holy Cross.

Heretofore, in my folly, I thought it would be a fine thing
if a General Council were to decree that the sacraments
should be administered to the laity in both kinds.[2] But our
exceedingly learned friar corrects this view, and says that
the offering of both kinds to the laity is neither commanded,
nor advised, by Christ or the Apostles, but that it was left
to the judgment of the church whether to do it, or leave it
undone; and the church must be obeyed. That is his contention.

Perhaps you will ask, What extravagances are upsetting
him? or Whom is he attacking? I myself have never condemned the use of one kind, and I have deferred to the
judgment of the church whether it should decree the use of
both kinds. This is just what he himself is trying to assert
in order to attack me. My reply is that that way of conduct-
ing an argument is the same as that adopted by all those who
write against me. They attack either what they themselves
affirm, or some enemy of their own invention. This was the
way of Sylvester, Eck, Emser, and of the people in Cologne
and Louvain. The present friar would have been a renegade
to their spirit if he had not written against me.

But this good man has been more fortunate than the rest;
he set out to prove that the use of both kinds was neither
decreed nor advised, but left to the decision of the church.

---

[1] The Observants wore sandals with wooden soles

[2] *Vide* Luther's *Sermon des hochwürdigen sacrament des Leichnams
Christi,* 1519. *W.,* Vol. II, 738ff.

Then he adduces Scripture, out of which he proves that the use of one kind by the laity was decreed by Christ. The result is, according to this Biblical exegete, that the use of one kind was both commanded, and yet, at the same time, not commanded by Christ. You understand of course that this new way of arguing is peculiar to the usage of the logicians of Leipzig. In his earlier booklet,[1] Emser professed he would be fair to me. Yet when convicted by me of base envy and dirty falsehoods, he confessed in his later book,[2] which was intended to confute me, that both writings were true, and that what he had written had been fair and also foul. A fine fellow for you—as you are aware!

But listen to this specious advocate of the use of one kind, who professes to follow the will of the church and also the commandment of Christ, and yet again, both the commandment of Christ and the absence of such commandment. With this dexterous twist, he proves that the one kind is to be given to the laity by the commandment of Christ, i.e., the will of the church. He uses capital letters for this truth and calls it: THE INFALLIBLE FOUNDATION. He then proceeds to handle John 6 with incredible skill. In this passage,[3] Christ speaks of Himself as the bread of heaven and the bread of life. But our scholar applies these words to the bread of the altar, and goes further. Because Christ had said: "I am the living bread", and not, "I am the living cup", he concludes that this passage institutes, for the laity, the sacrament in one kind. But he learnedly avoids touching the words that follow. These say: "My flesh is truly food, and my blood is truly drink"; and, again: "Unless you eat the flesh of the Son of Man, and drink His blood". But when it entered the friar's head that these words supported the use of both kinds, and irrefutably discountenanced the use of only one kind, with what felicity and learning did he explain it away! He said that "Christ meant by these words simply that he who partook of the one kind, partook under this kind of both the body and the blood"! He puts this forth as the "infallible

---

[1] *De disputatione Lipsicensi*, 1519
[2] *A venatione Luteriana Aegocerotis Assertio*, 1519
[3] John 6:48–63

foundation" of a structure well worthy of holy and heavenly
"Observance".

But let us continue taking lessons from this man; he says
that, in John 6, Christ commands the use of one kind, and
yet prescribes it in such a way that He left it to the will of
the church; and that, moreover, in this chapter, Christ is
speaking only of the laity and not of the priests. Apparently
the bread of life from heaven is not meant for the latter,
but perhaps the bread of death from hell! What, also, of
the case of the deacons and subdeacons, who are neither
laymen nor priests? According to this distinguished writer,
they ought to use neither one kind only, nor both. You will
now understand, my dear Tulich, the new method of apply-
ing Scripture that is found current among the Observants.

But you will also be shown that, in John 6, Christ was
speaking of the sacrament of the Eucharist, although He
Himself teaches that He was speaking of faith in the Incarnate
Word when He said: "This is the work of God, that you
should believe in Him whom He sent."[1] Truly we must grant
that the Leipzig professor of the Bible can prove anything
he pleases from any passage of Scripture whatever. He is
a theologian of the breed of Anaxagoras, if not Aristotle;
nouns and verbs have the same meaning, even when replacing
one another, and they signify anything you like.[2] Throughout his book, he so conjoins passages of Scripture that, if
he wishes to prove that Christ is in the sacrament, he might
well begin by saying: "The lesson is from the Book of Revelation of the blessed John the Apostle."[3] Everything he says
would be as appropriate as this, and the wise fellow thinks
that it will enhance the value of his own drivel to quote
passages copiously.

I pass over other matters lest I drown you in the sludge

---

[1] John 6:29

[2] After being appointed to the new university of Wittenberg in 1508,
one of Luther's most important duties was to lecture on Aristotle's *Ethics*,
just as he had been doing at Erfurt since 1505. Though acquainted with
Aristotle only through a Latin translation—like almost everyone else—
Luther must have acquired a thorough knowledge of his subject, as is
shown by many of his criticisms; cf. *Appeal to the Ruling Class*, § 25, *vide
supra*, p. 186

[3] The title as given by Luther

of this foul drain. Finally, he adduces Paul, who says in
I Corinthians II that he received from the Lord, and handed
on to the Corinthians, the use of the bread and the cup.
Here once more this distinguisher of kinds, as everywhere
in his egregious application of Scripture, teaches that Paul,
in this passage, permitted, but did not hand on, the use of
both kinds. Do you ask where he found the proof? In his
own head, just as he did with regard to John 6. For it does
not become our lecturer to give reasons for what he says,
as he is one of the kind who prove and teach everything on
the basis of their own imagination. Accordingly, we are
taught, in this connection, that the Apostle did not write
that passage for the benefit of the whole church at Corinth,
but only for the laity. Apparently, therefore, he gave no
permission to the priests in that passage, but, we gather,
deprived them of the whole of the sacrament. Then, by the
new grammar, "I have received of the Lord" becomes the
same as "It is permitted by the Lord"; and "I have handed
on to you" means "I have permitted you". Please make a
special note of this, because it would be a logical inference
that not only the church but any passing poltroon would
be in order in turning any and all of the commandments,
institutions, and ordinances of Christ and the Apostles into
"things permitted".

Therefore I regard this man as instigated by an angel of
Satan, and I include those in collusion with him. They seek
the worldly fame of being able to enter into a disputation
with me. But their hope will be disappointed, and they will
be despised by me to the extent that I shall never even
mention them by name. I shall be content with this one
reply to all their books. If they are worthy of being brought
back to sanity by Christ, I pray He will do it, in His mercy.
But if they are not worthy, my prayer is that they may
never cease writing such books, and that the enemies of the
truth may never deserve to read any others. It is a common
and faithful saying:

Strive I with the filthy, I know, not in vain,
That, victor or vanquished, dark spots I retain.

Then, as I perceive they have abundance of leisure and plenty of paper, I will see to it that they have ample cause for writing. I will keep ahead of them just to such an extent that, while they are celebrating a most glorious victory over what they conceive to be one of my heresies, I shall be constructing a new one in the interim; for I, like them, desire that these mighty leaders in battle should be decorated with many honours. Thus, they complain that I commend the use of both kinds in Holy Communion; and so, while they are happily engaged in a subject most worthy of themselves, I shall be on ahead, trying to show that it is most impious to deny to the laity the use of both kinds in Holy Communion. To do this the more conveniently, I shall write in a preliminary way on *The Pagan Servitude of the Church of Rome*, reserving more to a future date when these most learned Romanists shall have refuted that book.

I shall adopt this method lest any religious-minded reader comes my way and takes offence at the unclean things with which I have dealt. He may rightly object that he finds nothing here hard to follow, or particularly new; or at all events nothing of a scholarly nature. You know how impatient my friends are with me for bothering myself with the paltry propositions of these persons. My friends say that the mere reading of their writings suffices to confute them; they say that they are looking for better things from me, things which Satan is trying to obstruct through the agency of these men. At last, I have resolved to follow their advice, and to leave to those hornets the business of brawling and denigration.

I shall say nothing about the Italian friar of Cremona.[1] He is an untrained and simple fellow attempting to write a few rhetorical pages to "revoke" me to the Holy See. I am not aware of having ever withdrawn from it, nor has any one shown that I have done so. His main concern in these silly pages is to show that, on account of my vows, and for the sake of the empire which has been granted to us Germans, I ought to be moved elsewhere. The object of his writing does not by any means appear to have been to "revoke"

[1] Cf. *supra*, p. 209

me, but rather to extol the French people and the Roman pontiff. He has my permission to write this little book, such as it is, and testify to his own obsequiousness. Nothing here merits serious discussion, since he does not seem to be moved by ill-will; nor is the book worthy of a scholarly review, since, in his complete ignorance and inexperience, he only trifles with the whole subject.

The first thing for me to do is to deny that there are seven sacraments, and, for the present, to propound three: baptism, penance, and the Lord's Supper.[1] All these have been taken for us into a miserable servitude by the Roman curia and the church has been robbed of all her liberty. If, however, I were to use the language of Scripture, I should say that there was only one sacrament,[2] but three sacramental signs of which I shall speak in detail in the proper place.

(1) *The Lord's Supper*

In regard to the sacrament of the Lord's Supper, which is the most important of all, I shall discuss in what way my ideas have progressed while meditating on the administration of this sacrament. For, at the time, when I published my tractate on the Eucharist,[3] I held to the common usage, quite undisturbed by what was right or wrong according to the pope. But now that I have been cited and attacked, and even forcibly thrust into the arena, I shall give free expression to my ideas, no matter whether the Papists all join together to mock or reproach me.

In the first place, John 6 is to be totally set on one side, on the ground that it does not utter a syllable about the sacrament. The sacrament was not yet instituted; and, a more important point, the chapter is plainly and obviously speaking about faith, as is shown by the warp and woof of the words and thoughts. For Jesus said: "My words are spirit

---

[1] Lat. *panis*: bread, because the wine was withheld from the laity. But Luther is discussing the sacrament as a whole, and the corresponding English term is therefore as given above

[2] Cf. 1 Tim. 3:16

[3] *On the Holy Sacrament*, 1519. *W.*, Vol. II, p. 738ff.

and they are life", showing that He was speaking of spiritual eating, by doing which any partaker would live; whereas the Jews understood Him to mean eating His flesh, and so raised the dispute. No sort of eating gives life except eating in faith. This is the true eating, the spiritual. Accordingly, Augustine says: "Why do you make your teeth and stomach ready? Believe, and thou hast eaten." In itself, sacramental eating does not give life, for many eat unworthily. Therefore Jesus cannot be understood to have spoken of the sacrament in this passage.

This passage has often been wrongly thought to teach the sacrament, as, e.g., in the decretal *Dudum*, and many others.[1] But it is one thing to use the Scriptures wrongly, and another to understand them properly. Otherwise, if Jesus had intended it to be a commandment to eat of the sacraments when He said: "Unless you eat my flesh and drink my blood, you will not have life", He would have condemned all infants, all the sick, all those kept back by any cause and prevented from partaking of the sacraments, no matter how firm their faith. Hence Augustine, in the second book of *Contra Julianum*, proves from Innocent[2] that even infants, who do not yet partake of the sacrament, eat the flesh and drink the blood of Christ; i.e., they communicate through the faith of the church. Let us then regard this proposition as proved, and that John 6 is not relevant here. Elsewhere,[3] I have written that the Bohemians had no assured support in this passage when they sought to prove the use of the sacrament in both kinds.[4]

Thus there remain two records which deal, and that very clearly, with this subject, viz.: the gospel passages on the Lord's Supper, and St. Paul in 1 Corinthians 11. Let us consider them. For, as Matthew, Mark, and Luke all agree, Christ gave all His disciples both kinds. And that Paul gave both kinds is so certain that no one has had the effrontery to

[1] Cf. *infra*, p. 231 and n.
[2] Pope Innocent I; died A.D. 417
[3] *Verklärung etliche Artikel in dem Sermon von heiligen sacrament*, 1520; *W.*, VI, p. 78
[4] One ancient edition inserts at this point the cross-heading *De Coena Domini* (The Lord's Supper). The Erlangen edition followed this example, but it is not Luther's

say anything to the contrary. A further fact is that, according to Matthew, Christ did not say of the bread: "All of you eat of this"; but he does say of the cup: "All of you drink of this"; and in Mark He does not say: "All of you ate", but "All of you drank from it". Each writer attaches the mark of universality to the cup, but not to the bread. It is as if the Spirit foresaw the coming division forbidding the communion of the cup to some, though Christ would have had it common to all. You may be sure the Romanists would let us feel their anger smartly if they found the word "all" applied to the bread and not to the cup. They would leave us no loophole; they would cry aloud, brand us as heretics, and damn us as schismatics. But now, when Scripture is on our side and against them, they refuse in their perversity to be bound by logic, even in those things which be of God; they change, change again, and tangle everything together.

Now, suppose I were to approach my lords the Romanists, and ask them whether the whole sacrament, under both kinds, at the Lord's Supper[1] is to be given only to the priests, or also to the laity. If, as they wish, only to the priests, then logically neither kind is to be given to the laity on any excuse; for it is not to be lightly given to anyone to whom Christ did not give it when He first instituted the rite. Otherwise, if we allow an alteration in one institution of Christ's, all His ordinances are immediately brought to nought, and any one whatever is in a position to say that he is not bound by anything Christ ordained or instituted; for a single exception, especially in the Scriptures, disproves any universal law. But, if the cup was given to the laity also, the logical consequence is that no one can deny both kinds to the laity. If, nevertheless, the administration is denied to those who desire it, that is done impiously and against Christ's act, example, and institution.

This argument seems unassailable, and I confess that it has convinced me. I have neither heard of, nor discovered, anything opposed to it. Christ's word and example stand

[1] Lat. *coena domini*, and frequently, instead of *panis* as at first in this discussion, but without difference of meaning; see *supra*, p. 215, n. 1

here as firmly as possible. When He says, "All ye drink of it", He is not giving a permission, but issuing a command. Everyone ought to drink of it, and that commandment ought not to be understood as addressed only to the priests. Hence, it is undoubtedly impious to deny it to the laity who ask for it; yes, even if an angel from heaven were to do so. To support the Romanists' view that it was entrusted to the free judgment of the church to administer which kind she preferred, they bring forward no reasons, and no proofs from Scripture. The question is more easily passed over than proved; but their contention avails nothing against an opponent who faces them with the words or the works of Christ. Such a person must be refuted with the Word of Christ, the very thing we Romanists lack.[1]

If, however, in the Lord's Supper, either kind could be denied to the laity, so also might a part of the rites of baptism and penitence be withheld from them, equally, at the free dispensation of the church; because in each instance they have equal grounds and authority for so doing. Therefore, just as the rites of baptism and absolution are administered to the laity in their complete form, so also should the complete sacrament of the Supper,[2] if asked for. I am greatly astonished that the Romanists insist that, under pain of mortal sin, the priests must never receive only one kind at mass. The reason given by them all, with one voice, is that the two kinds constitute a full and complete sacrament, and should not be sundered. I would like them to tell me why the two kinds are separated for the laity, whereas the undivided sacrament must be administered only to themselves. Do they not acknowledge, by their own practice, either that both kinds should be given to the laity, or that the true and genuine sacrament is not in fact given them under the one form? Or is it that, in the case of the priests, the sacrament in one kind is not complete, but is complete in the case of the laity? Why do they appeal at this point to the free choice of the church and the power of the pope?

---

[1] I.e., we who belong to the Church and uphold its doctrines, cannot find words of Christ forbidding the use of both kinds

[2] *Panis*, but necessarily in the sense of *coena domini*

Yet no such appeal abolishes either the Word of God or the testimony of the truth.

Further, if the church has authority to withhold the wine from the laity, she can also withhold the bread; and, on the same basis, she could withhold the whole sacrament of the altar from the laity, and deprive the laity altogether of what Christ instituted. But, I deny that she has such authority. If, on the other hand, she is commanded to administer either the bread alone, or both kinds (according to the desire of the communicant), it is not in her choice to withhold the wine. No attack on this position can succeed. Either the church has authority over both kinds, and the same authority applies to each separately; or else it is not valid over both together, and neither is it valid over each separately.[1] I am hoping to hear what answer the toadies of Rome will give to that.

The most important proof, and, to me, a fully cogent one, is that Christ said: "This is my blood, shed for you and for many for the remission of sins." Here you may see very plainly that the blood was given to all, and that it was shed for the sins of all. No one will dare to say that it was not shed for the laity, for it is clear who was addressed, when Jesus was speaking of the cup. Did He not address all? He used the words "for you". Good, let us grant these words referred to the priests. Even so, the words Jesus added, viz., "and for many", cannot also apply to them only. Besides all this, He said: "All ye drink of it." I could easily make a little word-play here, and jest with Christ's words, as does that trifler whom I have already mentioned. But those who rely on Scripture to refute us, must be overcome by Scripture.

These considerations have kept me from condemning the Bohemians, who, whether in the right or the wrong, have certainly the words and works of Christ on their side. We Romanists have neither the words nor the works, but only that inane remark: "The church has so ordained." Yet it is not the church which ordained these things, but those who

---

[1] The terse scholastic phrases of this paragraph can be given a clear rendering in English only with a certain amount of expansion

tyrannize over the church without the consent of the church, which is the people of God.

My next question is: Why is it in any way necessary, why is it religious, what value is it, to deny both kinds to the laity? Why withhold the visible sign when all agree that they receive the content of the sacrament without that sign? If they grant them the content, the more important part, why do they not grant the sign, which is the less important? In every sacrament, the merely outward sign is incomparably less important than the thing symbolized. What prevents the less important from being administered when the more important is administered? It almost seems to me that matters have been allowed to go thus far by the wrath of God, in order to give occasion for a schism in the church; which would mean that, long ago, we had lost the content of the sacrament while contending for the outer sign; and that while striving for what is of minor importance, we are hostile to the things of greatest value and alone worth while. In the same way, some Romanists fight for ceremonial but oppose love. Indeed, this monstrous state of affairs arose at the time when, contrary to Christian love, we began, in our folly, to pursue worldly wealth. God showed it by that terrible sign, namely, that we preferred the outer signs rather than the things themselves. How perverse it would be if you were to concede that a candidate received faith in baptism, but you were to refuse him the sign of faith, i.e., water!

But, in the end, Paul is impregnable, and he stops the mouth of everyone when he says, in 1 Corinthians 11: "I have received of the Lord, that which I have handed on to you."[1] He does not say: "I permitted you", as our mendacious friar asserts. Nor is it true that it was because of the contentions in the church at Corinth that Paul gave both kinds. Firstly, the document still shows that the contention was not about the two kinds, but about the mutual contempt and envy between the rich and the poor. The text says clearly: "One is hungry and another is drunken, and ye put to shame those that are poor." A further point on the same side is that Paul is not speaking of the time when he first administered the

[1] 1 Cor. 11:23

sacraments to them. He does not say: "I am receiving from the Lord", and "I am giving to you"; but "I received" and "I handed on"; this was when first he preached to them, and long before the rise of these disputes. He meant that he had handed on the use of both kinds, because "handed on" means "passed on the commandment", with the same meaning as when he uses the same word elsewhere. Not even a vestige remains here of the friar's "permission", which he raked up apart from Scripture, reason, or other foundation. His opponents do not ask what he dreamed of, but what verdict Scripture pronounces here. He cannot produce a letter of Scripture in support of his pretences, whereas they can produce mighty thunderbolts on behalf of their faith.

Come forward, then, all ye fair-speaking toadies of the pope; make ready, and rid yourselves of impiety, tyranny, treason against the Gospel, and the crime of slandering your brothers. You proclaim them to be heretics if they do not agree with the very fabrications of your own brains, or if they do not think them inherently right and proper even where contrary to Scripture—as is both patent and potent. If any are to be called heretics and schismatics, it is neither the Bohemians, nor the Greeks, who take their stand on the gospel; rather, you Romanists are heretics and impious schismatics, who presume on your figments alone, and fly contrary to plain passages in divine Scripture. Get rid of these things, my friends.

What could be more ridiculous and more worthy of our precious friar's intellect than to say that the Apostle wrote that passage, and gave that permission, not to the church universal, but to the church at Corinth, a local church? Whence does he derive this proof? From one and only one storeroom, viz., his own impious head. When the church universal accepted and read the epistle, and obeyed it completely, did it not also obey this passage? If we admit that any epistle of Paul's, or a single passage in them, does not pertain to the church universal, all Paul's authority is nullified. On that basis, the Corinthians might aver that what Paul had taught the Romans about faith did not apply to them. Could anything more blasphemous be imagined? Away

with the idea that there is a single syllable in the whole of
Paul which the whole church is not obliged to follow and
obey. That was not the view of the Fathers, up to the perilous
present. It was of our day that Paul spoke when he foretold
that men would be blasphemers, and blind, and without
understanding. This friar is one, if not the chief, of them.

However, for the sake of argument, let us proceed with
this intolerable lunacy. If Paul gave permission to a particular church, then, from your Romanist point of view, the
Greeks are in the right, and so are the Bohemians, for they
too are particular churches. Hence, the situation is satisfactory, so long as they do not act contrary to Paul, who
at least gave permission. Moreover, Paul could not permit
anything contrary to what Christ had instituted. Accordingly, I hold it against you, O Rome, and all your hangers-
on, that these words of Christ and Paul speak on behalf of
the Greeks and the Bohemians. You cannot show by a tittle
of evidence that power has been given you to change these
things; and far less that you can accuse of heresy those who
disregard your proud pretensions. You yourself deserve to
be criminally accused of impiety and oppression.

Cyprian is strong enough, even when alone, to refute all the
Romanists. He discusses the point at issue in his work, *On
the Lapsed*, book V. He testifies that it was the custom in
the church at Carthage to give both kinds to many of the
laity, even children; and he provides many examples. Among
other points, he reproves some of the people as follows: "The
sacrilegious man is wrath with the priests when he is not
forthwith given the body of the Lord though his hands are
unwashed; or allowed to drink the blood of the Lord though
with unclean lips." Would you find anything here, you
miserable toady, at which to snarl? Would you declare that
this holy martyr, a teacher in the church, and filled with
the apostolic spirit, was a heretic and that he used that
permission in a particular church?

In the same book, Cyprian recounts the story of something that happened in his presence, and that he himself
witnessed. A deacon was administering the cup to a young
girl, but she drew back shyly; whereupon he poured the blood

of the Lord into her open mouth. Similarly, we read of St. Donatus at the time when his chalice had been broken; but this wretched toady of ours easily disposes of the incident by saying: "My record says the chalice was broken, but not that the blood was administered."[1] No wonder. A man who can give his own meaning to Scripture can also read what he wishes into history. But that is no way to establish the authority of the church, or to confute heretics.

Enough! for I did not begin writing in order to reply to that man, who is not worth replying to, but in order to bring the truth of the matter into the open.

I conclude, therefore, that to deny both kinds to the laity is impious and oppressive; and it is not in the power of any angel, nor of any pope or council whatever to deny them. Neither does the ruling of the council of Constance disturb me. If its authority were valid, why not that of Basel, which decreed the contrary, and permitted the Bohemians to receive both kinds? This result was reached after a lengthy argument, as is proved by the extant records and documents of that council, which our servile ignoramus adduces to support his own fabrications. It is with similar sagacity that he discusses the whole subject.

The question of its substance and completeness is what constitutes the first shackling of this sacrament. Of that substance and completeness, the Roman dictatorship has deprived us. Granted that it is not sin against Christ to partake of the sacrament under one kind only, for Christ did not decree the use of either, but left the matter to each man's choice. He said: "This do ye, as oft as ye do it, in remembrance of me." It is sin to refuse to give both kinds to those who wish to exercise freedom of choice; and it is the priests, and not the laity, who must bear the guilt. The sacrament does not pertain to the priests alone, but to all; the priests are not lords but servants, and it is their duty to administer both kinds to those who so desire, and as often as they desire. If they deny and forcibly deprive the laity of this right, they are oppressive; the laity incur no guilt,

[1] The cup had been accidentally knocked from St. Donatus's hand by a passer-by. The saint repaired the cup miraculously. Cf. *W.*, VI, p. 506, n.1

whether they have to do without one or both; meanwhile they will be preserved from harm by their faith and by their desire for the whole sacrament. Similarly, because the priests are servants, they ought to administer baptism and absolution to one who makes the request as of right. If they do not so administer it, the seeker has full merit in his faith, whereas they will be accused before Christ as wicked servants. In former times, the desert Fathers for a long period did not receive the sacrament in any form.

Thus I am not arguing that force be used to seize both kinds, but I am seeking to instruct men's consciences, so that, when any one suffers under the tyranny of Rome, he may know that it is for his own sinful complicity that he has been deprived of his right in the sacrament. My desire is only that no one should be able to uphold the Roman dictatorship as rightly denying one kind to the laity. We ought rather to abhor it and refuse consent, although we should bear ourselves just as if we were prisoners among the Turks and not allowed to use either kind. This was my point when I said it would seem well that this servitude were abolished at a general council, and that our noble Christian liberty were restored to us, and that we were set free from the hands of the dictator at Rome. Each man should be allowed his free choice in seeking and using the sacrament, just as in the case of baptism and penance. At present, year by year, the tyrant exercises his despotism, and compels us to accept one kind only. That is the measure of the utter loss of the liberty which we received from Christ, and that is the due recompense for our impious ingratitude.

The second shackle[1] imposed on this sacrament is less serious as regards our conscience, but far more perilous to discuss, and yet worse to condemn. Here I shall be called a Wycliffite and six hundred times a heretic. But what does it matter? Now that the Romish bishop has ceased to be a bishop and has become a dictator, I fear none of his decrees at all; for I know that he has no power to make a new article

---

[1] While not specifically enumerated, the first shackle is the denial of the cup to the laity, cf. *supra*, pp. 217ff.

of faith, nor has a general council. Some time ago, when I was studying scholastic theology, I was greatly impressed by Dr. Pierre d'Ailly,[1] cardinal of Cambrai. He discussed the fourth book of the *Sententiae* very acutely, and said it was far more likely, and required the presupposition of fewer miracles, if one regarded the bread and wine on the altar as real bread and wine, and not their mere accidents—had not the church determined otherwise. Afterwards, when I saw what was the kind of church which had reached this conclusion, namely, the Thomist,[2] or Aristotelian church, I gained more courage. At last, after hesitating between conflicting opinions, I found peace in my conscience in accepting the earlier opinion, viz., that the true flesh and the true blood of Christ were in the true bread and true wine, and this not otherwise, nor less, than the Thomists regard them as under the accidents.[3] I adopted this view, because I saw that the opinions of the Thomists, even though approved by pope and council, remained opinions still, and would not become articles of faith even if decreed by an angel from heaven. For what is ascribed without a basis of Scripture or a proven revelation, may be held as an opinion, but is not to be believed of necessity. This opinion of Thomas's, being without a basis in Scripture or reason, is so uncertain that it seemed to me as if he understood neither his philosophy nor his logic. Aristotle speaks of accidents and their subject very differently from St. Thomas. I feel we ought to be sorry for so great a man, not only for drawing his views from Aristotle in matters of faith, but also for attempting to found them upon a man whom he did not understand, thus building an unfortunate superstructure on an unfortunate foundation.

I would therefore allow anyone to hold whichever opinion he prefers. The only thing I aim at for the present is to

---

[1] Born in northern France 1350, became a student in Paris, 1372, and became Chancellor of that university, 1388. He was chairman of the council which condemned John Huss, June 28, 1415; and exercised much political influence. He died at Avignon, Aug. 9, 1420

[2] Named after Thomas Aquinas, who died in A.D. 1274, and is still regarded as the great doctrinal authority in the Roman Catholic church

[3] The qualities which, in medieval thought, were held to adhere to the invisible "substance", and together with it, form the object

P

banish scruples of conscience, so that no one may fear being
called a heretic if he believes that the bread and wine on
the altar are real bread and wine. Let him understand that,
without endangering his soul's salvation, he may believe and
think and opine either the one or the other, because no
particular view is a necessary article of the faith.

But I shall now pursue my own opinion further.

1. I shall not give an ear, nor pay any attention, to those
who cry out that my opinion is Wycliffite or Hussite heresy,
and contrary to the decree of the church. This kind of device
is adopted only by those whom I have convicted many times
of heresy in questions of the indulgences, of free will and
God's grace, of good works and sins, etc. If Wycliffe was
a heretic in one degree, they are such in ten degrees. It is
a pleasure to be blamed and accused by heretics and perverse sophists, for to please them would be the worst sort
of impiety.

2. Moreover, they can neither prove their own contentions,
nor disprove the opposite, nor do other than say: "That is
Wycliffite, Hussite, or heretical." They carry this feeble
objection always on the tip of their tongues, but nothing
else. If you ask for a scriptural proof, they reply: "That is
our opinion, and the church (i.e., ourselves) has decreed it
so." That shows the extent to which men of reprobate faith,
unworthy to be believed, not only propound to us their own
imaginations as articles of faith, but do so under the authority of the church.

There is very good reason, however, for my standpoint.
Firstly, that the word of God does not need to be forced
in any way by either men or angels. Rather, its plainest
meanings are to be preserved; and, unless the context manifestly compels one to do otherwise, the words are not to
be understood apart from their proper and literal sense, lest
occasion be given to our adversaries to evade Scripture as
a whole. This is why Origen was rightly repudiated long ago;
he made allegories out of the trees and all else described in
Paradise, and ignored the plain, literal sense. One might have

inferred from what he said that God had not created trees.
Similarly, in the second place, in regard to our special subject, the evangelists plainly record that Christ took bread
and blessed it; the book of Acts and the apostle Paul call
it bread; therefore we are intended to understand it means
real bread; and so also true wine, and a true chalice. Even
our opponents do not say that the chalice is changed. Since,
therefore, it is not necessary to assume that divine power
effected a transubstantiation, this must be regarded as a
human invention, because it is not supported by Scripture
or reason, as we shall see.

It gives a new and foolish twist to the words to hold that
"bread" means the form, or the "accidents", of the bread;
and "wine" the form, or the accidents, of the wine. Why
then do they not take everything else to consist of forms
and accidents? Even if all else were consistent with that
idea, nevertheless the word of God ought not to be taken
so lightly, nor deprived of its original meaning, with so
little justification.

For over 1,200 years the church remained orthodox. On
no occasion, and in no place, do the Fathers mention the
word transubstantiation—monstrous whether as a locution
or as an idea—until the specious philosophy of Aristotle
took root in the church, and attained a rank growth in the
last 300 years. During this time, many other perverse conclusions were arrived at. Examples are: "That the divine
Being is not begotten, nor does it beget"; "That the soul is
the form to which the human body corresponds as the substance"; and the like. These assertions are made without
any reason or ground, as the cardinal of Cambrai himself
acknowledges.

The Romanists may perhaps object that the danger of
idolatry forbids that the bread and wine should be real. This
is a very ridiculous objection, because the laity have never
understood the hair-splitting philosophy of substance and
its accidents; nor, if they were taught it, could they grasp
it. Thus the danger remains the same whether it is the visible
accidents that are retained or the invisible substance. For
if they do not worship the accidents, but the Christ which

they conceal, why should they worship the bread which they do not see?[1]

Why could not Christ maintain His body within the substance of the bread as truly as within its accidents? Iron and fire are two substances which mingle together in red-hot iron in such a way that every part contains both iron and fire. Why cannot the glorified body of Christ be similarly found in every part of the substance of the bread?

What will they reply? Christ is believed to have been born from his mother's virgin womb. Let them aver, here also, that the flesh of the virgin was temporarily deprived of being, or, as they would more aptly have it put, "transubstantiated", in order that Christ, having been enfolded in the accidents, might come forth through the accidents. The same thing will have to be said of the shut door of the upper room and the closed mouth of the sepulchre, through which He went in and out without doing them injury. Out of this theory has arisen that Babel of a philosophy of a constant quantity distinct from substance, till the stage is reached when they themselves[2] do not know which are the accidents and which the substance. No one has given a certain proof that heat, colour, cold, luminosity, weight, and shape, are accidents. Further, they have been forced to pretend that a new substance is created by God and added to the accidents on the altar. This has been required because Aristotle said: "The nature of accidents is to be in something." They have been led to an infinite number of monstrous ideas, from all of which they would be free if they would simply grant that the bread was truly there. And I rejoice to think that, at least among the ordinary people, simple faith in this sacrament still abides. Because they do not understand the dispute, they do not argue whether the accidents are there without the substance; rather, they believe, in simple faith, that the body and blood of Christ are truly contained there, and they leave the business of arguing what contains them to those who have time to spare.

[1] I.e., the bread whose actual substance, apart from the accidents, is invisible. To follow Luther's argument easily, one requires a certain familiarity with scholastic philosophy and terminology
[2] I.e., the Romanists

Perhaps the Romanists will say: "Aristotle teaches that, in an affirmative sentence, the subject and the predicate ought to mean the same thing"; or, to quote this beast's own words in the *Metaphysics VI*, "An affirmative proposition requires the agreement of the extremes." It would then follow that when Christ said, "This is my body", the subject cannot stand for the bread, but for the body of Christ. What is our response when Aristotle, and the doctrines of men, are made the arbiters of these very sublime and divine things? Why not hiss these ingenious inquiries off the stage, and hold to the words of Christ in simple faith, satisfied not to understand what takes place, and content to know that the true body of Christ is there by virtue of the words of institution? We do not need to understand completely the mode of the divine operation.

But what do the Romanists say when Aristotle attributes a subject to all the categories of accidents, although he grants that the substance is the prime subject? According to him "this white", "this great", "this something", are all subjects because something is predicated of them. If this is true, then, since *transubstantiation* has to be propounded in order to avoid declaring the bread to be the body of Christ, I ask: Why not propound a *transaccidentation* and so avoid affirming that an accident is the body of Christ? The danger remains the same if one were to understand the "subject" to be "this white or this round object",[1] and to be the body of Christ. On whatever grounds transubstantiation is taught, on the same grounds transaccidentation might be taught, the principle being that the two terms of a proposition refer to the same thing.

But if, by a *tour de force*, you rise above the accident, and do not wish to regard it as signified by the subject when you say, "This is my body"; why not, with equal ease, transcend the substance of the bread when you do not wish to regard it as the subject? Then to say, "This is my body", will be as true in the substance as in the accident, especially as this would be a miracle performed by God's almighty power, which can operate to the same degree, and in the same way, in the substance as in the accident.

[1] The host or wafer is in Luther's mind, but his language is very obscure

But let us not carry on our dialectics too long; does it not seem that Christ used plain words in anticipation of these curious ideas? He did not say of the wine, "This substance is my blood", but "This is my blood". It was still clearer when He introduced the word "cup" and said, "This is the cup of the new testament in my blood." Does He not seem to have wished us to continue in simple faith, and believe only that His blood was in the cup? When I fail to understand how bread can be the body of Christ, I, for one, will take my understanding prisoner and bring it into obedience to Christ; and, holding fast with a simple mind to His words, I will firmly believe, not only that the body of Christ is in the bread, but that the bread is the body of Christ. My warrant is in the words which say, "He took bread and gave thanks and brake it, and said, Take, eat, this" (i.e., this bread which He had taken and broken) "is my body". Paul says: "The bread which we break, is it not participation in the body of Christ?" He does not say: "It is in the bread", but, "this bread is participation in the body of Christ." What if the philosophers do not grasp it? The Holy Spirit is greater than Aristotle. How can the Romanists maintain that their fine doctrine of transubstantiation is comprised in any system of philosophy at all, when they themselves confess that here all philosophy falls short? However that may be in Greek or Latin, the possessive adjective "this" is linked to "body" by identity of gender; in Hebrew, which has no neuter gender, "this" refers to the bread. The meaning in Hebrew is: "This (bread) is my body", when Jesus said: "This is my body". The idiom of the language and also common sense show that the subject indicated by Jesus was the bread, and not His body, i.e., when Jesus said, "This is my body", he meant, "this bread is my body".

Thus what is true in regard to Christ is also true in regard to the sacrament. It is not necessary for human nature to be transubstantiated before it can be the corporeal habitation of the divine, and before the divine can be contained under the accidents of human nature. Both natures are present in their entirety, and one can appropriately say: "This man is God"; or, "This God is man". Though philosophy cannot grasp it, yet faith can. The authority of the word of God goes beyond the capacity of our mind. Thus, in order that the true body and the true blood should be in the sacrament, the bread and wine have no need to be transubstantiated, and Christ contained under the accidents; but, while both remain the same, it would be true to say: "This bread is my body, this wine is my blood", and conversely. That is how I would construe the words of divine Scripture and, at the same time, maintain due reverence for them. I cannot bear their being forced by human quibbles, and twisted into other meanings. Nevertheless, in my view, other men must be allowed another opinion, e.g., that laid down in the decretal *Firmiter*.[1] But, as I have said, let them not press their opinions on us to be accepted as articles of faith.

The third shackle imposed upon this sacrament is by far the most wicked abuse of all. The result of it is that there is no belief more widely accepted in the church to-day, or one of greater force, than that the mass is a good work and a sacrifice. And this abuse has brought in its train innumerable other abuses; and these, when faith in the sacrament has completely died away, turn the holy sacrament into mere merchandise, a market, and a business run for profit. This is the origin of the special feasts, the confraternities, intercessions, merits, anniversaries, and memorial days. Things of this kind are bought and sold in the church, dealt in and bargained for; the whole income of priests and monks depending on it.

It is difficult, perhaps impossible, to do away with the abuse which I shall now discuss. It is a matter which has been confirmed by so many centuries of ancient custom, and has become so ingrained, that to alter or abolish it would require that the great majority of the books which are to-day regarded as authoritative, and almost the whole form of church life, should be changed and done away with. Entirely different rites and ceremonies would have to be introduced, or rather reintroduced. But the Saviour lives, and the word of God must be obeyed with greater care than any nice notions,

[1] *Decret. Greg., lib.* I, tit.; cap. 3

human or angelic. I will discharge my office by bringing the facts to light, and teaching the truth as I have understood it; I shall do this neither under compulsion nor for the sake of money. In other matters, let each work out his own salvation. I mean to labour faithfully as one who must stand before Christ's judgment seat, and in such a way that no one will be able to blame me for his unbelief, or his ignorance of the truth.

Firstly, in order to be happy and assured, and to reach a true and unconstrained understanding of this sacrament, we must be careful to begin by setting aside all the later additions to the first, simple institution. Those additions have been made by men's devotion and through their zeal, and include such things as vestments, ornaments, chants, prayers, organs, candles, and the whole pageantry of things visible. Let us turn our eyes and devote our minds purely and simply to that alone which Christ Himself instituted. Let us confine ourselves to the very words by which Christ instituted and completed the sacrament, and commended it to us. For these words alone, and apart from everything else, contain the power, the nature, and the whole substance of the mass. All the rest are human productions, additions to the words of Christ, things without which the mass could still continue, and remain at its best.

These are the words with which Christ instituted this sacrament:

"As they were eating, Jesus took bread and blessed and brake, and gave to His disciples, and said: Take and eat; this is my body which is given for you. And taking the cup, He gave thanks, and gave to them, saying: All ye drink of it. This cup is the new testament in my blood which is poured out for you and for many for the remission of sins. This do in remembrance of me."[1]

St. Paul hands these words down in 1 Corinthians 11, and explains them at greater length. We ought to rest on them, and stand upon them as firmly as upon a rock, if we do not

[1] Matt. 26:26ff.; Luke 22:19

wish to be carried about by every wind of doctrine, as we have been carried about till now by irreverent doctrine, man-made, and contrary to the truth. This passage omits nothing pertaining to the integrity, the usefulness and the fruitfulness of this sacrament; and nothing is introduced which is superfluous or not necessary for us to know. Anyone who passes these words by, and yet meditates on or teaches the mass, teaches a monstrous impiety. This is, in fact, done by those who make an *opus operatum*,[1] and a sacrifice of it.

The first point stands infallibly fast. The mass or sacrament is Christ's testament which He bequeathed to be distributed after His death, among those who believed on Him. For His words run: "This cup is the new testament in my blood." I say this truth stands firm, and is the unchanging foundation on which to build everything else we have to say. For you will see how we shall undermine all the sacrilege which men have imported into this sweetest of all sacraments. Christ, who is the Truth, truly said: "This is the new testament in my blood which is shed for you." I do not stress this without reason; the matter is not a small one, and is to be received in the depths of our heart.

Let us inquire, therefore, what a testament is, and, at the same time, it will also become clear to us what is the mass, what its use, its fruit, and its abuse.

Without question, a testament is a promise made by a man in view of his death. In it, he bequeaths his heritage, and appoints heirs. A testament, therefore: (a) anticipates the death of the testator; (b) embodies the promise of the heritage; and (c) appoints the heirs. That is how Paul discusses a testament at length in Romans 4, Galatians 3 and 4, and Hebrews 9. The words of Christ show the same quite plainly. Christ testifies of His own death when He says: "This is my blood which is given. This is my blood which is shed." He names and designates the bequest when He says, "In remission of sins." Similarly, He appoints the heirs when He says, "For you and for many", i.e., those who

---

[1] Luther's own words, "a finished work", is the usual translation in the German form

accept, and believe in, the promise of the testator. Faith here makes men heirs, as we shall see.

You will see, therefore, that what we call the mass is a promise made by God for the remission of our sins; a promise which was confirmed by the death of the Son of God. Now a promise and a testament only differ in so far as a testament contemplates the death of the promiser. The testator is the same as the promiser with his death in view, whereas a mere promiser is, so to speak, a testator who is not contemplating death. Now Christ's death was foreshadowed in all the promises of God from the beginning of the world. Indeed, whatever value the ancient promises had, depended on that new promise in Christ which lay in the future. Hence the very frequent use in Scripture of the words, "covenant", "compact", "testament of the Lord". Their meaning was that God would die at some future date; because, before a testament comes into effect, the testator's death must take place (Hebrews 9). But it was God who made the testament, and therefore He needs must die. But He Himself could not die unless He became man. Therefore the one comprehensive word, "testament", envisages both the incarnation and the death of Christ.

These things having been said, it becomes obvious what is the right and the wrong use of the mass, and what constitutes a worthy or an unworthy preparation for it. If, as I have argued, it is a promise, we cannot prepare ourselves for it by any works, by the use of force, or by any merits; but only by faith. For where there is the word of a promise-keeping God, there is needed the faith of a man who accepts it. It is plain that our salvation begins in our faith, and this clings to the word of the God of the promises. And God, apart from and before all that we can do, manifests His mercy, which is unearned and unmerited, and proffers His words of promise: "For He sent His word and healed them."[1]

He does not first accept our works, and then save us. The word of God is prior to all else; faith follows it; then love succeeds faith, and gives rise to every good work. Love does

[1] Ps. 107:20

not cause evil, for it is the fulfilling of the law. There is no way by which a man can commune with God, or treat with Him, except by faith; that is to say, no man by his works, but God by His promises, is the author of our salvation. All things depend on His authoritative word, and are upheld and maintained by it. He begot us by it that we might be, as it were, the first-fruits of His creative work.

Thus, when Adam came to be restored after the Fall, God gave him this promise, and said to the serpent: "I am putting enmity between you and the woman, between your seed and her seed. She shall bruise your head, and you shall lie in wait to bruise her heel."[1] According to this word of promise, Adam and his family were carried for a long time in God's bosom, and kept by faith in Him. He patiently waited for the woman who was to bruise the serpent's head as God had promised. He died in this faith and expectation, not knowing when or how she would come, but not doubting that she would come. For such a promise, being the truth of God, preserves, even in hell, those who believe and wait for it. After this there was another promise, made to Noah, and reaching to Abraham. Its sign was the rainbow of the covenant placed in the clouds. Noah and his posterity had faith in it, and found God beneficent. Afterwards, He promised Abraham that all the nations should have blessing in his seed. It was into Abraham's bosom that his posterity were received when they died. Then to Moses and the children of Israel, and especially to David, He plainly made the promise of Christ, and so revealed what the earlier promise had implied.[2]

Thus we come to the most perfect promise, that of the new testament. The words used are plain: life and salvation are promised without price; they are given to those who believe in the promise. God plainly distinguishes this testament from the former by calling it the new testament. For the older testament, mediated through Moses, was not a promise of remission of sins, or of eternal life, but of temporal things, to wit, the land of Canaan. No one was renewed in spirit by this promise so as to lay hold on a heavenly heritage.

[1] Gen. 3:15   [2] Deut. 18:18; 2 Sam. 7:16

For this reason, an unthinking beast had to be slain as a figure of Christ, and the testament was confirmed by its blood. Thus the blood corresponded to the testament, and the victim to the promise. Now Christ said: "The new testament in my blood"; not another's, but His own; and, by this blood, grace is promised through the spirit for the remission of sins, that we might receive the inheritance.

Therefore the mass, in essence, is solely and simply the words of Christ just quoted, viz., "Take and eat," etc.; as if He had said, "Lo! thou sinful and lost soul, out of the pure and free love with which I love thee, and in accordance with the will of the Father of mercies, I promise thee with these words, and apart from any deserts or undertakings of thine, to forgive all thy sins, and give thee eternal life. In order that thou mayest be most assured that this my promise is irrevocable, I will give my body and shed my blood to confirm it by my very death, and make both body and blood a sign and memorial of this promise. As often as thou partakest of them, remember me; praise and laud my love and bounty, and be thankful."

From all of which you will see that nothing else than faith is needed for a worthy observance of the mass, and the mass is truly founded on this promise. Faith believes Christ to be truthful in these words, and does not doubt that she has had these immeasurable blessings bestowed upon her. Given this faith, there immediately follows the most precious affection of the heart, enlarging and deepening the human soul, i.e., love as given by the Holy Spirit through faith in Christ. Thus the believer draws near to Christ, that loving and bounteous testator, and becomes a new and different man through and through. Who would not weep inward tears and in very joy surrender himself entirely to Christ, if he believed firmly and without doubt that this inestimable promise of Christ's belonged to him? How could he help loving so great a benefactor, who offered, promised, and presented to him, in his unworthiness and while deserving something quite different, this great wealth and also an eternal inheritance?

The one and only pity about it all is that there are many

masses said, while none, or few of us, recognize, consider, and apprehend, the promises and riches they set before us. Of a truth, during mass, nothing else should be done with greater zeal, indeed with all our zeal, than to give all our attention to these words, these promises of Christ, for they truly constitute the mass itself. We should meditate on these words, ponder them, exercise and nourish our faith in them, make it grow and add to its strength, by daily commemoration of it. This is to fulfil Christ's command when He said, "This do in remembrance of me." Preachers ought to do the same thing in order to impress the promise faithfully on the people, to commend it and awaken their faith in it.

But, to-day, how many know that the mass is Christ's promise? I pass over those irreverent men who recount fables, teaching man-made traditions instead of these great promises. Even when they do teach these words of Christ, they teach them, not as a promise or a testament, nor in order to rouse faith by their means.

What we deplore, in the servitude of the church, is that the priests take every care nowadays lest any of the laity hear these words of Christ. It is as if they were too sacred to be uttered to the common people. For we priests have no more sense, as to the terms which we call the words of institution, than to arrogate them to ourselves alone. We say them privately, and in such a way that they do us no good; for we ourselves do not feel them as promises, nor regard them as a testament to nourish our faith. But I know not whether it is superstition or blasphemy for us to repeat the words after we have lost belief in them. Satan has taken advantage of this lamentable condition of ours to remove every trace of the real mass from the church. At the same time, he has taken care that every corner of the world is full of spurious masses, i.e., abuses and travesties of God's testament. He burdens the world more and more with sacrilege, that gravest of sins, and so increases its guilt; for what more sinful sacrilege could there be than to replace God's promises by perverse opinions, or to neglect them, or to extinguish all faith in them?

As we have said,[1] God never has dealt, and never does deal, with mankind at any time otherwise than by the word of promise. Neither can we, on our part, ever have to do with God otherwise than through faith in His word and promise. He does not hold works in high esteem, nor does He need them. We use them in dealing with one another and with our own selves. But He does require that we should regard Him as faithful to His promises; we should pray without ceasing, and worship Him in faith, hope, and love. In this way, He is glorified in us, since it is not of us who run, but of Him who shows mercy, and who promises and gives, that we receive and possess all good things. Lo, this is the true worship and service of God which we ought to offer in the mass. But when the words of the promises are not handed on, how can faith be exercised? And, without faith, what of hope? What of love? and, without faith, hope, and love, what of service? Thus without any doubt, all the priests and monks to-day, together with the bishops and all their other superiors, are idolaters and in a state of peril on account of this ignorance, abuse, and mockery of the mass, i.e., sacrament, i.e., promise of God.

For anyone readily understands that these two, promise and faith, are necessarily yoked together. No one can believe if there is no promise. If there is no faith, a promise is useless, because faith is its counterpart and completion. From these considerations, any one can easily deduce that the mass, which is simply a promise, can only be attended and celebrated in faith. Without that faith, any ancillary thing by way of prayer, self-preparation, good works, outer signs, and genuflections, are far rather instigations to irreligion than religious exercises. It readily happens that those who have prepared themselves in this way think they have a right of access to the altar, whereas in reality they are more unfit than at any other time, or by any other means; and this on account of the unbelief which they bring with them. How many priests you may see everywhere and every day offering the sacrifice of the mass, who, if they have made some error in vestment, or have unwashed hands, or if they

[1] Cf. *supra*, pp. 233ff.

stumble in the prayers, or blunder in some small way, make themselves very miserable, as if guilty of a great crime! But, on the other hand, they are not in the least conscience-stricken if they do not reverence or believe the mass itself, i.e., the divine promise. Oh, the unworthy religion of our times, the most irreligious and thankless of all times! There is, therefore, no other worthy self-preparation and no other proper observance of the mass than by faith, the faith by which we believe in the mass, i.e., in the divine promise. Therefore, let him who desires to approach the altar, or to receive the sacrament, beware lest he appear empty before the face of the Lord our God. But he will be empty without faith in the mass, i.e., in this new testament. By what state of mind, other than this unbelief of his, could he sin more grievously against the divine truth? As far as it lies in his power, he is making God a liar and a promiser of vain things. The safest course, therefore, would be to attend mass in the same spirit as in hearing some other promise made by God, i.e., in such a way that, while you would not be ready to do or contribute much yourself, you would be ready to believe and accept all that was promised you there, i.e., the promises pronounced by the priest in discharging the office. If you do not come in this spirit, beware of drawing near at all, for you will undoubtedly draw near to the judgment seat.

Thus I was right in saying[1] that the whole virtue of the mass consisted in the words of Christ, when He gave testimony to the remission of the sins of all who believed that His body had been given for them and His blood shed for them. On this account, nothing is more important for those who hear mass than to meditate on His words carefully, and in fullness of faith. Unless they do that, all else they do is in vain. Nevertheless it is true to say that God's way is almost always to add some sign as a mark or reminder of His promise, that thus we might serve Him the more faithfully, or that He might admonish us the more effectually. When He made the promise to Noah that the earth should not again be destroyed by flood He gave His bow, and placed

---

[1] Cf. *supra*, pp. 230ff.

it in the clouds, as the sign that He would be mindful of His covenant. After promising Abraham that his seed should gain the inheritance, He gave circumcision as the seal of justification by faith. Similarly, He gave Gideon at first a dry and then a wet fleece, in confirmation of His promise of victory over the Midianites. Through Isaiah, He offered Ahaz a sign of his victory over the kings of Syria and Samaria, to confirm his faith in the promise of it. And so we read of many other signs accompanying the promises of God in the Scriptures.

Similarly in the mass, the greatest promise of all, He adds a sign as a memorial of this great promise, His own body and His own blood in the bread and wine, when He says: "This do in remembrance of me." So, at baptism, He adds the sign of immersion in the water to the words of the promise. From these instances we learn that, in every promise, God presents two things to us, a word and a sign, in order that we may understand the word to be a testament, and the sign a sacrament. In the mass, the word of Christ is the testament, the bread and wine are the sacrament. Since greater power resides in a word than in a sign, so more power resides in a testament than in a sacrament; for a man may have, and use, a word or testament without a sign or sacrament. "Believe", says Augustine, "and thou hast eaten." But what is believed is nothing less than the word of the promiser. Thus I am able daily, indeed hourly, to have the mass; for, as often as I wish, I can set the words of Christ before me, and nourish and strengthen my faith by them. This is the true spiritual eating and drinking.

You will not understand the nature or importance of the things which our theologians have produced in the *Sentences*.[1] (1) The crux and sum of the whole matter is that the testament, or word of promise, is not discussed by any of them; consequently they abrogate faith and the whole virtue of

---

[1] The reference is to the famous work of Peter Lombard (1105 (?)–60): *quattuor libri sententiarum*, which was the text-book of dogma throughout the Middle Ages. As a text-book it did not seek to express the author's own views; rather, it gave brief statements of the main views and of the main arguments pro and con. Hence the name—and the value of the book to students

the mass. Then (2) they discuss only the second part of the mass, the sign or sacrament. But they do it in such a way that, here once more, they teach nothing about faith, but only about its presuppositions; or about *opera operata*, participations, and the fruits of the mass. At last (3) they come to the profundities, and talk trumpery stuff about transubstantiation, and other metaphysical nonsense without end. Meantime they have done away with the true knowledge and use of both the testament and the sacrifice, together with the whole of faith. In addition, as the prophet declared, they have caused the people of Christ to forget their God "days without number".[1]

But you should let others recount the various benefits of hearing mass. Give it your attention that you may say and believe, with the prophet, that here is a table which has been made ready for you by God in the face of all who cause you anxiety, and at which your faith may feed and grow strong.[2] Your faith feeds only on the word of the divine promise, for "man doth not live by bread alone, but by every word that proceedeth out of the mouth of God."[3] Hence, at mass, you ought, first of all, to be a most minute observer of the words of the promise, as forming the richest banquet, with every variety of food and holy nourishment. You must esteem it greater than all else, trust in it above all else, cleave to it most firmly in spite of every sin, and unto death. If you do so, you will obtain not only those tiny drops and crumbs of fruits of the mass, which some have fabricated superstitiously, but the principal fountain of life itself. By this I mean faith in the very word, the source of all good; as it says in John 4,[4] "He that believeth in me, out of his belly shall flow living waters"; and again: "Whosoever drinketh of the water that I shall give him, there shall be in him a well of living water springing up into eternal life."[5]

Now there are two defects from which we commonly suffer, and which prevent our understanding the fruits of

---

[1] Jer. 2:32   [2] Ps. 23:5   [3] Matt. 4:4; Deut. 8:3
[4] Really John 7:38; one of the few of Luther's slips in giving a scriptural reference
[5] John 4:14

Q

the mass. The first is that we are sinners; and our profound unworthiness makes us unfit for such great things. Secondly, even if we were worthy, these things are so highly exalted that our timorous nature would not dare either to seek or to hope for them. Forgiveness of sins and eternal life!—who would not be overawed by them, rather than dare to hope for them, if the great benefits issuing from them were given their due importance. By them, we may have God as our Father, and ourselves become sons and heirs of all God's riches. To outweigh this twofold defect of our nature, we must lay hold of the word of Christ, and look to Him more steadily than to our sense of weakness. For great are the works of the Lord; they are all full of His purposes, and He is able to give beyond what we ask or-think. If they did not exceed our worth, our capacity, and indeed every talent of ours, they would not be divine. Christ also encourages us in the same way when He says: "Fear not, little flock, for it is the Father's good pleasure to give you the Kingdom."[1] This incomprehensible wealth of God, showered upon us through Christ, causes us to love Him, in return, most ardently and above all else. We are drawn to Him with the fullest confidence, despising all things else, and being made ready to suffer all things for Him. Thus the sacrament is aptly called "a fount of love".

In this connection, consider an example from human affairs. Suppose a very rich nobleman were to bequeath 1,000 guilders to a beggar, or even a worthless and wicked fellow. The man would assuredly claim them boldly and take them without regard to his own worthlessness, or the magnitude of the bequest. If someone should accost him in the road, and remind him of his own worthlessness and the magnitude of the bequest, what do you think he would reply? Presumably: "What business is that of yours? I am receiving what I receive, not as my deserts, nor on account of any special claim on my part. I know I do not deserve it and that I am getting more than I have earned; in fact, I have earned the opposite. But by the generosity of my benefactor, I am making a perfectly valid claim through the processes

[1] Luke 12:32

of the law which deals with wills and bequests. If it was not an unworthy act on his part to make a bequest to a man as unworthy as me, why should I make my unworthiness a reason for not accepting it? Nay, unworthy of it though I am, the more thankfully should I accept this gracious gift of a stranger." Every one ought to fortify his conscience with such considerations against all doubts and fears, in order to hold this promise of Christ with an unwavering faith. Take great care that no one goes to mass trusting in confession, or prayer, or self-preparation; but lacking confidence in all these things, let him rather go in high confidence in the Christ who gives the promise. As already said at sufficient length, the word of the promise must reign unchallenged here in pure faith, which faith in itself constitutes the sole and sufficient preparation.

I have shown how God, in His great wrath, has permitted the perfidious teachers to hide from us the words of this testament, and thereby to eradicate faith as far as they could. It is easy to see now what would inevitably follow on blotting out faith, viz., the most ungodly superstition of works. For when faith dies, and the word of faith is dumb, works soon take its place, and the tradition of works. This substitution results in our soon being taken prisoner out of our own land, exiled to Babylon, and robbed of all our treasures. That is what has happened to the mass; it has been transformed, by the teaching of godless men, into a good work. They themselves call it an *opus operatum*. Through it, they presume themselves to be all-powerful with God. From that starting-point they have gone on to the last folly of falsely asserting that, because the mass avails by virtue of its *opus operatum*, it is no less beneficial to others even if it be hurtful to a celebrant priest who is a wicked man. That is the foundation of sand on which they base their "applications", "participations", sodalities, anniversaries, and an infinite number of other profitable, money-making schemes of that kind.

These spectres are so strong, numerous, and firmly ensconced, that you will scarcely be able to stand against them unless you exercise unceasing vigilance, and remember what the mass is, and what I have said about it. I have said that the mass is simply the divine promise or testament of Christ confirmed in the sacrament of His body and blood. That being so, you will understand that it is impossible for it ever to be an outward work; nor does anything happen in it, nor can any benefit be attained in it, except by faith alone. Faith is not a work, but it teaches us to do good works, and is their soul! Can any one be found so foolish as to regard a promise he has received, or a testament he has been given, as a good work of his own? What heir thinks he is doing good to his father when he receives the instruments of the bequest along with the bequest he has inherited? How then shall we describe our impious temerity when we act as if we were going to perform a good work for God in coming to receive the divine testimonies? This ignorance of the testament, and this servitude of the sacrament, are things that go beyond tears. When we ought to be grateful to accept, we come arrogantly to give the things that are to be accepted. With unheard-of perversity, we mock at the mercy of the Giver; for we give as a work what we should be accepting as a gift, till the Testator now no longer distributes the largesse of His own good things, but becomes the recipient of ours. Alas for such sacrilege!

Who has ever been so lacking in sense as to consider baptism to be a good work? Has any candidate for baptism believed he was doing a good work which he was offering and communicating to God for himself and others? If, therefore, no good work is communicable to others in a sacrament and testament of any kind, there cannot be one in the mass, for the mass itself is simply a testament and a sacrament. Hence it is plainly an impious error to offer or apply a mass for sins, for satisfactions, for the benefit of the departed or any necessity of one's own or that of another. You will easily understand this as the plainest truth, if you hold it firmly that the mass is a divine promise which can benefit no one, be applied to no one, intercede for no one, be communicated to no one, except only to the believer himself by the sole virtue of his own faith. Who can receive or accept, on another's behalf, the promises of God, which require faith from each one individually? Can I give the promises of God to another, even if he be an unbeliever? Or can I believe on behalf of another, or cause another to believe? But these powers are needed if I am to be able to apply and communicate the mass to others, since the mass contains only those two things: the divine promise and the human faith, the latter accepting what the former promises. If this were not the case, I should be able to hear the gospel for others, and believe for them; I could be baptized for someone else; I could communicate in the sacrament of the altar for another, and, to go through the list of their sacraments, I could marry a wife for another, be ordained for another, be confirmed for another, and receive extreme unction for another.

But if this can be done, why did not Abraham believe on behalf of all the Jews? Why was faith in the same promise as was believed in by Abraham, demanded of every Jew individually? Therefore, this truth is irrefragable: each one stands for himself where the divine promise is concerned. His own faith is required. Each must respond for himself, and bear his own burden, as Mark says in chapter 16: "Every one who believes and has been baptized will be saved; but he who does not believe, will be condemned."[1] So also each one can take mass only for his own good, through his own faith; and he can communicate for no one else at all. So also, the priest cannot administer the sacrament to any one in another's stead, but administers the same sacrament to each one individually. In consecrating and administering, the priests are our servants. We do not offer a good work through them or actively communicate; rather, through them we receive the promises and the sign, and we communicate passively; and that has remained the case to this day as far as the laity are concerned. For the laity are not said to do good, but to receive it. But the priests have gone astray in their impieties, and have made a good work of their own out of the fact that they communicate, and administer, the sacrament and testament of God, in which the good shall be received by the laity.

[1] Mark 16:16

But, you will say: What is this? Surely your contentions will overturn the practices and purposes of all the churches and monasteries, and destroy those by which they have waxed rich for many centuries, since they have been founded on masses at anniversaries, intercessions, "applications", "communications". You will deprive them of their largest incomes. My answer is: That is the very thing which led me to write that the church has been taken prisoner. For this sacred testament of God has been forced into the service of impious greed for gain by the opinions and traditions of irreligious men. They have passed over God's word; they have laid before us the thoughts of their own hearts, and led the world astray. To point to the numbers or the eminence of those whom I assert to be in error carries no weight with me. The truth is mightier than all else. If you were able to refute Christ who taught that the mass was a testament and a sacrament, I would admit them to be in the right. Further, if you could show that to receive the benefit of a will and testament, or to receive the sacrament of promise, is to do a good work, then I would be ready and willing to condemn my own teachings. Since you can do neither, why do you hesitate to treat with contempt the mob who are going from bad to worse? Give God the glory and confess His truth. His truth is, in particular, that to-day all those priests have perverted views who regard the mass as a good work which will help them and others out of their difficulties even in matters of life or death. This is to say things unheard-of hitherto and repellent now. But examine the mass as it is to-day, and you will know that I have spoken the truth. The misfortune is that we have now gained a sense of security which prevents our realizing that the wrath of God is being visited upon us.

But I gladly agree that the prayers, which we pour out before God as soon as we assemble to partake of the mass, are good works and appropriate acts. In them, we confess to one another, utter our own desires, pray for the common weal, and for each other. It is thus that James taught us to pray for each other that we might be saved;[1] and that Paul

[1] Jas. 5:16

commanded, in 1 Timothy 2, that there should be "supplica-
tions, prayers, intercessions for all men; for kings and all
that are in high places."[1] Yet the prayers are not the mass,
but the works of the mass, if the prayers of the heart and
the mouth can be properly called works, since they issue
from the faith received or increased in the sacrament. For
the mass, or otherwise God's promise, is not fulfilled by
praying, but only by believing; and it is as believers that
we pray and do every good work. Yet what priest sacrifices
the mass in such a way that his object is only to offer the
prayers? All of them imagine that they are offering Christ
Himself to God the Father, as a fully sufficient sacrifice;
and that they are doing a good work on behalf of all whom
they wish to help. They trust in the efficacy of the mass,
and they do not ascribe its efficacy to prayer. The error has
gradually increased in this way until they ascribe to the
sacrament what belongs to the prayer, and they bring to
God what they ought to receive from Him as a gift.

We must therefore make a clear distinction between testament and sacrament on the one hand; and, on the other,
the prayers which we offer at the same time. Not only so,
but we ought also to bear in mind that the prayers are of
no avail either for him who offers them, or for those on whose
behalf they are offered, unless the testament be first received
in faith. It is faith which prays, and its voice alone which
is heard, as James teaches in his first chapter.[2] Thus, prayer
is something quite different from the mass. Prayer can be
extended to comprehend as many people as I choose; the
mass covers none other than him who exercises his own
faith, and then only in so far as he exercises it. Nor can the
mass be given to God or to other men; rather God bestows
it on men through the agency of the priest; and men receive
it through faith alone, apart from all works or merits. There
will be few persons so foolish as to assert that a poor man
does a good work if he comes in his poverty to receive a gift
from the hand of a rich man. But the mass is, as I have
said,[3] the gift of the divine promise, offered to all men by
the hand of the priest.

[1] 1 Tim. 2:1ff.   [2] Jas. 1:6   [3] *Supra*, p. 233

It follows that the mass is not a work in which others can share, but an object of faith, as I have already explained; and it is meant for nourishing and strengthening the personal faith of the individual.

But there is another misconception to be done away with which is much more serious and more specious, viz., the common belief that the mass is a sacrifice offered to God. This belief seems to be expressed in the words of the canon[1] which speak of "these gifts, these offerings, these holy sacrifices"; and, later, "this oblation". Moreover, the request is very definite that the sacrifice will be accepted as was Abel's sacrifice, etc. Then, too, Christ is said to be the victim[2] on the altar. In support of these false views, there are many sayings of the holy Fathers, and the whole custom of the church as observed throughout the world.

We must resolutely oppose them all with the words and example of Christ, in spite of the fact that they are so strongly entrenched. For if we do not hold firmly that the mass is the promise, or testament, of Christ, as His words plainly show, we shall lose the whole gospel, and all its comfort. We must not allow anything to prevail contrary to these words, not even if an angel from heaven were to teach otherwise. Those words contain nothing about a good work or a sacrifice. Moreover, Christ's example is on our side. At the Last Supper, when Christ initiated this sacrament, and instituted this testament, He did not offer Himself to God, or perform any "good work" for others. He took His seat at the table, He offered the same testament to each, one by one, and gave the same sign. Now the closer our mass resembles that first mass of all, which Christ celebrated at the Last Supper, the more Christian it will be. But the mass which Christ celebrated was extremely simple, without any display of vestments, genuflections, chants, and other ceremonies. If it was necessary to offer Himself as a sacrifice, then He did not institute it completely.

Not that any one ought to speak evil of the universal church, because it has embellished and amplified the mass

---

[1] Between the *Sanctus* and the *Pater Noster* in the canon of the mass
[2] Lat. *Hostia*; Eng. "host"

with many other rites and ceremonies. But the point is that no one should be deceived by the outward splendour of the ceremonies, and hindered by the impressive pomp. This would be to pass over the simple form of the mass and, in fact, practise a kind of transubstantiation; for it would be a case of passing over the simple substance of the mass, and of clinging to the various elements accidental to its outward appearance. Everything additional to the words and the example of Christ is an "accident" of the mass. Nothing of this must we regard otherwise than we are accustomed to regard the "monstrances" and the altar cloths, within which the host itself is contained. Hence, as it is a self-contradiction to speak of distributing a testament, or accepting a promise on the one hand, and on the other, of offering a sacrifice, so it is a self-contradiction to call a mass a sacrifice; for a mass is something we receive, but a sacrifice is something we offer. But one and the same thing cannot be both received and offered at the same time, nor can it at once be given and accepted by the same person, any more than a prayer can be the same thing as that which we pray for; nor is it the same to pray and to receive the thing prayed for.

What then are we to say of the Canon,[1] and of the patristic authorities? I answer, in the first place, that even if we had no objection to raise, it would be safer to deny everything rather than to grant that the mass is either a good work or a sacrifice. For we must not deny Christ's word and destroy both faith and mass at the same time. Nay, in order to retain the mass, we shall declare that we have been taught by the apostle, in I Corinthians II, how the Christian believers, when they assembled for mass, used to bring food and drink with them.[2] These they called "the collections", and they used to distribute them among all who were in need, after the example of the apostles in Acts 4.[3] A portion of this food was taken and consecrated as the bread and wine of the sacrament.[4] Just because all this was consecrated by word

---

[1] I.e., the Canon of the Mass   [2] I Cor. II:20f.   [3] Acts 4:34f.
[4] Cf. Luther: *On the Blessed Sacrament*, c. 12, A.D. 1519, *W.*, Vol. VI, p. 742ff.

and prayer in accordance with the Hebrew custom, namely, by being "lifted up", as we read in the Pentateuch, therefore the terminology and the custom of "lifting up" or offering remained in use long after an end had come to the custom of bringing and collecting together what was to be sacrificed and "lifted up". Thus, according to Isaiah 37, Hezekiah commanded Isaiah to lift up his prayer before God's face on behalf of the remnant.[1] In the Psalms, we read: "Lift up your hands in the Sanctuary"; and again, "Unto thee will I lift up my hands". I Timothy 2 says: "Lifting up pure hands in every place."[2] That is why the words "sacrifice" and "offering" ought to be used, not in reference to the sacrament or testament as such, but to the collections themselves. This is also the source whence comes the word "collect" which is still used of the prayers at mass.

For the same reason, the priest consecrates the bread and wine, and immediately elevates them. But this does not show that he is offering something to God, for no word he uses reminds one of a sacrifice or an offering. Rather, this is either a survival of the Hebrew custom according to which the gift, which had been received with thanksgiving, was brought back to God, and then "lifted up"; or, on the other hand, it may be an exhortation to stimulate our faith in this testament. The priest has expounded and described it in the words of Christ in order to exhibit the sign of the testament at the same time. In this case, the offering of the bread really corresponds to the demonstrative adjective "this", in the words: "This is my body"; and the priest, in a way, uses this sign as an allocution to those of us who are standing round him. Similarly, the offering of the cup properly corresponds to the demonstrative adjective in the words: "This cup of the new testament". For the purpose of the rite of elevation is that the priest should arouse faith in our hearts. But I wish that, at the same time as he "elevates" the sign or sacrament openly before our eyes, he would pronounce, in an audible and clear voice, the words of the testament; and that he would do it in the vernacular, whatever that may be, in order that faith may be the more effectively

[1] Isa. 37:4   [2] I Tim. 2:3

awakened. For why should it be permissible to celebrate mass in Greek, Latin, and Hebrew, but not in German or any other language?

Therefore let the priests who offer the sacrifice of the mass in these corrupt and most perilous times, take care, firstly, that the words of the greater and lesser canons of the mass, together with the collects, which all too plainly re-echo the sense of sacrifice, do not refer to the sacrament but either just to the bread and wine which the words consecrate, or to their own prayers. Indeed, the bread and wine were formerly offered in order to receive the blessing, and so become sanctified by the word and by prayer. After the blessing and consecration, they are no longer offerings, but gifts received from God. Throughout the rite, let the priest bear in mind that the gospel is superior to all the canons and collects, which are but man-made; and the gospel offers no warrant for calling the mass a sacrifice, as you have heard.

Further, when a priest is celebrating mass publicly, his intention should be only to "communicate" himself and let others "communicate" through the mass. At the same time, he may offer prayers for himself and others, but he must take care lest he presume to offer the mass. But if a priest is saying a private mass, he must conceive his act as one of communicating himself. For a private mass differs in no way from, and operates to no greater extent than, the simple communion which every layman receives from the hand of the priest. The difference is in the prayers, and in the fact that he himself consecrates the elements and then administers them to himself. In the matter of the mass and the sacraments, we are all equals, whether priests or laity.

If a priest be requested by others to celebrate "votive" masses, let him not dare to accept payment for them, or presume to offer any votive sacrifice. Let him be careful to confine himself entirely to prayers, whether for the living or the dead. Let his thought be: "Lo! I am to go and take the sacrament for myself alone; but while I am taking it, I will pray for so and so." In this way the money he receives will be, not for the mass, but for the prayers, and to buy himself food and clothing. Do not be disturbed if the whole

world is of the contrary opinion and practice. Thou hast
the utmost certainty in the gospel. Trust in it, and thou
canst well afford to despise man-made beliefs and opinions.
But if thou rejectest my words, and goest to offer a mass,
and not the prayers only, bear in mind that I have warned
thee faithfully, and I shall be held guiltless on the Day of
Judgment. Thou thyself wilt bear the penalty of thine own
sins. I have said what I was under compulsion to say to
thee as brother to brother for the sake of thy salvation.
Observe it and it will be to thy advantage; neglect it, and it
will be to thy hurt. If man would condemn what I have
said, I would reply in Paul's words: "But evil men and
impostors shall wax worse and worse, deceiving and being
deceived."[1]

All the above enables any one to understand the frequently
quoted saying of Gregory's:[2] "The mass said by a wicked
priest is not less effective than that said by a good one; nor
was one said by Saint Peter any better than one said by
Judas the traitor, if they indeed say masses." With this saying as a cloak, many have sought to hide their godlessness;
and, in so doing, they have drawn a distinction between
opus operatum and opus operans, in order to be free to live
an evil life themselves, and yet to do good to others.

What Gregory says is true, but they take him wrongly.
It is quite certainly true that ungodly priests give and receive
the testament and sacrament no less completely than do the
most godly; and no one doubts that even ungodly priests
preach the gospel. But the mass is a part of the gospel, nay
the sum and substance of the gospel; for the whole gospel is
simply the good news of the forgiveness of sins. And whatever can be said about forgiveness of sins and the mercy of
God, in the broadest and richest sense, is comprehended, in
brief, in the word of the testament. For this reason, popular
sermons ought to be nothing else than expositions of the
mass, or explanations of the divine promise contained in
this testament. This is the way to teach faith and to edify

[1] 2 Tim. 3:13
[2] Pope Gregory I died A.D. 604; famous for the saying (in regard to some
fair-haired Anglo-Saxon youths in the slave market) "non Angli sed angeli"

the church. But those who to-day expound the mass, play and make mockery with allegorical human ceremonies.

Hence, just as an ungodly priest may baptize, i.e., apply the word of promise and the sign of water to the candidate for baptism, so also may he administer the promise of this sacrament to the partaker, and also himself partake—as did also Judas the traitor at the last supper of the Lord. Nevertheless it remains the same sacrament and testament, which does its own work in the believer, but a "strange work" in the unbeliever. But in the case of offering a sacrifice there is a complete difference. For it is not the mass, but the prayers, which are offered to God; and so it is obvious that the prayers offered by an ungodly priest are without avail; but, as Gregory likewise said, when an unworthy person is the intercessor, the heart of the judge is only turned to greater sternness. Those two things, mass and prayer, or sacrament and work, or testament and sacrifice, must not be confused. The first comes from God to us through the intermediation of the priest, and demands faith. The second issues from our faith, ascends to God through the priest, and requires One who hears. The former descends; the latter ascends. The former, therefore, does not necessarily require a worthy and religious-minded minister; but the latter does require such an one, because God does not listen to sinners, although He knows how to give good gifts even through evil men. But He accepts no wicked man's works. He showed this to Cain, and, as we read in Proverbs 15, "The sacrifice of the wicked is an abomination to the Lord";[1] and Romans 14, "Whatsoever is not of faith is sin."[2]

Let us bring this first section to a close, but with the reservation that I shall have more to say if an enemy should arise. The conclusion we draw is, that, of all for whom the mass has been provided, only those partake of it worthily whose consciences make them sad, humble, disturbed, confused, and uncertain. The word of the divine promise in this sacrament offers forgiveness of sin; therefore let each come forward undisquieted, whoever he may be, even though troubled by remorse, or suffering from temptation. This

[1] Prov. 15:8   [2] Rom. 14:23

testament of Christ's is the only antidote for sins past, present, or future. But you must cling to Him with unwavering faith. You must believe that what the words of the testament declare is granted to you freely. If you do not believe this, then never, nowhere, by no good works, and by no kinds of efforts, can you gain peace of conscience. For faith alone means peace of conscience, and unbelief nought but distress of mind.

(2) *The Sacrament of Baptism*

Blessed be the God and Father of our Lord Jesus Christ who of His rich mercy has preserved at least this one sacrament in His church unspoiled and unspotted by man-made ordinances, and made it free to all races and classes of men; nor has He allowed it to be suppressed by foul money-grubbing and ungodly monsters of superstition. His purpose was that little children, who were incapable of greed and superstition, might be sanctified by it and initiated into simple faith in His word. To-day baptism is indeed of the highest advantage for them. For if this sacrament were administered only to grown-up people and older folk, I do not believe it could retain its power and beauty in the teeth of the overwhelming greed and superstition which have overthrown all religion among us. There is no doubt that carnal cunning would have devised its preparations and dignities, and then its reservations, restrictions, and what other traps there may be for catching money, until the font would have been sold for as high a price as parchment itself.[1]

But Satan, though unable to do away with the virtue of baptizing little children, has shown his power by putting an end to it among adults. To-day there is scarcely any one who calls to mind his own baptism, still less takes pride in it; because so many other ways have been found of getting sins forgiven and entering heaven. Jerome's dangerous saying, whether because it is ill-phrased or wrongly understood, has given occasion to these views. He speaks of penitence as the second plank after shipwreck,[2] as if baptism were

[1] A reference, of course, to the cost of the Indulgence tickets
[2] Cf. Epist. 130:9

not a sign of penitence. Hence those who have fallen into sin lose faith in the first plank, or the ship, as though it were lost; and they begin to trust and cling to the second plank, i.e., penitence. That situation has given rise to the innumerable impositions of vows, orders, works, satisfactions, pilgrimages, indulgences, and monastic sects; together with that torrent of books, questions, opinions, and man-made ordinances, for which the whole world has hardly room. The result is that the oppressiveness of this state of things reduces the church to an incomparably worse condition than was ever known to Jews or any other race under heaven.

The part of the pontiffs should have been to remove these things, and to strive with zeal to recall Christians to the integrity proper to baptized persons. These might then understand what manner of people they were, and how Christians ought to live. But, at the present time, the one endeavour of the popes is to remove the people as far away as possible from their baptism, plunge them all into an ocean of dictatorship, and cause the people of Christ, as the prophet said, to forget Him for ever.[1] Oh! unhappy are all they who bear the name of bishops nowadays; for not only do they not know what a bishop should be like, but they are not even aware what bishops ought to know or do. They fulfil what Isaiah 56 says: "His watchmen are blind; they are all ignorant; they are shepherds without knowledge; all have turned to their own way, each one to his gain."[2]

1. The first point about baptism is the divine promise, which says: "He that believeth and is baptized shall be saved."[3] This promise is far superior to all the outer show of works, vows, orders, and whatever else men have introduced. Our entire salvation depends on this promise, and we must be watchful to keep our faith in it knowing without any dubiety of mind that, once we have been baptized, we are saved. Unless faith is present, or comes to life in baptism, the ceremony is of no avail; indeed it is a stumbling-block not only at the moment we receive baptism but for all our life thereafter. For that kind of unbelief is equivalent

1 Jer. 2:32   2 Isa. 56:10f.   3 Mark 16:16

to accusing God of promises that cannot be trusted, and that is the greatest of all sins. When we first try to exercise faith in God's baptismal promises we shall immediately find how difficult it is to believe. Human nature in its infirmity and its consciousness of sin, finds it a most difficult thing to believe in the possibility of salvation. Yet, without believing it, men cannot be saved; and this just because they do not believe in the divine promise of salvation.

The people ought to have been taught this message, and this promise should have been assiduously repeated; baptism ought to have been constantly brought to mind, and faith should have been constantly aroused and cultivated. Once the divine promise has been accepted by us, its truth lasts till death; and similarly our faith in it must never falter, but must grow ever stronger until death, in abiding remembrance of the promise made to us in our baptism. Therefore, when we regain our faith, or repent of our sins, we are only returning to the strength and faith of baptism from which we fell when sin made us deserters. For the truth of this promise, once made, abides for ever, ready with outstretched arms to receive us when we return. And that, if I mistake not, is what they mean who say, but not clearly, that baptism is the prime sacrament, the foundation of them all, and without it none of the others can be received.

Hence it is no small benefit to a penitent first of all to remember his baptism. Let him recall the divine promise which he has abandoned, and confess it to the Lord. Let him rejoice to be still within the fortress of salvation, for it is still the case that he has been baptized; and let him abhor the impious ingratitude shown when he fell away from the faith and truth of his baptism. His heart will be wonderfully strengthened and inspired with the hope of mercy, if he will but keep in mind the divine promise which has been made to him. It is impossible for that promise to play false. Hitherto it has remained unbroken and unchanged, nor can it be changed by any sin. That is Paul's message in 2 Timothy 2: "If we do not believe, he remaineth faithful; he cannot deny himself."[1] This truth of God will preserve the penitent,

[1] 2 Tim. 2:13

so that if all else fail, this, if we believe in it, will not fail. In it, he possesses something which he can hold against a scornful enemy, something he can oppose to the sins which assault his conscience, something which is proof against the terrors of death and judgment. Finally, he has a solace in every temptation, in the unique truth, which he utters when he says: "God is faithful in His promises, and I received His sign when I was baptized. If God is for me who can be against me?"

When the children of Israel turned in penitence, they remembered, first of all, their exodus from Egypt; and in remembering this they returned to the God who had led them out. Moses constantly impressed this memory and this leadership on them, and David did the same. But how much more ought we to be mindful of our exodus from our Egypt, and, with that in mind, to return to Him who led us out through the baptism of rebirth which we are commanded to remember for this very purpose! This can be done most appropriately in the sacrament of bread and wine. Formerly the three sacraments of penitence, baptism, and the Lord's Supper, were celebrated with the same end; and they supplemented one another. Thus we read of a holy virgin, who, as often as she suffered temptation, made her baptism her sole defence; she said briefly, "I am a Christian." The enemy immediately perceived the power of baptism and of a faith which clings to the truth of a promise-keeping God, and fled from her.

In this way, you will see how rich a Christian is, i.e., one who has been baptized. Even if he wished, he could not lose his salvation however often he sinned, save only if he refused to believe. No sins have it in their power to damn him, but only unbelief. If his faith relies on the divine promise made at baptism, all things else are embraced by that same faith, nay by the truth of God; because He cannot deny Himself, if you confess Him and continue to cling to His promise. But "contrition" and "confession of sin" followed by "satisfaction", and all the other devices thought out by men, will desert you suddenly and leave you in distress, if you forget this divine truth and batten upon those things. Whatever

R

is done apart from faith in the truth of God, is vanity of vanities and vexation of spirit.

Similarly, you will see how dangerous, indeed false, it is to imagine that penitence is a plank to which you can cling after shipwreck; and how pernicious is the error of supposing that the power of baptism is annulled by sin, and that even this ship is dashed in pieces. Nay, that one ship[1] remains, solid and indestructible, and its timbers will never be broken to pieces. All who voyage in it are travelling to the haven of salvation, namely, the divine truth promised in the sacraments. True, it often happens that many people foolishly leap out of the ship into the sea, and perish. These are they who abandon faith in the promise and plunge themselves in sin. But the ship itself survives and, being seaworthy, continues on its course. If any one, by some gracious gift, is able to return to the ship, he is carried into life not by some plank, but by the well-found ship itself. One who returns to the abiding and enduring promise of God through faith is such a man. On this account, Peter, in 2 Peter 1, rebukes those who sin, because they are forgetful of the time when they were cleansed from their former sins;[2] doubtless reproving them for their ingratitude after accepting baptism, and for their disloyal impiety.

What is the use then of writing so much about baptism, and yet not teaching this faith in its promises? All the sacraments were instituted to feed our faith, but ungodly men never deal with faith sufficiently, but declare that no man can be certain of the forgiveness of his sins or of sacramental grace. By this sacrilegious doctrine they deprive the whole world of understanding. They lay hold of, nay totally deny, the sacrament of baptism on which stands the first glory of our consciousness as Christians. Meanwhile they talk in extravagant terms to the miserable people about "contritions", anxious "confessions", "circumstances", "satisfactions",

---

[1] Luther is using the metaphor of a ship, which was, and still is, very familiar in "catholic" tradition, and often applied to the church itself. There is therefore a certain amount of polemic here; but it is noticeable that the actual allegory is as appropriate in Luther's use as in that of tradition. Model ships are hung in the nave of (Lutheran) churches in Denmark. There is also one in a chapel in Portsmouth cathedral

[2] 2 Pet. 1:9

"works", and other such absurdities without end. Let
us be cautious, then, or rather scornful, in reading the
"Master of the Sentences"[1] in his fourth book, and all those
who copy him. At best they only write about the material
and form of the sacraments, that is they deal only with the
dead letter of the sacraments; but their spirit, life, and use,
or the truth of the divine promise and of our faith—this
they leave altogether untouched.

Be very cautious, then, lest you be deceived by the outward
show of works, and the deceitfulness of man-made ordinances, and lest you are thereby led to do wrong both to
the divine truth and your own faith. If you desire to be
saved, you must start from faith in the sacraments—anterior
to any works. The works will follow the faith, unless your
faith be too feeble. In fact, faith is the most excellent and
most difficult of all "works". You would be sustained by it
alone, if you were prevented from doing any others. For
faith is the work, not of man, but of God alone, as Paul
teaches. God does the other works through us and by us;
in the case of faith, He works in us and without our co-
operation.

These considerations show clearly the difference, as regards
the rite of baptism, between the ministry which man renders,
and the initiative which comes from God. For the man baptizes; and yet does not baptize. He baptizes in as far as he
performs the rite: he submerges the candidate. Yet, in
one sense, he does not baptize, but only acts on God's behalf,
and not on his own responsibility. Hence we ought to understand baptism at human hands just as if Christ Himself,
nay God Himself, baptized us with His own hands. The baptism which we receive through human hands is Christ's and
God's, just as everything else that we receive through
human hands is God's. Be careful, therefore, in regard to
baptism, to ascribe only the external rite to man, but the
internal operation to God. You may rightly ascribe both to
God, and regard the officiating person as the instrument
acting for God, through whom the Lord, sitting in heaven,

[1] Peter Lombard, who died A.D. 1160; one of the most famous of the
Schoolmen; *vide supra*, p. 240, n. 1

submerges you in the water with His own hands, and promises you forgiveness of your sins by a human voice speaking to you through the lips of His servant on earth.

The words themselves bear this out: "I baptize you in the name of the Father, and the Son, and the Holy Spirit, Amen." The minister does not say: "I baptize you in my name"; he says, as it were: "This which I am doing, I am not doing by my own authority, but in the stead and in the name of God; and what you receive is just the same as if the Lord Himself had given it visibly. The One who effects the work, and the one through whose agency it is done, are different; but the work of the two is the same; nay, I but minister on behalf of Him who is the sole Author." What is meant, in my view, is that the words, "in the name", refer to the person of the Author in such a way that it is not merely the case that the name of the Lord is only uttered or invoked during the rite; rather, the rite itself, far from being an act of the minister's, is done in the name and the stead of another. In Matthew 24 Christ speaks in the same mode: "Many shall come in my name";[1] and Romans 1 says: "Through whom we have received grace and apostleship, for the sake of obedience to the faith among all peoples, for His name's sake."[2]

I am glad to adopt this point of view because it gives a very complete support to our confidence and a real incentive to faith, to know that we are not baptized by human hands, but by the Holy Trinity itself through the agency of the man who performs the rite in Their name. This puts an end to that tiresome dispute about the words employed, and which are called the "form"[3] of the baptism. The formula of the Greek Church is: "May a servant of Christ be baptized"; and that of the Latin: "I baptize." Others again, sticking rigidly to their pedantry, condemn the use of the words, "I baptize thee in the name of Jesus Christ", although it is certain that the Apostles used that form in baptizing, as we read in the Acts of the Apostles.[4] They refuse to

[1] Matt. 24:5   [2] Rom. 1:5
[3] As distinct from the act of baptism which was called the "material"
[4] Acts 10:48

regard any as valid except: "baptize in the name of the Father, and of the Son, and of the Holy Spirit, Amen." The Romanists urge their point of view in vain; they bring no proofs, but only assert their own fabrications. The truth is that no matter in what words baptism is administered, as long as it is not in a human name but in the Lord's name, it surely saves. Indeed, I have no doubt that any one who receives it in the name of the Lord, even if the ungodly minister were not to give it in His name, would be truly baptized in the Lord's name. For the virtue of baptism lies not so much in the faith or practice of the administrator, as in that of the recipient. An instance is even recorded where an actor was baptized for a joke. Pointless disputes about questions of this kind are raised for us by those who lay no emphasis on faith, but all on works and the proper rites; whereas we lay all the stress on faith alone, and none on a mere rite; and this makes us free in spirit from all these scrupulosities and distinctions.

2. The second point in regard to baptism is that it is a sign or sacrament: an immersion in water, whence the name. For the Greek word *baptizō* means "immerse", or "plunge", and the word *baptisma* means "immersion". I have already said[1] that the divine promises were accompanied by signs to set forth what the words mean; or, as the moderns say, the sacrament has an effective significance. Let us consider what that means.

A great majority maintain that there is a certain spiritual virtue hidden in the word and the water, which operates in the soul of the recipient by the grace of God. Others, however, contend that there is no virtue in the sacraments themselves, but that grace is given by God alone, who is present by covenant at the sacraments which He has instituted. Yet all agree that the sacraments are effective signs of grace. They are moved to this conclusion by the single argument that they see no other reason why the sacraments of the New Law should take precedence over those of the Old Law if they are only signs. Hence they have been driven to

[1] Cf. *supra*, pp. 239ff.

attribute to the sacraments of the New Law something which makes them beneficial even to those who are in mortal sin. Neither faith nor grace are needed, it being enough if there is no obstacle imposed, i.e., no actual intention to sin anew.

Such contentions, however, are lacking in both reverence and faith; they are contrary to faith and to the nature of the sacraments, and therefore should be carefully avoided and shunned. For it is wrong to hold that the sacraments of the New Law differ from those of the Old Law in point of their effective significance. Both have the same meaning; for the God who now saves by baptism and the Supper, saved Abel by his sacrifice, Noah by the rainbow, Abraham by circumcision, and the others by their own signs. With regard to the meaning of the sacraments, there is no difference between those of the Old Covenant and those of the New, except that you may describe as belonging to the Old Law everything which God did among the patriarchs and their fathers at the time of the Law. For the signs which were given to the patriarchs and fathers should be widely distinguished from the legal form in which Moses instituted his law, such as the priestly customs regarding vestments, vessels, foods, houses, and the like. For these are very different, not only from the sacraments of the new law, but also from the signs which were given by God from time to time to the fathers who lived under the law; e.g., the fleece to Gideon,[1] the sacrifice in Noah's case, and that which Isaiah offered Ahaz in Isaiah 7.[2] Each of these was accompanied by a promise of some kind, and this demanded faith in God.

Thus the legal formulas differ from both the old and the new signs in that the legal forms are not accompanied by any word of promise which calls for faith. They are not signs of justification because they are not sacraments of faith, which alone justifies, but merely sacraments of works. Their entire force and nature consisted in the rite, not in faith. He who performed them fulfilled them, even when he performed them without faith. But our signs, and those given

---

[1] Judges 6:36ff.   [2] Isa. 7:10ff.

to the fathers, are accompanied by a word of promise demanding faith, the fulfilment being impossible by any other work. They are signs, or sacraments, of justification because they are sacraments of a justificatory faith, and not of works. The whole of their effectiveness lies in faith, and not in anything that is done. He who believes in them, fulfils them, even if nothing is done. This is the root of the saying: "Not the sacrament, but the sacramental faith, is what justifies." Accordingly, it was not circumcision that justified Abraham and his seed, although the apostle calls it the seal of the righteousness of faith;[1] rather, faith in the promise to which circumcision was attached, gave righteousness and implemented what the circumcision signified. For faith was the spiritual circumcision of the heart which was figured by the literal circumcision of the flesh.[2] What justified Abel was by no means his sacrifice, but his faith; for by this he gave himself up to God, and of this his sacrifice was only the outward figure.

Thus, baptism justifies nobody, and gives advantage to nobody; rather, faith in the word of the promise to which baptism was conjoined, is what justifies, and so completes, that which the baptism signified. Faith is the submersion of the old self and the emersion of the new self. Hence the new sacraments cannot differ from the old; both alike have the divine promises, and the spirit of faith is the same. But they differ incomparably from the old imagery by the word of promise which is the sole, but very effective, means of distinguishing them. So also at the present time, the showy display of vestments, the holy places, or the meals, together with the innumerable ceremonies, doubtless imply things that are to receive an impressive fulfilment in the realm of the spirit; yet, because they contain no word of a divine promise, they cannot be compared with the signs of baptism and the Supper. Neither do they confer righteousness, nor are they of any other advantage of that kind; because their purpose is fulfilled in the very use, or practice, of them, apart from faith. The apostle speaks of them accordingly in Colossians 2: "All which things are to perish in the using

---

[1] Rom. 4:11   [2] Deut. 10:16; Jer. 4:4

after the precepts and doctrines of men."[1] The sacraments are not fulfilled by the ritual, but only when they are believed.

Therefore it cannot be true that there resides in the sacraments a power capable of giving justification, or that they are the "signs" of efficacious grace. All such things are said to the detriment of faith, and in ignorance of the divine promises. They must be called efficacious, however, in the sense that, when faith is indubitably present, they most assuredly and effectively impart grace. That this is not the sense in which the Romanists say they are efficacious is proved by the assertion that sacraments do good to all, even to wicked and unbelieving men, provided these latter impose no obstacle to them. But this contention is as much as to say that unbelief itself is not the most obstinate and hostile of all obstacles to grace. In this way, the Romanists have put precepts in place of the sacraments, and works in place of faith. Now, if a sacrament were to give me grace just because I receive that sacrament, then surely I should obtain the grace, not by faith, but by my works. I should not gain the promise in the sacrament, but only the sign instituted and commanded by God. Thus you can see quite clearly that the sacraments have been completely misunderstood by the theologians who follow the *Sentences*. They offer no reason for either the sacramental faith or the sacramental promises. They stick to the sign, and to the use of the sign, thus seducing us from faith to works, and from the word to the sign. As I have said, they have not only taken the sacraments into servitude, but as far as possible abolished them.

Therefore, let us open our eyes, and learn to pay more attention to the word than to the sign, to faith than to works or ritual. We know that, wherever we meet a divine promise, there faith is required of us; and moreover that both are necessary, for neither is efficacious without the other. Belief is impossible without a promise to believe in, and a promise is void when it is not believed. But if both react on each other as they should, they bring about the true and indubitable

[1] Col. 2:22

efficacy of the sacraments. Therefore it is futile to look for an efficacious sacrament apart from promise and faith; it is, indeed, to fall into condemnation. Christ said: "He that believeth and is baptized shall be saved; but he that disbelieveth shall be condemned."[1] Here He points out that, in the sacrament, faith is necessary to such a degree that it can save even apart from the sacrament; that is why He did not add, after "He who disbelieveth", the words *"and is not baptized"*.

There are two things which baptism signifies, namely, death and resurrection, i.e., the fulfilling and completion of justification. For, when the minister submerges the child in the water, that signifies death; but, when he again lifts it out, that signifies life. That is how Paul explains it in Romans 6: "We were buried therefore with him through baptism into death; that, as Christ was raised from the dead through the glory of the Father, so we also might walk in newness of life."[2] We call this death and resurrection a new creation, a regeneration, a spiritual birth; and it ought not to be understood, allegorically, of the death of sin and the life of grace, as is the custom of many, but of a real death and a real resurrection. For the significance of baptism is not a matter of our imagination. Sin is not dead, nor is grace fully received, till the sinful body which we inhabit in this life is no more, as the apostle says in the same passage. For, while we are in the flesh, the desires of the flesh are active, and often stirred up. When we begin to have faith, at the same time we begin to die to this world and to live to God in the future life. Thus, faith is verily both death and resurrection; and this is that spiritual baptism into which we are submerged and from which we rise.

It is permissible to regard baptism as a washing away of sin, but this meaning is too slight and mild to express the full meaning of baptism, which is, rather, symbolical of death and resurrection. For this reason I would that those who are to be baptized were wholly submerged in the water, as the term implies and the mystery signifies; not that I consider it necessary to do so, but that I consider it to be a

[1] Mark 16:16   [2] Rom. 6:4

beautiful act to give the sign of baptism as fully and completely as possible. It represents something complete and full, and without doubt it was so instituted by Christ in the form of total immersion. A sinner requires, not so much to be washed, as to die. This is in order that he should be reborn and made another creature, and that the rite may correspond with the death and resurrection of Christ. Then through baptism the sinner would, as it were, also die and rise again. Though you may say that Christ was washed clean of His mortality when He died and rose again, yet the expression is less forceful than if you were to say that He was totally transformed and renewed. Thus there is more vigour in our form of words if we say that to us our baptism means to die utterly and in every way, and to rise to eternal life, than merely that we are washed from our sins.

Here again you will see that the sacrament of baptism, even as a sign, is not a momentary action, but something permanent. While the rite itself is quite transitory, yet the purpose which it signifies lasts till death; indeed till the resurrection at the last day. That which baptism signifies, operates as long as we live, i.e., every day we die, and every day we rise again. We die, I say, not merely mentally and spiritually, in that we renounce the sins and vanities of the world; but, rather, we begin in fact to leave this mortal body and to lay hold on the future life. In this way, we experience what they call a "real" and bodily transition from this world to the Father.

We must beware of those who have weakened and diminished the force of baptism, and, while declaring it true that grace is infused into us, yet maintain that, through our sin, this grace gradually disappears. Then we are compelled to go to heaven by some other route—as if our baptism had now become quite inoperative. You must not adopt that view. You must understand baptism to mean something by which evermore you die and live; and, therefore, whether you use the confessional, or any other means of grace, you must still return to the very power that baptism exercises, and begin again to do what you were baptized for, and what your baptism signified. But baptism never does lose its efficacy—not so long as you refuse to despair of reaching salvation. It is true that you may wander awhile from the sign, but that does not make the sign impotent. Although you only receive the sacrament of baptism once, you are continually baptized anew by faith, always dying and yet ever living. When you were baptized, your whole body was submerged and then came forth again out of the water. Similarly, the essence of the rite was that grace permeated your whole life, in both body and soul; and that it will bring you forth, at the last day, clothed in the white robe of immortality. It follows that we never lose the sign of baptism nor its force; indeed we are continually being rebaptized, until we attain to the completion of the sign at the last day.

You will perceive, therefore, that whatever kind of life we live, if it serves for the mortification of the flesh and the vivification of the spirit, it is relevant to our baptism. The sooner we depart this life, the more quickly we bring our baptism to its completion; and the worse our sufferings, the more fully we conform to our baptism. Similarly, the church was soundest when martyrs suffered death every day, and were accounted as sheep for the slaughter. At that time, the virtue of baptism was in full force in the church, whereas to-day we are actually unaware of that force, overwhelmed as we are by works and man-made doctrines. All our experience of life should be baptismal in character, viz., the fulfilment of the sign or sacrament of baptism. We have been freed from all else that we might devote ourselves to baptism alone, that is to say, death and resurrection.

Our splendid freedom, and our proper understanding of baptism, are in shackles to-day, and the blame can be laid at the door of the autocratic pontiff of Rome. As chief shepherd, it ought to be quite emphatically his first duty to preach this doctrine and defend this freedom; as Paul says, 1 Corinthians 4: "Let a man so account of us, as of ministers of Christ, and stewards of the mysteries or sacraments of God."[1] But the pontiff's only concern is with oppressing us with his decrees and laws, and in ensnaring and keeping us captive

[1] 1 Cor. 4:1

under his absolute authority. Without discussing the impious and indefensible fact that the pope omits teaching these mysteries, I ask most earnestly, By what right does he impose laws upon us? Who gave him power to deprive us of this liberty of ours which was given to us in our baptism? As I have already said, there is no greater duty set before us in the whole of our life than to be baptized, and so to die and live by our faith in Christ. This is the sole thing that should be taught, especially by the chief shepherd. But, to-day, faith is passed over in silence; the church is smothered by endless regulations about rites and ceremonies; the virtue and the knowledge of baptism have vanished; faith in Christ is obstructed.

Therefore I declare that neither pope, nor bishop, nor any one else, has the right to impose so much as a single syllable of obligation upon a Christian man without his own consent. Whatever is done otherwise is done autocratically. Therefore the prayers, fastings, donations, and whatever else the pope ordains and demands in the whole body of his decrees, which are as numerous as they are iniquitous, he has no right to demand and ordain; and he sins against the liberty of the church in so doing. The churchmen of to-day are most energetic guardians of "ecclesiastical liberty", in the sense of their freedom to use and possess the stones, timber, lands, and rents; for "ecclesiastical" has come to mean the same as "spiritual". By this same false terminology, they not only put the true liberty of the church into bonds but utterly destroy it. They have done worse than the Turks, and contrary to the apostle when he said: "Be ye not the servants of men."[1] But it is indeed to become servants of men when we are made subject to their statutes and tyrannical laws.

The disciples of the pope help on this impious and sinful despotism when they twist and debase in their own support Christ's words: "He that heareth you, heareth me."[2] For they puff out their cheeks, and cry up this passage on behalf of their usages. Yet Christ spoke these words to the apostles when they were going forth to preach the gospel and He meant them to refer to the gospel only; but the Romanists

[1] 1 Cor. 7:23   [2] Luke 10:16

leave out the gospel and apply the words only to their own fabrications. It says again, in John 10: "My sheep hear my voice, and the voice of another they do not hear."[1] The Romanists, therefore, leave out the gospel so that the popes may sound forth their own voice as if it were the voice of Christ Himself; nevertheless, it is their own voice which they sound, and yet they expect to get a hearing. But the apostle said that he had not been sent to baptize but to preach the gospel.[2] Therefore no one is subject to the papal traditions, nor is he required to obey the pope except when he is teaching the gospel and proclaiming Christ; and the pope ought not to teach anything except faith, and this is the freest of all things. Christ said: "He that heareth you, heareth me"; why then does not the pope hear others? It was not to Peter only that Christ said: "He that heareth you". In fine, where true faith abides, there of necessity must be also the word of faith. Why does not the pope, who is no believer, sometimes hear a servant of his who does believe, and who preaches faith? The pontiffs are nought but blind.

Other Romanists are even more shameless in their deductions from the passage in Matthew 16: "Whatsoever ye shall bind", etc.[3] They claim that here the pope is given authority to decree laws, whereas, in that passage, Christ was dealing with those sins which were to be retained, and those to be forgiven; He was not giving authority to take the whole church into captivity and oppress it by any laws. But this dictator of ours takes and falsifies everything with his lies, and forcibly twists and deforms the word of God. Yet, I must acknowledge that even this absolutism, accursed though it be, ought to be borne with by Christians, as is the case with every other act of violence in this world. Christ said: "Whosoever shall smite thee on thy right cheek, turn to him the other also."[4] But my complaint against those ungodly priests is that they can, and do, perform these deeds legally; and also they pretend, while doing so, to be seeking the welfare of Christendom with this Babylon of theirs; and they try to persuade everyone to believe this pretence. If they, on their part, do these things, and we, on our part, suffer their

[1] John 10:27   [2] 1 Cor. 1:17   [3] Matt. 16:19   [4] Matt. 5:39

violence, both sides being aware of its wicked and oppressive nature, then we should rightly count it among the things which contribute to the mortifying of this life, and the fulfilling of our baptism. In that case, our conscience might remain unhurt, and even rejoice in the wrongs we had suffered. But as it is, they wish to deprive us of our consciousness of liberty in such a way that we believe that what they do is well done; and that it is not permissible to censure it, or complain that what they do is evil. Just because they are wolves, they pretend to work like shepherds; and just because they are Antichrist, they wish to be honoured as Christ.

It is solely on behalf of this liberty that I cry aloud; and I do so with good conscience, and in the faith that it is not possible for either men or angels rightfully to impose even a single law upon Christians except with their consent; for we are free from all things. Yet, whatever the impositions may be, they are to be borne in such a way that we preserve liberty of conscience; the conscience that knows and affirms unhesitatingly that an injury is being done to it, even though it glories in bearing that injury. In this way we take precautions not to justify the tyranny, even though we do not murmur against it. "For who is it", asks St. Peter, "that will harm you if ye be followers of that which is good?"[1] "All things work together for good for the chosen."[2] Yet but few are aware of this glorious aspect of baptism, or know how happy is this practice of Christian freedom; the majority cannot know them on account of papal oppression. I hereby disentangle myself, and redeem my conscience, by laying this charge against the pope and all the Romanists, and say: If they do not abrogate their laws and traditions, restore proper liberty to the churches of Christ, and cause that liberty to be taught, then they are guilty of all the souls which perish in this miserable servitude; and that the papacy is identical with the kingdom of Babylon and the real Antichrist. For who else is the "man of sin" and the "son of perdition"[3] than he who, by his doctrines and statutes, increases sin and multiplies the loss of souls in

[1] 1 Pet. 3:13   [2] Rom. 8:28   [3] 2 Thess. 2:3

Christendom, while himself enthroned in the church as if he were God? All of this has been done to excess for many generations by papal absolutism. It has extinguished faith, beclouded the sacraments, suppressed the gospel, decreed laws which are not merely impious and sacrilegious but even barbarous and ignorant; and it has multiplied them without limit.

Consider, then, the wretchedness of our servitude. "How doth the city sit solitary that was full of people, and the mistress of the gentiles is become as a widow, the princess of provinces is laid under tribute! There is none to comfort her, even her friends spurn her", etc.[1] There are to-day as many ordinances, as many rites, as many sects, as many votaries,[2] as many anxieties and works, as there are Christians busied with them; and the result is that Christian people forget they have been baptized. Because of the multitude of locusts, caterpillars, and cankerworms, I say, no one is able to remember that he has been baptized or what benefits follow on baptism. We ought, when baptized, to have been like little children, who are not preoccupied with any cares or any works, but entirely free, redeemed, and safe merely through the glory of their baptism.

As against what I have been saying, it may be objected that, when infants are baptized, they cannot receive the promises of God; are incapable of accepting the baptismal faith; and that, therefore, either faith is not a requisite, or else it is useless to baptize infants. On this matter I agree with everyone in saying that infants are helped by vicarious faith: the faith of those who present them for baptism. The word of God, whenever uttered, is powerful enough to change the hearts even of the ungodly, and these are not less unresponsive and incapable than any infant. Further, all things are possible in response to the prayers of a believing church when it presents the infant, and this is changed, cleansed, and renewed, by their infused faith. Nor should I doubt that an irreligious adult could be transformed by any of the sacraments, if he were presented and prayed for by such a church; just as we read in the Gospel that the

<hr>

[1] Lam. 1:1f.   [2] Lat. *professiones*

paralytic was healed by vicarious faith.[1] For these reasons, I would readily admit that the sacraments of the new law are efficacious in giving grace, not only to those who offer no resistance, but even to those who resist most obstinately. What cannot the faith of the church and the prayer of believers remove, seeing it is believed that Stephen converted the apostle Paul by this power? In that case, however, the sacraments accomplish what they do, not of themselves, but by virtue of faith, without which they are without any effect, as I have said.

The question has been raised whether a child yet unborn could be baptized, if a hand or a foot were projecting from the womb.[2] On this point, I am uncertain what to say, and I confess my ignorance. Nor do I know whether it is satisfactory to assume, as the Romanists do, that the whole soul is in every part of the body; for it is not the soul, but the body that receives the outer baptism of water. But neither do I agree with those who say, quite insistently, that it is impossible for one not yet born to be reborn.[3] Therefore I leave this question to the further teaching of the Spirit; meanwhile, let each one follow his own judgment.

But there is one point I should like to add, of which I wish I could persuade the world, namely, that all vows whatsoever should be abolished or ignored, no matter whether "spiritual" vows,[4] or those about pilgrimages, or other works; and that we should remain in that most spiritual and active freedom which is given us by baptism. No one can say how much this excessively widespread delusion about vows detracts from the due value of our baptism, and darkens our knowledge of Christian freedom; to say nothing, for the time being, about the utterly innumerable and immeasurable dangers which are increased every day by the passion for vows, and by the unthinkable lightheartedness in which they are undertaken. Oh! you most ungodly priests and

---

[1] Matt. 9:2ff.; Mark 2:1ff.

[2] A curious example of arguments dear to the Schoolmen; actually put forward by Aquinas

[3] A quotation from Augustine: *non potest quisquam renasci antequam sit natus*

[4] E.g., on joining one of the religious orders

unfaithful pastors slumbering in security and wanton in greed, without any sympathy for the most serious and perilous "affliction of Joseph"![1]

A general edict would be needed in this case, abolishing all vows, especially those of a life-long character, and recalling everyone to his baptismal vows; either this, or else all should be earnestly advised not to take a vow temerariously. None should be invited to take them. It would be better if difficulties and delays were put in the way of taking vows. For the vows we took at our baptism were ample, more than we are able to keep. We shall have enough on our hands if we give ourselves to this duty alone. As matters stand, we compass sea and land to convert many, to fill the world with priests, monks and nuns, and to incarcerate them all under vows in perpetuity. On this point, there are some who assert and argue that a work done within the ambit of a vow is more valuable than a work outside, and takes precedence of it; and in heaven will be preferred to the others, and receive no one knows what reward. Oh! blind Pharisees who measure righteousness and sanctity by size, or number, or some such standard; although, in God's sight, it is measured solely by faith. In His sight, there is no difference between works except that of the measure of faith which they express. Ungodly men are very facile in the use of language, employing their own inventions to deck out man-made views and works, and to draw the unthinking masses on. These can usually be led on by the outer show of works, to the great detriment of faith, the oblivion of baptism, and the hurt of Christian freedom. Since a vow is a kind of law or obligation, it follows of necessity that, when vows are multiplied, laws and works are multiplied; whereas faith is blotted out, and our baptismal freedom is made captive. Others, not content with these alluring evils, add that the entry into a religious order is a kind of new baptism, and baptism may afterwards be repeated as often as the purpose of the "spiritual" life itself is again renewed. In this way, these votaries must take credit to themselves alone for their righteousness, holiness, and glory; and leave nothing at all

[1] Amos 6:6

S

whereby those who have only been baptized may bear comparison with themselves. To-day, the Roman pontiff, the fount and source of all superstitions, has used pompously-worded bulls and indulgences to confirm, approve, and embellish these ways of life; while no one thinks baptism worthy even of being remembered. And, as I have said, the Romanists drive the guileless people of Christ, by this specious outer show, into whatever giddy dangers are chosen for them, until the latter lose all gratitude for their baptism, and begin to think they are becoming better Christians by their works than others by their faith. Therefore God, on His part, shows Himself froward with the froward;[1] and punishes the ingratitude and pride of those given to vows; and so orders it that they do not fulfil their own vows, not even by the most strenuous labours, and although the votaries remain swamped under by them. Meanwhile they remain unaware of the grace given by faith and by baptism. And, because their spirit is unworthy in God's sight, He ordains that they persist in their hypocrisy to the end of time, yet never reaching righteousness. Thus they fulfil what Isaiah said, "The land is full of idols."[2]

Of course, I should not prohibit or discourage any one who, of his own choice, wished to make some vow in private, for I am far from despising or condemning vows as such; but I am altogether against the kind of votive life which is publicly established and instituted. To have a private liberty to make vows at one's own peril is enough. But I regard it as pernicious, both to the church and to ordinary people, to urge and commend a system of living publicly under the obligation of discharging a vow. I do this, first, because it is in no small degree repugnant to the Christian life; because a vow is a kind of ceremonial law, a mere human tradition, and arrogation of rights, from which the church has been delivered by baptism. Secondly, because the votive life is not commended in the Scriptures; particularly the vows of perpetual celibacy, obedience, and poverty. Now whatever cannot be supported by Scriptural example is fraught with danger; it should never be urged on any one, much less

---

[1] Ps. 18:26   [2] Isa. 2:8

set up for the public in general as a recognized mode
of life. On the other hand, it must be permitted to any one
to venture on it at his own peril. For certain special
works are wrought by the Spirit in a few, but such works
should not be cited as examples, or as a mode of life for
all.

But I fear very much that these ways of living under a
vow, as among the monastics, are of the sort which the
apostle foretold: "They shall teach lies in hypocrisy, forbidding to marry, and commanding to abstain from meats which
God hath created to be received with thanksgiving."[1] Nor
let any one face me with St. Bernard, St. Francis, St.
Dominic, and others who have founded orders, or augmented
them. God is terrible and marvellous in His counsels in
regard to the sons of men. He could preserve Daniel, Ananias,
Azarias, and Misael, one and all, when they were engaged in
administering the kingdom of Babylon (and when they were
surrounded by paganism); therefore, He is able to sanctify
those whose way of life is full of peril, or to control them
by some strange work of His Spirit, while yet not desiring
this to be a precedent for others. Further, it is certain that
not one of them was saved by his vows and his religiosity,
but only by faith, through which indeed all are saved. Pretentious lives, lived under vows, are more hostile to faith
than anything else can be.

However, on matters like these, everyone is fully entitled
to his own opinion. But let me continue the discussion I
have already begun. I now wish to speak up for the liberty
of the church and the glory of baptism. I feel that, for the
general good, I ought to give the counsel which I learnt
under the guidance of the Spirit. With this in mind, I would
suggest to those in high places in the church, firstly, that
they should do away with all vows and religious orders; or
at least not speak of them with approval or praise. If they
are unwilling to do this, I would urge all who wish to be
more certain of being saved to refrain from taking any vows,
especially those of great and life-long consequence, particularly in the case of youths in their teens and early

---

[1] 1 Tim. 4:2f.

twenties.[1] My first reason, as I have said, is that this kind
of life finds no testimony or support in Scripture, but has
been made to look imposing solely by the works of monks
and priests. However numerous, sacred, and arduous they
may be, these works, in God's sight, are in no way whatever
superior to the works of a farmer labouring in the field, or
of a woman looking after her home. Rather, all are measured
by Him by faith alone; as it says in Jeremiah 5, "O Lord,
thine eyes have respect unto faith",[2] and Ecclesiasticus 32,
"In all thy works believe with faith in thy heart, for this is
to keep the commandments of God."[3] Indeed, it occurs quite
frequently that the common work of a serving man or a
maid is more acceptable than all the fastings and other works
of monks and priests where faith is lacking. That is in fact
our present situation; vows only tend to the increase of pride
and presumption. It would almost seem, indeed, that nowhere
is there less of faith, or of the true church, than among the
priests, monks, and bishops; and that, in fact, these persons
are gentiles or hypocrites although they consider themselves
the church, or the heart of the church, and spiritual men
and rulers of the church, when really they are far from it.
These are in fact "the people of the captivity", who hold in
captivity the gifts given freely to us in baptism, while the
few poor "people of the land"[4] appear contemptible in their
eyes,[5] as also do those who are married.

From the foregoing, we may deduce two major errors of
the pope of Rome:

Firstly, that he grants dispensations from sworn vows, and
does it as if he alone among all Christians had authority,
such is human temerity and audacity. Surely, if he is able

[1] Luther took the vows at 22, and only after 20 years did he finally
abandon them. This was about the time of his marriage, and later than
several of his fellow reformers

[2] Jer. 5:3

[3] Ecclus. 32:27. The passage occurs in different places in different MSS.
of the Vulgate

[4] "People of the land" sounds very much like a reference to the "humble"
of the N.T., and to the position they occupied in the national economy;
poor (on the whole), despised, ignorant of, or in practice indifferent to,
the law, and therefore outside the Rabbinic scheme of salvation

[5] Cf. Ps. 64:1 and 2 Kings 24:14, in the Vulgate, for this vague reference
and parallel

to grant dispensations, then any Christian whatever may grant them, either to his neighbour or even to himself. If, however, the ordinary Christian has no power of dispensation, the pope has no right to it. Whence does he derive "authority"? From the possession of the keys? But the keys belong to all, and have to do only with the question of sin, Matthew 18.[1] Since the Romanists themselves admit that vows come within the divine law, why then does the pope cheat and ruin wretched men by granting dispensations in matters falling within the divine laws where there are dispensations? On the basis of the section in the decretals entitled "Of vows and their redemption",[2] he babbles away and claims that he has the power to alter vows. Formerly the Mosaic law taught that the firstling of an ass might be exchanged for a lamb; and the pope uses this permission as an analogy—as if the firstling of an ass were the same thing as a vow which requires to be fulfilled. Again, if the Lord in His own law decreed that a lamb should be exchanged for an ass, it scarcely follows that the pope, who is a man, has the same power of dealing with a law which not he, but God had made. It was not the pope who made this decretal, but, since it is so exceptionally crazy and impious, it must have been an ass masquerading as the pope.

Secondly, he greatly errs in decreeing that a marriage should be terminated if one of the parties enters a monastery without the consent of the other, and before the marriage has been consummated. By all that is holy, I ask which of the devils gave the pope this portentous power? God commanded men to keep faith, and to guard the truth towards each other; and, further, that a man should do good with what is his own, for God hates robbery for burnt offering, as He says through the mouth of Isaiah.[3] Now, in marriage, each of the parties owes fidelity to the other by their compact, and no longer is either his own. Neither has any right or power to break faith, and what either does alone,

---

[1] Matt. 18:15ff.
[2] *Decret. Greg.*, *lib.* III, tit. 24, cap. 7. The Decretals were amongst the first subjects on which Luther lectured when qualified in theology. By now he had been a close student of them for many years
[3] Isa. 61:8

against the will of the other, is a kind of robbery. And, further, why should it not be permitted, by the same ruling, that a man heavily in debt should enter, and be welcomed, into a religious order, and be freed from his debts, and be at liberty to break faith? O blind, blind men! Which is greater, fidelity commanded by God, or vows worked out and assumed by men? You, O pope, are a pastor of souls; and you, who teach these doctrines, are Doctors of Sacred Theology. Then why do you teach them? It is because you have extolled the votive life to appear superior to marriage, but not faithfulness, which is such as to exalt all things. Rather, you exalt works, which are as nothing in God's sight, or are all of equal worth as far as merit is concerned.

For myself, therefore, I am sure that neither men nor angels can grant dispensation in regard to vows rightly so called. On this point I am, for myself, not fully persuaded that all the vows that are made nowadays belong to the category of a vow. An example of this is that astonishingly ridiculous piece of folly wherein parents vow on behalf of a child, perhaps a baby and still unborn, that it should enter a religious order, or observe perpetual chastity. It is quite certain that this cannot be classed as a vow. Rather it seems to be a kind of mockery of God, since the parents' vows in no way lie within their province to perform. As to the religious orders, candidates themselves take three vows, which the more I study the less I understand; and I am puzzled to know the origin of the custom of taking these vows. Still less by far do I understand in what year of one's age it is possible to take vows, properly so called, and of a valid kind. It is a good thing that all agree that no vows are valid if taken before the age of puberty. Yet the Romanists deceive a large number of children on this point, who know nothing of the age of puberty, or of what they are vowing. Those who are receiving them leave the age of puberty out of account; nevertheless when these children make their profession, they are kept captive just as if their consent had been given in riper years; then they become the prey of uneasy consciences—it is all as if an invalid vow became valid at last by the passage of time.

To me it seems foolish for one group of people to fix a date when the vows of others will become operative, or to do this at a time when the votaries cannot prescribe for themselves. Nor do I see why a vow should be valid if taken after the eighteenth birthday, but not after the tenth or twelfth. It is not enough to say that, at eighteen, a person is aware of his sensual impulses. What about it if he scarcely feels them at twenty or thirty, or if they are stronger at thirty than twenty? And why not fix a date in respect of the vows of poverty and obedience? What age will you set for the feelings of greed and pride, seeing that even very spiritually-minded persons are scarcely aware of possessing these motives? It follows that there is no special age at which any vow becomes valid and binding, unless and until we shall have become spiritually-minded; but then, however, we should have no need of vows. It is obvious therefore that this is an uncertain and very dangerous matter; and it would be a counsel of safety to keep these lofty ways of life free of vows, and leave them to the Spirit only, as used to be done. They should never be transformed into ways of life to which one is bound for ever.

For the time being, however, I have said enough about baptism and the liberty pertaining to it. In due time, perhaps, I shall discuss the matter of vows at greater length,[1] and in very truth there is an urgent need of discussing them.

(3) *The Sacrament of Penance*

In the third section we are to discuss the sacrament of penance. I have already expounded at length my views on this subject in tracts and discussions which have been published but which have given considerable offence to many.[2] In the present instance, and for the sake of unveiling the tyranny which is as aggressive here as in the case of the sacrament of the bread, I must briefly repeat what I have said. On account of the many opportunities afforded by these two sacraments for money-making and self-seeking, the greed

---

[1] Cf. Luther's *de votis*, *W*., Vol. VIII, 573–669
[2] *Ablass und Gnade*; cf. *supra*, pp. 49ff.; *Sermo de Poenitentia*, *W*., Vol. I, 317–324; *Freiheit des Sermons*, *W*.,Vol. I, 380–393; etc.

of the shepherds has raged with unbelievable activity against Christ's sheep. As we have already seen in discussing vows,[1] baptism has largely lost its place among adults, with the result that papal greed has further opportunities of indulgence.

The first and principal evil connected with the sacrament of penance is that the sacrament itself has been made so utterly void that not a vestige of it remains. Like the other two sacraments I have already discussed, this also consists, on the one hand, of the words of the divine promise, and, on the other, of our faith. But the Romanists have undermined both. In conformity with their arrogance, they have adapted the words of promise in which Christ said, in Matthew 16, "Whatsoever thou shalt bind", etc.;[2] in 18, "Whatsoever ye shall have bound", etc.;[3] and in John 20, "Whose soever sins ye remit, they are remitted unto them", etc.[4] These words evoke the faith of penitents, and make them fit to receive forgiveness of sins. But in none of their books, teachings, or sermons, do the Romanists explain that these words of Scripture contain promises made to Christians; nor do they explain what things are to be believed, and what great comfort may be gained by doing so. Rather, their only object has been to extend their own dictatorship by force and violence as far, as widely, and as deeply as possible. At length, some have begun to command the angels in heaven;[5] they give themselves airs, in their incredibly rampant impiety, as if they had received in these words the right of ruling in heaven and earth, and of possessing the power of "binding" even in heaven. They say nothing about saving faith required of the people, but are garrulous about the absolute powers of the popes. Christ, however, said nothing at all about power, but spoke only of faith.

For Christ established in His church neither emperors, nor potentates, nor despots, but ministers—as we learn when the apostle says: "Let a man account of us as ministers of Christ and dispensers of God's mysteries."[6] When Christ says:

---

[1] Cf. *supra*, pp. 272ff., 275f., 279, n.1; *infra*, pp. 302, 303
[2] Matt. 16:19   [3] Matt. 18:18   [4] John 20:23
[5] Cf. The probably spurious bull of Clement VI in 1350, "We command the angels in paradise, &c"   [6] 1 Cor. 4:1

"Whosoever believes and is baptized, shall be saved",[1] this
is to evoke the faith of those about to be baptized, so that
they might have the assurance, based on this promise, that,
if they were baptized as believers, they would receive salvation. And, in founding this ceremony, He imparted no power
whatever. The only thing instituted was the service rendered
by those who perform the act of baptizing. Similarly, in the
place where it says: "Whatsoever thou shalt bind", etc.,[2]
Christ is calling out the faith of the penitent, by giving a
certitude based on the words of the promise, that, if he be
forgiven as a believer here below, his forgiveness holds good
in heaven. This passage makes no mention at all of conferring
power, but only deals with the service performed by the
administrator promising the words of forgiveness. It is very
remarkable that, by some chance, these blind and overbear-
ing men have not arrogated to themselves an oppressive
authority out of the baptismal promise. But if they have
not done so there, why have they presumed to do it in the
case of the penitential promise? Both are equally cases of
ministry, the promises being alike, and the sacraments of
the same sort. If baptism is not the right of Peter alone,
then it is a wicked imposition to arrogate the power of the
keys to the pope alone.

Similarly, when Christ says: "Take, this is my body which
is given for you. This is the cup in my blood", etc.,[3] the
eating calls forth the faith of the partakers, so that, when
their conscience has been confirmed by faith in these words,
they may have the certitude, as they eat, that their sins
are forgiven. Nor is there anything said here about power,
the administration being alone mentioned. Whereas the baptismal promise is still held valid so far as infants are concerned, the promise connected with the bread and the cup
has been annulled to minister to their avarice; instead
of faith we find works; and, for the testament, a sacrifice.
The penitential promise has been transformed into a most
outrageous instrument of tyranny, and a power of control
has been established greater than any in the temporal sphere.

Not content with this, our Babylon has so nearly put an

[1] Mark 16:16   [2] Matt. 16:19   [3] 1 Cor. 11:24f.

end to faith that it barefacedly denies the latter to be necessary in this sacrament. With an antichristian impiety, it even
defines as heretical any assertion that faith is necessary.
What more could be done by the arbitrary use of power
than they have already done? Truly, "by the rivers of
Babylon we sat and wept when we remembered thee, O Zion.
We hanged our harps upon the willows in the midst thereof."[1]
May the Lord curse the sterile willows growing by the rivers
which belong to men like that. Amen.

Promise and faith having thus been blotted out or sub-
verted, let us see what the Romanists have put in their place.
They have divided penance into three parts: contrition,
confession, and satisfaction; but they have done it in such
a manner as to set aside what was good in them in detail,
and have set up in each part the form of oppression which
they preferred.

In the first place, they teach contrition in such a way
that it not only takes precedence of faith in the promises,
but is held far superior. Indeed, they never mention faith.
They stick closely to works, and to those examples of it in
Scripture which tell of many who obtained rewards on
account of their heartfelt contrition and humility; but they
do not advert to the faith which effected that contrition
and remorse of heart; as it is written of Nineveh in Jonah 3,
"And the people of Nineveh believed in the Lord and proclaimed a fast."[2] Being more audacious and more wicked
than the Ninevites, these men have invented a kind of semi-
contrition which, by virtue of the keys (which they do not
understand), becomes contrition proper. This they present
to the ungodly and the unbelieving, and thereby entirely
abnegate the true contrition. O the unbearable wrath of God
in that these things are taught in the very church of Christ![3]
Faith and its works having been destroyed, we feel secure
when we adopt man-made doctrines and opinions, and so
we simply perish. For a contrite heart is a matter of very
great importance, but it is only found in connection with
an ardent faith in God's promises of reward and punishment.

[1] Ps. 137:1f.   [2] Jonah 3:5
[3] I.e., these false doctrines are themselves a punishment for sin

This faith, divining the unchangeableness of the truth of God, disturbs and reproves the conscience, and so renders it contrite; but, at the same time, it exalts and comforts that conscience, and so keeps it contrite. Wherever faith is found, the certainty of punishment causes contrition, and the trustworthiness of the promises is the means of consolation; and through this faith a man merits forgiveness of sin. Hence, faith takes precedence of all else as a thing needing to be taught and called forth. Once faith is present, contrition and divine comfort follow naturally and inevitably.

Therefore, although the Romanists are partly right in teaching that you will become contrite if you enumerate and examine your sins; yet that is a hazardous and perverse method of teaching. For they should previously teach the prime elements in, and causes of, contrition: the unchangeable character of the divine verities, whether of warning or promise. This teaching should be given in the way that will induce faith, so that they may understand the importance of having their minds centred on the divine truth; then they will be made humble and yet lifted up. This is far better than to meditate on one's seething sins, which, if considered before taking God's truth into account, will rather refresh and increase the desire for sin than produce contrition.[1] I shall not discuss at the present juncture that insurmountable and chaotic heap of labours which they impose upon us, when they formulate a special contrition for each and every sin; for this is to ask the impossible. Besides, we can only know the minor part of our sins; and, further, even our good works are found to be sins according to Psalm 143: "Enter not into judgment with thy servant; for in thy sight shall no man living be justified."[2] It is enough if we sorrow for those sins which are actually gnawing our consciences, and which can be easily recognized in the mirror of our memory. Anyone in this mood is undoubtedly prepared to feel sorrow and fear for all his sins; and he will sorrow and be afraid whenever they recur to his mind in the future. Therefore beware of confiding in your own contrition, or of attributing the forgiveness of your sins to

[1] An important contribution to the psychology of sin   [2] Ps. 143:2

your own remorse. God does not esteem you on account of these feelings, but on account of the faith by which you have believed in His admonitions and His promises, and which causes its own kind of remorse. From all that I have said, it follows that none of the virtue of penitence is due to the diligence with which we have recollected and enumerated our sins, but only to God's fidelity and to our faith.[1] All the rest are works and fruits which are produced afterwards spontaneously. These do not reform a man's character; rather, they are the things a man does after he has been regenerated by faith in God's faithfulness. So it is that "a smoke went up in his wrath, and because he was wroth he shook the mountains and kindled them", as it says in Psalm 18.[2] Fear of His warnings comes first, and this burns up the wicked; but faith, which accepts the warnings, sends up contrition like a cloud of smoke, etc.

Contrition, however, has suffered less from unbridled power and greed than from ungodliness and pestilential doctrines, to which, indeed, it has fallen a total prey. Confession and satisfaction, on the other hand, have been made into an egregious factory of money and power.

First, in regard to confession:

Without doubt, confession of sins is necessary, and in accordance with the divine commandments. In Matthew 3, we read that they "were baptized by John in the Jordan confessing their sins";[3] and I John I, "If we confess our sins, he is faithful and just to forgive us our sins. If we say that we have not sinned, we make him a liar, and his word is not in us."[4] If it was not permissible for the saints to deny their sins, how much more obligatory is it for those guilty of great and open sins to confess them. Most conclusively of all, the institution of confession is proved by Matthew 18, where Christ teaches that a brother who is doing wrong should be reproved, brought before the church, and accused; and then excommunicated if he will not listen. But he can be said "to hear" when, heeding the correction, he acknowledges and confesses his sin.[5]

---

[1] This doctrine of penitence is often neglected in spite of its perspicacity. It also adds much to our understanding of Luther's doctrine of faith
[2] Ps. 18:8, 7   [3] Matt. 3:6   [4] I John 1:9f.   [5] Matt. 18:15ff.

As for secret confession as practised to-day, though it cannot be proved from Scripture, yet it seems a highly satisfactory practice to me; it is useful and even necessary. I would not wish it to cease; rather I rejoice that it exists in the church of Christ, for it is a singular medicine for afflicted consciences. If we lay bare to a brother what lies on our conscience, and in confidence unveil that which we have kept hidden, we receive, through the mouth of a brother, a comfort which God has spoken. When we accept this in faith, it gives us peace by the mercy of God through the words spoken to us by a brother. What I reject is solely that this kind of confession should be transformed into a means of oppression and extortion on the part of the pontiffs. For they "reserve" to themselves even the secret sins, and order them to be made known to confessors nominated by themselves, of course to the torment of consciences. They not merely play at being pontiffs, but utterly scorn the true duties of a pontiff, which are to preach the gospel and to care for the poor. Nay, the impious despots reserve to themselves those trespasses which are mostly of little moment; while the greater, sure enough, they leave everywhere to the common run of priests. Of the former class are the ridiculous kind fabricated in the bull, *"Coena domini"*. Indeed, as if in order that their wicked perversity might become the more obvious, not only do they not reserve, but even teach and approve, things which are adverse to the worship of God, to the faith, and to the chief commandments. One might specify such things as running about on pilgrimages, the perverse worship of saints, the mendacious legends of saints, various beliefs in works and in the practice of ceremonies; by all of which, faith in God is lessened, while idolatry is fostered, as is the case nowadays. The result is that, now, all our pontiffs are of the kind that Jeroboam formerly instituted in Dan and Beersheba.[1] They were to serve the golden calves, but they knew nothing of God's laws, of faith, or of anything that pertained to shepherding Christ's sheep. But, by practising what they themselves invented, they oppressed the people by fear and violence.

[1] I Kings 12:26ff.

Now, I urge that these "reservations", that have been imposed upon us by force, should be borne patiently, just as Christ commanded us to bear all forms of oppression, and taught us to obey such despots. Nevertheless I deny, and I refuse to credit, that Romanists have any right to make these reservations, or that they can prove a single jot or tittle of them; whereas I myself can prove the opposite. In the first place, in Matthew 18, when speaking of known transgressions, Christ taught us that we had gained the soul of our brother if he listened when corrected; and that he was not to be haled before the church unless he refused to hear us. It must therefore be all the more relevant to secret sins, that they would be forgiven if voluntarily confessed by one brother to another. It follows that it is unnecessary for this kind of sin to be brought before the church: the prelate or priest as they pretentiously interpret the term. We have Christ's authority in this passage, as also in another, where He says, to the same effect: "Whatsoever ye shall bind on earth shall be bound in heaven and whatsoever ye shall loose on earth shall be loosed in heaven."[1] This is said to Christians individually and collectively. He said the same thing again when He declared: "Again I say unto you, that if two of you shall agree on earth as touching anything that they shall ask, it shall be done for them of my Father which is in heaven."[2] Similarly, in the case of the brother who lays bare his secret sins before his fellow and seeks forgiveness, he is assuredly at one in the truth with his brother on earth, and that truth is Christ. Christ speaks even more plainly on this point, confirming what has been said, when He declares: "Of a truth I say unto you, where two or three are gathered together in my name, there am I in the midst of them."

In view of the foregoing, there is no doubt in my mind that a man's secret sins are forgiven him when he makes a voluntary confession before a brother in private, and, on reproof, he asks for pardon and mends his ways. No matter how much any pope may rage against these contentions, the fact is that Christ manifestly gave the power of pronouncing forgiveness to anyone who had faith in Him. As

[1] Matt. 18:18   [2] Matt. 18:19

a minor argument in support, it may be said that, if it were valid to "reserve" any secret sins in such a way that, unless they were forgiven, the transgressor were not saved, then the good works and superstitious acts of worship noted above would prove the greatest hindrance to attaining salvation, in spite of their being inculcated by the popes at the present day. Because if the very weighty matters are not a hindrance, surely there is far less reason for foolishly reserving the smaller matters. Such are the astonishing things which the ignorance and blindness of the shepherds bring about in the church. Therefore, I would admonish those princes in Babylon, and bishops in Bethaven,[1] firstly, to refrain from making reserved cases of any kind; and, secondly, to give free permission for any brother or sister to hear confessions of secret sins. The result would be that one who has done wrong might lay bare his sin to whomsoever he chooses, and beg absolution, comfort, and Christ's very word from the mouth of his neighbour. For the only object of the Romanists, in their temerity, is to entrap the consciences of the weak-willed, to confirm their own powers of oppression, and to gain satisfaction for their greed out of the sins and failures of their brethren. Thus they stain their hand with the blood of men, with souls, and children are devoured by their parents. Ephraim shall devour Juda, and Syria Israel, and not be satisfied, as Isaiah says.[2]

To these evils they have added the "circumstances", in detail; the "mothers", "daughters", "sisters", "sisters-in-law", "branches" and "fruits", worked out, if you please, by these most perspicacious men who have nothing else to do, into a kind of family tree of sins, with consanguinities and relationships; such is the fertility of irreligion and ignorance. No matter what good-for-nothing may have invented it, this kind of conception passes into the public law, like much else. The shepherds watch over the church of Christ in such a way that, whatever new superstitions or works may have entered the heads of these stupid devotees, they are immediately published, and even decked out with indulgences, or fortified by bulls. That shows how remote they

[1] Hos. 4:15 and 10:5   [2] Isa. 9:20f.

are from prohibiting these things, and guarding faith and liberty for the people of God. For what is there in common between liberty and a despotic Babylon?

I would urge, no matter what the "circumstances", that they should be altogether passed over. Among Christian people there is only one "circumstance": it is, that a brother has sinned. No other person can be compared in importance with a Christian brother; nor will any reference to places, seasons, days, or any other rank superstition, do anything else than magnify things which matter nothing, to the hurt of those which matter everything. It is impossible for anything to be of greater weight and importance than the glory of Christian fellowship. But they tie us down to places and days and persons till the name of "brother" loses its value, and we serve, not in freedom, but in bondage, we to whom days, places, persons, and whatever else is external, are all on the same level.

In regard to "satisfaction", how unworthily the Romanists have dealt with it! I have discussed it in detail in dealing with indulgences.[1] They have abused it to an extraordinary extent, to the ruin of Christians in body and soul. In the first place, they have expounded it in such a manner that the people in general have not the slightest understanding of the true satisfaction, although it means the renovation of life. Moreover, they are so insistent on satisfaction, and construe it as necessary in such a way, that they leave no room for faith in Christ. With consciences pitilessly tortured by scruples on this point, one person runs to Rome, another here, and yet another there; this man to Chartreuse,[2] that to some other place; one flays himself with rods, while another is mortifying his body with vigils and fasting. Under the same delusion, all are crying: "Lo! here is Christ, and lo! there", and thinking that the kingdom of Christ, though it is within us, will come with observation. These monstrous things we owe to thee, O thou whose seat is in Rome, together with thy soul-destroying laws and rituals. By these enormities,

---

[1] Cf. *supra*, pp. 49ff.
[2] Where the first Carthusian monarchy was founded in 1086. Luther often attacked its strict rules: perpetual silence, solitude, complete vegetarianism

thou hast brought the world into such disorder that men think they can propitiate God for their sins by means of their works, whereas He is propitiated only by faith in the contrite heart. But thou dost not only silence faith by means of this restlessness, but even suppress it. Thy insatiable horse-leech then has some to whom it may cry, "Give, give", and to whom it may now sell sins.

Some Romanists have gone further, and have contrived machinations for driving souls to despair. They have decreed that if the satisfactions enjoined for any sins have not been duly fulfilled, all those sins must be confessed afresh. But there is no limit to the temerity of men who were bred to imprison their victims ten times over. Further, what is the proportion of those imbued with the idea that they are among the saved, and have made atonement for their sins if they have mumbled the words of the prayers enjoined by the priest, although, meanwhile, it never struck them to amend their mode of life? Their belief is that their lives were changed at the time of their contrition and repentance, the only further condition being that they should make satisfaction for the sins they have committed. How can they think otherwise when they have not been taught anything else? Not a thought is given to the mortification of the flesh. No value is attached to the example of Christ who, when He forgave the woman taken in adultery, said: "Go and sin no more",[1] thus imposing the cross, which meant mortifying the flesh. Considerable excuse has been given for perverted notions by the custom of pronouncing absolution to sinners before they have completed their "satisfaction". Hence it comes about that they are more concerned about fulfilling their "satisfaction", which is a lasting thing, than they are about contrition, which they believe was over and done with when they confessed. In the early church, on the other hand, absolution was posterior, and was only given when satisfaction had been completed. Thus it arose that, once the works had been completed, the penitents were exercised more fully in the faith and newness of life.

But, in regard to these matters, it must suffice to repeat

[1] John 8:11

T

what I have said in greater detail in connection with the subject of indulgences.[1] In any case I have said enough for the time being about these three sacraments, which are both discussed, and yet not discussed, in so many noxious books on the Sentences and the laws. It remains to say a few words on the rest of the sacraments, lest I should needlessly appear to have rejected them.

(4) *Confirmation*

It is difficult to understand what the Romanists had in mind when they made the sacrament of confirmation[2] out of the laying on of hands. We read that Christ touched the children in that way, and by it the apostles imparted the Holy Spirit, ordained presbyters, and cured the sick;[3] as the apostle wrote to Timothy: "Lay hands hastily on no man."[4] Why have they not made a "confirmation" out of the sacrament of the Lord's Supper? It is written in Acts 9, "And he took food and was strengthened";[5] and, in Psalm 104, "And bread strengtheneth man's heart."[6] On this reasoning, confirmation would include three sacraments—the Supper, ordination, and confirmation itself. But this argument suggests that anything whatever that the apostles did was a sacrament; but, in that case, why did the Romanists not make a sacrament of preaching?[7]

I am not saying this because I condemn the seven sacraments as usages, but because I deny that it can be proved from Scripture that these usages are sacraments. O would that there were in the church the kind of laying on of hands that obtained in the time of the apostles, whether we preferred to call it confirmation or healing! But nothing of this

---

[1] Cf. *supra*, pp. 49ff.
[2] "Confirmation" means "strengthening", and much of Luther's argument in this section depends on an almost Elizabethan play on the conventional and the etymological meanings of the term. As usual, he prefers the original meaning, and argues for its validity now
[3] Mark 10:16; Acts 8:17, 19:6, 6:6
[4] 1 Tim. 5:22
[5] Acts 9:19
[6] Ps. 104:15
[7] The language is very terse, and requires much expansion for clarity when translated into English. The full depth of the argument cannot be plumbed, until the whole of this section has been read

remains nowadays, except what the Romanists have devised to embellish the duties of bishops, lest they be entirely without function in the church. For, after the bishops had ceased themselves to administer those sacraments which, together with preaching the gospel, would have been truly work of value, but which they regarded as inferior; and after they had handed these functions to assistants (probably because what the divine Majesty had instituted must be contemptible to men!), it was only right that something new should be introduced, that would be easy and not so very vexatious to these high and mighty supermen; and also that we should never treat the innovation as if it were something common, and commit it to subordinates. The argument is that what has been set up by the wisdom of men ought to be reverenced by men. The ministry any priest exercises, and the office he fills, should correspond in quality to that of the man himself. A bishop who neither preaches nor practises the cure of souls is nothing at all but an idol, in spite of the name and appearance of a bishop. This, however, is a digression; our present inquiry has to do with the nature of the *sacraments of divine institution, and we find no reason for enumerating confirmation among them.*[1] What is required above all else for constituting a sacrament is that it should be accompanied by a divine promise, and this, of itself, calls for our faith. But nowhere do we read that Christ gave a promise in regard to confirmation, although He placed His hands on many people. Among other relevant passages, we read in Mark 16, "They shall lay hands on the sick and they shall recover."[2] But no one has turned this into a sacrament, because it is impossible.

For these reasons, it is enough to regard confirmation as a rite, or ceremony, of the church, like the other ceremonies of the consecration of water, and similar things. If in all other cases physical objects may be sanctified by preaching and prayer, surely there is greater reason for thinking that a man may be sanctified by them. Nevertheless, since sermons and prayers for these purposes are not mentioned in Scripture as accompanied by a divine promise, they cannot

[1] The italics, in effect, are Luther's   [2] Mark 16:18

be called sacraments in which we must have faith; nor are they helpful in promoting salvation from sin. On the other hand, by their very nature, sacraments save those who believe the divine promises always attaching to them.

(5) *Marriage*

There is no Scriptural warrant whatsoever for regarding marriage as a sacrament; and indeed the Romanists have used the same traditions, both to extol it as a sacrament, and to make it naught but a mockery. Let us look into this matter.

We have maintained that a word of divine promise is associated with every sacrament, and anyone who receives the sacrament must also believe in that word of promise, for it is impossible that the sign should in itself be the sacrament.[1] But nowhere in Scripture do we read that anyone would receive the grace of God by getting married; nor does the rite of matrimony contain any hint that that ceremony is of divine institution. Nowhere do we read that it was instituted by God in order to symbolize something, although we grant that all things done in the sight of men can be understood as metaphors and allegories of things invisible. Yet metaphors and allegories are not sacraments, and it is of sacraments that we are speaking.

There has been such a thing as marriage itself ever since the beginning of the world, and it also exists amongst unbelievers to the present day. Therefore no grounds exist on which the Romanists can validly call it a sacrament of the new law, and a function solely of the church. The marriages of our ancestors were no less sacred than our own, nor less real among unbelievers than believers. Yet no one calls marriage of unbelievers a sacrament. Also, there are irreligious marriages even amongst believers, worse than among any pagans. Why then should it be called a sacrament in such a case, and yet not among pagans? Or are we talking the same sort of nonsense about marriage as about baptism and the church, and saying it is only a sacrament within the

---

[1] Cf. *supra*, pp. 239f.

church? Is it the case that some people speak as if they were demented, and declare that temporal power exists only in the church? Yet this is so childish and laughable as to expose our ignorance and foolhardiness to the ridicule of unbelievers.

The Romanists will reply that the apostle says in Ephesians 5, "The twain shall become one flesh; this is a great sacrament."[1] Do you mean to contradict this plain statement of the apostle? My reply would be that to put forth this argument shows great negligence, and very careless and thoughtless reading. Nowhere in Holy Scripture does the noun, "sacrament", bear the meaning which is customary in the church, but rather the opposite. In every instance, it means, not "a sign of something sacred", but the sacred, secret, and recondite thing itself. Thus in 1 Corinthians 4, Paul says: "Let a man so account of us, as of ministers of Christ, and stewards of the mysteries of God", that is the sacraments.[2] Where the Vulgate uses *sacramentum*, the Greek text reads *mysterion*, a word which the translator sometimes translates, and sometimes transliterates. Thus in the present case, the Greek says: "The twain shall become one flesh. This is a great mystery." That explains how it came about that they understood it as a sacrament of the new dispensation, and this they would have been far from doing if they had read *mysterion*, as it is in Greek.

So also in 1 Timothy 3, Paul calls Christ Himself a sacrament, when he says: He was evidently a great sacrament (i.e., *mysterion*), for He was manifested in the flesh, justified in the spirit, seen of angels, preached among the nations, believed on in the world, received up in glory.[3] Why have the Romanists not made an eighth sacrament out of this, when Paul's authority is so plainly there? Although they restrained themselves in this instance, when they had abundant opportunity to contrive sacraments, why are they so extravagant in the others? Plainly, they have been betrayed by their ignorance both of the facts and of the vocabulary; going simply by the sound of the words, they have founded their own opinions on them.[4] Once they had arbitrarily taken

[1] Eph. 5:31f. The English versions reproduce the Greek word, *mystery*, which Luther in fact proceeds to discuss
[2] 1 Cor. 4:1   [3] 1 Tim. 3:16   [4] Lit., "they stick to their own opinions"

"sacrament" to mean "sign", they immediately, and without
further criticism or closer examination, set down the word
"sign" every time they read "sacrament" in Holy Scripture.
In this manner also, they have brought verbal meanings,
human customs and such like, into the sacred writings, trans-
forming the proper meaning into what they themselves have
fabricated, turning anything into anything else. Thus it
comes about that they are always making a vague use of terms
like "good works", "evil works", "sin", "grace", "justification", "virtue", and almost all the main terms and subjects.
For they employ the whole of these arbitrarily, on the basis
of writings which are merely human, to the detriment of
God's truth and our salvation.

According to Paul, sacrament, or mystery, is the very wisdom of the Spirit, and this is hidden in the mystery, as he
says in 1 Corinthians 2: "This wisdom is Christ, and, for the
reason just given, He is unknown to the rulers of this world;
and therefore they crucified Him. To them, He is still foolish-
ness, a scandal, a stumbling-block, and a sign to be contro-
verted."[1] "Stewards of the mysteries" is the name given by
Paul to those preachers who preach Christ and proclaim Him
as the power and the wisdom of God,[2] and this in such a way
that, unless you believe, you will not understand. Thus a
sacrament is a *mysterion*, a secret thing described by words,
but seized by faith in the heart. That is what is said in the
passage under discussion: "The twain shall be one flesh, this
is a great sacrament" (Greek—*mysterion*). The Romanists
think this was said of matrimony, whereas Paul himself is
using these words about Christ and the church, as he himself goes on to explain clearly when he says: "But I speak
of Christ and of the church."[3] You see, then, the nature of
the agreement between the Romanists and Paul? Paul says
that he is speaking of the great sacrament in Christ and the
church; they, however, preach it in terms of male and female.
If it were permissible to handle Scripture in this unbridled
fashion, there would be no room for surprise whatever sacrament they found in it, nor even if they found a hundred.

We conclude that Christ and the church are a "mystery",

[1] 1 Cor. 2:7ff.   [2] 1 Cor. 4:1   [3] Eph. 5:32

or something at once hidden and of great importance, a thing which can, and should, be spoken of metaphorically, and of which matrimony is a sort of material allegory; but matrimony ought not to be called a sacrament on this account. The heavens are meant to represent the apostles in Psalm 19, and the sun is metaphorically Christ, and the seas the people;[1] but this does not mean that they are sacraments. There is no mention of either a divine institution, or a promise, which together would constitute a sacrament. Therefore Paul, in Ephesians 5, either quotes Genesis 2 for the words about marriage, and applies them on his own initiative to Christ;[2] or else, according to prevailing opinion, he teaches that the spiritual marriage of Christ is contained here, when he says: "Even as Christ cherisheth the church, because we are members of His body, of His flesh, and of His bones. For this cause shall a man leave his father and mother, and shall cleave to his wife; and the twain shall become one flesh. This mystery is great, but I speak in regard of Christ and of the church."[3] You see that Paul means this whole passage to have been spoken by him about Christ, and he takes pains to warn the reader to understand that the sacrament is not in the marriage but in Christ and the Church.[4]

[1] Ps. 19:1ff.　　[2] Eph. 5:23ff.; Gen. 2:24　　[3] Eph. 5:29ff.

[4] At this point, a passage from some other writing of Luther's has been interpolated. It clearly breaks the context, and is out of position here. A footnote in *W.*, VI, p. 552, says it appears to have been introduced here by mistake. I have therefore followed the example of modern scholars in relegating the interpolation to a footnote as follows:

"Of course, I agree that there was a sacrament of penance in the Old Law, and that it was so from the beginning of the world. But the new promise for penitence and the gift of the keys are peculiar to the New Law. Instead of circumcision, we now have baptism, and, similarly, instead of sacrifice, or other signs of repentance, we have the keys. I have already said that the same God gave different promises and different signs at different times, in regard to the forgiveness of sins and the salvation of men; yet all received the same grace. Thus, in 2 Cor. 4 Paul says: 'Having the same spirit of faith, we also believe, and therefore also we speak.' And in 1 Cor. 10: 'Our fathers did all eat the same spiritual meat and did all drink of the same spiritual drink; for they drank of a spiritual rock that followed them; and the rock was Christ.' Similarly, Heb. 11: 'And these all, being dead, received not the promise, God having provided some better thing concerning us, that apart from us they should not be made perfect. For Christ is yesterday, to-day, and forever, Himself the head of His Church from the beginning even to the end of the world.' Thus the signs vary, but the faith is the same in every case, because without faith it is impossible to please God, yet it is that by which Abel pleased Him, Heb. 11."—ED.

Granted, therefore, that matrimony is a figure for Christ and the church, yet it is not a sacrament of divine institution; it was introduced into the church by men who were misled by their ignorance both of the subject and the record. But, if this fact is not a hindrance to faith, it ought to be borne with in a charitable spirit, just as many other human devices due to weakness and ignorance in the church are to be tolerated so long as they do not stand in the way of faith and the Holy Scriptures. But at the present moment we are arguing on behalf of the certainty and purity of faith and the Scriptures. Our faith would be exposed to scoffing if we affirmed that something was contained in the Holy Scriptures or in the articles of our faith, which was later proved not to be there. Then we should be found unversed in our own special province, causing difficulties to our enemies[1] and to the weak; but most of all we should detract from the authority of the Holy Scriptures. For there is a very great difference between what has been handed down about God in the Holy Scriptures, on the one hand; and, on the other, that which has been introduced into the church by men of no matter what sanctity or learning. Thus far about matrimony as a rite.

What then shall we say about those impious, man-made laws in which this divinely instituted way of life has become enmeshed, and which have sometimes exalted, and, at others, debased it? Merciful God! what a dreadful thing it is to examine the temerity of the Romanizing oppressors who divorce couples, or enforce marriages, just according to their own sweet will. I ask in all earnestness: Has the human race been handed over to the good pleasure of these men to be made sport of, to be subjected to any sort of misuse, and for the sake of whatever filthy lucre they can make out of it?

A greatly esteemed book entitled the *Summa Angelica*[2]

[1] The meaning of this clause is obscure; cf. *Martin Luther Ausgewählte Werke*, ed. Borcherdt and Merz, Vol II; 1520. Munich, 1948, p. 228

[2] The *Summa Angelica* of Angelus de Clavassio Chiavasso in Liguria (died 1495), published 1486, one of the favourite handbooks of casuistry, in which all possible cases of conscience were treated in alphabetical order. It was among the papal books burned by Luther, together with the bull, Dec. 10, 1520 (cf. Luther's letter to Spalatin on the same day, *Br.* Vol. II, pp. 234f., and 235, n. 2). The work has now gone to the limbo of things forgotten and unwept

enjoys a wide circulation, but it consists of a jumbled collection, a kind of bilge-water, of the offscourings of all that
men have handed down. It would more appropriately be
called the *Summa worse than Diabolical*. It contains numberless horrible things by which confessors think they receive
instruction, whereas they are led into most pernicious confusion. It enumerates eighteen impediments to marriage; but,
if you will examine them with the unbiassed mind and the
uncensored view given by faith, you will see that a number
of them are foretold by the apostle when he said: "They
shall give heed to the spirits of devils, who shall speak lies
in hypocrisy, forbidding to marry."[1] Is not the invention of
so many impediments, and the setting of so many traps,
the reason that people do not marry; or if they are married,
the reason why the marriage is annulled? Who gave this
power to man? It may be that they were religious men,
zealous and devout, yet by what right does another man's
saintliness put limits on my own liberty? Let any one who
is so minded be a saint and a zealot to any extent he likes,
but let him not harm any one else in doing it, or steal my
freedom.

Yet I rejoice that these man have got their due in these
disgraceful regulations. By their means the Romanists of
to-day have become market-stall holders. What is it they
sell? It is male and female pudenda, goods most worthy of
these merchants whose avarice and irreligion are worse than
the most sordid obscenity imaginable. For there is no impediment to marriage nowadays which they cannot legitimize
for money. These man-made regulations seem to have come
into existence for no other reason than raking in money and
netting in souls, to serve these greedy and rapacious hunters.
It is all done in order that the "Abomination" might stand
in the church of God, and publicly sell to men the pudenda
of both sexes; or, in Scriptural language, their "shame and
nakedness",[2] of which they had already robbed them by the
effect of these laws. O traffic worthy of our pontiffs who,
being given up unto a reprobate mind, carry on that traffic
with extreme baseness and utter lack of decency, instead of

[1] 1 Tim. 4:1ff.   [2] Lev. 18:6ff.

exercising the ministry of the gospel, which their greed and ambition make them despise!

You will probably ask me what I can say or do. If I were to enter into detail, I should go on without end. Everything is in such confusion that you do not know where to begin, in which direction to turn, or where to stop. But this I know, that the body politic cannot be felicitously governed merely by rules and regulations. If the administrator be sagacious, he will conduct the government more happily when guided by circumstances rather than by legal decrees. If he be not·so wise, his legal methods will only result in harm, since he will not know how to use them, nor how to temper them to the case in hand. Hence, in public affairs, it is more important to make sure that good and wise men are in control than that certain laws are promulgated. Men of this kind will themselves be the best of laws, will be alert to every kind of problem, and will resolve them equitably. If knowledge of the divine laws accompanies native sagacity, it is obvious that written laws will be superfluous and noxious. Above all else, remember that Christian love has no need of any laws at all.

Similarly, with regard to those impediments to marriage in respect of which the pope claims power to grant dispensations, but which are not mentioned in Scripture, I would urge it upon every priest and friar with all the power I possess, to declare, without more ado, that all those marriages are valid, the only objection being that they have been contracted merely against one or other of the ecclesiastical or pontifical canons. Let them arm themselves with the divine law which says: "What God hath joined together, let no man put asunder."[1] The union of man and wife is in accordance with divine law, and this holds good no matter how it may contradict any regulations made by men; and these same regulations ought therefore to be disregarded without any hesitation. If a man ought to leave his father and mother, and cleave to his wife, so much the more ought he to trample upon frivolous and wicked human regulations, in order to cleave to his wife. And if the pope, or bishop, or

[1] Matt. 19;6

official, should dissolve a marriage contracted contrary to one of these man-made laws, then he is an Antichrist; he does violence to nature, and is guilty of contempt of the divine Majesty; for the text still remains true that: "What God hath joined together let no man put asunder."

Remember, also, that no man has a right to promulgate such laws, that Christ has given Christians a freedom which rises above all human laws, especially when the divine law intervenes. Similarly, it says in Mark 2, "The Son of Man is also lord of the Sabbath, for man was not made for the Sabbath, but the Sabbath for man."[1] Further, Paul condemned such laws in advance when he foretold that there would be those who prohibited marriage.[2] Therefore, as far as the Scriptures permit, there should be an end to the validity of those impediments which arise from spiritual or legal affinities,[3] or from consanguinities. The Scriptures forbid only the second degree of consanguinity, as in Leviticus 18.[4] Here twelve persons are within the prohibited degrees, viz.: mother, step-mother, full sister, half-sister by either parent, grand-daughter, father's sister, mother's sister, daughter-in-law, brother's wife, wife's sister, step-daughter, uncle's wife. Thus only the first grade of affinity and the second of consanguinity are prohibited, and not even these in every respect, as is clear on close examination. The daughter and granddaughter of a brother or sister are not mentioned as prohibited, although they fall in the second grade. Therefore, if at any time a marriage has been contracted outside these grades, than which none other has at any time been prohibited by the divine laws, then it should never be dissolved on the ground that it is contrary to any laws of human origin. Marriage itself, as a divine institution, is incomparably superior to any laws, so that it ought not to be broken for the sake of laws, but laws for its sake.

In the same way, the nonsense about compaternity, commaternity, confraternity, consorority, and confiliety, ought to be completely blotted out, and the marriage contracted.

[1] Mark 2:28, 27   [2] 1 Tim. 4:3
[3] Those due to sponsorship at baptism, or by legal adoption
[4] Lev. 18:6ff.

These spiritual affinities are due purely to superstition. If neither the one who administers the baptism, nor the godparent at the baptism, is permitted to marry the one who has been baptized, then why is any Christian man permitted to marry any Christian woman? Does a fuller relationship arise from the rite or the sign of the sacrament, than from the sacrament itself? Is not a Christian man the brother of a Christian sister? Is not a baptized man spiritual brother to a baptized woman? What silly stuff they talk! If any husband teaches the gospel to his wife, and instructs her in faith in Christ, whereby he in very truth becomes her spiritual father—then ought she no longer to remain his wife? Would Paul not have been allowed to marry one of the Corinthian girls, all of whom he claims to have begotten in Christ?[1] See how Christian liberty has been oppressed by the blindness of human superstition!

Even more trifling are the legal affinities, and yet the Romanists have made these superior to the divine right of marriage. Nor would I grant that there is any impediment in what they call "disparity of religion". This means that a Christian man is not permitted to marry an unbaptized woman, either as such, or only on condition that she be converted to the faith. Was it God or man who set up this prohibition? Who has given men the authority of prohibiting this kind of marriage? It was a spirit "speaking lies in hypocrisy", as Paul says.[2] It would be to the point to say of them: "The wicked have related fables to me, not according to thy law."[3] Patritius, a pagan, married the Christian Monica, the mother of St. Augustine; why should not a similar marriage be allowed nowadays? The same obstinate, if not sinful, harshness is seen in the "impediment of crime", e.g., if a man marries either a woman with whom he had previously committed adultery, or the widow of a man whose death he had contrived in order that he might marry her. I beg you, in all earnestness, to tell me whence comes this harshness of man towards men, such as God has nowhere demanded? Or do they pretend not to know that David, a man held in the highest reverence, married Bathsheba,

[1] I Cor. 4:15   [2] I Tim. 4:2   [3] Ps. 119:85

Uriah's wife, after both the above crimes had been committed? I mean her previous adultery, and the murder of her husband. If the divine law operates in this way, why do men act despotically against their fellow servants?

What Romanists call the "impediment of a tie"[1] is also recognized: whereby a man is engaged to one woman, but has sexual relations with another woman. In such a case their ruling is that his engagement to the first is ended. This I simply do not understand. My view is that a man who has betrothed himself to a woman is no longer his own, and though he has had sexual relations with the second, he belongs to the first by the divine commandment, even though he has had no sexual relations with her. He cannot give away the self he does not possess; rather, he has deceived the first, and in fact committed adultery with the second. The reason the Romanists see it differently is that they give more weight to the carnal union than to the divine command according to which the man has "plighted his troth" already, and ought to keep it for ever. For you can only give what is your own. God forbid that anyone should circumvent his brother in any matter that ought to be kept in good faith above and beyond all human traditions whatever. I do not believe that he could live with the second with a good conscience, and therefore I think that this impediment ought to be completely done away with. For if the vow of one of the religious orders takes away one's self-disposal, why not also a troth plighted and received? This is indeed one of the precepts and fruits of the spirit according to Galatians 5,[2] whereas these vows derive from the human will. Moreover, if a married woman can claim her husband

---

[1] *Impedimentum ligaminis.* The following argument depends on the significance attaching to betrothals in canon law and common practice, much of which is still valid, not least in Germany. A betrothal was either a true, though irregular, marriage (*sponsalia de praesenti*), or became regular on consummation (*s. de futuro*). The laws governing betrothals were ill-defined; practice required a definite, formal occasion, the essence of the ceremonial consisting in the public nature of the mutual promises and an exchange of gifts; such betrothals were legal contracts. In Germany, the couple are still called bride and bridegroom from that day *until* the day of marriage. Actions for breach of promise in England still reflect the nature of betrothals before the Act of 1753

[2] Gal. 5:22

back, in spite of the fact that he has taken a monastic vow, why is it not allowed that an engaged woman should claim her betrothed back, even though he has had sexual connections with another woman? Rather, as I have already said, anyone who has plighted his troth to a woman cannot rightly take a monastic vow. His duty is to marry her, because it is his duty to keep faith. This precept comes from God, and therefore cannot be superseded by any human decree. In a case like this, he is under a far greater obligation to keep faith with the first woman, because he could only plight his faith with the second with a lie in his heart, and therefore it would not be plighted. What he has done, in God's sight, is to deceive her. For these reasons, the "impediment of error"[1] operates here, and makes marriage with the second woman null and void.

The "impediment of ordination" is also a purely manmade regulation, especially when the Romanists blatantly say that it overrides a marriage which has already been solemnized; for they always exalt their own rules as superior to the divine ordinances. I am not criticizing ordination to the priesthood as known to-day, but I see that Paul commands that "the bishop be the husband of one wife."[2] Therefore it is not possible to annul the marriage of a deacon, priest, bishop, or anyone who is ordained; although, of course, it must be admitted that Paul knew nothing of the kinds of priests and ordinations that pertain to-day. Perish then those accursed man-made regulations which seem only to have entered the church to multiply the dangers, the sins, and the evils there! Between a priest and his wife, therefore, there exists a valid and inseparable marriage, as is proved by the divine commands. What of it, then, if men who fear not God prohibit, and even annul, such a marriage entirely on their own authority? Nevertheless, what men have prohibited God permits, and His laws take precedence when at variance with human regulations.

The "impediment of public propriety", by which marriage contracts can be annulled, is a similar fiction. I am angered by the irreligious audacity which so speedily separates those

---

[1] *Erroris impedimentum*   [2] I Tim. 3:2

whom God has joined, that you can recognize the Antichrist
who attacks everything Christ said or taught. In the case
of an engaged couple, if one of them should die before their
marriage, what reason is there why the survivor should not
marry one of the deceased's relatives who comes within the
fourth degree of consanguinity? To forbid this is not a case
of the vindication of public propriety, but ignorance of it.
The people of Israel possessed the best laws, because they
were divinely instituted, and yet there was none of this kind
of vindication of public propriety. On the contrary, God
commanded the next of kin to marry a woman left a widow.
Otherwise, the question might be asked: Ought the people
who possess the liberty of Christians to be burdened with
more onerous laws than the people in bondage to the Mosaic
law? To sum up my discussion of what should be called
fictions rather than impediments: there appears to me at
present to be no impediment which can annul a legal contract of marriage, except sexual impotence, ignorance of a
marriage already existing, or a vow of chastity. Concerning
such a vow, my uncertainty up to now is such that I do
not know at what age it ought to be regarded as valid, as
I have already said with reference to the sacrament of baptism.[1] Matrimony, therefore, is an example sufficient in itself
to show up the nature of the present unhappy and hopeless
state of confusion. It also shows that any and all of the
practices of the church are impeded, and entangled, and
endangered, on account of the pestilential, unlearned, and
irreligious, man-made ordinances. There is no hope of a cure
unless the whole of the laws made by men, no matter what
their standing, are repealed once for all. When we have
recovered the freedom of the gospel, we should judge and
rule in accordance with it in every respect. Amen.

Now it is needful to discuss sexual impotence,[2] for, by

[1] Cf. *supra*, pp. 254ff.

[2] The following discussion has been the subject of much controversy,
and has received severe adverse criticism. Many editors and translations
omit it; yet its inclusion is unavoidable for a true understanding of Luther
and his times. It should, of course, be remembered in reading this section
that the whole treatise was written in Latin, and so not intended for the
general public; but also, in particular, that this section was intended to
be of special import in the confessional (*vide infra*, p. 305), where priests

so doing, it may be easier to give advice to those whose minds are labouring and in peril. But I would preface this with the remark that what I have said above about impediments applies to marriages already solemnized; and none of these should be annulled on account of such impediments as I have discussed. But in regard to a marriage which has yet to be solemnized, I will briefly repeat what I have already said.[1] When if youthful passion makes the case urgent, or if there are other needs that the pope would meet by granting a dispensation, then any Christian can grant one to his brother, or he can grant one to himself. This opinion means that he is given permission to carry his wife off in the teeth of any oppressive laws whatsoever. Why should I be deprived of my freedom by someone else's ignorance or superstition? Or, if the pope would grant a dispensation for a fee, why should not I grant one to myself or my brother for the good of my salvation? Is it the pope who decrees laws? Let him decree them for himself, but leave my freedom to me, or I will take it without his knowing.

On the question of impotence:

Let us examine such a case as this. A woman is married to an impotent man, but cannot, or perhaps will not, prove in court her husband's impotence, because of the numerous items of evidence, and the notoriety, which would be

were simply bewildered as to the advice they should give. Luther's advice, even where obviously wrong, was in accordance with German common law (so Steinhauser, in Holman, *op. cit.*, Vol. II, p. 271 n.). It should also be remembered that divorce was absolutely forbidden, as is still the case in the Roman church. Further, Luther's own historical background was at once franker, and even more tangled, as regards sex questions, than our own. Finally, he accepted the Bible as uttering God's word in both Testaments. He was without knowledge of the significance of its relation, book by book, and often chapter by chapter, to the times in which they were written, as distinct from those to which they referred. Thus the danger to public law and order was hidden from Luther when he gave this advice. It is to Luther's credit that he discussed the question with obvious reluctance, without any prurience, and under an urgent sense of necessity. He keeps close to the facts of nature, and of the objective historical situation as he knew it. Here, as in the *Appeal* (cf. *supra*, pp. 161), he may be open to the accusation of "no statesman", but no worse charge could, perhaps, be sustained. His suggestions, however, are never merely doctrinaire: they represent an attempt, root and branch, to find some remedy for a clamant social evil; the alternative being an increase of the widespread cynicism and human misery

[1] *Vide supra*, pp. 164ff.

occasioned by a legal process. Still she wishes to have a child, and is unable to remain continent. In addition, suppose I had advised her to seek a divorce in order to marry another, as she was content, in her conscience, to do, and after ample experience on the part of herself and her husband, that he was impotent; if, then, however, her husband would not agree to her proposal, I myself would give the further advice,[1] that, with her husband's consent (although now really he is not her husband, but only a man who lives in the same house) she should have coition with another man, say her husband's brother, but keeping this "marriage" secret, and ascribing the children to the putative father, as they call such a one. As to the question whether such a woman is "saved" or in a state of salvation, I would reply, Yes, because in this case a mistake due to ignorance of the man's impotence created a false situation which impedes the marriage proper; the harshness of the law does not allow divorce; yet by the divine law the woman is free, and so cannot be forced to remain continent. Therefore the husband ought to concede this right to her, allowing her coition with another, since she is his wife in a formal and unreal sense only.

Further, if the man will not consent, and if he does not wish to be separated, then, rather than let her burn or commit adultery, I would counsel her to contract matrimony with someone else, and flee to some distant and unknown region. What other counsel can be given to one constantly struggling with the dangers of her own natural emotions? I know, of course, that some will be disturbed because it would be unfair for the children of a secret marriage of this kind to be the heirs of the putative father. But, on the one hand, if it were done with the husband's consent, there would be no unfairness. If, on the other hand, he were ignorant of it, or had refused his consent, then let an unfettered, and therefore Christian, reasonableness, if not charity itself, judge the case and say which of the two was the more harmful to the other. The wife alienates her husband's estate, but the husband deceives the wife, and is defrauding her totally in body and life. Does not the man

[1] In the confessional, was doubtless meant by Luther

U

commit the greater sin by wasting the body and life of his wife, than the woman in alienating a quantity of temporal property? So either let him agree to a divorce, or else let him bear with children not his own. The fault is his in having deceived an innocent girl, and defrauded her of the full use of both her life and her body, besides giving her an almost unbearable cause for committing adultery. Let these two cases be weighed in a just balance. According to any legal code, forsooth, fraud ought to recoil on the fraudulent, and any one doing harm should make it good. In what respect does a husband, such as we are discussing, differ from a man who keeps another's wife in prison along with her husband? Would not such a bully be compelled to support the wife and children as well as the husband, or else set them free? And this should happen in the case under discussion. Hence, in my judgment, the man ought to be compelled either to accept divorce, or support his putative child as his own heir. Without doubt that is the judgment which charity calls for. In that case, the impotent man, because not really a husband, should support his wife's issue in the same spirit as if his wife were ill, or suffered some other indisposition, and he had to nurse her at great cost. For it is by his own fault, and not his wife's, that she labours under this wrong. I have set out my views to the best of my ability for the sake of giving instruction to those whose consciences are disquieted, for my desire is to bring what little comfort I can to my afflicted brethren who are in this kind of captivity.[1]

In regard to divorce, it is still a subject for debate whether it should be allowed. For my part, I have such a hatred of divorce that I prefer bigamy to divorce, yet I do not venture an opinion whether bigamy should be allowed.[2] Christ's own command, as chief pastor, is given in Matthew 5, "Every one that putteth away his wife, saving for the cause of fornication, maketh her an adulteress; and whosoever shall marry her when she is put away committeth adultery."[3] Hence,

---

[1] For the foregoing section, see footnote on p. 303, *supra*
[2] He was later greatly perturbed by the cases of Philip of Hesse and King Henry VIII, in both of which the verdict was grudgingly conceded largely on political grounds
[3] Matt. 5:32

Christ permitted divorce, but only in case of fornication. It follows that the pope is in error where he grants divorce for other causes. No one, therefore, should think his case sound if he has been granted a divorce by a papal dispensation, for that shows presumptuousness rather than authority. But I marvel even more that the Romanists do not allow the re-marriage of a man separated from his wife by divorce, but compel him to remain single. Christ permitted divorce in case of fornication, and compelled no one to remain single; and Paul preferred us to marry rather than to burn, and seemed quite prepared to grant that a man may marry another woman in place of the one he has repudiated.[1] But this is a subject that ought to be fully discussed, and a decision reached, so that it would be possible to give counsel to those who, though surrounded by an infinite number of dangers, are forced to remain unmarried to-day through no fault of their own; cases where wives or husbands have run away and deserted their partners, to return perhaps ten years later, or even never. This kind of thing distresses and depresses me, for there are instances day by day, whether due to some special piece of wickedness of Satan's, or to our neglect of God's word.

For my own part, and speaking entirely for myself in this matter, I cannot make any rules and regulations; yet I wish that passage in 1 Corinthians 7 were applied, which reads: "If the unbelieving departeth, let him depart; the brother or the sister is not in bondage in such cases."[2] Here the apostle rules that the unbeliever who deserts his wife should be divorced, and he pronounces the believer free to marry another. Surely the same principle should hold good if a believer (i.e., nominally a believer, but in fact an unbeliever) deserts his wife, especially if he never intends to return. At least I can see no difference between the two cases. On the other hand, I believe that if, in the apostle's time, an unbeliever had returned, and had either become a believer, or promised to live together with his believing wife, he would not have been given that permission; rather, he would have been given permission to marry someone else. As I have

[1] 1 Cor. 7:9   [2] 1 Cor. 7:15

said, however, in these matters I am not enunciating any
principles, although there is nothing which I desire more to
see settled; for there is nothing that disquiets me more to-day,
and many others with me. Nevertheless, I would not have
the matter settled by the mere fiat of the pope or the bishops.
Rather, if two learned and good men were to agree, in Christ's
name and in Christ's spirit, and issue a pronouncement, I
myself would prefer their verdict even to that of a council.
For the kinds of council which usually assemble nowadays
are more notable for their numbers and power than for their
learning and sanctity. So I hang up my harp,[1] until I can
discuss the subject with another and wiser man than myself.

(6) *Ordination*

This was unknown as a sacrament to the church of Christ's
time, the doctrine having been devised by the church of the
popes. A promise of grace is nowhere given, nor does the
whole of the New Testament contain a passage with any
allusion to it. It is ridiculous to assert that what can nowhere
be proved to have been instituted by God is nevertheless
a sacrament. My point is, not that I wish to condemn a
rite which has been celebrated ever since the church was
founded, but that I refuse to place a man-made fiction among
things divine; I refuse to construe anything as if it were of
divine institution when it has not been divinely ordained.
Otherwise we shall appear ridiculous to a hostile critic; and
we ought to try, as far as we ourselves are concerned, to
have everything assured, unassailable, plainly confirmed by
Scripture, before it is put forward as an article of the faith.
But in the present "sacrament" we cannot satisfy these
requirements with a single tittle of evidence.

The church has no power to initiate and institute divine
promises of grace, as is the case when the Romanists pretentiously claim that anything instituted by the church has
no less authority than what has been ordained by God, since
the church is governed by the Holy Spirit. For the church
was born by virtue of her faith in the word of promise, and

---

[1] Luther was writing a "prelude"—a musical term

by that promise she is both fed and maintained. In other words, she was instituted by God's promises, and not God's promise by her. For the word of God is beyond comparison superior to the church. She is a created thing, and, being such, has no power to institute, to ordain, or to make; but only to be instituted, to be ordained, and to be brought into being. No man can beget his own parents or settle the author of his own being.

Of course, the church has the power of distinguishing the word of God from the word of man. This is borne out by Augustine, who confesses that, moved by the authority of the church, he believed in the gospel, because it proclaimed that this was the gospel. But this does not make it superior to the gospel, for by the same argument the church would be superior to the God in whom it believes, since the church's message is that He is God. Rather, as Augustine says elsewhere, the mind is so laid hold of by the truth itself, that, by virtue of that truth, it is able to reach certainty in any judgment. Nevertheless, the mind is unable to judge the truth as such, although it is compelled to say, when entirely confident, This is true. For example, the mind declares with infallible assurance that three and seven make ten, and yet it cannot adduce any reason why that is true,[1] although it cannot deny its truth. The fact is that, rather than being itself the judge, the mind has been taken captive, and has accepted a verdict pronounced by the Truth herself sitting on the tribunal. Similarly by the illumination of the spirit, when doctrines come up for decision and approval, the church possesses a "sense" whose presence is certain, though it cannot be proved. Just as no philosopher attempts to appraise the conceptions of common sense, but is rather judged by them, so, among ourselves, there is a spirit of which we are aware, which judges all things, but is judged by none,[2] as the apostle says. But I digress.

[1] This is part of the theory of numbers, which is still the subject of recondite argument, cf. e.g., Bertrand Russell, *The Principles of Mathematics, sub voce*

[2] 1 Cor. 2:15. Luther shows himself well acquainted with the existence of the difficult problem of the theory of knowledge, and no one but an acute philosopher could have written this paragraph. For a recent statement, cf. Bertrand Russell, *Human Knowledge* (1948), esp. pp. 439ff.

For these reasons we can be sure that, because it belongs to God alone to do so, the church has no power to promise grace, and, by the same sign, none to institute a sacrament. Even if she possessed these powers in the highest degree, it would by no means follow that ordination was a sacrament. For when these decrees were passed, it was customary for only a few bishops and doctors, and no others, to be present; and who knows if they constituted a church possessing the spirit? It was possible they did not constitute a church, and that they all erred. Councils have often erred, especially that of Constance,[1] which was the most wicked of them all. There is reliable proof only of what has received the assent of the church universal, and not merely that of Rome. On this basis, I would go as far as to say that ordination is an ecclesiastical ceremony, like many others which have been introduced by the Church Fathers, e.g., consecration of vases, houses, vestments, water, salt, candles, herbs, wine, and the like. No one suggests that any of these cases constitutes a sacrament; nor is a promise attached to any of them. Hence, neither anointing a man's hands, shaving his poll, nor anything else of the sort, can be made into a sacrament, for they convey no promise; they are merely rites employed solely to prepare men for certain duties, as in the case of vases or implements.

The question may be asked: What, then, have you to say about Dionysius (Areopagiticus),[2] who enumerates six sacraments, and includes ordination among them in his *Ecclesiastica Hierarchia*? My answer is, that I know this is the only ancient writer who argues on behalf of seven sacraments, although, by omitting to speak of matrimony, he gives only six. Apart from him, among the rest of the Fathers there is no mention of these as sacraments. On no occasion when they speak of these subjects do they regard them as sacraments, for the innovation of sacraments is a modern phenomenon. And, if I may dare to say so, it is by no means to my liking to assign much importance to this particular Dionysius; who-

[1] A.D. 1414–18. It condemned John Huss and Jerome of Prague to be burned, and thus it treacherously revoked their "safe-conduct"

[2] Really the pseudonym of a fourth-century writer of *The Celestial Hierarchy*, *The Ecclesiastical Hierarchy*, etc.

ever he may have been, he shows hardly any signs of solid learning. I would ask: On whose authority or by what logic does he prove the statements about angels which he has jumbled together in the *Coelesti Hierarchia*—a book over which inquisitive and superstitious minds have pored? If read and judged without prejudice, all the fruits of his meditations seem very much like dreams. In the *Theologia Mystica*—rightly so-called—of which certain pretentious, but very unscholarly, theologians make so much, Dionysius is very pernicious, being more of a Platonist than a Christian. In sum, I myself do not want any believer to give the least weight to these books. So far indeed from learning about Christ in them, you will be led to lose what you know. I am speaking from experience. Rather, let us listen to Paul, that we may learn of "Jesus Christ and Him crucified".[1] "He is the way, the truth, and the life."[2] He is the ladder[3] by which we may come to the Father; as He Himself said: "No one cometh unto the Father, but by me."

Similarly, in the *Ecclesiastica Hierarchia*, Dionysius only describes a number of rites of the church; he plays with his allegories, but this does not make them realities. The same sort of thing has been done amongst us by someone who has written a book called *Rationale Divinorum*.[4] This business of allegorizing is only for men who have nothing else to do. I am sure that I myself would not find it difficult to trump up allegories round any thing in creation. Did not Bonaventura use allegory to convert the liberal arts into theology?[5] Then Gerson turned the smaller *Donatus*[6] into a mystical theology. It would not give me much trouble to write a better *Hierarchy* than that of Dionysius; but he knew nothing of pope, cardinals, and archbishops, and so he put a bishop at the head of the church. And whose ingenuity is so slight that he could not try his hand at allegorizing? In my view, no theologian should waste time on allegories until

---

[1] I Cor. 2:2   [2] John 14:6   [3] Cf. Jacob's dream, Gen. 28:12ff.

[4] Guillaume Durand the elder (*c.*1230-96) bishop of Mende, and canonist; called "the Speculator", from his principal work, *Speculum Judicale*

[5] I.e., John of Fidenza, 1221-74, in *reductione artium ad theologiam*

[6] As a result of the popularity of the Latin grammar of Donatus, published in numberless editions from about A.D. 350 till the Renaissance, the term *Donatus* became the equivalent of *grammar* in Western Europe

he has become expert in the proper and simple sense of Scripture.[1] Otherwise, as in Origen's case, he will endanger his theological thinking.

Therefore, nothing ought without more ado to be held as a sacrament merely because Dionysius so describes it; or else why not make a sacrament of the procession which he describes in the same passage, and which is practised to the present day? Why not as many sacraments as rites and ceremonies which have grown up in the church? On this same weak basis, the Romanists have attributed to the sacrament of ordination a certain fictitious "character", which is said to be indelibly impressed upon an ordinand.[2] I would ask whence do such ideas arise, and on whose authority and for what reason have they become established? Not that we are unwilling for the Romanists to be free to invent, to say, or to assert, whatever they like; but we also insist on our own freedom, lest they arrogate to themselves the right of making articles of the faith out of their own ideas, as they have hitherto presumed to do. It is sufficient that, for the sake of concord, we should accommodate ourselves to their ceremonies and idiosyncrasies; but we refuse to be compelled to accept them as necessary for salvation, which they are not. Let them do away with the element of compulsion in their arbitrary demands, and we will yield free obedience to their wishes in order that we may live in peace towards each other. For it is mean, iniquitous, and servile for a Christian man, with his freedom, to be subjected to any regulations except the heavenly and divine.

At this point, the Romanists adduce their strongest argument, in that, at the Last Supper, Christ said: "This do ye in remembrance of me." Look, they say at this point: "Christ ordained His disciples as priests." From this, also,

---

[1] It is difficult to overestimate Luther's stand against allegorization, a practice which had dominated, and increasingly perverted, Biblical exegesis from at least the time of Origen (c. A.D. 184–253), and which is too far from extinct even yet. To demand and insist on the determinative value of the plain sense of Scripture is the greatest single contribution made by Luther to modern Biblical scholarship. He himself was a supreme master in eliciting the plain sense plainly, a most excellent example being found in section 7 of the *Pagan Servitude*, cf. *infra*, pp. 319ff.

[2] I.e., "Once a priest, always a priest"

they infer, among other things, that the elements in both kinds are only to be given to the priests. After that, they deduce from it anything at will, with the effect that, once they have arrogated to themselves the right of making free decisions, they assert what they like on the basis of Christ's word no matter what the occasion. But is that what is meant by expounding the word of God? Answer me, I beg you. Christ promised nothing on this occasion, but only commanded that this was to be done in memory of Him. Why do they not argue that He ordained as priests those on whom He laid the office of the word and of baptism when He said: "Go ye into all the world and preach the gospel to every creature, baptizing them in the name", etc?

It is the very duty of priests to preach and baptize. Further, since it is the primary, and, they say, the indispensable duty of the priests to-day to read the canonical hours, why have the Romanists not discovered a sacrament of ordination in those passages where Christ gives a command to pray? There are many such occasions, but especially one in the garden, where He says: "Pray, lest ye enter into temptation."[1] They may object that this is no commandment to pray, and that it is enough to read the canonical hours. If so, nowhere can it be proved from Scripture that praying is a duty of the priests. By the same mark, the sacerdotal kind of praying is not of God, as indeed it is not.

Not one of the ancient Fathers asserts that priests were ordained when those words were used. What then is the origin of this new piece of intelligence? Perhaps they sought by this means to establish a seed-bed of unappeasable discord, through which clergy and laity were to be more widely separated than heaven and earth; yet this has proved to be unbelievably hurtful to baptismal grace, and to the confusion of fellowship based on the gospel. Here is the root of the terrible domination of the clergy over the laity. In virtue of a physical anointing, when their hands are consecrated, and in virtue of their tonsure and vestments, the clergy claim to be superior to the Christian laity, who, nevertheless, have

[1] Matt. 26:41

been baptized with the Holy Spirit. The clergy can almost be said also to regard the laity as lower animals, who have been included in the church along with themselves.

Thus it arises that they make bold to command and demand, to threaten and urge and oppress, as they please. In sum, the sacrament of ordination is the prettiest of devices for giving a firm foundation to all the ominous things hitherto done in the church, or yet to be done. This is the point at which Christian fellowship perishes, where pastors become wolves, servants become tyrants, and men of the church become worse than men of the world.

Now we, who have been baptized, are all uniformly priests[1] in virtue of that very fact. The only addition received by the priests is the office of preaching, and even this with our consent. If the Romanists had to grant this point, they would have to admit that they had no right to lord it over us, except in so far as we, of our own free will, allowed them to do so. Thus it says in 1 Peter 2, "Ye are an elect race, a royal priesthood, and a priestly kingdom."[2] It follows that all of us who are Christian are also priests. Those whom we call priests are really ministers of the word and chosen by us; they fulfil their entire office in our name. The priesthood is simply the ministry of the word. So in 1 Corinthians 4 it says: "Let a man so account of us as of ministers of Christ and stewards of the mysteries of God."[3]

That being the case, it follows (i) that any one who has been called by the church to preach the Word, but does not preach it, is in no way a priest; and (ii) that the sacrament of ordination cannot be other than the rite by which the church chooses its preacher. That is how Malachi 2 defines a priest: "The priest's lips should keep knowledge, and they should seek the law at his mouth; for he is the messenger of the Lord of Hosts."[4] Be assured that anyone who is not a messenger of the Lord of Hosts, or any one who is called to do something other than be such a messenger is, if I may say so, by no means a priest. Accordingly, Hosea 4 says: "Because

[1] Cf. *supra*, *Appeal to the Ruling Class*, pp. 113f.
[2] 1 Pet. 2:9   [3] 1 Cor. 4:1   [4] Mal. 2:7

thou hast rejected knowledge, I will also reject thee, that thou shalt be no priest to me."[1] Moreover, the reason they are called pastors is that their duty is to find pasture for, or, to teach, their flock. From this, it follows that those men who are ordained merely to read the canonical hours and to celebrate mass may be papal priests, but they are not Christian priests; for not only do they not preach, but they are not even appointed to preach. Indeed, our contention is that a priesthood of this kind has another status than that of the office of preaching. Thus, they are the priests of the Hours and the Missals, merely a kind of living idols which bear the name of the priesthood; they are exactly the kind of priests whom Jeroboam ordained at Bethaven,[2] and whom he had taken from the lowest dregs of the people, and not from the tribe of Levi.

Lo! how far the glory of the church has departed! The whole world is full of priests, bishops, cardinals, and clergy, not one of whom, as far as his official responsibilities go, is a preacher, unless, apart from the sacrament of ordination, he is called upon to preach by virtue of some other requirement different from that of his ordination. He considers that he fulfils the requirements of his ordination completely by mumbling through the "vain repetition" of the prayers which he has to read, and by celebrating the masses. But in repeating the "hours" he never prays, or if he prays, he does so to himself. And the mass, by an extreme perversity, is offered as if it were a sacrifice, whereas it is just the celebration of a sacrament. Thus it is plain that ordination, which is used as a sacrament to consecrate this type of man, and make a cleric of him, is really and truly, purely and simply, a man-made ceremonial. Those who compacted it knew nothing of the church in its essence; nothing of the priesthood; of preaching the word; or of the sacraments. The result is that this sacrament and those priests stand on the same level. In addition to these errors and stupidities, is that closer incarceration by which they separate themselves more widely still from other Christians, now regarded as profane; like the Galli, who were the priests of Cybele,

[1] Hos. 4:6   [2] 1 Kings 12:31 and Hosea 10:5

they unman themselves by assuming the burden of a very spurious celibacy.

Nor was it enough to satisfy this piece of hypocrisy and the operation of this error, that bigamy[1] should be prohibited, i.e., that no man should have two wives at the same time, as was forbidden in the law, and as is the common meaning of bigamy. The Romanists have interpreted bigamy to mean marrying two virgins in succession, or one widow. Indeed, so very sacred is the sanctity of this most sacrosanct sacrament, that it is impossible for a man to be ordained if he has married a virgin and while she still remains alive as his wife. In order to attain the very summit of sanctity, a man is prohibited access to the priesthood if he has married a girl who was not a virgin, though he may have done so in ignorance, and by an unfortunate mischance. But he may have had vile commerce with six hundred prostitutes, and seduced countless matrons and virgins, and kept many mistresses, yet nothing of this would be an impediment, and prevent his becoming a bishop, or a cardinal, or a pope. As a consequence, it has become needful to expound the apostle's saying, "husband of one wife",[2] as "prelate of one church". Out of this arises the principle of "incompatible benefices".[3] But the pope, who magnanimously grants dispensations, may allow three, twenty, or a hundred wives, i.e., churches, to count as one, after he has been bribed with money, or induced by some favour; I should say, of course, moved by godly generosity, and constrained by concern for the churches.

O pontiffs worthy of this venerable sacrament of ordination! O prince, not of the church universal, but of the synagogues of Satan and of Darkness itself! Now is the time to cry out with Isaiah: "O ye scornful men, that rule my people which is in Jerusalem";[4] and with Amos 6: "Woe to you that are at ease in Zion, and are secure in the mountain of Samaria, notable men, heads of the people, going in state into the house of Israel."[5] O! the disgrace which these monstrous priesthoods bring upon the Church of God! Where can you find priests who know the gospel, not to mention

---

[1] Cf. *supra*, pp. 298ff.   [2] 1 Tim. 3:2
[3] Cf *supra*, *Appeal to the Ruling Class*, pp. 135ff.   [4] Isa. 28:14   [5] Amos 6:1

preach it? Why then do they boast of being priests? Why do they wish to be regarded as holier, and better, and more powerful, than other Christians who pass as laymen? As for reading the "hours", what ordinary person, or, as the apostle says, what man that speaketh with tongues,[1] is not equal to that? The prayers of the hours are suitable for monks, hermits, and private persons, although laymen. The function of the priest is to preach; if he does not preach, he is no more a priest than the picture of a man is a man. Or does it make a man a bishop if he ordains this kind of clapper-tongued priest, or consecrates churches and bells, or confirms children? Never! These are things that any deacon or layman might do. What makes a priest or a bishop is the ministry of the Word.

Do not accept my standpoint if you wish to live at ease. Be off with you, young men. Refuse to accept this kind of ordination;[2] refuse, unless you want to preach the gospel, and unless you can believe that you will become superior to a layman by the sacrament of ordination. Reading the "hours" is of no consequence. And, again, to offer mass is only to receive the sacrament. What function, then, is left for you as a priest which is not equally appropriate for a layman? Tonsure and vestments? It is a poor sort of priest that is made up of tonsure and vestments! Or is it the oil that anointed your fingers? But every Christian whatsoever has been anointed with the oil of the Holy Spirit, and sanctified in body and soul. Formerly laymen used to administer the sacraments as often as priests do now. Yet the superstitious of our day regard it as a great offence if a layman touch the bare chalice, or even the cover of it. Nor is a nun, though a consecrated virgin, allowed to wash the altar cloth or the sacred linen. O my God! this shows how far the sacrosanct sanctity of this sacrament has gone! I expect the time will come when the laity will not be allowed even to touch the altar—except with money in their hand. I almost burst with indignation when I think of the wicked impositions of these most brazen monsters, who, with their tricks and puerile

---

[1] I Cor. 14:14
[2] Cf. *supra*, pp. 312f.; *Appeal to the Ruling Class*, p. 199

traps, make sport of the Christian religion, and bring its liberty and glory into ruin.

Therefore every one who knows that he is a Christian should be fully assured that all of us alike are priests,[1] and that we all have the same authority in regard to the word and the sacraments, although no one has the right to administer them without the consent of the members of his church, or by the call of the majority (because, when something is common to all, no single person is empowered to arrogate it to himself, but should await the call of the church). Moreover, the sacrament of ordination, if it has any validity at all, is only the rite through which someone is called to the ministry of the church, since the priesthood is simply the ministry of the word; the word, I say; not the law, but the gospel. The diaconate, on the other hand, is not a ministry for reading the gospel, or the epistle, as the present custom is, but for distributing the church's bounty to the poor, in order that the priests might be relieved of the burden of temporal matters, and be more at liberty for prayer and the word. It was on this plan, as we read in Acts 6, that deacons were installed;[2] and therefore a man who neither knows nor preaches the gospel is not a priest or a bishop, but only a kind of nuisance in the church. Under the false title of priest or bishop, or dressed in sheep's clothing, he does violence to the gospel and acts as a wolf in the church.

Therefore, unless those priests or bishops, with whom the church abounds to-day, work out their own salvation in another way, and unless they recognize that they are neither priests nor bishops, let them bemoan the fact that they bear the name. They are ignorant of the duties and unable to fulfil them. Let them deplore their pitiable lot, appropriate to their hypocrisy, with prayers and tears. Otherwise, of a truth, they will be the sons of eternal perdition. It was only speaking the truth about them when Isaiah said: "Therefore my people are gone into captivity, for lack of knowledge; and their honourable men are famished, and their multitude

---

[1] Luther discusses fully this doctrine in the *Appeal to the Ruling Class*; cf. *supra*, pp. 113ff., and *Freedom of a Christian*, *infra*, pp. 366ff.

[2] Acts 6:1ff.

are parched with thirst. Therefore hell hath enlarged her desire, and opened her mouth without measure: and their glory, and their multitude, and their pomp, and he that rejoiceth among them descend into it."[1] What a dreadful prophecy of our times when Christians are being swallowed up in such an abyss!

According to what Scripture teaches us, what we call priesthood is a form of service. I quite fail to see the reason why a man, who has once become a priest, cannot again become a layman, since he only differs from the laity by his ministry. Further, it has not hitherto been impossible for him to be deposed from the ministry, seeing that this punishment is actually imposed from time to time on priests found in fault; they may be either suspended temporarily, or deprived permanently of office. The fiction of the "indelible character" has long been ridiculous.[2] I agree that the pope imparts this character to the man, though it was unknown to Christ; and that thereby the man is consecrated for ever as the servant and prisoner, not of Christ but of the pope, as is the case nowadays. Further, unless I am mistaken, if at any time this fictitious sacrament should decay and disappear, the papacy itself would scarcely continue and retain its "characters". A joyful liberty would come back to us, in which we should understand that we are all equal by any law whatever; and, when the oppressive yoke had been cast aside, we should know that he who is a Christian possesses Christ; that he who possesses Christ possesses all things that are Christ's, and is able to do all things. This is a subject on which I shall have more to say, and with more emphasis,[3] when I perceive that the above has displeased my friends the papists.

(7) The Sacrament of Extreme Unction

The theologians of the present day have made two additions, well worthy of themselves, to the ceremony of anointing the sick. In the first place, they call it a sacrament; and in the second, they make it the last. Thus we

---

[1] Isa. 5:13f.   [2] Vide supra, p. 115
[3] Luther refers to his Freedom of a Christian, which followed the Pagan Servitude a couple of months later; cf. infra, pp. 351ff.

have nowadays a sacrament of extreme unction which is only
to be administered to those who are on the brink of death.
As the theologians are very acute in argument, perhaps they
relate it to the first unction of baptism, and the two sub-
sequent unctions of confirmation and ordination. This time,
they have something to throw in my face; it is that, on the
authority of the apostle James, here are both promise and
sign: things by which, as I have hitherto contended, a sacrament is constituted. The apostle says: "Is any among you
sick? let him call for the elders of the church; and let
them pray over him, anointing him with oil in the name
of the Lord: and the prayer of faith shall save him that
is sick, and the Lord shall raise him up; and if he
have committed sins, it shall be forgiven him."[1] Behold,
they say, the promise of forgiveness of sins, and the sign
of the oil.

My reply is: If nonsense is spoken anywhere, this is the
very place. I pass over the fact that many have maintained,
with much probability, that this epistle was not written by
the apostle James,[2] and is not worthy of the spirit of an
apostle. Nevertheless, no matter who may have been the
author, it has the authority due to custom. Yet, even if it
were by the apostle James, I would say that no apostle was
licensed to institute a sacrament on his own authority, or,
to give a divine promise with an accompanying sign. This
pertains to Christ alone. That is why Paul says that it was
from the Lord that he received the sacrament of the
eucharist;[3] and that he had not been sent to baptize, but
to preach the gospel.[4] Nowhere in the gospels is there any
mention of this sacrament of Extreme Unction. But, allowing that to pass, let us look at the actual words of the
apostle, or whoever was the author, and we shall see, at

[1] Jas. 5:14f.
[2] This remark, which is in accord with modern scholarship, does not
occur in the introduction which Luther wrote to the epistle in his translation of the New Testament, first published in 1522. Cf. *Bi.*, Vol. VII,
383f. The famous judgment about the "epistle of straw", usually quoted
in a truncated form, occurs only in the Introduction to the New Testament as a whole, and was withdrawn after the first edition. This general
Introduction, however, nowhere denies James's authorship. Cf. *Bi.*, Vol.
VI., 1-11
[3] 1 Cor. 11:23   [4] 1 Cor. 1:17

once, that those who have multiplied the sacraments have paid no real attention to his words.

Firstly, if they hold that what the apostle said in the present instance is true, and ought to be kept, by what authority have they changed and restricted it? Why do they make an extreme unction, to be administered only once, out of what the apostle intended to be of general application? It was not the apostle's intention that it should be extreme, or that it should be given only to those at the point of death. Rather he says, purely and simply: "Is any among you sick?"; he does not say: "Is any among you at the point of death?" I shall ignore the sapient remarks on this subject in Dionysius's *Ecclesiastica Hierarchia*;[1] the apostle's words are plain; Dionysius and the Romanists alike rely on them—but without obeying them. It appears, therefore, that, without any other authority than their own choice, they have wrongly interpreted the words of the apostle, and transformed them into the sacrament of Extreme Unction. This has been to the harm of the other sick persons whom they have deprived, on their own authority, of the benefit of the anointing as appointed by the apostle.

Here is a nicer point: the promise of the apostle expressly says: "The prayer of faith shall cure the sick, and the Lord will grant him recovery", etc.[2] You will have noticed that, in this passage, the apostle commands anointing and prayer in order that the sick man may be made well and recover, i.e., not die; and the anointing, therefore, is not that of extreme unction. This point is also proved in that, to the present day, while the Romanists are administering the last unction, prayers are said asking for the sick man's recovery. But the Romanists maintain, in spite of those prayers, that the unction is only to be administered to the dying, i.e., not in order that such a person may get well and recover. If this were not a serious matter, who could help laughing at this pretty, neat, and sensible comment on the apostle's words? Do we not here plainly detect that stupid sophistry which, both in this passage as well as in many others, affirms what Scripture denies, and denies what it affirms? Shall we

---

[1] Cf. *supra*, p. 310 and n.2.   [2] Jas. 5:13–15

W

pass a vote of thanks to these egregious masters of ours?
Surely I was right in saying that nowhere else have they
spoken such utter folly as in dealing with this passage!

Furthermore, if Extreme Unction is a sacrament, there
should be no doubt that it is (as they say) an efficacious
sign of what it signifies and promises. Now, it promises the
health and recovery of the sick man, as the words plainly
say: "The prayer of faith shall cure the sick, and the Lord
will heal him."[1] But every one knows that this promise is
seldom, or never, fulfilled. Scarcely one in a thousand is
restored, and then no one thinks it is by the sacrament, but
by the help of nature or medicine. Indeed, they attribute to
the sacrament the opposite effect. What, then, is our conclusion? It is that either the apostle did not speak the truth
when he made this promise, or else that this unction of theirs
is not a sacrament. A sacramental promise is certain, whereas
this is usually fallacious.

But let us again take cognizance of the care and insight
of these theologians; we may note that they mean it to be
"extreme unction" just in order that the promise shall not
hold good, or, lest the sacrament be a sacrament. For if it
is extreme, it does not heal, but increases the infirmity. If
it healed, it would not be extreme. Thus, it comes about,
according to the exegesis of these masters, that James is to
be understood to have contradicted himself: he instituted
a sacrament to avoid instituting a sacrament! and the
Romanists wanted to have the unction just in order that it
should be untrue that the sick were healed by it, as James
decreed! If this is not talking nonsense, then what is?

A remark of the apostle Paul is apposite here, when he
says, 1 Timothy 1, "Desiring to be teachers of the law,
though they understand neither what they say, nor whereof
they confidently affirm",[2] since they read and follow everything uncritically. With the same carelessness, they have also
deduced auricular confession from the apostle's words: "Confess your sins to one another."[3] But they do not keep the
apostle's command that the elders of the church should be
brought in, and that they should pray over the sick.[4] To-day,

1 Jas. 5:15   2 1 Tim. 1:7   3 Jas. 5:16   4 Jas. 5:14

they will hardly send even one of the minor ranks of priests, although it was the apostle's will that many persons should be present, and this not to administer the unction, but to pray. That is why he said: "The prayer of faith will heal the sick", etc.;[1] although I am uncertain whether he meant "priests" to be understood when he said *presbyteroi,* or elderly men, nor does it follow that a priest or minister is an elderly man. Therefore we may suppose that the apostle's intention was that the older and graver members of the church should visit the sick. They would be doing a work of mercy, and, by praying in faith, would heal the sick. This is an interpretation of the apostolic injunction which cannot be denied, for the church was formerly governed by the older members without any being ordained and consecrated; and they were elected for this purpose on account of their years and long experience of affairs.

From this standpoint, I take it that this early unction is the same as that when Mark 6, speaking of the apostles, says: "And they anointed with oil many that were sick and healed them."[2] This appears to have been a rite, now long obsolete, in the first church, by which they worked miracles on the sick. In the same way, the last chapter of Mark's gospel tells how Christ gave power to believers to pick up serpents, lay their hands on the sick, etc.[3] It is surprising that the Romanists did not make sacraments out of this passage, for the essential power and promise here are very like that which James speaks of. The fictitious "Extreme Unction" of these Romanists is not a sacrament, but a piece of James's advice which anyone who wishes may follow. As I have said, it is based on Mark 6, and so handed down. Moreover, since the glory of the church is seen where there is weakness, and since death is gain, I do not believe that this counsel was given for the sake of sick persons in general; rather, it was meant for those who were bearing their illness too impatiently, and with an immature faith; from whom, therefore, the Lord had departed. In such cases, the miraculous power of faith would show up more conspicuously.

James purposely and carefully made provision for the view

---

[1] Jas. 5:15   [2] Mark 6:13   [3] Mark 16:17f.

I am propounding, for he did not ascribe the promise of healing and of the forgiveness of sins to the unction, but to the prayer of faith. His words are: "And the prayer of faith shall heal the sick, and the Lord shall cure him; and if he have committed sins, it shall be forgiven him."[1] A sacrament, so it is said,[2] does not require the administrant to pray or to have faith; for an ungodly man may administer baptism, and need not pray in order to consecrate. It depends for its validity entirely on being instituted by God, and on what He then promised; and it requires faith on the part of the recipient. But in Extreme Unction as practised in our day, there is no prayer of faith. No one prays in faith over the sick, confidently expecting their restoration. Yet James describes that kind of faith in this passage, and he had already spoken of it in Chapter I: "But let him ask in faith, nothing doubting."[3] Christ also had said: "All things whatsoever ye pray for, believe that ye have received them, and ye shall have them."[4]

There is no doubt at all that if, at the present day, this kind of prayer were offered over the sick, i.e., by the older and graver men, men saintlike and full of faith, as many as we desired would be healed. Nothing is impossible for faith. Yet we neglect this faith although, on apostolic authority, it is most necessary. Further, we interpret "elders", i.e., men outstanding on account of age and faith, to mean any sort of ordinary priest; and we go on to convert the unrestricted anointing, i.e., the unction meant to be administered at any time, into an Extreme Unction. Not only do we not pray for healing to be granted, as promised by the apostle, but actually render the promise void by doing the very contrary. Nevertheless, we take pride in thinking that our present sacrament, though really a figment, is founded on, and proved by, this passage from the apostle; although, in fact, it is further apart from it than two octaves on the organ. What theologians!

But, let it be understood that I am not condemning the present practice of the "sacrament" of Extreme Unction; but I do firmly deny that Extreme Unction was prescribed

---

[1] Jas. 5:15   [2] Lat. *enim*   [3] Jas. 1:6   [4] Mark 11:24

by the apostle James. His anointing was in no way congruent with our "sacrament", either in form, or usage, or effectiveness, or purpose. Rather, we should class Extreme Unction among those "sacraments" which we ourselves have instituted, such as the blessing and sprinkling of salt, or holy water. We cannot deny that any creature whatever may be sanctified by the word and by prayer, a fact taught us by the apostle Paul.[1] Similarly, we cannot deny that forgiveness and peace are given through Extreme Unction. This, however, does not take place because it is a sacrament divinely instituted, but because he who receives it, receives it believing that forgiveness and peace are now his. The receiver's faith makes no error, however much the administrant may go astray. Even if the latter were baptizing or absolving in jest, i.e., not absolving at all as far as he himself was concerned, yet, in fact, he does absolve and baptize in as far as the man seeking baptism and forgiveness has faith. How much more truly will he who administers extreme unction give peace, even though the rite itself does not give peace, because it is no sacrament. The faith of the anointed man can receive even what the administrant either cannot give, or does not want to give. It is enough if the anointed man hears the word and believes; for whatever we believe we shall receive; in fact, we do receive, no matter what the minister does and leaves undone; whether he feigns or jests. For Christ's pronouncement holds good: "All things are possible to him that believes";[2] and, again: "As thou hast believed, so be it done unto thee."[3] Yet none of our sophisticators mention faith when discussing the sacraments, but strive only to talk what is, in fact, mere nonsense about the virtues of the sacraments as such, "ever learning but never coming to the knowledge of the truth".[4]

By being made the extreme or *last* unction, it has had the advantage that it has been less abused than any other sacrament, and that the benefit it confers has been less subject to the Romanists' insufferable conduct and greed. This one mercy has been left to the dying: to receive the unction without charge, without even confessing, or communicating.

[1] 1 Tim. 4:5   [2] Mark 9:23   [3] Matt. 8:13   [4] 2 Tim. 3:7

If unction had continued in daily use, and especially for curing the sick, even if not for the forgiveness of sins, one could not imagine what stretches of territory the popes would have possessed by now. Merely by abuse of the sacrament of penitence, the power of the keys, and the sacrament of ordination, they have far outvied emperors and princes. But now, fortunately, they so despise the prayer of faith that they never undertake the cure of the sick; rather, out of the old rite they have trumped up another sacrament.

I know that what I have said so far about these four sacraments used by the Romanists will be quite enough to displease those persons who think that the number and the employment of the sacraments derive, not from Scripture, but from papal authority. Their view is that these particular sacraments were bestowed by the papacy. In fact, however, they originated in the universities; and it cannot be contested that every one of the papal "sacraments" comes from that source. Nor would the papal oppressiveness have attained its present intensity if Rome had not accepted many things from the universities; for among the famous bishoprics, there is scarcely one which has had so few scholars enthroned as in the case of Rome. Hitherto the Roman pontiffs have been pre-eminent, indeed unrivalled, in violence, craftiness, and superstition. Those who occupied that throne a thousand years ago were very different from their successors, who have become so mighty in the interim; so much so that one cannot help saying that, either the early popes were not true pontiffs of Rome, or else those of the present day are not true pontiffs.

There are several other rites which it would have seemed possible to class among the sacraments, particularly all those to which a divine promise has been attached, such as prayer, the word, and the cross. There are many passages in which Christ promised that those who prayed would be heard; especially in Luke 11, where many parables admonish us to pray.[1] Concerning the word, we read: "Blessed are they who hear the word of God, and keep it."[2] And none can tell how often He promised help and blessedness to all the troubled,

[1] Luke 11:5ff.   [2] Luke 11:28

the suffering, and the humble. In particular, it is true that no one can count all God's promises, seeing that the whole of Scripture is concerned to rouse faith in us, now urging us with commandments or retributions, and again encouraging us with promises and consolations. In fact, the whole of Scripture consists of either precepts or promises. The precepts make demands which humble the haughty, whereas the promises lift up the lowly by forgiving their sins.

It seemed most proper, however, to give the name of sacrament to those ordinances which consisted of promises conjoined with signs. The others, to which no signs are attached, are promises pure and simple. It follows that, strictly speaking, there are but two sacraments in the church of God: baptism and the Lord's Supper, since we find in these alone a sign divinely instituted, and here alone the promise of the forgiveness of sins. I added the sacrament of penance to these two; but it lacks a visible sign, and was not divinely instituted; and, as I said, it is simply a means of reaffirming our baptism. Not even the Scholastics can claim that their definition of a sacrament covers penance, because they, too, require a sacrament to have a visible sign which impresses on the senses the nature of the operation which is taking place invisibly. Since neither penance nor absolution have any such sign, they are compelled by their own definition either to deny that penance is a sacrament, and so to reduce their number; or else to propose another definition of a sacrament.

I have shown that baptism applies to the whole of our life, and that it suffices for whatever sacrament we require in the course of our journey through life. On the other hand, the Supper is really the sacrament for mortal men, and for those departing this life. In it, we commemorate Christ's departure from the present world, so that we may become like Him. Thus we apply these two sacraments in such a way as to apportion baptism to cover the beginning and the whole course of our life, while the Supper has in view our life's end in death. But let a Christian use both while he inhabits this mortal frame, until his baptism having reached its fullness and his strength its summit, he then

passes out of this world as one born into a new and everlasting life, where he will eat with Christ in the kingdom of
His Father. This is in harmony with His promise at the Last
Supper, when He said: "Verily I say unto you, I will not
drink henceforth of the fruit of the vine, until it is fulfilled
in the Kingdom of God."[1] Thus it seems clear that He
instituted the sacrament of the Supper with a view to our
entry into the future life. Then both sacraments will have
fulfilled their purpose, and baptism and Supper will be no
more.

Here I come to the end of my Prelude. I place it freely
and gladly at the disposal of all those religious-minded people
who desire to have an unbiassed understanding of the Scriptures and the proper use of the sacraments. To know what
God has given us, as it says[2] in 1 Corinthians 2, and to
know how the gifts ought to be used, are matters of no mean
importance. For, if we have learned to judge spiritually, we
shall not make the mistake of relying on things that are
wrong. Contemporary theologians have never explained these
two sacraments to our understanding, even if they have not
actually tried to hide them. If I, for my part, have not
explained them, at least I have managed not to hide them;
and I have given to others an opportunity of thinking them
out to better conclusions. At any rate, I have tried to bring
them both out into the light. But none of us can do everything. In confidence and without reserve, I proffer what I
have written and fling it at the ungodly and those who,
arrogantly and insistently, teach us their own ideas instead
of the divine. I am indifferent to their coarseness, but I
wish that they would come to the right understanding.
I do not despise their efforts, but I differentiate their efforts
so far from what is really and truly Christian.

I have heard a rumour that once more a bull and other
maledictions are being prepared against me by the papal
authorities, by which I shall be pressed to recant, lest I be
declared a heretic. If the rumour is true, then I want this
little book to be part of the recantation that I shall make,
lest these arrogant despots complain of having spent their

[1] Matt. 26:29; Mark 14:25; Luke 22:18   [2] 1 Cor. 2:12

breath in vain. I will publish a sequel shortly,[1] and in such kind, please Christ, as the popes of Rome have neither seen nor heard hitherto. I will give ample testimony of my obedience. In the name of Jesus Christ, our Lord, Amen.

> Why, impious Herod, shouldst thou fear
> Because the Christ is come so near?
> He who doth heavenly kingdoms grant
> Thine earthly realm can never want.[2]

[1] I.e., the *Freedom of a Christian*, cf. pp. 351ff., *infra*

[2] Hostis Herodes impie
Christum venire quid times?
Non arripit mortalia
Qui regna dat coelestia.

From Coelius Sedulius, *c.* A.D. 450.
The translation is according to *The English Hymnary*

AN OPEN LETTER TO POPE LEO X

1520

Introduction

Two years had elapsed since Karl von Miltitz[1] had arrived in Germany as the Apostolic Nuncio. He came armed with many papal briefs, and his object was to smother the movement of protest against the authority of the church. This movement had gathered head mainly because of the publication of Luther's *Ninety-five Theses* and various other writings of a similar standpoint by him and other leaders. Eck's arrival with the ban against Luther in the summer of 1520, threatened to make a fiasco of Miltitz's diplomacy. The latter therefore attempted once again to keep control.

John von Staupitz, vicar-general of the German Augustinians, had summoned the chapter of the order to meet at Eisleben on August 28, 1520. Miltitz attended with a view to devising with "the brethren" some means of persuading Luther to write in a different manner.[2] He suggested that Staupitz, who had resigned the vicariate, and Lenck, who had succeeded him, together with a few "brothers", should interview Luther. The suggestion was accepted, and the group met in Wittenberg at the beginning of September. Luther agreed to explain in a humble spirit that he had never intended to attack the pope personally, and undertook to exercise greater self-restraint; but before the end of that very month, when Eck began to publish the papal bull excommunicating Luther, he felt himself freed from his promises.

Meantime, Miltitz was planning to meet Luther personally. At the former's request, Frederick the Wise, Elector of Saxony, directed his councillor, Fabian von Feilitzsch, to order Luther to meet Miltitz and listen to what he had to say. The conversation between them took place at Lichtenberg on October 12. They agreed on the contents of the letter which Luther was to write to the pope; and, in order that none should be able to say that Eck had published the bull and in this way forced his hand, it was also agreed that the date of the letter was to be given as September 6, the day when the chapter of his order "had requested him to write to the pope". A pamphlet was to be

---

[1] A German nobleman, born 1490, and trained in the law. He became a trusted papal diplomat while still in his twenties. He negotiated with Luther at Altenburg early in January 1519, and, on his own authority, suggested that a German bishop should act as arbitrator

[2] Luther's *Schreiben in einen anderen Stil zu wenden*

333

appended, whose contents had probably already been discussed. Each document was to be published in both German and Latin.

The letter, written in Latin and intended for the pope, was composed by Luther before the end of October; he immediately made a German translation, and published it before the Latin form, under the title: *An Open Letter to Pope Leo X*. The German edition was in print before November 16, for on that date Miltitz sent a printed copy to Willibald Pirckheimer[1] in Nüremberg. The pamphlet, *On the Freedom of a Christian*, in its German form, was a separate publication, but was included in the same parcel (cf. *infra*, p. 351).

The instructed reader can scarcely avoid being confused, or even offended, by his first glance through the *Open Letter*: Luther's personal attitude to the pope may appear self-contradictory, perhaps insolent; and his discussion of public affairs immoderate as well as largely irrelevant. But account must be taken of the critical pass to which matters had come, and of the promise which Luther had given to Miltitz. These circumstances meant that Luther felt compelled to write, and also to keep in mind the general terms of his last conversation with Miltitz. Approached from this angle, the *Letter* becomes clear, self-consistent, timely, and of great importance in the reforming movement now getting under way. In his own mind, Luther tries to make a distinction between Leo X, on the one hand, and the papacy in its evil repute on the other. Taken in the strictest sense, this distinction is maintained, but it is doubtful if this is what was popularly understood; for the indictment of the papacy is so severe and so well merited that it is difficult to escape the impression that Luther regarded Leo to some extent as a consenting party, and that, by implication at least, Luther depicts him as such. Still, in passages where Leo is directly addressed, Luther's tone is sufficiently respectful.

But the *Letter* is dominated by the fact that Luther was determined to stand his ground in regard to his charges against the gross abuses which were being practised in Rome, which were spreading everywhere and which were poisoning the whole church. Since he had promised to write to Leo, he would try to write as if Leo were not only innocent, but also ignorant, of the scandalous state of affairs; as if Leo would be glad of the information, however

---

[1] One of the outstanding humanists (1470–1530). His large library and collection of artistic treasures at Nüremberg was the pivot of the town's culture. At first on Luther's side, he wrote against Eck. He abandoned the Reformation in 1524 as "too demagogic and radical". .

disagreeable in itself; and as if he would be the first to punish wrong-doers, and initiate reforms. Such a standpoint was far too artificial to be consistently maintained. Luther could not in fact do other than write with the general public in view, and continue the polemic he had carried on with devastating force in the *Appeal to the Ruling Class* and in the *First Inquiry into the Pagan Servitude of the Church.*

But it should never be forgotten that the *Open Letter* was sent to the pope along with the *Freedom of a Christian*, a fact which gives new depth to the *Letter* and fresh point to the *Freedom*.

The present translation is made from the German text as given in the Weimar Edition, Vol. VII, pp. 1–3, 3–11. The Latin text is given on pp. 39–42, 42–49.

Text and Notes

To the most holy Father in God, Leo X., Pope in Rome, all blessedness in Christ Jesus, Our Lord. Amen.

Most Holy Father in God. The bitter dispute in which I have been engaged for almost three years past[1] with certain dullards, has caused me from time to time to think of appealing to Your Holiness. Indeed, because it is held that you alone are the real subject of this dispute, I cannot help thinking of you continually. Some of the smooth-tongued and unchristian hangers-on at your Court are groundlessly incensed with me. Their conduct is driving me to appeal, not to your Throne and Court, but to a free council of the church, to which I would submit my contentions.[2] Yet I have never become estranged from you in my affection; at all times, I have most earnestly desired all that is good for you and the Roman see; and I seek that blessing from God with earnest, heartfelt prayer, and with all my powers. It is true that I have tried very hard to set at nought those who have often attempted to frighten me by invoking the majesty attaching to your name and the greatness of your power. But a matter has come forward which I do not dare to ignore, and which is the cause of my writing you once more,[3] viz., it has come to my notice that I have been misrepresented, and spitefully described as not having spared even your own person.

I wish to declare, freely and frankly, that I am not conscious of having done other than speak most loyally and

[1] I.e., since Luther nailed the 95 theses on the church door at Wittenberg, Oct. 31, 1517. Hence the time of writing to the pope was Autumn, 1520

[2] Luther had actually published an *Appellatio ad Concilium* in Nov., 1518 (*W.*, II, 34ff.), and had reiterated his appeal in a revised form the following November (*W.*, VII, 74ff.). If these publications had actually been brought to Leo's notice, the present reminder would serve to add weight to this letter

[3] Luther had written a humble letter to the pope after a conference with Karl von Miltitz at Altenburg in Jan., 1519, following a letter of defence on May 30, 1518; cf. *supra*, pp. 6off.

highly of your Holiness, whenever I have thought of your name. Had I done otherwise at any time, then, far from being proud of my action, I should feel myself compelled fully to acknowledge and support the verdict of my accusers; and I should have been very anxious to retract such presumption, to correct any misrepresentation on my part, and to revoke any culpable words. I have called you a Daniel in Babylon; and, as to how zealously I have defended your innocence against Sylvester,[1] your defamer, everyone who reads what I have written can fully understand.

Indeed your reputation and the fame of your blameless life are so widely spread in all the world, praised so generously and highly by many scholarly men that no one, however great he might be, could injure you by any sort of innuendo. I am not so foolish as to set out alone to attack one whom all praise. Moreover, my way has always been, and I intend it always shall be, not to injure even those who are already held in evil repute by everyone. I take no pleasure in the sins of others, for I am well aware that I also have a beam in my own eye; and indeed I cannot be the one to cast the first stone at the woman taken in adultery.[2]

Granted, I have sharply attacked certain unchristian doctrines, although only in general terms. I have also used bitter words about my opponents, not because of their wicked lives, but for their unchristian doctrines and arguments. Far from regretting this in any way, I intend to go on actively making attacks, and pressing them home, no matter how certain persons construe my actions; for in this matter I have Christ's example. He Himself was keenly hostile to His opponents, and called them a brood of vipers, hypocrites, blind,[3] children of the devil.[4] Again St. Paul calls Simon Magus a son of the devil, and full of all subtlety and mischief;[5] and he reviles certain false apostles as dogs, deceivers, and corrupters of the word of God.[6] If soft and

[1] Probably Sylvester Mazzolini of Prierium, who had written a *dialogus in presumtuosas Martini Lutheri conclusiones.* Luther replied by sending an explanation of his theses to the pope on May 30, 1518. In another writing, he went as far as to say that the pope was the head of the whole world, indeed, in essence, the whole world! Cf. *De potestate papae (W.,* Vol. I, 644–86); *vide supra,* p. 28, n.1   [2] John 8:1ff.   [3] Matt. 23:33 and 3:7   [4] John 8:44   [5] Acts 13:10   [6] Phil. 3:2; 2 Cor. 11:13 and 2:17

X

tender-hearted people had heard such expressions, they also would probably have said that there was none so bitter and impatient as St. Paul. And who are more biting than the prophets? But to-day, our hearts have become so very soft and tender owing to the multitude of shameless toadies, that, unless we are praised for every little thing, we cry out "How abusive he is." If we cannot do anything else to escape the truth, we break into fictitious pleas about his bitterness, impatience, and rudeness. But what is the use of salt if it is not in fact salty? What is the use of the edge on the sword if it is not sharp enough to cut? The prophet says, "Cursed be he that doeth the commandment of God carelessly, and spareth too much."[1]

Therefore, Holy Father Leo, I beg that you will accept this explanation of mine, and regard me confidently as one who has never thought any wrong towards you personally. I wish you all that is good from the bottom of my heart. I desire no quarrel or dispute about the evil life of any one; I am only striving for the truth of the divine word. I have no wish except to yield gladly to any man; but neither do I wish to abandon, nor am I able to deny, the word of God. If any one has a different opinion of me, or has taken my writings in another sense, he errs and has not understood me rightly.

True, I have vigorously attacked the see in Rome, and what is known as the Roman court; and you yourself, like every one else on earth, must admit that it is more wicked and shameful than Sodom, Gomorrah, or Babylon ever was. And, as far as I can see, its wickedness can henceforward be neither remedied nor ignored. Everything has become altogether hopeless and beyond repair. It has angered me that, in your name and under the mask of the Roman church, poor people everywhere have been deceived and made to suffer; this is what I have set myself against, and I shall set myself against it as long as a Christian spirit lives in me. Not that I think I can do the impossible, nor do I hope to accomplish anything in that most detestable Sodom and Babylon called Rome, especially as so many toadies are

[1] Jer. 48:10

wroth against me. But because I confess myself to be under obligation to serve all Christian people, it behoves me to advise and to warn them in order that few of them may suffer, and all of these suffer less, from their Romish oppressors.

It cannot have been hidden from you yourself what has been happening now and for many years in Rome, and extending everywhere. There has grown to be a corruption of body, soul, and goods; every kind of wickedness has seized upon and overwhelmed all men alike. All of this is open to the day and known to every one. Thereby the Roman church, which in past ages was the holiest of all, has now become a den of murderers beyond all other dens of murderers, a thieves' castle beyond all other thieves' castles, the head and empire of every sin, as well as of death and damnation. Indeed one can hardly imagine what further wickedness could be added if the very Antichrist himself were to come.

Meanwhile, Holy Father Leo, you seem like a sheep amongst the wolves,[1] and like Daniel among the lions,[2] you seem to be with Ezekiel among the scorpions.[3] What can you do alone amongst so much that is vile and shocking? Even if three or four learned and pious cardinals came to your aid, what is that among such a multitude? You would certainly all be poisoned[4] before you could begin to mend matters. It is all over with the Holy See of Rome; God's anger has fallen upon it, and will not relent. That see is hostile to the general councils; it will let itself be neither taught nor reformed, and is not even able to restrain its own rankly unchristian nature. Thereby what Jeremiah said of its mother, the old Babylon, is fulfilled: "We have often healed Babylon, but she is not healed; we shall let her go."[5]

It should be your duty and that of your cardinals to cure this state of woe, but the disease spurns the medicine; horse and waggon no longer obey the driver. That is the reason why

---

[1] Matt. 10:16   [2] Dan. 6:16ff.   [3] Ezek. 2:6

[4] This remark is neither exaggerated, nor without foundation. An attempted plot on Leo's life by poisoning had in fact been discovered only just in time during the summer of 1517; and it is still uncertain whether his sudden death in Dec., 1521, was not due to poison; cf. *supra*, 128, 165

[5] Jer. 51:9

it has always been a grief to me, that your Holiness became pope in this age; you were surely worthy to be pope in a better age. The see of Rome is not worthy of you and those like you.[1] The Evil One is the veritable pope, for he certainly rules in this Babylon more truly than you.

Would God that, relieved of the honour (as your most mischievous enemies call it), you lived in a benefice or on your paternal heritage; for surely no one would be fitly honoured by such an honour except Judas Iscariot and his compeers, whom God has overthrown. What good is done by you in virtue of the papacy? It becomes the more wicked and incorrigible the more often and the more widely it either misuses your power and title, hurts the people materially and spiritually, increases sin and shame, or stifles faith and truth. O most unhappy Leo, you who sit on the most dangerous of all thrones, truly I am telling you the truth, and I yearn for your good.

Thus St. Bernard[2] bewailed Eugenius, who became pope in his time, because, although the Roman See was even then extremely wicked, he nevertheless ruled in good hope of its improvement. How much more ought we to bewail you in that, three centuries later, evil and corruption have increased irresistibly and gained the upper hand! Is it not true that nothing under heaven is more wicked, more poisonous, more hateful than the court of Rome? It has surpassed the immorality of the Turks so far, indeed, that Rome, formerly a gate of heaven, is now the wide-open throat of hell, and, unhappily, such a throat as, by the wrath of God, no man can shut. We have no other recourse than that we should warn and support certain persons, lest they too be swallowed down into the abyss called Rome.

[1] While Leo X was guilty of nepotism and of political duplicity quite in accordance with the age, his private life exhibited a refreshing elevation and his personal character a purity of morals which distinguished him markedly from his more immediate predecessors, and contributed to the inauguration of a worthier tradition after his death

[2] The celebrated Bernard of Clairvaux, one of whose pupils became Eugenius III. When Eugenius was chosen pope in 1145, Bernard wrote the cardinals: "In God's name, I ask, what have you done? You have called back into the world one who had withdrawn from the world; you have cast back again into cares and business matters one who had withdrawn himself from cares and business matters" (*Ad Eugenium papam*)

Lo! Holy Father, that is the final and the efficient cause[1] why I have made such attacks upon this pestilential see. So far was I from intending to gird at you personally, that I even hoped to earn your goodwill and thanks, and be recognized as labouring for your highest good by virtue of the very lustiness and sharpness of my attack upon your prison, for your Throne must seem like hell to you. I believed that everything which any reasonable and educated men could bring to bear against the rank, unchristian disorders of your court would be welcomed as advantageous to you and many others. All who do every possible harm and every possible hurt to such a court are, of course, doing a work which you should do; all who disgrace the court as much as possible are doing honour to Christ. In short, all good Christians are bad Romanists.

I wish further to add that, in the ordinary course, it would never have come into my mind to inveigh against the Roman court or to raise controversy about it. But, when once I saw that money and strength were wasted without bettering it, I despised it, gave it the *congé*, said "Adieu, dear Rome. What stinks there, let it go on stinking, and what is filthy there, let it go on being filthy."[2] So I devoted myself to the quiet and peaceful study of the Holy Scriptures, that I might be helpful to those among whom I lived. As I was not labouring in vain, however, the Evil One opened his eyes and took notice. He bayed and awakened his servant, John Eck, to a foolish project. This man is a special enemy of Christ and the truth. He drew me into a discussion, in which I was incautious. He seized on me in regard to a minor word, uttered about the papacy, which almost as it were slipped from me.[3] Then the great, boastful braggart jumped up, snorting and gnashing his teeth, as if he had already arrested me. He gave out that he would venture and perform all things to the honour of God and to the praise of the holy

[1] Parts of the scholastic system of causation derived from Aristotle
[2] Rev. 22:11
[3] In reply to certain theses published by John Eck dealing with the supremacy of the pope in the first century, Luther entered into the famous disputation with Eck in Leipzig in July, 1519, the result being that Luther no longer recognized the authority of the Roman church in matters of faith, but only that of the Bible

Church of Rome. He puffed himself up and protested your authority, which he used to get himself the repute of being the foremost theologian in the world—a matter which lay nearer his heart than did the good of the papacy. He ventured to think that it would be a considerable advantage to this end if he triumphed over poor me. When that failed, however, the quibbler pretended not to understand, for he then felt that, by his own fault alone, the shame and disgrace of the Roman See had been laid open to my gaze.

Now, Holy Father, let me further plead my own affairs before you, and arraign your real enemies before you. Without doubt you know how your legate,[1] Cardinal St. Sixti, negotiated with me at Augsburg.[2] Admittedly he was indiscreet and incorrect, nay unfaithful; yet for your sake I placed all my affairs in his hands on condition that he should impose peace on both sides. I wanted an end of the matter and to be at peace if my antagonists would also keep the peace. He could easily have secured this by a word. But the itch of temporal fame tickled him so much that he despised my offer. He thought it well to justify my antagonists, to give them a longer rein, and to order me to recant; although he had no instructions to that effect. Thus it has come about, through his mischievous blundering, that those affairs, which at that time were quite satisfactory, have since then become much worse. The further consequences, therefore, are not my fault, but that same cardinal's, who would not permit me to maintain silence as I earnestly requested. What else ought I to have done?

Afterwards came Karl von Miltitz,[3] who also was your Holiness's emissary. He travelled here and there at much trouble, and tried hard to bring matters back into the good order from which they had been arrogantly and criminally thrown by the cardinal. At length, with the help of his Serene Highness the Elector, Frederick, Duke of Saxony,

---

[1] I.e., Cajetan (really Thomas de Vio of Gaeta); cf. *supra*, p 65; and p. 209

[2] In July, 1518 (cf. *W.*, Vol. II, p. 1ff.)

[3] Miltitz was a Saxon nobleman. He undertook to write to the pope and persuade him to send a scholarly bishop and lay upon him the responsibility of settling matters. Meanwhile both sides were to maintain silence

etc., he managed to arrange a few conferences[1] with me. I let myself once more stand corrected and be silenced, out of respect for your name. I agreed that the case should be tried by the archbishop of Trèves or the bishop of Naumberg. This was arranged and ordered. When these matters were agreed on, and the outlook was hopeful, John Eck,[2] who is really your worst enemy, broke in with the debate at Leipzig,[3] which he had undertaken against Dr. Carlstadt. In the course of his speeches, which were as changeable as the wind, he found a tiny point[4] about the papacy, and suddenly turned upon me with might and main, completely destroying the plan for the intended peace.

Meanwhile Karl von Miltitz was waiting. The debate proceeded; judges were chosen; but nothing was settled. This did not surprise me. For Eck with his lies, special pleas, and secret devices, embittered, confused, and beclouded the issue until no matter to which side the verdict had been given, a greater fire would undoubtedly have been lighted; for he sought fame and not the truth. Thus throughout, I have done my duty, and left undone nothing I was under obligation to perform. I acknowledge that by these means no small part of the unchristian ways at Rome has been brought to light. The responsibility for that is not mine but Eck's, for he undertook a task beyond his ability, and, by his ambition, the Romish vices have been laid bare everywhere, and have brought shame.

Holy Father Leo, this man is your enemy and the enemy of the Roman see. From the example of this one man, all may learn that there is no more baneful enemy than a toady. All he has effected with his flattery is misfortune such as no king could have brought about. The name of the

---

[1] In Altenburg, Liebenwerda, and Lichtenberg

[2] Cf. *supra*, p. 28, n.3

[3] Cf. T. M. Lindsay, *op. cit.*, I, 236ff. J. Mackinnon, *op. cit.*, II, 126ff. Erasmus wrote to Fisher, bishop of Rochester, on Oct. 17, 1519: "I fear Martin will perish for his uprightness, but Eck ought to be called Geck (Dutch for fool). . . . The Elector of Saxony (by whose protection alone Luther lives), protested that he would not allow innocence to be oppressed in his dominions by those who sought their own profit, and not the things of Christ." Cf. *Br.*, Vol. I, 514; also compare H. P. Smith's *Life of Erasmus*, p. 224

[4] Cf. *supra*, p. 341

Roman curia now makes a stench in all the world, respect
for the pope is enfeebled, Romish ignorance stands in evil
repute. We should never have heard of any of these matters
if Eck had not destroyed the plans of Karl von Miltitz
and myself for peace.[1] He now feels this himself and, although
too late and in vain, he is indignant about the tractates I
have published.[2] He should have thought of that beforehand
when he neighed for fame like a spirited, ruttish horse; and
seeking nothing but his own advantage, in spite of your great
disadvantage. The silly man thought that I would be frightened if your name were mentioned, or that I would then
give way to him, and be silent; for I do not hold that he
was depending only on his skill and cleverness. Now, when
he sees that I have been encouraged, and have gained a
wider audience, he rues his rashness too late, and bethinks
him (if he thinks at all) that there is One in heaven Who
withstands the proud and humbles the presumptuous.[3]

Since the only result of the debate was to bring greater
dishonour to the Holy See, Karl von Miltitz came to the
fathers of my Order and sought advice how to smooth
affairs over and hush things up; for all was now in a most
unfortunate and dangerous state. Therefore they chose a few
of their fine fellows, and sent them to me. It was not to be
supposed that anything could be effected by using violence
against me, so they requested me to show due respect to
your self, Holy Father: I was to write submissively and
explain how you and I were alike innocent in the affair. They
were of the opinion that the matter was not yet entirely
forlorn and desperate if the Holy Father Leo would deal
with it, in accordance with the highly renowned kindness
characteristic of him. I have always offered and desired peace,
that I might apply myself to quieter and more useful studies;
so this delegation seemed to me valuable and welcome.
I received them gladly, and was happy to follow the lines
they suggested—I felt it would be a great blessing if only

---

[1] I.e., for a settlement by the agency of a German bishop
[2] Perhaps, e.g., *Resolutiones disputationum, W.*, I, 522–628; *sermo de virtute
excommunicationis, W.*, I, 634–43; *appellatio ad futurum concilium universale,
W.*, I, 34–40
[3] 1 Pet. 5:5; Judith 6:15

all should happen as we hoped. I have spoken forcefully in bold words and vigorous writings, just in order to overwhelm them and make them keep quiet; for, as I saw clearly, they were far from equal to serious argument.

I now come, Holy Father Leo, and fling myself at your feet. I beg that, if possible, you will be pleased to put out your hand and bridle the toadies who are the enemies of peace while proffering peace. But it is useless to demand that I should recant my teaching. Nor must any one else try forcing me to recant, for he would only make matters still worse. Moreover, I cannot bear with rubrics and regulations as to how I should explain the Scripture; because the word of God, which teaches full freedom, should not and must not be fettered. If these two points are granted, any other conditions that can be imposed upon me I shall welcome and most willingly observe. I hate contention, and desire neither to challenge nor provoke any one; neither do I desire to be provoked myself. But if I am incited, then, please God, I shall not lack utterance or refrain from writing. Your Holiness could, with a few brief words, call the whole of this controversy to your own presence and suppress it and, instead, command silence and peace, words which I have all along been most anxious to hear.

Therefore, Holy Father, I pray you, refuse to listen to those whose smooth tongues whisper in your ears, saying that you are not merely a man, but conjoined with God; and that it is your prerogative to command and require all things. That is not true, and you are not able to act as if it were. You are a servant of all the servants of God, and you are in more dangerous and deplorable circumstances than any other man on earth. Do not let yourself be deceived by those who lie to you and pretend you are lord of the world; who will not allow any one to be called a Christian unless he is subject to you; who prate that you have authority over heaven, hell, and purgatory. They are your enemies, and want to destroy your soul. It is as Isaiah says: "O my people, they who praise and exalt you, deceive you."[1] All are in error who say that you are superior to councils and to the

---

[1] Isa. 3:12

church universal. They err who accord you the sole authority of interpreting Scripture; one and all they seek nothing else than how, in your name, they might strengthen their unchristian projects in Christendom—as indeed the Evil One has unfortunately done through many of your predecessors. In brief: trust not even one of those who exalt you, but only those who make you feel humble. That is God's judgment, as it says in the Scriptures: "He has put down the mighty from their seats and exalted them of low degree."[1]

Consider the dissimilarity between Christ and His vicars or representatives;[2] if, indeed, all of them do want to represent Him. I fear it is only too true that they replace Him, for a representative only acts in a place from which his superior is absent. And the pope, unless Christ dwells in his heart, rules in the Lord's absence, and then only too truly does he replace Christ. Even a troop of men like that would not have Christ in their midst; and that kind of a pope would only be an Antichrist and idol. The apostles did far better when they only called themselves servants of the Christ[3] dwelling in them; and did not call, or allow themselves to be called, vicegerents acting for an absent Lord.

Perhaps I am presumptuous in daring to instruct one who is so highly exalted, by whom indeed every one else ought to be instructed, and from whom, as certain of the poisonous, smooth-tongued men around you boast, all kings and judges receive judgment. But herein I am following St. Bernard[4] in his book addressed to Pope Eugenius, which all popes ought by rights to know by heart. I follow him, indeed, but not with the intention of instructing you. My motive is purely one of loyalty and concern. There is a duty which

---

[1] Luke 1:52

[2] *Statthalter*, etymol: place-holders. It is almost impossible to translate this paragraph owing to the subtle play on the various nuances of this term, and of the phrase "Vicar of Christ". It may be noted, incidentally, that Ambrosiaster (an anonymous writer of the fourth century and a disciple of Ambrose) called the king the Vicar of God, and claimed that he had the image of God as the bishop had that of Christ, cf. G. Rupp, *English Protestant Tradition* (1947), p. 83 and H. Lietzmann, *The Era of the Church Fathers* (1951), Chap. IV

[3] Cf. Phil. 1:1

[4] Cf. *supra*, p. 340, n. 2

compels every one of us to take an interest in matters which are quite clear, and which have to do with our neighbours. This concern and duty should pay no regard to our neighbour's rank or station, but should cause us to do all we can to protect him against any danger or misfortune which may threaten him. I know how your Holiness lives and labours in Rome: among the numberless dangers and ceaseless storms of a rough sea; and how you live and work under such a strain that you would welcome the help of even the humblest Christian. I have therefore not allowed the exalted position, which your Holiness occupies, to deter me from discharging my duty of brotherly love. I cannot bring myself to play the flatterer in the midst of such a serious and dangerous state of affairs; if certain persons refuse to understand that in so abstaining I am your friend and more than a mere subject, at least he who does understand will find it true.

Finally, lest I come before Your Holiness empty-handed, I am sending herewith a little book[1] which I have dedicated to you. It comes with my good wishes, and as an earnest of the beginning of peace. I send it with the lively hope that Your Holiness may discern the kind of subject on which I would spend my time and strength, and it would be an advantage to do so, if it were possible to me in view of the unchristian toadies who hang about you. Going by the number of pages, it is but a pamphlet, but to grasp its meaning is to comprehend the whole sum of the Christian life. I am a poor man, having nothing else with which I can pay my respects; moreover you need nothing except to be enriched with spiritual gifts. Herewith I commend myself to Your Holiness.

May Jesus Christ ever preserve you. Amen.

Wittenberg. September 6th, 1520.

---

[1] *The Freedom of a Christian*, cf. *infra*, pp. 349ff.

6

THE FREEDOM OF A CHRISTIAN

Introduction

In accordance with the promise which he had given to Miltitz at Lichtenberg on October 12, 1520,[1] Luther at once began work on the *Open Letter* to the pope, Leo X, and the pamphlet on the *Freedom of a Christian* which was to accompany the *Letter* and explain Luther's essential position. He wrote, of course, in Latin, and immediately on completing this task, he set about making a German version. Here, as distinct from the Latin version, he presented the *Open Letter* and the pamphlet as two separate publications. In any case, the German versions were the first to see the light, and were published before November 16, on which date Miltitz is known to have sent a copy of each to Willibald Pirckheimer in Nüremberg.

In neither case is the German version a close translation of the Latin, though the substance is, of course, the same. It is generally agreed that Luther's German version is rather inferior to the Latin, not only in fullness, completeness, and clarity, but also in the firmness and precision with which the thought is expressed. Nevertheless, it was the German form which exercised the greater influence and which offered the average man, who laid no claim to be a scholar, a real understanding of Luther's essential message. As Luther said at the end of the *Open Letter*: "going by the number of pages, it is only a pamphlet, but to grasp its meaning is to comprehend the whole sum of the Christian life."[2] It is in fact the third of the crucial triad of Reformation writings.[3]

The fame of this brief document is well justified. It gathers up into a small compass what Luther had said in various ways many times before, and was to say many times again. As it stands, it is one of the most beautiful of Luther's writings, and in itself sufficiently warrants the name, "Swan of Wittenberg", often given by contemporaries to Luther. It is one of the classic documents of the Christian faith, and shows the positive, evangelical basis of the Reformation.

The title is rather misleading, and is due to the paradox with which Luther begins. Essentially, the writing deals with the question: What is it that makes a man acceptable to God? or, What is it to be good in God's sight? The answer is: When

---

[1] Cf. *supra*, pp. 333f.; 342ff.   [2] Cf. *supra*, p. 347
[3] The other two writings are: *The Appeal to the Ruling Class*, and *The Pagan Servitude of the Church*

God Himself has worked a miracle of grace in his heart. That is
an act which cannot be induced, nor can it ever be merited. God
does it Himself, of His own free will, and out of His own merciful
grace. The utmost the believer can do is to prepare himself for
it when God sees the time is ripe. He can prepare himself, and
then humbly accept it as a gift of which he is still utterly
unworthy, but which he will now use in whatever way God wills.
We become Christian because and when we are willing to let
God have His way with us, in His own time, and in His own
manner. That willingness on our part is what Luther means by
faith. Faith implies trust, receptivity, and response; and these
are so bound into a "bundle of life" that each depends on, and
inspires, the other two. A unity develops which gradually makes
its own nature clear to the intelligence, and comes to expression,
not only in "the countless unremembered acts of kindness and
of love", but also in the higher conduct of life. Its noblest
expression is to be seen in those who act as God's prophets, or,
perhaps equally, as humble missionaries of the gospel.

All this is clear enough, and has been the commonplace of
Protestant teaching for over four centuries; it has linked the
essential spirit of Protestantism direct with the New Testament
and the first generation of Christians, and this linkage has been
conscious and of set purpose.

Luther makes his own position clear in the first few sentences
which deal with the paradoxical antithesis of bondage and freedom, a paradox which really derives from St. Paul.[1] Nevertheless,
with many problems of detail very much in men's minds, and
with the habit of moral casuistry very much in possession of the
church, Luther was compelled to enter on a detailed discussion;
but, in his further advance, it must be confessed, he plunges
into a morass. He struggles with it, flounders in it, and barely
gets himself clear of it. Even in the final paragraph, he cries
aloud that all is well, and that he is through; but, in fact, he is
still there.

The explanation is that he never defined, and set in a place
apart, exactly what he intended to convey by his two key-words,
faith and works. Each term is, in fact, very complex, and he
uses now one connotation and then another, until the strands of
his argument are inextricably interlaced. Happily, the plain man
can see the plain meaning, even if he should completely fail to

[1] E.g., I Cor. 9:19; compare Rom. 1:1, ". . . a slave of Jesus Christ"
with Rom. 8:21, "the glorious liberty of the children of God"

express it plainly. The term faith is used by Luther in the following principal senses: (i) a humble trust in God in the spirit of Jesus; (ii) a glad obedience to the will of God as revealed in the Holy Scripture and as grasped by the trained intellect when comparing passage with passage and intention with intention: in cases where the most stubborn efforts do not reach clarity of understanding on this basis, then there is nothing for it but blind obedience to the written word of God; (iii) a grace received personally and mystically in one's heart, but also accepted with the criticism of one's best understanding. Perhaps the help of the experience of others must be sought, and the widest social implications must be kept in mind.

Luther would distinguish his understanding of faith from that of his opponents mainly in so far as the latter dutifully accept the customs and decrees of the church and the papal court. In effect, Luther would confine the operation of faith to religious issues, and his opponents would find no difficulty in joining Luther here; but they would include in these issues the humble acceptance of all the traditions of the church and the authority of the hierarchy. Luther makes faith essentially moral and, therefore, personal and masculine. His opponents make it essentially a matter of acceptance or obedience, and therefore an outward assent and a feminine compliance.

By works, Luther means an even more complex group of ideas. The fundamental proposition is simple and unexceptionable: a genuine ethical intention is the sole criterion of an act which deserves to be called good. Only the good tree can produce good fruits. These fruits form one of the groups to which Luther applies the term *Werke*, or works. But this basic proposition can be spread over many degrees of difference, until it is made to cover acts that are ethically indifferent, or even reprehensible. Thus obedience to the "inner voice" may deteriorate into a lifeless conformity to custom; then, *Werke* means conduct, a connotation about which Luther has very little to say. Or it may come to mean things done in blindly accepting the authority of the priest, the confessor, the curia, or the pope. These requirements may be innocuous or even praiseworthy in themselves, or they may be the reverse; in either case, they are equally unspiritual. In this sense, *Werke* means religious observances, and may include the rites and ceremonies of the church, or the mechanical performance of penances, or the purchase of indulgences, or going on pilgrimages, or the like.

Y

Confusion becomes worse confounded, however, when the same term, *Werke*, is also made to include acts of charity, brotherly helpfulness, self-sacrifice for the common good, and goodwill in general; as well as the personal qualities of patience, kindliness, and all the virtues which St. Paul includes among the fruits of the spirit. Unfortunately for the clarity and the brevity of many of Luther's writings, he never makes this complex connotation, or these broad and deep distinctions, clear in advance; but actually, like St. Paul, uses the same term to cover all the different kinds of religious actions, both the conventional and the moral, both the ecclesiastical rites and conformities, and also those fruits of the spirit which are at once ethical and religious in the highest sense.

A further, and much more subtle, meaning of the term *Werke* concerns not the thing actually done, not religious observance or altruistic conduct, but the volition, the motion of the will. Here we reach the heart of the matter. Luther's point is that this act of the will, to be ethically good, can only come from a man who is already good; and a man can only be good *in this sense* if he has been made so by the miracle of the grace of God, grace which by definition can only be grace when it is free, unbought, and unmerited: a gift which can only be prayed for. This is the very heart of the evangelical conception of religion; apart from it, the whole Protestant position is a mere matter of taste and preference.

As distinct from this view, Luther's opponents, basing themselves at once on Aristotle[1] and naïve common sense, believed that if a man accustomed himself, whether by his own choice or in obedience to some mentor, to doing the right things, he would gradually acquire the habit of good conduct, and so become good in himself.[2] Hence this obedience of his was to be approved and, proleptically, he was to be called good from the moment of his first obedience. No one can deny that this contention contains much psychological truth; it is the very basis of training. "Train up a child in the way he shall go, and when he is old he will not depart from it."[3] Moreover, Luther knew it to be true, and never lost sight of its truth. He himself acted upon it, e.g.,

---

[1] *Nicomachean Ethics*, Bk. II, chap. i, ed. Chace; so, too, Erasmus's *Encheiridion*, which shows that he had no true understanding of the evangelical position

[2] Aristotle, ed. Chace, *op. cit.*, "law-givers make the individual members good men by habituation", *loc. cit.*

[3] Prov. 22:6

in enjoining the use of some such system of religious education as is outlined in his *Catechisms*[1] and in the many, widely varying, editions of his *Betbüchlein* of 1522.[2] But this position, which is at least as old as Aristotle, had been grossly misunderstood and greatly abused in the medieval church. Far and wide, the church that Luther knew, and the religion that it sanctioned, had become the engine of a secularized hierarchy. In blunt, modern terminology, it was a "racket". This was an unspeakable calamity for Europe as a whole, for the nature and quality of its civilization, and for individual persons down into the most secret places of their hearts. It was against this "racket" and this "racket" alone, but with all that it implied in theory and practice, that Luther protested; and it was solely to establish a purer religion and a nobler ethic, i.e., the religion and ethic of the New Testament and the early Fathers, that Luther took his stand. The *Freedom of a Christian* was written when Luther was immersed in controversy, and labouring amid tense excitement; when the papal ban meant that all who obeyed it were authorized to use violence against him, and when even to kill him would not be murder. Yet, in these extraordinary conditions, he preserved his concern for the people at large. If we understand these circumstances, the writing becomes clear and forceful from first to last.

Luther dedicated the German version to the town provost of Zwickau, Hermann Mülport, whom he erroneously called Jerome. He had been told by John Silvius (Wildenauer) of Eger that Mülport was a great Bible-lover, delighting in the Scriptures. Silvius seems to have visited Luther in Wittenberg during the time the MS. was under his hand (October, 1520), and when Silvius, too, had come under the papal ban. By dedicating the *Freedom* in this way, Luther's intention was to begin a new friendship on a high level. The relation lasted, however, only a brief time, for the quarrels which broke out, in 1522, in the church at Zwickau,[3] caused estrangement between them.

The present translation has been made from the German text as given in the Weimar Edition, Vol. VII, pp. 12–19, 20–38.

---

[1] Cf. Vol. II of the present series; cf. *W*., Vol. XXX; pp. 1–425
[2] Cf. *W*., Vol. X, pt. ii, p. 331–482
[3] This quarrel was the first sign of what later became known, in 1525, as the Anabaptist movement. Zwickau is in Saxony, 40 miles south of Dresden, and in Luther's time it was a small but growing town on the main trade route between Saxony and Bohemia. Silver mines were discovered there in 1470, and were bringing wealth, importance, and excitement

THE FREEDOM OF A CHRISTIAN

Text and Notes

To the sagacious and learned gentleman, Jerome Mühlpfordt, Mayor of Zwickau, a very kind friend and patron, I, Martin Luther, Augustinian, present my compliments and best wishes.

Wise and learned sir, and my dear friend, your excellent civic chaplain, the reverend John Egran,[1] has spoken in very warm terms of the love and delight with which you regard Holy Scripture, and, indeed, how you readily avow and heartily commend it before men. That is why he wished to introduce me personally to you, and I am indeed very eager and happy that it should be so, for it gives me special pleasure to hear of any one who holds the divine truth so dear. Unfortunately there are very many others, especially those who are proud of some title, who use pressure and cunning of all kinds in striving against that truth. Indeed, it is ordained that many must come into collision with Christ, and fall; but rise again to renewed attacks, because He is set as a stumbling block and a sign that must be spoken against.[2]

Wherefore, in order to initiate our acquaintance and friendship, I would dedicate the German form of this tractate and homily to you. I have already dedicated the Latin version to the pope, in order to explain the grounds of my teachings and writings about the papacy; and I hope to have made them unexceptionable to all. I present to you herewith my respects and pray all God's blessing upon you. Amen.

Wittenberg, 1520.

[1] Johannes Egranus was one of the earliest adherents of Luther in Zwickau, where he was an influential preacher. He visited Luther in Nov., 1520, in Wittenberg, and this seems to have been the occasion when the mayor's name was mentioned

[2] Cf. Luke 2:34

Jesus

1. In order that we may have a true and proper understanding of what it is to be a Christian, or what is the freedom which Christ has won for us and given to us, and of which St. Paul often writes, I propose to begin with two propositions.

A Christian is free and independent in every respect, a bondservant to none.

A Christian is a dutiful servant in every respect, owing a duty to everyone.

These two axioms are clearly found in 1 Corinthians 9, where St. Paul says: "Though I am free from all men, I have made myself a servant to all."[1] Again, Romans 13: "Owe no one anything, except to love one another. But love owes a duty, and is a bondservant of what she loves";[2] in the same way also in regard to Christ, Galatians 4: "God sent forth His Son, born of a woman, and made Him a bondservant of the law."[3]

2. In order to understand these two antithetic assertions concerning freedom and bondage, we ought to remember that in every Christian there are two natures, a spiritual and a bodily. In as far as he possesses a soul, a Christian is a spiritual person, an inward, regenerate self; and in as far as he possesses flesh and blood, he is a sensual person, an outward, unregenerate self. Because of this difference, the Scriptures, in passages which directly contradict each other, speak of his freedom and bondage in the way I have just said.

3. When we consider the inner, spiritual man and see what belongs to him if he is to be a free and devout Christian, in fact and in name, it is evident that, whatever the name, no outer thing can make him either free or religious. For his religion and freedom, and, moreover, his sinfulness and servitude, are neither bodily nor outward. What avail is it to the soul if the body is free, active, and healthy; or eats, drinks, and lives as it likes? Again, what harm does it do to

[1] 1 Cor. 9:19   [2] Rom. 13:8   [3] Gal. 4:4

the soul if the body is imprisoned, ill and weakly; or is hungry, thirsty, and in pain, even if one does not bear it gladly? This sort of thing never touches the soul a little bit, nor makes it free or captive, religious or sinful.

4. Thus it does not help the soul if the body puts on sacred vestments as the priests and clergy do. It does not help even when the body is in church or in holy places, or when busy with sacred affairs; nor when the body is offering prayers, keeping fasts, or making pilgrimages, and doing other good works, which are performed only in and through the body. It must surely be something quite different which brings religion and freedom to the soul. For even a sinful man, or a hypocrite and pretender, may have all the afore-named things, do these works, and follow these ways. Also, this is the way to make men nothing but sheer hypocrites. Further it does no harm to the soul if the body wears worldly clothes, tarries in worldly places, eats, drinks, does not go on pilgrimages, nor keep the appointed hours of prayer; and if it neglects all the works that hypocrites perform, as already said.

5. The only means, whether in heaven or on earth, whereby the soul can live, and be religious, free, and Christian, is the holy Gospel, the word of God preached by Christ. He Himself says in John 11, "I am the resurrection and the life. He that believeth in Me shall live eternally";[1] and John 14, "I am the way, the truth and the life";[2] and Matthew 4, "Man does not live by bread alone, but by every word that proceeds out of the mouth of God."[3] Therefore, we can be certain that the soul can do without anything but the word of God; and apart from the word of God it has no means of help. When it has the word, however, it has no need of anything else. In short, it possesses food, joy, peace, light, ability, righteousness, truth, wisdom, freedom, and sufficient to overflowing of everything good. Thus we read in the Psalms, especially in Psalm 119, that the prophet cries only for the word of God.[4] And in the Scriptures, the worst calamity, the worst sign of God's wrath, is when He withdraws His

[1] John 11:25   [2] John 14:6   [3] Matt. 4:4   [4] Ps. 119:113

word from man.[1] On the other hand, it is held the greatest grace when He sends forth His word, as it is written in Psalm 107: "He sent His word and helped them thereby."[2] Christ came for no other object than to preach the word of God. Moreover all apostles, bishops, priests, and the whole clergy, were called and instituted only for the sake of the word; although, unfortunately, things happen differently nowadays.

6. You may ask, however: "What then is that word which gives such signal grace, and how shall I use it?" The answer is: It is nothing else than the message proclaimed by Jesus, as contained in the gospel; and this should be, and, in fact, is, so presented that you hear your God speak to you. It shows how all your life and labour are as nothing in God's sight, and how you and all that is in you, must eternally perish. If you truly believe this, and that you are indeed guilty, you necessarily despair of yourself; you believe that Hosea was right when he said: "O Israel, there is nought in you except your corruption, but in Me is your help."[3] In order that you may come out of yourself and flee from yourself, i.e., escape your corruption, He sets you face to face with His beloved Son, Jesus Christ, and says to you by means of His living and comforting word: "You should surrender yourself to Him with firm faith, and trust Him gladly." Then, for your faith's sake, all your sins shall be forgiven and all your wickedness overcome. You yourself will be righteous, upright, serene, and devout. You will fulfil all commands, and be free from all things, as St. Paul says in Romans 1: "A justified Christian lives only by his faith";[4] and in Romans 10: "Christ is the end and the fulfilment of all commandments for them that believe in him."[5]

7. Therefore it is reasonable to say that the only purpose for which all Christians should labour, is that they should build up both the divine word and Christ in themselves, by exercising and strengthening their faith continually. No

---

[1] Amos 8:11ff.   [2] Ps. 107:20   [3] Hos. 13:9
[4] Rom, 1:17   [5] Rom. 10:4

other works can make a man a Christian. Thus Christ answered the Jews (John 6), when they asked Him what they should do in order to do works of a godly and Christian kind. He said: "That is the only divine work, that you believe in Him whom God has sent",[1] whom God the Father has alone ordained to that end.

Therefore a right faith in Christ is, truly, superabundant wealth, for He brings with Himself all felicity, and takes away all infelicity. Thus Mark says, in the last chapter: "Therefore he who believes and is baptized is saved, and he who does not believe is condemned."[2] The prophet Isaiah (Chapter 10) surveyed the wealth of the same faith, and said: "God will make a small remnant on earth, and into the remnant righteousness will flow like a flood",[3] namely the faith, in which the fulfilling of all commands is quite briefly contained, will abundantly justify all who have it, till they need nothing more to become righteous and religious. Thus St. Paul says in Romans 10: "That which a man believes in his heart, makes him righteous and devout."[4]

8. But how does it come about that faith alone can make one religious, and give such exceeding wealth apart from any works, seeing that so many laws, commandments, works, and other means are prescribed in the Scriptures? In this connection we must be sure to note and carefully remember that, as we shall see later, faith alone, apart from any act of ours, makes us religious, sets us free, and saves us. We should understand that the entire Holy Scriptures can be divided under two heads: Commandment or God's Law, and Promise or Covenant. The commandments teach and prescribe many good works, but this does not mean that they are fulfilled by us. They give good instructions, but no assistance. They teach what man should do, but give no power to do it. Hence they are only fitted to show a man his own incapacity for goodness, and to make him learn to doubt himself. For this reason they are called the Old Testament, and all belong to the Old Testament. The commandment:

[1] John 6:28ff.   [2] Mark 16:16
[3] Compare Isa. 10:22   [4] Rom. 10:10

"Thou shalt not have sinful appetites",[1] shows that all
of us are sinners, and there can be no man without sinful
appetites, let him do what he may. Thereby a man learns
not to depend on himself, but to seek help elsewhere in order
that he may be without sinful appetites. Thus he may fulfil
the commandment through another, although he could not
do so of himself. In the same way, all other commandments
are impossible to us.

9. Now when a man has learned from the commandments,
and perceived his own incapacity, then he will be anxious
to know how to keep the commandment, for unless he fulfils
the commandment he will be damned. This will take away
all his pride, and he will become as nothing in his own eyes;
he will find nothing in himself to make him acceptable to
God. Then comes the other word, the divine promise, the
covenant which says: If you would fulfil all the commandments, and escape from your evil passions and sins, as the
commandments urge and require, lo! believe on Christ. In
Him I promise that you will find all the needful grace,
righteousness, peace, and freedom. If you believe, you will
possess; if you do not believe, you will not possess. What is
impossible to you in attempting all the works of the commandments, which are necessarily many and yet of no avail,
will come to you quickly and easily through faith. I have
summed everything up in faith alone, so that whoever has
faith shall have all, and be saved; without faith, no one
shall have anything. Thus God's covenants give what the
commandments require, and bring about that for which
the commandments are intended; all this is in order that
everything, both commandment and fulfilment, might be
God's own. He alone commands and alone fulfils. Therefore
the covenants of God are the words of the New Testament,
and their proper place is the New Testament.

10. Now these, and all God's words, are holy, true, right,
peace-giving, free, and entirely good. The soul of the man
who cleaves to them with a true faith will be so completely

[1] Exod. 20:17

united with God that all the virtues of the word will become the qualities of his soul. Through faith and by God's word, the soul will become holy, righteous, true, peaceful, free, and entirely good, and he will become a true child of God. Thus it says in John 1: "He gave power to all them that believe in His name to become children of God."[1]

From this standpoint it is easy to see why faith can do so much, and why good works can never be equivalent to it. For works of merit are not such as to depend on the divine word as in the case of faith, nor can they live in the soul. Only the word and faith exercise sway in the soul. Just as iron becomes red like fire through its union with the fire, so does the soul become like the word through its union with the word. Thus we see that a Christian has sufficient in his faith. Works are not needed to make him become acceptable to God. And if such works are no longer a prerequisite, then assuredly all commandments and laws are like broken chains; and if his chains are broken, he is assuredly free. That is Christian freedom, gained by faith alone. It is wrong to think this means that we can either be idle or do evil; rather it means that we have no need to perform works of merit in order to attain godliness and salvation. But we shall deal further with this matter later on.

11. Again it is to be noticed[2] in regard to faith, that when one man believes in another, he does so because he holds him to be duteous and trustworthy, which is the greatest honour that one man can pay another. On the other hand, it is the greatest insult if he holds him to be loose, untruthful, or shallow. Thus also, if the soul firmly believes in God's word, she holds Him trustworthy, good, and righteous; and thereby she pays Him the greatest honour in her power. For then she acknowledges Him to be in the right, obeys His law, and honours His name, and lets Him do with her what He will, because the soul has no doubt that He is good and trustworthy in all His words. Further, no one can show

[1] John 1:12

[2] Luther makes close use of this paragraph in his commentary on the *Magnificat*, in the following year; cf. *W.*, Vol. VII, p. 554

God greater disrespect than not to trust Him. By lack of reverence and faith, the soul holds Him to be incompetent, deceptive, and shallow, and, as far as she is concerned, she disclaims Him by such unbelief. She sets up in her heart a false god of her own imagination, as if she understood better than He. But when God sees that the soul acknowledges Him to be true, and honours Him by her faith, He honours her in return and holds her to be devout and trustworthy on account of such faith. For to hold God to be good and true, is itself good and true, and makes a man good and true; this is not done by those who have no faith, even though they are busily concerned doing many meritorious works.

12. Faith not only gives the soul enough for her to become, like the divine word, gracious, free, and blessed. It also unites the soul with Christ, like a bride with the bridegroom, and, from this marriage, Christ and the soul become one body, as St. Paul says.[1] Then the possessions of both are in common, whether fortune, misfortune, or anything else; so that what Christ has, also belongs to the believing soul, and what the soul has, will belong to Christ. If Christ has all good things, including blessedness, these will also belong to the soul. If the soul is full of trespasses and sins, these will belong to Christ. At this point a contest of happy exchanges takes place. Because Christ is God and man, and has never sinned, and because His sanctity is unconquerable, eternal, and almighty, He takes possession of the sins of the believing soul by virtue of her wedding-ring, namely faith, and acts just as if He had committed those sins Himself. They are, of course, swallowed up and drowned in Him, for His unconquerable righteousness is stronger than any sin whatever. Thus the soul is cleansed from all her sins by virtue of her dowry, i.e., for the sake of her faith. She is made free and unfettered, and endowed with the eternal righteousness of Christ, her bridegroom. Is that not a happy household, when Christ, the rich, noble, and good bridegroom, takes the poor, despised, wicked little harlot in marriage, sets her free from all evil, and decks her with all good things? It is not possible

[1] Eph. 5:30

for her sins to damn her, for now they rest on Christ, and are swallowed up in Him. In this way she has such a rich righteousness in her bridegroom that she can always withstand sins, although they indeed lie in wait for her. Paul speaks of this in 1 Corinthians 15: "Praise and thanks be to God, who has given us that victory in Christ Jesus, in which death is swallowed up together with sin."[1]

13. From this you will understand on what ground it is rightly attributed to faith, that it fulfils all laws, and makes us godly without the help of anything else. You will see that, of itself, it fulfils the first commandment, which decrees: "Thou shalt honour thy God."[2] If you were constituted entirely of meritorious works from top to toe, you would still not be a godly man, nor do God honour; nor would you have fulfilled the very first commandment. For God is not honoured unless truth and good and all are ascribed to Him, their true source. Meritorious works do not make that ascription, but only genuine faith. Therefore faith alone is the means of man's righteousness, and the fulfilment of all commandments; for he who fulfils the first and chief commandment, will also fulfil all other commandments with certainty and without strain. Works, however, are lifeless things. They can neither honour nor praise God, although they may be done, and admit of being done, to God's honour and glory. But we are not discussing works just now, for they are mere consequences; rather our subject is the initiator, the shipwright, himself. The active agent is the one who discharges his duty to God and who does the works. That active agent is none other than faith, and it resides in our hearts. Faith is the beginning and the end of religion. It is therefore a dangerous and dubious proceeding to teach that God's commandments can be met by performing works of merit. They are met by faith, and this before any works have been done. Works follow, once the commandments have been met, as we shall see.

14. The next point to consider is the treasure we possess in Christ, and how valuable is the right kind of faith. Let

[1] 1 Cor. 15:57   [2] Exod. 20:2ff.; Deut. 6:5

us be clear that, before Old Testament times, as well as during them, God chose and reserved for Himself all the first-born, whether human or animal. Moreover, the eldest son was of special dignity, and had two great privileges as distinct from all the younger children: he was given authority, and he was a priest. The kingship and the priesthood were his. Thus, in practice, the eldest son was the master of all the other brothers; he was also a priest, or pope, of God. This is a figure symbolizing Jesus Christ, who is that self-same, human Son of God the Father by the Virgin Mary. He is therefore a king and a priest—but in the spiritual sense. His kingdom is not earthly, nor does it consist in earthly things, but in those of the spirit, such as truth, wisdom, peace, joy, salvation, and the like. Temporal goods are not excluded, however, for all things in heaven, earth, or hell are subject to Him, although He is unseen owing to the fact that He rules spiritually and invisibly.

Thus even His priesthood does not consist in rites and vestments such as we see among men. Rather it consists in the spirit, and is invisible, in order that He may stand continually before God's face, and offer Himself on behalf of those who are His, and do all that a devout priest should do. He prays for us, as St. Paul says[1] in Romans 8; and also teaches us inwardly in our hearts. These two offices are right and proper for a priest; and therefore ordinary, human, and temporal priests pray and teach in the same manner.

15. Since Christ has the primogeniture with all appropriate honour and worth, He shares it with all Christians who are His, that, through faith, all may be kings and priests with Christ, as St. Peter says in 1 Peter 2: "You are a priestly kingdom and a royal priesthood."[2] The result is that a Christian is lifted up by faith so high above all things that he becomes the spiritual lord of all, for nothing can hinder his salvation. Rather, everything is subject to him, and helps him to reach salvation. Thus St. Paul teaches in Romans 8: "Everything must help to secure the good of the elect",[3] whether life, death, sin, piety, good or evil, or whatever it

[1] Rom, 8:34   [2] 1 Pet. 2:9   [3] Rom, 8:28

may be. So also, 1 Corinthians 3: "All things are yours, whether life or death, present or future",[1] etc. It is not to be understood that we exercise material authority over all things, so that we possess or use them like ordinary men. Indeed as far as the body is concerned, we must die, for no one can avoid death. In the same way, we are necessarily subject to many other things, as we see exemplified also in Christ and His saints. For ours is a spiritual rulership, exercised even to the extent of repressing the body. Thus I can gain benefit in my soul quite apart from material things, and I can make even death and suffering of service to my salvation. That is surely a high and noble dignity, a proper and all-powerful lordship, a spiritual royalty. Nothing is so good or so evil but that it must serve me for good, if I have faith. Indeed, I need none of these things. My faith is sufficient for me. How precious then is the freedom and potency which Christians possess!

16. In addition, we are priests,[2] and thus greater than mere kings, the reason being that priesthood makes us worthy to stand before God, and to pray for others. For to stand and pray before God's face is the prerogative of none except priests. Christ redeemed us that we might be able spiritually to act and pray on behalf of one another just as, in fact, a priest acts and prays on behalf of the people. But nothing avails to the benefit of a person who does not believe in Christ. He is nought but a slave; he is always worried; it is hard for him to pray, and his prayers do not come under God's eye. By contrast, who can fully conceive the honour and the elevation of a Christian? By virtue of his kingship he exercises authority over all things, and by virtue of his priesthood he exercises power with God, for God does what he asks and desires. Thus it is written in the book of Psalms: "God does the will of those that fear Him, and hears their prayers."[3] This is an honour to which Christians attain through faith alone and not through any works. Thereby it

[1] 1 Cor. 3:21ff.
[2] Cf. *supra, Appeal to the Ruling Class*, pp. 113ff.; *Pagan Servitude*, pp. 318ff.
[3] Ps. 145:19

becomes clear that a Christian always enjoys freedom, and is always master. He requires no good works to make him godly or to save him; faith brings everything in abundance to him. If he were so foolish as to think that by good works he would become godly, free, blessed, or a Christian, he would lose both faith and all else. He would be like the dog which, while carrying a piece of meat in its mouth, snapped at its reflection in the water, and thereby lost the meat and spoiled the reflection.

17. Should you ask: "What is the difference between the priests and the laity in Christian standing, if all are priests?" the answer is that spiritual mischief and other wrongs have been done to the little words "priest" or "pastor". These words have been taken away from the community in general and handed over to those little communities which we now call "the clergy". The Holy Scriptures make no distinction beyond calling the instructed or the consecrated, *ministros, servos, œconomos*, i.e., helpers, servants, stewards, whose duty is to preach Christ, and faith, and Christian freedom to others. For although we are all equally priests, still not all of us can serve and minister and preach. Thus St. Paul says in I Corinthians 4: "We do not desire to be held by the people to be other than servants of Christ and stewards of the gospel."[1] But there has now grown out of the stewardship such a worldly, outer, gorgeous and awe-inspiring lordship and authority that the worldly powers proper cannot compare with them. Indeed, it is as if the laity were something other than Christian people. The whole meaning of Christian grace and liberty and faith is taken away, together with everything we have in Christ, and, indeed, we are robbed of Christ Himself. Instead, we have received much man-made law and many man-made works, and we have become altogether the servants of the most unsuitable people on earth.

18. From all this we understand that it is not enough just to take the life and work of Christ, and, in preaching, merely tell the story and the chronicle of events. It is even worse

[1] I Cor. 4:1

to pass over these altogether, and preach about ecclesiastical law or other man-made rules and doctrines. There are also many who preach and understand Christ as if they rather pitied Him, and were angry with the Jews; they carry on in some other childish manner.[1] But He should and must be preached in such a way that, in both you and me, faith grows out of, and is received from, the preaching. And that faith is received and grows when I am told why Christ came, how men can use and enjoy Him, and what He has brought and given me. This takes place whenever a proper explanation is given of that Christian freedom which we have from Him: how we are kings and priests with power over all things; and how everything we do is well-pleasing to and granted by God, as I have already said. For when our heart hears about Christ in this way, it must rejoice through and through. It yearns for Christ, receives consolation, and loves Him in return. Neither regulations nor good deeds can effect as much as that. For who can do hurt to such a soul, or terrify it? If sin or death fall upon it, it has faith that the spiritual worth of Christ is its own, and that its sins are no longer its own, but Christ's. Thus sin must vanish away through the goodness of Christ in faith, as I said above. The heart learns with the apostle to defy death and sin, and say: "Where is thy victory, O death? Where, death, is now thy sting? Thy sting is sin. But praise and thanks be to God who has given us the victory through Jesus Christ our Lord. Death is swallowed up in His victory",[2] etc.

19. We have now probably said sufficient about the inner man, about his liberty and the principal features of his righteousness which requires neither laws nor "good works". Indeed, it is harmful to that righteousness when any one pretends to have been made righteous on that basis.

We now come to the second part, namely, to the outer man. Here we must deal with all those who take offence at the

---

[1] The "childishness" of the attitude to Christ's Passion has been only too frequent since the time of the earliest Christian ascetics, and was prominent in much medieval art. Luther felt it childish to be wroth with the Jews on account of Christ's crucifixion by their ancestors, or to stress the pathos of His innocent sufferings; cf. *Sermon . . . des Heiligen Leidens Christi* (*W.*, Vol. II, p. 136)   [2] I Cor. 15:55ff.

foregoing arguments, and are wont to say: "Oh! then if faith is the whole thing and sufficient in itself to make one religious, why are good works demanded? We shall be in good case without doing anything at all." No, my dear man, not so. That would perhaps be true if you were nothing but your inner self, and had become pure soul and pure spirit, a thing which will never happen before the last day. There will never be anything else on earth than a beginning and a growth; these will only be completed in the next world. That is why the apostle called it *primitias spiritus,* or the first-fruits of the spirit. From this fact we can understand what was said above: "*A Christian man is a dutiful menial, a bondservant to everyone*", which is as much as to say: "In as far as he is free, he requires to do nothing. In as far as he is a servant, he must do everything." How that happens we shall now see.

20. Inwardly, and as regards his soul, a man is sufficiently justified by faith. He possesses all he ought to have, except that his very faith and sufficiency must always increase until his entry into the next life; nevertheless he still remains on earth during his bodily life. Therefore he must rule his own body, and he must mix with other people. That is where the need for good works enters. He must not be idle. Yes, the body must be disciplined and exercised with fasting, watching, labouring, and all due training, in order that it may be obedient to, and in harmony with, both the inner man and with faith; and not hinder nor oppose, as is its nature when it is not restrained. For the inner man is one with God. He is joyful and glad on account of Christ who has done so much for him. All his pleasure consists in serving God in return, without reward, and out of unconstrained love. It is true that a man finds in his body a refractory will which wants to seek and serve the world, and which finds pleasure in doing so. Faith cannot tolerate that. She eagerly lays hold of it by the throat to subdue it and keep it in order. Thus St. Paul says in Romans 7: "In the inward man I have a desire for God's will, but I find another will in my flesh, which would make me prisoner together with sin";[1]

[1] Rom. 7:22ff.

Z

and again: "I discipline my body and bring it to obedience lest I myself become culpable, who should teach others";[1] and again, in Galatians 5: "All who belong to Christ crucify their body with its evil desires."[2]

21. But none of these works must be done under the impression that a man becomes devout in God's sight thereby. Faith cannot tolerate this false view; for faith alone is, and cannot be anything else than, godliness in God's sight. Works must be understood only in the sense that doing them makes the body obedient and keeps it clean from its evil desires; and the eye may only look on evil desires in order to drive them out. Through faith, the soul is made pure, and caused to love God; yet she wishes that all things were pure, especially her own body, and that every one loved and praised God along with her. Thus, for his own body's sake, a man may not be idle. He must do many good deeds in order to constrain it. Nevertheless the deeds are not the real essence of being good, and it is not true that they make a man dutiful and righteous before God. Rather he does them voluntarily and freely, out of love, in order to please God. His only object is to seek to do what pleases God, whose will he gladly does as well as ever he can. As a consequence, such a man can form his own rule and judge for himself about mortifying his body; for he will fast, watch, and labour as much as he sees his body needs, in order to neutralize its wantonness. The rest, however, who believe they will become religious by virtue of what they do, pay no attention to the self-discipline, but only to the actions. They believe that, if they only do many impressive works, all is well, and they will be godly. They sometimes go to great trouble, and even harm their bodies in the attempt. But it is undoubtedly very foolish, and a complete misunderstanding of the Christian life, to think that they can become religious and be saved by what they do apart from faith.

22. To give a few illustrations of the matter, we should consider what a Christian does, who is justified and saved by faith, and by the free grace of God. These acts must be

[1] 1 Cor. 9:27   [2] Gal. 5:24

regarded as exactly like those which were done by Adam and Eve in the garden of Eden. It is written in Genesis 2 that God took the man whom He had created and put him in the garden to till and guard it.[1] Now God created Adam duteous and acceptable, and without sin. He had no need to become godly or to be justified by working or guarding. But lest he be idle, God gave him something to do. He gave him work to do: plant the garden, cultivate and look after it. These labours were performed for themselves alone, and for no other reason than to please God. They were not for the purpose of attaining godliness, since Adam had that already, like all of us, naturally and inherently. Thus is to be understood also the life of a believing man who, by his faith, is planted once more in the Garden of Eden and created anew. He has no need to do certain things to make himself devout; but only that he be not idle, and that he discipline and care for his body. That is the only reason why such self-imposed duties are good for him; and thereby he pleases God.

Further, when a consecrated bishop consecrates churches, confirms, or discharges other duties of his office, these duties do not make him a bishop. Indeed, were he not already consecrated a bishop, these same duties would be useless and foolish. In the same way, a Christian who is consecrated by faith, and who also does good, is not made a better or more consecrated Christian by his works, for only an increase of faith effects that. Indeed, if he had no faith and were no Christian beforehand, all his works would be valueless; they would be merely foolish, culpable, and damnable sins.

23. Hence both expressions are true: "Good and devout works never make a man good and duteous; but a good and religious man does good and religious works." Nor do sinful works make a man sinful. Rather it is a sinful man who does sinful works. Thus every argument proves that the person must first be good and godly; after that come all the works that are good.[2] Good works proceed logically from a godly and good person. It is as Christ said: "An evil tree bears no good fruit, a good tree bears no evil fruit."[2] It

[1] Gen. 2:15   [2] Matt. 7:17f.

is evident that the fruits do not bear the tree, nor do the trees grow on the fruits, but rather the trees bear the fruits, and the fruits grow on the trees. Since the trees must precede the fruits, and since the fruits do not make the trees good or evil, for the trees make the fruits, so also must a man be personally godly or sinful in himself, before what works he does can be good or sinful, as the case may be. It is not his works that make him either good or sinful, but he himself that makes them good or evil. We see the same thing in all kinds of handicrafts. A good or bad house does not make a carpenter good or bad, but a good or bad carpenter makes a good or bad house. No work makes a workman of the same quality as the work, but as the workman is, so is his work. Thus also are a man's (religious) works to be understood: his actions are good or sinful just according as it stands with him in faith or unbelief. The reverse is not true: it is not true that he is good or believing according to his kind of works. Just as works do not make a man a believer, so also they do not make him godly. But just as faith makes one godly, so also does it produce good works. Therefore, it is not what one does that makes one religious. A man must be religious before he can do the works of religion. And it is evident that only faith, coming from pure grace through Christ and His word, is sufficient to make a person religious and save him; neither works nor commandments are necessary to a Christian before he can be saved. He is free from all commandments. He does all that he does quite voluntarily without recompense, and apart from seeking his own advantage or salvation. He already has sufficient, and he is already saved through his faith and the grace of God. What he does is done just to please God.[1]

---

[1] So also Boethius, translated by King Alfred, Chap. XVI, section iv: ". . . Hence thou mayest understand that if the good things of this present life through themselves, had power of themselves, and were of their own nature good, then would they also cleave to him who did good with them, not evil. But, wheresoever they are good, they are good through the good of the good man, who works good with them, and he is good through God. If, then, an evil man hath it, it is evil through man's evil, who doth evil with it, and through the devil. . . . Though anyone gives to an evil man power, the power does not make him good or meritorious, if before he were not. . . ." (Translated and edited by S. Fox, 1895)

24. Further, no meritorious works are of any avail to the godliness or salvation of one who is without faith; neither do sinful actions make him sinful or damn him; but the unbelief which makes the person and the tree sinful, is what does the sinful and damnable things. Therefore, when a man becomes either devout or sinful, the process does not begin with his actions, but with his faith. Thus Solomon says: "The beginning of sin is in departing from God, and in not trusting Him."[1] So also Christ teaches that one must not begin with conduct. He says: "Either make the tree good, and its fruits good, or make the tree evil and its fruits evil";[2] which is much as if He said: "Whoever wishes to have good fruits must first begin with the tree and make that right." Similarly, whoever wants to do what is good must not begin with the actions, but with the person who does them. But nothing makes that person good except his faith, and nothing makes that person evil except his unbelief. It is true, of course, that his conduct makes a man appear either good or evil in other men's eyes, i.e., it shows who is outwardly devout or sinful. Thus Christ said, in Matthew 7: "By their fruits you shall know them."[3] But all that is a matter of appearance and outward show. This outward show leads many people astray. They write and teach that we must do meritorious works and so become godly, but they never give a thought to faith. They go on in that way, and one blind man leads another. They load themselves with many duties, and yet never reach the real religion of which Paul speaks in 2 Timothy 3: "They have an appearance of godliness, but the foundation is not there. They go away, and learn more and more, and yet never come to knowledge of true godliness."[4] He who does not wish to go astray with those blind people must look beyond the works, the commandments, and the doctrines concerning what a man must do. A man must look into his own heart before everything else, and see how it may become godly. But the heart becomes devout and is saved, not by commandments or works, but by the word of God, that is, by His promise of grace, and by faith. In this way, His divine honour will stand firm, and

[1] Ecclus. 10:12ff.   [2] Matt. 12:33   [3] Matt. 7:20   [4] 2 Tim. 3:5ff.

He will save us, not by what we do, but by His gracious word. He will do it freely and out of pure mercy.

25. From all this it is easy to understand how meritorious works are to be condemned, and how they are not to be condemned; and also how one must understand all doctrines enjoining meritorious works. For, wherever are found the false addition and the perverse opinion that we become devout and are saved by means of our conduct, this is already far from good, and quite to be condemned; for a life of that kind is not free, and it contemns the grace of God. This grace alone makes men religious and saves them through faith. Works cannot do this; nevertheless they propose to do it, and in this way attack grace in its work and in its honour. Thus we condemn works of merit, not for their own sakes, but because of the evils they bring in, and their false perverse tendency to appear good in a way in which they are not good. Thus these people deceive themselves and everyone else at the same time, like ravening wolves in sheep's clothing. But that evil addition and that false tendency on the part of meritorious works are insuperable unless faith be present. This is of necessity the experience of those people who are "sanctified" by works, until faith comes and destroys the edifice. Nature by herself can neither cure nor even recognize the evil. She holds the appearance of good as precious and blessed, and thereby many are led astray. On that account, although it is good to write and preach about repentance, confessions, and restitution, yet, if one does not go on to deal with faith, they are simply impious and seductive doctrines. We must preach neither one nor the other alone, but both together. We must preach the word of God and the commandments of God, to alarm sinners, and make their sins plain so that they repent and are converted. But we must not stop there. We must also preach the second word, the promise of grace, and teach the faith without which commandments, repentance, and everything else are useless. There are some preachers, of course, who preach repentance from sin and proclaim grace; but they do not emphasize the commandments and promise of God for

us to learn either whence or how repentance and grace do come. For repentance flows from the commandments of God, and faith flows from His promises. Thus a man who is cast down by fear of the commandments of God, and so has reached knowledge of Him, is justified and exalted by faith in the divine word.

26. All this concerns meritorious works in general and those which a Christian may perform as far as his own self is concerned. But now we would speak of other actions, those which he does in relation to other men. For a man does not live alone, in his own body, but among other men, in the world. Therefore, he cannot remain without works in his contacts with others; he must speak to and co-operate with them, although none of these actions is necessary for his own godliness or salvation. In all such works his will should be subject to no constraint, and should only be directed to the way in which he may serve other people, and be helpful to them. He should have no other thought than of what is needful to others. That would mean living a true Christian life; and that is the way in which faith proceeds to work with joy and love, as St. Paul teaches the Galatians.[1] Also, in Philippians, after he has taught how they had all grace and sufficiency through their faith in Christ, he teaches them further, and says: "I exhort you by all the comfort which you have in Christ, and by all the comfort which you have by our love towards you, and by all the fellowship which you have with all spiritual and devout Christians, that you would cause my heart altogether to rejoice, by henceforth willing to be all of one mind, and showing love towards each other. Let each serve the other, and each have care, not for himself and his own concerns, but for others and what they need."[2] Consider how clearly Paul thereby depicted the Christian life. All that we do must be designed for the benefit of our neighbour, because each one has sufficient for himself in his faith. Other deeds or another kind of life are unnecessary to himself, and so he may serve his neighbour out of unconstrained love. In

[1] Gal. 5:6   [2] Phil. 2:1ff.

addition, St. Paul cites the example of Christ and says:
"Have the same mind as you see in Christ who, although
He was filled with the divine form and had sufficient for
Himself, and His life and works and suffering were not
necessary to Him in order that He might become devout
and be saved, nevertheless, He emptied Himself of all these
things, and assumed the form of a servant. He did and
suffered everything with no other object than our advantage. Thus, although He was free, for our sakes He became
a servant."[1]

27. It follows that, like Christ his head, a Christian must
let himself be completely and sufficiently content with his
faith, always increasing in this which is his life, his religion,
and his salvation. It gives him everything that Christ and
God possess, as is said above, and also as St. Paul says in
Galatians 2: "The life which I now live in the body, I live
in the faith of Christ the Son of God."[2] And although he is
now quite free, yet a Christian ought voluntarily to make
himself a servant and help his neighbour. He should associate
and deal with him as God has done with himself through
Christ, everything being free, and nothing being sought
except to please God. He should therefore think within himself: "Unworthy and guilty man that I am, and without any
desert, yet my God, quite freely and out of pure mercy, has
given me, in and through Christ, the full wealth of all religion
and salvation, so that henceforth I need nothing except faith.
So let it be. Yes, for the sake of such a Father, who has
heaped upon me His superabundant good things, will I
freely, gladly, and without reward, do what pleases Him.
To my neighbour, I will be, as a Christian, what Christ
has become to me, and do just what I see is needful, helpful,
or acceptable to him, for I have enough of all things in Christ
through my faith." Lo, that is how love and joy in God
flow out of faith, and how love gives rise to a free, eager,
and glad life of serving one's neighbour without reward. For
just as our neighbour is needy, and requires our excess, so we
were needy in God's eyes, and required His grace. Therefore,

[1] Phil. 2:5ff.   [2] Gal. 2:20

just as God helped us without payment through Christ, so ought we, through our body and its works, always to help our neighbour. Thus we see that the Christian life is a truly noble life. Unhappily it is now not merely held in poor esteem everywhere, but is neither known nor preached any longer.

28. Accordingly, we read in Luke 2 that the Virgin Mary went to church, after six weeks, for her purification according to the law, like all other women,[1] although she was not unclean like them, nor under the same obligation of purification; nor did she need it. But she did it voluntarily, out of love, that she might not look down upon other women, but remain on the level of the rest. Similarly also, St. Paul had St. Timothy circumcized[2] not because it was necessary, but lest he gave cause to Jews weak in faith to think evil thoughts. On the other hand, he refused to allow Titus to be circumcized[3] because some urged that he must needs be circumcized, and that it was necessary for salvation. And when toll was required of His disciples (Matthew 17), Christ discussed with St. Peter whether the children of the king were not free from paying toll. Yet when St. Peter agreed, He told him to go to the sea, and said: "Lest we vex them, go and take the first fish you catch, and you will find a penny in its mouth; pay it for me and you."[4] That is a notable example of the case in point, for Christ called Himself and His disciples free children of the king, under no compulsion; and yet He voluntarily submitted. He acted as a subject and paid toll. Now just to the extent that that act was necessary to Christ, and of use to His own godliness or salvation, so all His other deeds, and the deeds of His Christian followers, are necessary for their salvation. But this means that everything will be done freely, and only to please and benefit others. Therefore all that is done by the priests, monasteries, and religious foundations should be done in a similar manner. Let each one discharge the duties of his rank or order, only to assist others, to discipline his own body, or to give an example to others in mastering their own bodies as they find it necessary.

[1] Luke 2:22ff. [2] Acts 16:3 [3] Gal. 2:3 [4] Matt. 17:24ff.

But all the time we must beware lest we suppose ourselves to become devout or attain salvation by doing so, for that is within the power of faith alone. St. Paul also teaches in Romans 13 and Titus 3 that we should be subject and well-disposed to the secular power,[1] not for the sake of becoming godly by these means, but that we may freely serve our neighbours and the authorities, and do their will in love and freedom. Those who have this understanding of things can easily find their right attitude to the numberless rules and regulations of the pope, of bishops, of monasteries, of religious houses, of princes and lords, regulations which certain foolish prelates press on us as if they were needful to salvation. These are called laws of the church, although unjustifiably. But a free Christian says: "I will fast and pray, I will do this or that as is commanded, not because I need to do so, or would thereby become devout or attain salvation; but I will comply with the will of the pope, the bishop, the ordinary priest, or my fellow man, as if he were my master. I will set an example, and do a service, just because Christ did and suffered much greater things for my sake, although it was far less needful for Him to do so. And, although the tyrants do injustice in requiring such a thing, nevertheless it does not hurt me so long as it is not against God's will."

29. On this basis, each man may form a sure judgment, and make a clear distinction in regard to all works and laws. He can also tell which prelates are blind and foolish, and which are wise and right-minded. For unless the enjoined works tend to serve another man or to comply with his will, even if they do not compel us to act against God, they are not sound Christian works. Therefore it comes about, I fear, that few religious houses, churches, monasteries, altars, masses, or endowments are Christian; and, in particular, the observance of fasts, or the offering of prayers to certain saints. For I fear that, as a rule, each seeks only his own interest, yet believes he is atoning for his sins and being saved. But all this springs from ignorance of the nature of faith and Christian freedom. Certain blind prelates lead the

---

[1] Rom. 13:1ff.; Titus 3:1

people astray, and praise such doings, pile on indulgences, but never once teach faith. But I advise you if you wish to pray, or fast, or make an endowment, let it not be with the idea that you will benefit yourself. Rather do it freely in order that others may benefit; do it for their advantage— then you will be a real Christian. What is the value of your property or your merits if they are more than you require to enable you to master and provide for your body? You have a sufficiency in the faith through which God has given you all things. Remember that all the good things of God should flow from one man to another, and become common to all, so that each one may be as concerned for his neighbour as for his own self. All good things come to us from Christ, who has received us into His own life as if He had been what we are. From us they should flow to those who are in need of them. This should be so completely true that I must offer even my faith and righteousness before God on behalf of my neighbour, to blot out his sins, and take them upon myself. I must act as if they were my own, just as Christ has done for us all. Indeed, that is the nature of love if it is real. And it is real if faith is real. Therefore, in I Corinthians 13, the holy Apostle says that love is of such a kind that it does not seek its own advantage, but its neighbour's.[1]

30. From all the foregoing, the conclusion follows that a Christian lives not in himself, but in Christ and his neighbour; in Christ by faith and in his neighbour by love. By faith he rises above himself unto God; from God he stoops below himself by love, and yet he remains always in God and in divine love, just as Christ says in John 1: "You will see the heavens open and the angels ascending and descending upon the Son of Man."[2] Yes, that is the true, spiritual, and Christian freedom. It liberates our hearts from all sins, laws, and commandments. It exceeds all other freedom as much as heaven the earth. God grant that we rightly understand and retain this freedom. Amen.

[1] I Cor. 13:5   [2] John 1:51

A CHRONOLOGICAL TABLE OF LUTHER'S WRITINGS (TO DECEMBER, 1520) AND OF CONTEMPORARY EVENTS

(With acknowledgments to Weingarten, Koestlin, Grisar and the Cambridge Modern History, Vols. I and II)

The references are to the Weimar Edition of Luther's Works

Up to 1516. Accession of Leo X, 1513; Maximilian I, 1493; Frederick of Saxony, 1486; George of Saxony, 1500; William IV of Bavaria, 1508; Joachim I, Elector of Brandenburg, 1499; Albert, abp. of Mainz, 1514; Scultetus, bp. of Brandenburg, 1507

In 1502. Univ. of Wittenberg founded

1503. Death of Andreas Proles

1511. John Lang, professor in Wittenberg

1515–16. John Lang returns to Erfurt

1510. John Eck professor at Ingolstadt

1511. Nicolas Amsdorf becomes Licentiate in Theology

1513. George Spalatin, court chaplain and secretary to Frederick the Wise

1515. *Epistolae Obscurorum Virorum,* by Crotus Rubeanus

Luther's Writings

1. 1510–11. Marginal notes on the Sentences (Bks. i–iii), and certain works of Augustine (First pub. 1893) *W.* 9, 2ff.; 28ff.

2. 1513–15. Lectures on the Psalms (pubd. 1743, and 1876, complete 1885) *W.* 3, 1/11–652 4, 1–462 9, 116–21

3. 1514–17. Sermons on the Lessons (Latin) (pubd. 1720) *W.* 1, 18/20–141

4. 1514–20. Sermons (ed. Roth. 1886) *W.* 4, 587/90–717 9, 203ff.

5. 1515–16. Lectures on Romans (ed. J. Ficker, 1908) *W.* 56 and 57

6. **?** 1515. *Sermo praescriptus . . . in Litzka* (pubd. 1708)
   W. 1, 8/10–17
   plus sermons; and letters

A.D. 1516. Hermann v. Wied, abp. of Cologne; Lang, prior
   of Erfurt
   Publication of *Epistolae Obscurorum Virorum*, part I
   Erasmus: *Colloquia*; his 1st ed. of NT in Greek, with new
   Latin translation.
   Carlstadt's Theses
   Luther busy on Galatians and Titus, 1516–17

7. 1516–17. *Decem praecepta...praedicata populo* (pubd.
   1518) *W.* 1, 394/98–521

8. (Sept.) *Quaestio de viribus et voluntate hominis....W.* 1,
   142/45–51

9. *ad. Galatas* (lectures pubd. 1519) *W.* 2, 436/51–618; cf.
   57, 10

10. 1st ed. of *Eyn Geystlich edles Buchleynn* (The *Theo-
    logia Deutsch*) with Vor Rede *W.* 1, 152/3ff.
    plus sermons; and letters

A.D. 1517.
   Attempt to poison Leo; 31 cardinals newly created, July 1;
      17 cardinals executed by being strangled
   Hutten settles in Germany; his new edition of *Donatio
      Constantini*; *Epistolae Obscurorum Virorum*, part II
   Erasmus; paraphrases on the Epistles, and later, the
      Gospels; the old exegesis fares badly
   Tetzel visits Magdeburg, Halberstadt, and (Oct.) Berlin
   Luther: 95 Theses (Oct. 31)

Luther's Writings

11. *Die sieben Puszpsalm mit Deutscher Auslegung . . .*
    (the earliest original work pubd. by L.) *W.* 1,
    154/58–220

12. *Auslegung Deutsch des Vater Unnser fuer dye einfelti-
    gen Leyen* (pubd. by Agricola, and by L. himself in
    1518; cf. 31, *infra*)

13. Lectures on Hebrews (first pubd. 1938, cf. *W.* 57)

14. *Disputatio contra scholasticam theologiam* (Theses for Franz Guenther) *W.* I, 221/24–228
15. *Die zehen Gepot Gottes . . . mit einer kurtzen Aussle-gung* (pubd. 1518) *W.* I, 247/50–256; cf. No. 64
16. The 95 Theses *W.* I, 229/33–38
    plus sermons, letters, etc.

A.D. 1518.

Philip II, landgrave of Hesse
Von Sickingen and his men desert the French for the emperor (May 16)
Melanchthon goes to Wittenberg (Aug. 25) as professor
Early in 1518, archbishop Albert reports to Rome on 95 theses
Tetzel's counter-theses (Jan. 18)
Leo X directs the Augustinian superiors to take steps
Zwingli attacks indulgences as preached by Bernhard Sampson
Heidelberg Chapter and Disputation in Luther's favour
Lang takes Luther's place as district-vicar
Charges formulated at Rome against Luther (mid-June)
Luther summoned to Rome (Aug. 7)
Interview with Cardinal Cajetan at Augsburg
Papal Bull defending indulgences (Nov. 9)
Luther appeals to general council (Nov. 28)

Luther's Writings

17. *Ablass und Gnade* *W.* I, 239/43–246; cf. No. 23
18. *Resolutiones Disputationum de indulgentiarum virtute* *W.* I, 522/25–628 9, 171–5
19. *Sermo de poenitentia* *W.* I, 317/19–24
20. Theses for the Heidelberg disputation (Leonard Beyer's) *W.* I, 350/53–355 also *W.* 9, 160/61–170
21. *Asterisci . . . adv. Obeliscos Eckii* (pubd. 1545) *W.* I, 278/81–314
22. Preface to the complete edition of *Theologia Deutsch* *W.* 374/78–379
23. *Eyn Freiheit dess Sermons Bepstlichen Ablass und Gnad belangend* *W.* I, 380/83–93; cf. No. 17

24. *Ausslegung des 109 Psalmen* W. 1, 687/89–710
25. *Ad dialogum* . . . *Prieriatis de potestate Papae responsio* W. 1, 644/47–86
26. *Sermo de virtute excommunicationis* W. 1, 634/38–43
27. *Sermo in festo S. Michaelis in arce Wimariensi* (pubd. 1556)
28. *Acta Augustana* W. 2, 1/6–26 9, 205ff.
29. *Appellatio a Caietano ad Papam* W. 2, 27/28–33
30. *Appellatio ad Futurum Concilium universale* W. 2, 34/36–40
31. *Auslegung Deutsch des Vater Unnser fuer dye einfeltigen leyen* (cf. No. 12, *supra*) W. 2, 74/80–130 9, 122/23–159; cf. No. 42
32. *Sermo de triplici Justitia* . . . W. 2, 41/43–47; cf. No. 39 Also *decem praecepta*, cf. No. 7; Brief explanation of the Ten Commandments, cf. No. 15; Sermons; letters; etc.

A.D. 1519.

Death of Maximilian I; Charles V succeeds (June 28)
Ulrich becomes duke of Württemburg
Death of Tetzel (Aug. 11)
Capito becomes cathedral preacher at Mainz
Zwingli begins his ministry at the cathedral in Zürich (Jan.)
Miltitz: interview with Luther (Jan.)
Disputations at Leipzig (June–July) between Eck and Carlstadt on the freedom of the will; and between Eck and Luther on the primacy of the pope

Luther's Writings

33. Preface to Prierias's *Replica* W. 2, 48/50–56
34. *Kurtz Unterweyzung wie man beichten sol* W. 2, 57/9–65
35. *Untericht auff etlich Artikell* W. 2, 66/69–73
36. *Sermon* . . . *des Heyligen Leydens Christi* W. 2, 131/36–142
37. Publishes commentary on Galatians (cf. No. 9, *supra*)

38. Second course of lectures on Psalms. (A.D. 1519–21)
   W. 5, 1/19–673
39. *Sermo de duplici justitia W.* 2, 143/45–152; cf. No. 32
40. *Disputatio et excusatio adv. criminationes Eccii W.* 2
   153/58–61 9, 206/07–212
41. *Sermon . . . Elichen Standt W.* 9, 213–20 Revised
   text: 2, 162/66–171
42. *Kurtze Form des Pater noster zu versteen unnd zu
   betten W.* 6, 9/11–19; cf. No. 31
43. *Kurtze nutzliche Ausslegung des Vatter Unsers*, etc.
   W. 6, 20/21–2
44. *Sermon von dem Gepeet unnd Procession . . . W.* 2,
   172/75–179
45. *Eyn Sermon von dem Wucher W.* 6, 1/3–8
46. *Resolutio super propositione sua (Lipsiensi)* XIII de
   potestate papae W. 2, 180/83–240
47. *Scheda adversus Hochstraten W.* 2,384/6–87
48. *Resolutiones super propositionibus Lipsiae disputatis
   W.* 2, 388/91–435
49. *Tessaradecas consolatoria*, etc. (pubd. 1520) *W.* 6,
   99/104–134
50. *Contra malignum Ioh. Eccii iudicium W.* 2, 621/25–
   654
51. *Ad . . . Emserianum W.* 2, 655/58–79
52. *Sermon v. d. Sacrament der Puss W.* 2, 709/13–23
53. *Sermon v. d. Bereytung z. Sterben W.* 2, 680/84–97
54. *Ad Eccium super expurgatione . . . W.* 2, 698/700–8
55. *Sermon v. d. . . . . Sacrament d. Tauffe W.* 2, 724/27–37
56. *Sermon von dem . . . Sacrament des Heylingen waren
   Leychnams Christi W.* 2, 738/42–58
57. *Scholia in . . .* Genesis (pubd. 1893) *W.* 9, 329–415
58. *. . . postillas . . .* (pubd. 1893) *W.* 9, 415–676
59. Latin advent postils (pubd. 1521) *W.* 7, 458/65–637
   plus sermons, letters, etc.

A.D. 1520.
   Suleiman II begins his career The war in Hungary
   Chas. V crowned, Aachen (Oct. 23)
   Hutten and Sickingen both offer to protect Luther

A I

Münzer in Zwickau (May 17)
Link succeeds Staupitz as Vicar-general (Aug. 28)
Eck goes to Rome; the first Consistory against Luther
(Jan. 9)
The Stolpen Decree of the bp. of Meissen (Jan. 24)
Luther's letter to Chas. V (Aug. 30)
Luther's third and last epistle to Leo X (after Oct. 13)
The Bull *Exsurge* (June 15) condemns 41 theses; pubd. in
Germany by Eck (in Sept.), and burned by Luther
Dec. 10
Luther's open attack on the freedom of the will

Luther's Writings

60. *Sermon von dem Bann* W. 6, 61/63–75
61. *Sermon von dem Wurcher* W. 6, 33/36–60
62. *Erklerung etliche Artickel . . . vondem heyligen Sacrament* W. 6, 76/78–83
63. *Antwort auff die Tzedel . . . zu Stolpen* Lat. form, *Ad schedulam inhibitionis* W. 6, 135/36–141; 142/44–153
64. *Sermon von den guten Wercken* W. 6, 196/202–76 9, 226/29–301
65. *Responsio . . .* (to the condemnation of Louvain and Cologne) W. 6, 170/74–195
66. *Confitendi ratio* W. 6, 154/57–169
67. *Eyn Kurcz Form der czehen Gepott. Eyn kurcz Form des Glaubens. Eyn Kurcz Form des Vatter Unsers* W. 7, 194/204–229
68. *Von dem Bapstum zu Rom wider dem hochberumpten Romanisten tzu Leiptzk* (i.e., Alveld) W. 6, 277/5–324
69. *Epitoma responsionis . . . Prieratis* W. 6,325/28–348
70. *An den Christl. Adel . . .* W. 6, 381/404–69
71. *Sermon von dem newen Testament, d. h. von der heyligen Messe* W. 6, 349/53–78
72. *De captivitate Babylonica . . .* W. 6, 484/97–573
73. *Erbieten* (*Oblatio sive Protestatio*) W. 6, 478/80–481 482–3; early draft of same: 6, 476–8 9, 302–4
74. Pref. to *"Adv. constitutionem de cleri coelibatu"* W. 7, 677

75. *Von den newen Eckischenn Bullen und Lugen* . . . *W.* 6, 576/79–594
76. *Von der Freyheit eynes Christen Menschen* . . . *W.* 7, 12/20–38
77. *Eyn Sendbrief an den Bapst Leo X W.* 7, 1/3–11
78. (Latin versions of Nos. 76 and 77) *W.* 7, 39/42–73
79. *Adv. execrabilem Antichristi bullam W.* 6, 595/97–612
80. (German version of above) *W.* 6, 613/14–629
81. *Appellatio ad Concilium repetita W.* 7, 74/75–82
82. (German ed. of above) *W.* 7, 83/85–90
83. *Das Magnificat verteuschet und ausgelegt* (pubd. 1521) *W.* 7, 538/43; 544–604
84. *Warum . . . Bucher vorbrant seyn W.* 7, 152/60; 161–86; 24, ii, 154–66
85. *Assertio omnium articulorum . . . damnatorum W.* 7, 1–151
    plus *Tessaradecas* (cf. No. 49); Sermons; Letters.

A1*

Index of Scriptural References and Allusions

Index of Personal Names

Honstein, William of, 134, n.
Huss, John, 178, 179, 180, 310, n.1
Hutten, Ulrich von, 150, n.3, 170, n.

INNOCENT I, POPE, 216
Innocent III, pope, 41, n.2, 42, n.1
Isolani, Isidoro, of Cremona, 209, 214

JAMES, APOSTLE, 325
Jehu, 195
Jeroboam, 315
Jerome of Prague, 178, 179, 310, n.1
Jerome, St., 254
Jesus Christ, 16, 46, 85, 86, 216, 337, 365, 367, 368
  as the Head of the church, 115
  as the bread of life, 94
John, apostle, 212
Judas Iscariot, 340
Julius II, pope, 111, 151, n.2

KALKOFF, 45, 61, n.1
Köhler, W., 25, n., 29, n.
Kooiman, W. J., 19, n., 29, n.

LANG, JOHN, 28, 107
Laurence, St., 39
Leo III, pope, 191, n.1
Leo X, pope, 44, 59, 60f., 62, 65, 170, n.1, 205, 331, 334, 336, 339
  Giovanni dei Medici, 60f., 128, n.1
  plot to poison, 128, n.1
  creates cardinals, 128, n.1
Lietzmann, Hans, 157, n.2, 346, n.2
Lindsay, T. M., 25, n.1, 27, n.2, 343, n.3
Lombard, Peter, 50, 187, n.3, 240, n., 259, n.
Lotther, Melchior, 107
Louis, king of France, 178
Luther, annus mirabilis, 16
  and the Bible, 13, 18, 209, n.5
  character, 13ff.
  clear and homely speech, 17
  croak like a crow, 64
  discusses indulgences, 26
    and see Ninety-five Theses
  district-vicar, 26, 107
  doctor of Holy Scripture, 54, n.1
  enigma of, 11ff.
  fame, 203
  first reforming interest, 26
  and his fool's cap, 110
  and God's righteousness, 14
  heretical, 45, 55
  honesty, 13
  hymns, 19

Luther—continued
  indictment of Rome, 106
  journey to Rome, 55
  as leader of the people, 20
  as leader of reforming teachers, and preachers, 105, 109f.
  his memory, 15
  and orthodox tradition, 56
  pamphlets, Basel edition, 50
  as pastor, 54, n.2
  re penance and penitence, 55
  Penitential Psalms, 13
  personal struggles, 15
  the "philosopher", 23
  polemics, 101, 205, 206
  Primary Works, 6
  as professor of theology, 55
  not refuse to die, 61, 65, 200
  relation to humanism, 104
  ruling class, 109
  religious experience, 13
  Resolutio, 149, n.2
  Revocatio by Isolani, 209
  sermons, 17
  Sermon des Leichnams, 210, n.2
  and social amelioration, 106
  spelling of the name, 32, n.1
  his theology, 16, 18, 27
  translation of the New Testament, 19
  Verklärung etlicher Artikel, 216, n.3
  writes in Latin, 5
  and, later, more often in German, 6

MACKINNON, J., 25, n.1, 343, n.3
Mary Magdalene, 51
Mary, Virgin, 85, 86, 365, 377
Maximilian, emperor, 170, n., 178
Mazzolini. See Prierias
Melanchthon, Philip, 30, 70, n.1, 107
Miltitz, Karl von, 333, 334, 336, n.3, 342, 344, 351
Monica, St., 300
Moses, 257
Mülport, Hermann, 355, 356
Murner, Thomas, 205, 207

NATHAN, PROPHET, 195
Nimrod, 209
Nützel, Caspar, 30

ORIGEN, 18, 226, 312
Ottilia, St., 166

PASCHAL, ST., POPE, 35
Patritius, 300

Index of Subjects

Printed in the United States
1114000001B/142